Nicolussi-Köhler (Ed.): Change and Transformation of Premodern Credit Markets

Stephan Nicolussi-Köhler (Ed.)

Change and Transformation of Premodern Credit Markets

The Importance of Small-Scale Credits

UNIVERSITÄTS-
BIBLIOTHEK
HEIDELBERG

Bibliographic information published by the Deutsche Nationalbibliothek
The Deutsche Nationalbibliothek lists this publication in the Deutsche Nationalbibliografie; detailed bibliographic data are available in the Internet at http://dnb.dnb.de.

UNIVERSITÄTS-
BIBLIOTHEK
HEIDELBERG

Published at heiBOOKS,
Heidelberg University Library 2021.

The online version of this publication is freely available on the ebook-platform of the Heidelberg University Library heiBOOKS https://books.ub.uni-heidelberg.de/heibooks (open access).
URN: urn:nbn:de:bsz:16-heibooks-book-593-5
DOI: https://doi.org/10.11588/heibooks.593

Funded by the Deutsche Forschungsgemeinschaft (DFG, German Research Foundation) – 399266981 and by the Ministry of Science, Research and the Arts of the State of Baden-Württemberg (Ministerium für Wissenschaft, Forschung und Kunst des Landes Baden-Württemberg).

Layout and Typesetting: text plus form, Dresden

Cover Illustration: Detail of the Imbreviatura of the notary Jakob of Haas, Bolzano (1237). Archivio di Stato di Trento. https://commons.wikimedia.org/wiki/File:Imbreviatur_Jakob_Haas_1237.jpg. This file is licensed under the Creative Commons Attribution-Share Alike 4.0 International license.

ISBN 978-3-948083-13-7 (Softcover)
ISBN 978-3-948083-12-0 (PDF)

CONTENTS

Notes on Contributors VII

Introduction 1
Stephan Nicolussi-Köhler

Change and Transformation of Premodern Credit Markets.
The Importance of Small-Scale Credits 23
Gilles Postel-Vinay

Colonisation and Credit in Medieval Wales 39
Matthew Frank Stevens

Small Credit in a Small Town: Clerical Institutions and the Credit Market
in Kaufbeuren in the Fifteenth Century 65
Sven Rabeler

Between City and Countryside: Moneylending and Settling Debts
in and around Meran (1388–1392) 89
Stephan Nicolussi-Köhler

Credit Networks between City and Countryside
in Late Medieval Lucca 133
So Nakaya

Webs of Credit and Uses of Civil Justice.
The Case of 15th-Century Basel 157
Benjamin Hitz

The Other Side of Banking. Private Lending and the Role of Women
in Early Modern Italy 193
Marcella Lorenzini

High Finance, Banking and Small-Scale Moneylending:
A New Trinity of Financial Functions for Lombards in the Late-Medieval
Low Countries? 215
David Kusman

Trading Networks, Credit, and Trust: The Hansards' Capital
Raising Revisited 251
Ulf Christian Ewert

Contract and Trust in Fifteenth-Century Church Courts 275
Hannah Robb

Strategies of Survival: Pawn-broking and Credit Relations in Rome
and Perugia (15th and 16th centuries) 293
Tanja Skambraks

NOTES ON CONTRIBUTORS

Ulf Christian Ewert studied History, Sociology, Political Sciences, Business Administration and Econometrics at the University of Kiel. He holds a doctorate in Medieval and Modern History by the same university, and received his post-doctoral qualification, the Habilitation, from Chemnitz University of Technology, this including the Venia legendi in Medieval History as well as in Economic and Social History. He taught Medieval History, Economic and Social History, and Empirical Economics at Chemnitz University of Technology, Helmut Schmidt University Hamburg, Free University of Berlin and the Universities of Munich, Münster, Halle, Regensburg and Erfurt. Currently, he is working at the University of Erfurt in an international research project on trade fairs in late-medieval and early-modern Europe.

Benjamin Hitz studied history in Lausanne, completed his doctorate in Lucerne on early modern mercenaries and then worked as a research assistant at the University of Basel with a habilitation project on the late medieval debt economy. He is currently researching the history of the city of Basel.

David Kusman is adjunct-archivist at the Records office of the Centre Public d'Action Sociale de Bruxelles and an associated researcher at the SOCIAMM (histoire, arts, culture des Sociétés Anciennes, Médiévales et Modernes) research centre at the Free University of Brussels. His current researches focus on credit and information during the late Middle Ages in the Late medieval Low Countries.

Marcella Lorenzini is researcher in Economic History at the University of Milan, Department of Economics, Management and Quantitative Methods, and Honorary Research Fellow at The Bartlett School of Construction & Project Management, UCL. She received her PhD from the University of Milan. Her research focuses on how credit markets develop in absence of formal institutions with a special interest on the role of notaries in the Early Modern Age. Her latest publications include Credit Market and Notaries in Verona in the Second Half of the Seventeenth Century, in *The Journal of European Economic History* (2015), and Infrastructure Financing in the Early Modern Age. The Beginning of a 'Little Divergence', in Infrastructure Finance in Europe. Insights into the History of Water, Transport, and Telecommunications (Oxford University Press, 2016).

So Nakaya is an associate professor at the Osaka University. His research focuses on society and justice in medieval Italian cities.

Stephan Nicolussi-Köhler studied history in Vienna and Mannheim. He is a research associate at the University of Innsbruck and conducts research on economic history issues, with a focus on credit markets. He current project is on premodern credit markets, small-scale credits and market participation in the Alpine regions.

Gilles Postel-Vinay is directeur d'Etudes, Ecole des Hautes Etudes en Sciences Sociales and Emeritus Professor at Paris School of Economics. He is the author of La terre et l'argent, and, with Philip Hoffman and Jean-Laurent Rosenthal, of Priceless Markets, and Dark Matter Credit.

Sven Rabeler studied Medieval and Modern History, Eastern European History and Art History in Kiel (Germany). Ph.D. 2005. Research associate at the Historical Seminar, University of Kiel, project "Residenzstädte im Alten Reich/Residential Cities in the Holy Roman Empire (1300–1800)" of the Göttingen Academy of Sciences and Humanities. Research areas: medieval history, especially from social, economic and cultural perspectives—towns, urbanity and urbanisation, nobility, courts and residences, poverty, charity and hospitals. Currently, he is preparing a habilitation thesis dealing with poor relief and charitable foundations in medieval towns of the southern Baltic Sea area.

Hannah Robb is a research associate at the University of Exeter on the project "Forms of Labour: Gender, Freedom and Experience of Work in the Preindustrial Economy". Her research focuses on credit, debt and commercial relations in late medieval and early modern England.

Tanja Skambraks is assistant professor of Medieval History at the University of Mannheim. She just finished her second book on "Poor-relief, caritas and small-scale credit in late medieval and early modern Italy: the Monti di Pietà" and is now working on a new project on medieval tally sticks. Her research interests include economic and social history in the longue durée, material culture, moral economy, rituals and every-day life. She studied Medieval History, English Literature and Culture as well as Communication Science at the TU Dresden and the University of Edinburgh."

Matthew Frank Stevens is associate professor of history, Department of History, Swansea University (Wales, UK), and Ulam Fellow, Faculty of History, Nicolaus Copernicus University in Toruń (Poland). His work focuses on the economic, legal and social history of later medieval Wales and Britain, and comparisons with other colonial zones of northern Europe, including Ireland and the State of the Teutonic Order. He has particular interests in the legal and economic position of women and ethnic minorities.

INTRODUCTION*

Stephan Nicolussi-Köhler

Medieval Credit Markets

The importance of credit for modern economic growth is an undisputed fact.[1] This claim of economic science is also assumed for premodern societies and has been investigated in the case of pre-industrial Europa but also for large parts of Asia or the Americas.[2] The widespread use of credit in the Middle Ages for different purposes has been emphasised by emerging research on different topics. The growing use of credit was accompanied by a commercialisation of medieval societies and a progressing market involvement.[3] Bruno Kuske was one of the first to reject the view that medieval man was entrenched in church morality and had a limited economic horizon.

He showed that various forms of credit usage for consumptions credits, business loans, and public debt existed as far back as the Middle Ages.[4] The empirical research conducted in the last 100 years has highlighted the richness of credit operations in premodern societies in Europe. Consequently, Peter Schuster, drawing on an older term coined by Delloyd Guth, called the Late Middle Ages "the Age

---

* The papers presented in this book were part of a conference held at the Heidelberg Academy of Sciences in October 2019. The publication of the conference proceedings could not have been carried out without funds from the Deutsche Forschungsgemeinschaft (DFG, German Research Foundation)—399266981 and from the Heidelberg Academy of Sciences.

1 For the premodern world, it is more accurate to talk about a quantitative change in the economic performance than about growth. Cf. Köster 2020, 25.

2 Hoffman, Postel-Vinay, and Rosenthal 1999, 69–71; Köhler and Skambraks 2019, 22–23; Van Bavel 2016, 16–17; Zuijderduijn 2009, 1; Lopez 1976.

3 Ghosh 2020, 207–213; Ghosh 2017; Van Bavel 2011, 516–521.

4 Kuske 1956, 59–50. For a variety of medieval credit instruments, see Gilomen 2010.

Published in: Stephan Nicolussi-Köhler (Ed.), Change and Transformation of Premodern Credit Markets. The Importance of Small-Scale Credits. Heidelberg: heiBOOKS 2021, 1–21. DOI: https://doi.org/10.11588/heibooks.593.c12688

of Debt".[5] Several innovative micro-historical research projects on the financial dealings of medieval and early modern societies broadened our understanding of premodern credit arrangements and practices.[6] The growing interest in this field of economic history led to the emergence of different strands of research, each focusing on different questions and offering new approaches to the topic.[7]

By focusing on a specific phenomenon of medieval and early modern credit markets—small scale credits—the attention of this book is drawn to a topic that is usually not in the centre of historic research, either because of a lack of sources, or because these practices were overshadowed by credit activities of big corporations, princes, kings, or the church. These credit operations were bigger in size, but not in quantity and because of that, the economic dealings of a large part of the historical population involved in petty moneylending and small loans is left out of such considerations. This book adds to the research about small-scale credits and presents original studies on small credit practices in a broad range of European regions (England, France, Germany, Italy, Low Countries, Hanseatic cities) from the Middle Ages to the Early Modern times.

Recent Studies on Credit Markets

Most prominent has been the question about the relationship between financial and economic development. Several studies suggest a correlation between the level of financial development and economic growth. If credit is available and money circulates easily then economic growth takes off.[8] The question here is, bluntly said, how capital can be reallocated swiftly in a society so that it can be put to economic use.[9] Of utmost importance for the functioning of such an exchange is the institutional framework that organises economic interaction and thus decreases or increases transaction costs. Exchange could be organised in many ways, and allocation via a market was only one possibility amongst many others.[10] Markets as the dominant system of exchange were quite rare in history. But factor markets, especially for capital, were already large in the Late Middle

5 Schuster 2008. In his article, he provides extensive examples for medieval Europe.
6 Clemens 2008, 9–11.
7 Neu 2019.
8 Cf. Levine 2005, 868; Hoffman, Postel-Vinay, and Rosenthal 2019, 1.
9 This includes cashless forms of credit. Bell, Brookes, and Moore 2017.
10 For a broader debate about the exploration of premodern markets with further references, see Kypta 2021.

Ages in Europe, and in some regions became the dominant system of allocation.[11] Thus, medieval capital markets seem to be the ideal research topic to answer questions about economic growth, but also about the everyday economic practices of medieval and early modern societies.

Studies on credit markets have produced several narratives and models that try to explain the development and functioning of credit markets, each highlighting different explanations for the historical development. As will be shown, several topics such as the emergence of banks or state regulations (i.e. the protection of property rights) are recurring topics of these studies. Other aspects, like informal credits, non-market operations, or small-scale credits played only a minor role in the analyses of credit markets until recently. The following section refers to the most important studies on credit markets.

According to Douglass North and the New Institutional Economy (NIE), the institutional arrangements—or market structures—are, alongside production costs, the chief determinant for any economic exchange to take place or not.[12] Thus, transaction costs, such as costs to overcome asymmetric information between contracting parties, costs for protection or for enforcing contractual obligations, affect the economic growth, the integration of economies, and the emergence of market economies.[13] The market structures are put into effect by private or public interest groups (powerful individuals like monarchs, organisations, etc.) to profit from economic exchange, and they are thus exponents of the political and social structure. This institutional framework—the so-called institutions—can be both formal and informal.[14] Whereas informal institutions include religious taboos, norms, customs, social habits, or moral values, formal institutions, for example contractual obligations or property rights, are enforceable by law.[15] Since formal institutions rely in many cases on legal systems and other long-lasting structures, they often create a certain path dependency.[16]

The emergence of (well-functioning) capital markets are thought to be of special importance for the economic development of Western Europe.[17] One corner-

---

11 Wickham 2021, 7; Van Bavel 2016, 12.

12 North 1990.

13 Zuijderduijn 2009, 2–5.

14 The New Institutional Economic approach was most prominently applied to the medieval period in Avner Greif's study about Mediterranean commerce and Jaco Zuijderduijn's book about medieval capital markets. Greif 2006. Zuijderduijn 2009.

15 Hoffman, Postel-Vinay, and Rosenthal 1999, 12.

16 Zuijderduijn 2009, 4; Coffman, Lorandini, and Lorenzini, 2018, 2.

17 Hatcher and Bailey 2001, 125; Van Bavel 2016, 14–18. However, the argument of long-lasting economic growth through the implementation of markets is questioned by Van Bavel. Cf. Huang and Kypta 2018, 103.

stone of this institutional framework for capital markets is the setting of secure property rights.[18] The choice of institutions and how free, or "perfect", these markets were, depended upon specific settings.[19] Therefore, no general meta-narrative about the development of capital markets can be made since every region had a unique development with its own historical setting. For Western Europe, some key financial institutions have been identified that lowered transactions costs and enabled economic growth: the emergence of trade companies, early banking facilities, the stock exchange, and public debt are seen as forerunners of the financial development of the nineteenth century.[20] However, this side of the story about medieval credit markets leaves out the everyday dealings of small households and businesses and small-scale credit activities.[21]

Especially the debate over institutions that linked economic growth to public finance has attracted the attention of many scholars. Political reforms strengthening property rights protection offered widespread opportunities for investments and at the same time brought about depersonalisation and objectivity to the financial market. The creation of a modern financial system, encompassing the consolidation of public debt with a secondary market where government bonds could be traded, marked a watershed in financial history.[22] This way, the emergence of the modern state is connected to the existence of funded public debt.[23] The earliest evidence of such (municipal) financial institutions can be identified in Northern Italy (Florence, Genoa, Venice), the Low Countries, Northern Germany, and England, appearing as early as the twelfth century.[24] Research on funded public debt has been inclined to consider the requirements and needs of both the savers and the investors. Whereas the savers wanted financial instruments that allow them to withdraw their savings and convert them into cash at short-notice and with low costs, investors were concerned with an assured continuity and a constant supply of capital. A lot of focus has been put on the demand side—that is the need of governments, merchants, and business corporations. Less attention has been paid to the supply side of the investors.[25] Once again, the questions here are

18 Zuijderduijn 2009, 2; Gelderblom and Jonker 2004, 645; De Soto 2000.

19 No historical or present-day market was ever fully open and free. Markets have always been embedded in their political and social environment. Van Bavel 2016, 8–11.

20 Coffman, Lorandini, and Lorenzini, 2018, 3.

21 This includes the dealings outside the market. The co-existence of the market economy and the "material culture" was already described by Braudel. Braudel 1985, 15–19.

22 Gelderblom and Jonker 2004, 642.

23 Stasavage 2011; Munro 2003; Tracy 1985; North and Weingast 1989; Hoffman, Postel-Vinay, and Rosenthal 1999.

24 Denzel 2008, 51–53; Munro 2003, 514; Fryde and Fryde 1963.

25 For this observation, see Gelderblom and Jonker 2004.

centred around people that have financial reserves at hand to invest, leaving out those people that lived from hand to mouth and depended on credit instruments not so much to invest but to bridge a shortage of cash and to survive.

Thus, the mechanisms that help to accumulate capital are of special interest for economic history. Closely connected to the topic of public debt is that of the functioning of a secondary market for rents or annuities. Here, several micro- and macro-historical studies have approached this topic dealing with different questions like the social background of the buyers and sellers of tradeable financial assets like annuities, the factors of determining the level of interest rates, or the question of capital market integration.[26] Closely connected to the organisation of funded public debt is the emergence of tax systems.[27] The interplay of taxation, possibilities of investment, and inequality has shown that it is worth investigating how rich but also poor people dealt with economic difficulties.[28] Low-scale credits have so far only played a minor role in such considerations.

Another benchmark of growing capital markets is the evolving merchant-banking sector. The exploration of the influence of early banking processes for the economic development established banking history as an independent field of study.[29] The emerging of deposit banking and transfer banking (*giro*) further stimulated the circulation of money and mobilisation of savings.[30] Next to international banking, specialised in money-changing and commerce, local banking developed. Soon, bankers extended their activities and also accepted deposits, created banking currencies and paper money, and were also engaged in the trading of financial instruments. This led to an expansion of lending activities, both in the private and the public sector. Standardised financial systems in modern banking allowed people to overcome the bonds of personal relationship and offered new possibilities of moneylending and of trading financial assets on a secondary market.[31] The credit intermediated by formal institutions, such as banks, continued in various forms until the present day and has received a lot of attention.[32]

More recently, economic historians have turned to study smaller and less formal financial institutions that provided access to credit and reallocated capital. Departing point for this was a study by Philipp Hoffman, Gilles Postel-Vinay, and Jean-Laurent Rosenthal of the role of notaries in Paris in 17th and 18th century

26 Chilosi, Schulze, and Volckart 2018, 638 (with further references); Boone, Davids, and Janssens 2003.

27 Van Schaik 2015; Ucendo and Limberger 2012, 2; Isenmann 2012, 516–542.

28 Alfani and Di Tullio 2019; Vries 2020.

29 Usher 1934; De Roover 1948; Cameron 1972; Blomquist 1985; Botticini 2000, 165.

30 Van Bavel 2016, 109–110; Spufford 1988, 255–263.

31 Coffman, Lorandini, and Lorenzini 2018, 2.

32 Signori 2021, 31–34.

France. In Paris, notaries facilitated the reallocation of huge sums on the capital market without the use of modern banks.[33] The findings of the study have shown that in pre-industrial France, and probably in other parts of Europe as well, credit activities were not hampered by a lack of formal institutions (i.e. banks) but instead credit flourished and was intermediated through informal credit institutions. This premodern (and pre-banking age) informal credit proved to be effective and to meet the needs of the people.[34] Moneylending through non-institutional channels was widespread and used both by individuals of all social classes as well as by institutions and businesses for various purposes, ranging from trade, business investments, consumptions to everyday necessities (paying rent, debts, etc.). Most of this credit was privately arranged.[35] Although these informal credit institutions differed quite a lot from formal ones, the former ones were not replaced by the later ones. Quite the contrary, both systems were rather complementary and did not compete with each other.

Traditional forms of moneylending did indeed survive until the 19th century and played an important role. Unlike formal credit, these informal credit practices depended on trustworthiness, reputation, and social relations between market participants.[36] In the process, informal credit practices were able to solidify both asymmetrical power relationships and reciprocal obligations. The coexistence of different lending practices has been studied in a broad range of European countries, and it is undisputed that the elements of informal credit practices were not abandoned during the financial revolution but continued to play an important role.[37] Very often, small-scale credit practices belonged to this informal sector. These findings widened our understanding of the functioning of medieval and early modern credit markets and show indeed that the exploration of formal institutions must also include the informal ones.

---

33 Hoffman, Postel-Vinay, and Rosenthal 1999; Hoffman, Postel-Vinay, and Rosenthal 2000; Hoffman, Postel-Vinay, and Rosenthal 2019.

34 A definition is given by Coffman, Lorandini, and Lorenzini: *"Informal credit in particular refers to transactions that are not intermediated by operators specialized in matching demand and supply, namely professionals whose specialization was other than this, like for instance notaries, scriveners, merchants and even religious institutions."* Coffman, Lorandini, and Lorenzini 2018, 3–4. See also Botticini 2001, 165; Carboni and Muzzarelli 2004; Van Zanden 2012;

35 However, this does not automatically mean that this credit was personal. Clemens 2008, 9–10; Hoffman, Postel-Vinay, and Rosenthal 1999, 71.

36 Muldrew 1998; Schlumbohm 2007; Signori 2014; Shaw 2018; Skambraks et al. 2020. For an anthropologic view of credit and debt practices, see Lipp 2007; Graeber 2011.

37 Coffman, Lorandini, and Lorenzini 2018, 16.

Change and Transformation of premodern Credit Markets

The "traditional story" about the development of modern credit markets is centred around the question of the emergence of new financial institutions, like modern corporations, the world's first stock exchange, or the first central banks, and depicts this development as a transition from a society used to personal money-lending to a society economising in an impersonal and capitalistic way.[38] This assumption has two consequences: first, it is often (implicitly) assumed that economic theory is only applicable for the (modern) capitalistic world. Hence, many scholars dealing with the economic history of premodern Europe do not apply an economic methodological approach because it seems not appropriate for medieval and early modern societies (or rather their sources).[39] Second, the "traditional story" narrows down the choice of the subject matter. If modern financial institutions mattered for economic growth then it would be only logical that—according to this assumption—research concerned with this topic should focus on the financial practices that survived the transition from the premodern to the modern world.[40] This view leaves out institutions that no longer exist and has a nearly exclusive focus on the high finance, that is banking, public debt, and merchant corporations. This issue has been tackled by recent research. Several studies of informal credit institutions have widened our knowledge about premodern financial markets and shown that medieval and early modern credit practices were in use until the 19th century.[41] Next to new forms of credit, these traditional credit institutions continued to be used and it seems as if different credit institutions often completed one another.

The narrative of a transition from premodern to modern capital markets certainly seems to be challenged. This may be exemplified by the history of early

38 This observation has been made in the pioneering works of Hoffman, Postel-Vinay, Rosenthal in their various studies about the French credit markets. Hoffman, Postel-Vinay, and Rosenthal 1999, 69–71 (with references) and especially 91–92. Gelderblom, Jonker, and Kool 2016, 1178.

39 That it can be indeed very fruitful to think about the economic logic of medieval societies is shown by Chris Wickham in an article about the Feudal Economy. He challenged the underlying rules of capitalist economics and instead put forward an argument based on the logic of Feudal mode of production. Wickham 2021, especially page 15.

40 Criticism of this approach is older. Concerning Medieval trade, Kathryn Reyerson pointed out that research has been led by a diachronic approach and economic historians *"searched relentlessly"* for precedents of modern economic institutions in the medieval period. Reyerson 2002, 1–4. Also, Wickham 2021, 15; Gelderblom and Jonker 2004.

41 Gelderblom and Jonker 2004; Coffman, Lorandini, and Lorenzini 2018; Hoffman, Postel-Vinay, and Rosenthal 2019; Skambraks 2021.

European banking. De Roover tried to reconstruct the evolution of banking techniques and identified three categories that existed in the Middle Ages. The first one, merchant-banking, evolved into exchange banking; the second one, money-changing, evolved into deposit and transfer banking; and the third one, pawnbroking, *"led to nowhere insofar as banking history is concerned since the service that the pawnbroker provided to impecunious borrowers were for the most part taken over by charitable public institutions".*[42] Indeed, from the supply side of credit—that is the perspective of banks—it may look like pawnbroking and petty lending led to nowhere (although the separation of business activities of medieval banking has been challenged by now).[43] But maybe we should start asking new questions: Could we not understand medieval banking techniques better if we looked at the credit practices used by a vast majority of people instead of the way we had been looking at it as a phenomenon of the development of European banking? Instead of focusing solely on the formal banking institutions, it might be interesting to look at nowadays obsolete credit institutions, like informal credit intermediaries like notaries or booksellers that dealt with financial transactions.[44] Besides, we should ask what people needed and which institutions suited their needs best. Finally, an exploration of credit markets must also include the so-called low finance, that is the everyday financial dealings of small households and businesses.[45]

Financial practices did not stay the same over time. Formal and informal credit practices used to exist along each other with new forms of credit emerging and old forms being adapted to the necessities of the people.[46] This change of credit techniques emerging in premodern credit markets was one of the topics of the conference in Heidelberg in 2019 and in the papers of this book. As several studies have shown, the implementation of new credit instruments could have a major impact on the economic behaviour of societies, as in the case of funded public debt financed through financial instruments like annuities, *renten* but also forced loans. At the same time, other forms of financial instruments could cease to exist.[47] Next to the emergence of new practices, the transformation of existing financial institutions is also of great importance. One example for this is the de-

---

42 De Roover 1948, 345–357; De Roover 1974; Blomquist 1985, 522.

43 Blomquist 1985; Botticini 2000; Kusman 2021.

44 Cf. Geldberlom, Jonker, and Kool 2016.

45 Several authors argued that in England changes in the private capital market proceeded the financial revolution. Van Zanden, Zuijderduijn, and de Moor 2012, 3. Cf. Epstein 2000; Clark 2005;

46 Shaw 2018, 624–625.

47 For example, there were some annuities based on mills and tolls in Hamburg, which disappeared during the 14th century. Cf. Baum 1976, 92–93.

velopment of a secondary market where financial assets could be traded.[48] However, the emergence or survival of institutions is not necessarily solely linked to the economic efficiency but can be explained by other factors.[49] Researchers like Laurence Fontaine and Jürgen Schlumbohm have shown that the importance of credit arrangements from a social point of view cannot be overemphasised.[50]

The study of change and transformation offers new insights into the functioning of premodern credit markets, without seeing premodern economies as basically primitive or backwards or—the other extreme—imagining them as more or less modern societies, run by "modern" economic rules.

Small-scale credit

It is a well-known fact that a large part of the credit dealings in premodern societies did not belong to the big commercial loans of merchant corporations, the financing of public debt, or the financial dealings of the ecclesiastical and secular lords. But unlike the credit practices of the economic and social elites, rather little is known about the credit dealings of other population groups.[51] It is therefore not enough to discuss only the formal credit institutions and instruments (i.e. early banking), exploring small-scale credit practices is equally necessary.[52]

The financial behaviour of the relatively poorer men and women, who depict in premodern Europe the major part of the historical population, is of great importance for the economic wellbeing of a society, and of course is of interest for any economic historian. The so-called "working poor" were the main users of these credits and used them to bridge gaps in their cash flow. One has to keep in mind that until the late 19th century, between 25 and 50 per cent of the European population lived in "poverty".[53] Poor households relied on makeshift solutions

---

48 Zuijderduijn 2009, 204–206.

49 Ogilvie 2007; Shaw 2018, 625–626.

50 Fontaine and Schlumbohm 2000; Fontaine 2014.

51 Several studies addressed this problem. Cf. Groebner 1993; Schlumbohm 2007, 7–8; Berthe 2008; Dirlmeier, Fouquet, and Andermann ²2009, 197–198; Van Zanden, Zuijderduijn, and de Moor 2012, 3; Signori 2014, 8–9; Skambraks et al. 2020; Signori 2021, 30–32.

52 That financial activity was not restricted to merchants and bankers is shown in various studies within the last few years, cf. for example Ogilvie, Küpker, and Maegraith 2012.

53 The working or labouring poor were those whose daily labour was necessary for their daily support. Cf. Fontaine and Schlumbohm 2000, 1–2; Deneweth, Gelderblom, and Jonker 2014, 80.

that enabled them to survive and to participate in the economy.[54] One of these solutions, which was not only taken up by the poor, was the access to credit.[55] But small-scale credit was often connected to high transactions costs, which must be covered by the interest rates. This could have several reasons like the lack of—or the inability (because of an absence of secured property rights) to use certain objects as—collateral or information asymmetries. If no collateral could be offered to the creditor, he had to assess the ability of his debtor to repay the loan and monitor his payments.[56] Thus, very often, the contribution of small scale credit belonged to the informal economy, being embedded in social relations or hierarchical networks that circumvented legal regulations.[57]

Now, what is a small-scale credit? A true definition does not exist and there are several approaches to this topic. For one, very often the size of the credit is related to the monthly wage. Some scholars used the quarterly wage of one year of a labourer as the upper limit for a small-scale credit.[58] Indeed, one could argue that in the Middle Ages, wages were only one part of the overall income of a large part of the population, and it is therefore difficult to put the size of the credit in relation to the salary of a labourer.[59] Another suggestion was put forward by Gabriela Signori, who described small-scale credits with five attributes: small size, short runtime, without collateral, no legally binding purpose of use, and repayment through instalments.[60] Whereas none of these attributes was intrinsic to small-scale credits alone, all these factors are important when analysing the wider financial situation in which loans were taken out.[61]

One problem of studying small-scale credits is a lack of sources. Since the debtors could usually not offer a collateral for these credits, they were usually not recorded like other debts—that is in written contracts—or negotiated in court. Instead, the economic and social lower classes often had to resort to informal credit practices, and small-scale credits can be found more often in other sources, like

---

54 Fontaine and Schlumbohm 2000; Tomkins and King 2003; Fontaine 2013; Shaw 2018, 624; Skambraks 2021.

55 The importance of access to credits for large parts of the population, but also public bodies, in the Middle Ages was shown by several publications. Cf. for example Fouquet, von Seggern, and Gilomen 2007; Fouquet and Andermann 2016.

56 Van Zanden, Zuijderduijn, and de Moor 2012, 4; Deneweth, Gelderblom, and Jonker 2014, 81.

57 Shaw 2018.

58 Hagen 2018, 48.

59 Cf. Wickham 2021, 11–16.

60 Signori 2021, 32.

61 For example, to calculate the interest rates actually charged in a methodologically correct way, one needs to know the principal of the sum, the size and payment dates of the instalments, and the runtime of the credit. Bell, Brookes, and Moore 2009.

accounts of the voluntary jurisdiction.[62] It is obvious that small-scale credits differed a lot over time and place. A loan taken out by a relative cannot be compared to the pledging of household items to a pawnbroker for cash. Similar to other credits (business or investment credits) of average size, there were many different ways to acquire petty loans. The mentioned characteristics may help to analyse and understand them better, but the transition from one form to another was a smooth one.

What is to be gained by studying small-scale credits? Most importantly, it broadens our understanding of the economic dealings of pre-modern societies. By integrating the credit activities of a large part of the historical population in the picture, it will help us to study the internal logic of medieval societies and economies. The studying of the financial behaviour of poor households in the Middle Ages and the Early Modern period may uncover new insights concerning economic history, and could offer new hints that help understand some of the big questions, i.e. about inequality or economic development and growth. The extent to which studies of past societies allow statements and comparisons with modern societies is controversial.[63] But understanding the logic—not necessarily the economic logic—of past societies may indeed help to understand historic developments better.[64]

Research studies across Europe

The studies conducted on small-scale credits in this book represent the richness and variety of this economic practice in pre-modern societies. There was a wide use of different forms of moneylending, which is described in the articles of this book: notarial credit, informal moneylending, pawnbroking, the buying and sel-

---

62 Signori 2021, 44.

63 Some authors are in favour of comparing the economic problems in past societies and today. This argument was put forward by Hoffman, Postel-Vinay, and Rosenthal. *"To be sure, the culture of early modern Paris was different, as were Old Regime institutions. But the problems in early modern finance often turn out to be the same as in the modern world [...]."* Hoffman, Postel-Vinay, and Rosenthal 1999, 91. A similar approach is put forward by Denewth, Gelderblom, and Jonker 2014. Of different opinion is Signori: *"Wir sollten die Gegensätze als solche belassen und die Komplexität der städtischen Realität im ausgehenden 15. Jahrhundert nicht quellenfernen Geschichtsbildern opfern. Die spätmittelalterliche Stadt ist weder eine Südseeinsel noch eine industrialisierungsbedingte soziale Problemzone."* Signori 2021, 50.

64 Ovilgie 2007, 659–661.

ling of annuities, commercial loans, loans offered by charitable institutions (Monti di Pietà), and credits offered by merchant bankers. The there are several overarching topics in the book. The first one is a spatial analysis of credit relationships, especially between city and countryside. Another one is the focus on the institutional framework of credit practices, including both formal and informal ones (and sometimes even orally conducted credit). Finally, different credit instruments are examined, showing that historical circumstances had a huge impact on the emergence of specific contract forms.

Gilles Postel-Vinay takes a broader perspective in his introduction by describing the possibilities offered by studying credit. He highlighted the economic reasoning behind historical developments and at the same time warns not to generalise certain results from well-studied regions. Instead, he points in a different direction and refers to unexplored topics in the wide research area of pre-modern credits.

In the contribution of Matthew Frank Stevens, the impact of the colonisation of Wales on the credit market is studied. By describing changes of credit practices in Wales after the English conquest (11th to 13th century), he is able to present a well-documented case of institutional change that had a big impact on the credit market. The implementation of new forms of credit did not only affect the emergence of a money economy but the Welsh princes' lack of access to credit placed them also at a strategic disadvantage when faced by their English aggressors.

In a micro-historical study, Sven Rabeler reconstructed credit relations in the small town of Kaufbeuren in the 15th century. He shows the close entanglement between the citizens and clerical institutions within the credit market of the town. His research suggests two things: first, that annuities were not only used for bigger loans, but also for small-scale credit operations. Second, that parish churches could play an important as credit institutions—an observation very often ignored by research.

The paper from myself is devoted to the exploration of small-scale credit in medieval Tirol. By comparing different sources, court protocols, and notary registers, I show that loans with a small principal were usually not recorded by a notary. But in contrast, the majority of unpaid debts brought to court dealt with small sums. This acts as a reminder to avoid an unwanted selection bias of the sources when studying small-scale credits.

A similar conclusion can be drawn from So Nakaya's paper about credit networks between city and countryside in late medieval Lucca. By using a memorandum, a record book from a wealthy landowner, he describes everyday practices of rural credit relationships between city and countryside, and shows the practice of giving out unsecured smaller loans that depended on many social and economic factors.

The effectiveness of using a vast database and methods such as network analysis is apparent in Benjamin Hitz's article about webs of credit and uses of civil justice in 15th century Basel. By using two samples of court records, the author is able to draw remarkable conclusions about the spatial distribution and social power relations of the creditors and debtors in late medieval Basel. This method allows for a better understanding of the relationship between creditor and debtor, and proves that people in 15th century Basel definitely had an idea who to ask for credit.

Another unknown chapter of pre-modern credit markets is addressed by Marcella Lorenzini. By studying the participation of women on the financial market in early modern Italy, another perspective is put on an economic sector that has long been dominated by men. That this is a worthwhile undertaking is proven by the results, which allow detailed insights into the vivid capital market of Northern Italy, where female participation in small-scale credits was growing—with all associated economic and social effects.

The different financial services offered by Piedmontese moneylenders in the late medieval Low Countries is the focus of David Kusman's chapter. By studying the commercial strategies of the bankers, the author shows their involvement in credit and money supply for a huge part of the population. The so-called usurious loans were usually recovered within several weeks and thus calculation of interest rate should take the actual runtime of the credit into account. The results suggest that interest rates should be considered anew on a weekly basis. A close reading of the sources allows for a more differentiated picture of their dealings.

The role of the contractual form of credits and investments is the topic of Ulf Christian Ewert's contribution about trading networks, credit, and trust in the German Hanse. Departing point is the problem of a scarcity of money and a lack of capital. Both could be circumvented with the institution of "reciprocal trade", a system of credit transfer that unlike the sophisticated financial instruments that emerged in Italy (*commenda, societas maris,* etc.) was not part of a venture capital market. The fundamental differences to the Mediterranean credit system are not so much connected to an anti-credit stance of Hanseatic merchants but can be explained by a path-dependency. This exemplifies the problematic of looking eagerly for forerunners of modern economic institutions.

The question of the transformation of credit practices, from a performative ritual to an impersonal exchange, is addressed by Hannah Robb. By looking at the practices and customs of credit in ecclesiastical courts in 15th century England, the author shows that oral contracts were still the norm by that time. There was no clear shift from oral to a written economy at that time, which proves that the co-existence of both oral and written agreements was the most effective means of creating a communal knowledge of the economic activities.

Different strategies of survival of the working poor in late medieval and early modern Italy is the topic of Tanja Skambraks' contribution. The services offered by the Monti di Pietà, ranging from pawnbroking to deposit banking, are analysed. The Monti were one of several credit institutions in the city, and were frequented by a large part of the population. By accepting different types of pawns and also allowing investments of smallest sums, the Monti established a niche in the financial environment, and point to the survival strategies of small households and the working poor.

The research presented in these studies shows that small-scale credit cannot be thought apart from other credit activities. It was a ubiquitous phenomenon that was not restricted to the informal economy or the dealings of the poorer economic spheres of the population. Small-scale credits could be granted in the form of annuities, given orally by relatives, or received against a pledge by pawnbrokers or charitable institutions. In many cases it was the very same institutions that intermediated small-scale credits, which were also engaged in other financial transactions. Pre-modern financial institutions made no clear distinctions between borrowing for investment and borrowing for consumption, probably because it belonged to everyday financial business. The economic (and social) impact of this credit is not to be underestimated. It did help to smoothen consumption and bridge shortcomings in cash for the poorer population. Besides, the credit enabled them to hold savings in financial assets and to participate in the market. This reveals important questions concerning the form credit took in different times and places: what financial services did poor households need and how were their needs satisfied. This might point to the connection between growth and finance.[65]

It emerges from the research carried out that small-scale credit practices were more stable than other financial institutions. Whereas high-finance saw an emergence of new institutions, many financial intermediaries concerned with petty moneylending did not become obsolete in the wake of the financial revolutions: clerical institutions, peer-to-peer moneylending, and pawnbroking still played a crucial role in raising capital in the 18th and 19th century. This might point to the direction that the needs of poorer households did not change too much over time. However, more research on this topic is necessary before this topic can be settled.

Finally, the editor would like to thank the many colleagues and friends who contributed to this book, and especially all participants of the conference held in Heidelberg in 2019: Change and Transformation of Pre-Modern Credit Markets, hosted by the Heidelberg Academy of Sciences. Special thanks go to Tanja

---

65 Cf. Deneweth, Gelderblom, and Jonker 2014.

Skambraks, Annette Kehnel, and Hiram Kümper for their detailed comments and critical input and to Laura Grabarek for the editorial tasks in preparing this volume, which she carried out with great accuracy.

References

Alfani G. and Di Tullio M. 2019. *The Lion's Share. Inequality and the Rise of the Fiscal State in Preindustrial Europe* [= Cambridge Studies in Economic History]. Cambridge: Cambridge University Press.

Baum H.-P. 1976. *Hochkonjunktur und Wirtschaftskrise im spätmittelalterlichen Hamburg. Hamburger Rentengeschäfte 1371–1410* [= Beiträge zur Geschichte Hamburgs. Herausgegeben vom Verein für hamburgische Geschichte, Band 11]. Hamburg: Hans Christians Verlag.

Bell A., Brooks C., and Moore T. 2009. "Interest in Medieval Accounts: Examples from England, 1272–1340". *History* 94: 411–433.

Bell A., Brooks C., and Moore T. 2017. "The non use of Money in the Middle Ages." In *Peter Spufford's Money and its Use in Medieval Europe.* [= Twenty-five Years On. Royal Numismatic Society Special Publication 52], edited by N. Mayhew, 137–151. London: Spink.

Berthe M. (ed.) 2008. *Endettement Paysan et Crédit Rural dans l'Europe médiévale et moderne.* [= Actes des XVIIes Journées Internationales d'Histoire de l'Abbaye de Flaran, Septembre 1995]. Toulouse: Presses Universitaires du Mirail.

Boone M., Davids K., and Janssens P. (eds.) 2003. *Urban Public Debts. Urban Government and the Market for Annuities in Western Europe (14th–18th Centuries)* [= Studies in European Urban History (1100–1800) 3]. Turnhout: Brepols.

Blomquist T. 1985. "The Early History of European Banking: Merchants, Bankers, and Lombards of thirteenth-century Lucca in the County of Champagne." *The Journal of Economic History* 14: 521–536.

Botticini M. 2000. "A Tale of "Benevolent" Governments: Private Credit Markets, Public Finance, and the Role of Jewish Lenders in Medieval and Renaissance Italy." *The Journal of Economic History* 60, no. 1: 164–189.

Braudel F. 1985. *Sozialgeschichte des 14. Bis 18. Jahrhunderts. Der Alltag.* Translated by Siglinde Summerer, Gerda Kurz, Günter Seib. Munich: Kindler Verlag.

Cameron R. (ed.) 1972. *Banking and Economic Development. Some Lessons of History.* New York: Oxford University Press.

Carboni M. and Muzzarelli G. M. (eds.) 2014. *Reti di credito: circuiti informali, impropri, nascosti (secoli XIII–XIX)*. Bologna: Il Mulino.

Chilosi, Schulze, and Volckart 2018. "Benefits of Empire? Capital Market Integration North and South of the Alps, 1350–1800." *The Journal of Economic History* 78, no. 3: 637–672.

Clark G. 2005. "The Interest Rate in the Very Long Run: Institutions, Preferences and Modern Growth." [Internet] London: Centre for Economic Policy Research (published April 2005). Available at: https://www.researchgate.net/publication/228426504_The_interest_rate_in_the_very_long_run_institutions_preferences_and_modern_growth [Accessed 28 July 2021].

Clemens G. 2008. "Einleitung. Die Omnipräsenz von westeuropäischen Kreditbeziehungen im Mittelalter und Neuzeit." In *Schuldenlast und Schuldenwert. Kreditnetzwerke in der europäischen Geschichte 1300–1900*, edited by G. Clemens, 9–20. Trier: Kliomedia.

Coffman D., C. Lorandini, and M. Lorenzini 2018. "Introduction. Formal and Informal Credit Across Europe: A Long-Run Perspective." In *Financing in Europe. Evolution, Coexistence and Complementarity of Lending Practices from the Middle Ages to Modern Times* [= Palgrave Studies in the History of Finance], edited by M. Lorenzini, C. Lorandini, and D. Coffman, 1–18. eBook: Palgrave Macmillan.

Denewth H., Gelderblom O., and Jonker J. 2014. "Microfinance and the Decline of Poverty: Evidence from the nineteenth-century Netherlands." *Journal of Economic Development* 39, no. 1: 79–110.

Denzel M. 2008. *Das System des bargeldlosen Zahlungsverkehrs europäischer Prägung vom Mittelalter bis 1914*. Stuttgart: Steiner, 2008.

De Roover R. 1948. *Money, Banking and Credit in Medieval Bruges. Italian Merchant-Bankers, Lombards and Money Changers: A Study in the Origins of Banking*. Cambridge, Ma.: Routledge.

De Roover R. 1974. "New Interpretations on the History of Banking." In *Business, banking, and economic thought in late medieval and early modern Europe: Selected studies*, edited by R. de Roover and J. Kirshner, 200–238. Chicago: University of Chicago Press.

De Soto H. 2000. *The Mystery of Capital: Why Capitalism Triumphs in the West and Fails Everywhere Else*. New York: Basic Books.

Dirlmeier U., Fouquet G., and Fuhrmann B. [2]2009. *Europa im Spätmittelalter 1215–1378* [= Oldenbourg. Grundriss der Geschichte 8]. Munich: R. Oldenbourg.

Epstein S. R. 2000. *Freedom and Growth. The Rise of States and Markets in Europe, 1300–1750*. London: Routledge.

Fontaine L. and Schlumbohm J. 2000. "Household Strategies for Survival: An Introduction." *International Review of Social History,* 45, no. 8, 1–17.

Fontaine L. 2013. "Survivre en temps de crise: Une perspective historique." *Revue Projet,* 336–337, 43–50. https://doi.org/10.3917/pro.336.0043.

Fontaine L. 2014. *Le Marché. Histoire et usage d'une conquête sociale.* Paris: Gallimard.

Foquet G. and Andermann K. (eds.) 2016. *Zins und Gült. Strukturen des ländlichen Kreditwesens in Spätmittelalter und Frühneuzeit* [= Kraichtaler Kolloquien, Bd. 10]. Epfendorf: Bibliotheca Scademica 2016

Fouquet G., von Seggern H, and Gilomen H.-J. (eds.) 2007. *Städtische Finanzwirtschaft am Übergang vom Mittelalter zur Frühen Neuzeit* [= Kieler Werkstücke, Reihe E, Beiträge zur Sozial- und Wirtschaftsgeschichte 4]. Frankfurt am Main: Peter Lang.

Fryde E. B. and Fryde M. M. 1963. "Public Credit, with Special Reference to North-Western Europe." In *The Cambridge Economic History of Europe: III: Economic Organization in the Middle Ages,* edited by M. Postan, E. E. Rich, and E. Miller, 430–553. Cambridge: Cambridge University Press.

Gelderblom O. and Jonker J. 2004. "Completing a Financial Revolution: The Finance of the Dutch East India Trade and the Rise of the Amsterdam Capital Market, 1595–1612." *The Journal of Economic History* 64, no. 3: 641–672.

Gelderblom O, Jonker, J. and Kool C. 2016. "Direct finance in the Dutch Golden Age." *Economic History Review* 69, no. 4: 1178–1198.

Ghosh S. 2017. "Rural Commercialisation in Fourteenth-Century Southern Germany: The Evidence from Scheyern Abbey". *Vierteljahrschrift für Sozial- und Wirtschaftsgeschichte* 104, no. 1: 52–77.

Ghosh S. 2020. "Rural Commercialization in Southern Germany, c. 1200–c. 1500: Sources, Problems, and Potential". *Mediaeval Studies* 82: 207–274.

Gilomen H.-J. 2010. "Kredit und Innovation im Spätmittelalter." In *Aufbruch im Mittelalter- Innovationen in der Gesellschaft der Vormoderne. Studien zu Ehren von Rain C. Schwinges,* edited by C. Hesse and K. Oschema, 35–68. Ostfildern: Jan Thorbecke Verlag.

Graeber D. 2011. *Debts. The First 5,000 Years.* New York: Melville House.

Greif A. 2006. *Institutions and the Path to the Modern Economy: Lessons from Medieval Trade.* Cambridge: Cambridge University Press.

Groebner V. 1993. *Ökonomie ohne Haus. Zum Wirtschaften armer Leute in Nürnberg am Ende des 15. Jahrhunderts.* [= Veröffentlichungen des Max-Planck-Instituts für Geschichte 108]. Göttingen: Vandenhoeck and Ruprecht.

Hatcher J. and Bailey M. 2001. *Modelling the Middle Ages. The History and Theory of England's Economic Development.* Oxford: Oxford University Press.

Hoffman P., G. Postel-Vinay, and J.-L. Rosenthal 1999. "Information and Economic History: How the Credit Market in Old Regime Paris Forces Us to Rethink the Transition to Capitalism." *The American History Review* 104, no. 1: 69–94.

Hoffman P., G. Postel-Vinay, and J.-L. Rosenthal 2000. *Priceless Markets: The Political Economy of Credit in Paris, 1660–1780*. Chicago: University of Chicago Press.

Hoffman P., G. Postel-Vinay, and J. L. Rosenthal 2019. *Dark Matter Credit. The Development of Peer-to-Peer Lending and Banking in France*. Princeton and Oxford: Princeton University Press.

Huang A. and Kypta U. 2019. "Europe, c. 1300–1600: Commercialisation and the Market Economy." In *Methods in premodern economic history: case studies from the Holy Roman Empire c.1300–c.1600* [= Palgrave Studies in Economic History], edited by U. Kypta, J. Bruch, and T. Skambraks, 101–104. London: Palgrave Macmillan.

Isenmann E. 2012. *Die deutsche Stadt im Mittelalter 1150–1550: Stadtgestalt, Recht, Verfassung, Stadtregiment, Kirche, Gesellschaft, Wirtschaft*. Vienna und Cologne: Böhlau.

Köhler S. and T. Skambraks 2019. "Commercial Revolution." In *Methods in premodern economic history: case studies from the Holy Roman Empire c.1300–c.1600* [= Palgrave Studies in Economic History], edited by U. Kypta, J. Bruch, and T. Skambraks, 22–24. London: Palgrave Macmillan.

Köster R. 2020. *Einführung in die Wirtschaftsgeschichte. Theorien, Methoden, Themen*. Paderborn: Ferdinand Schöningh.

Kuske B. 1956. "Die Entstehung der Kreditwirtschaft und des Kapitalverkehrs." In Bruno Kuske. *Köln, der Rhein und das Reich. Beiträge aus fünf Jahrzehnten wirtschaftsgeschichtlicher Forschung*. Cologne/Graz: Böhlau, 48–137 [published for the first time in Fritz Beckmann, Karl Diehl, Bruno Kuske, Alfred Müller, and Joseph Schumpeter. 1927. Die Kreditwirtschaft, vol. 1 [= Kölner Vorträge 1], 1–79. Leipzig: Gloeckner].

Kusman D. 2021. "High Finance, Banking and Small-Scale Moneylending: A new Trinity of Financial Functions for Lombards in the Late-Medieval Low Countries?" In *Change and Transformation of Pre-Modern Credit Markets. The Importance of Small-Scale Credits*, edited by S. Nicolussi-Köhler, 225–260. Heidelberg: Heidelberg University Publishing.

Kypta U. 2021. "How to Study the Premodern Market: The Concept of Market Exchange." In *Markets and their Actors in the Late Middle Ages*, edited by T. Skambraks, J. Bruch, and U. Kypta, 7–26. Berlin and Boston: De Gruyter.

Levine R. 2005. "Finance and Growth: Theory, Mechanisms and Evidence." In *Handbook of Economic Growth,* edited by P. Aghion and S. Durlauf, 865–934. Amsterdam: North Holland.

Lipp C. 2007. "Aspekte der mikrohistorischen und kulturanthropologischen Kreditforschung." In *Soziale Praxis des Kredits. 16.–20. Jahrhundert* [= Veröffentlichungen der Historischen Kommission für Niedersachsen und Bremen 238], edited by J. Schlumbohm, 15–36. Hannover: Hahnsche Buchhandlung Hannover.

Lopez R. 1976. *The Commercial Revolution of the Middle Ages. 950–1350,* Cambridge: Cambridge University Press.

Muldrew C. 1998. *The Economy of Obligation. The Culture of Credit and Social Relations in Early Modern England.* Hampshire: Palgrave.

Munro J. 2003. "The Medieval Origins of the Financial Revolution: Usury, Rentes, and Negotiability." *The International History Review* 25, no. 3: 505–562.

Neu T. 2019. "Geld gebrauchen. Frühneuzeitliche Finanz-, Kredit- und Geldgeschichte in praxeologischer Perspektive". *Historische Anthropologie* 27, no. 1: 75–103.

North D. C. 1990. *Institutions, Institutional Change and Economic Performance.* Cambridge: Cambridge University Press.

North, D. C. and Weingast, B. 1989. "Constitutions and Commitment: The Evolution of Institutions Governing Public Choice in Seventeenth-Century England." *Journal of Economic History* 49, no. 4: 803–32.

Ogilvie S. 2007. "Whatever Is, Is Right? Economic Institutions in Pre-Industrial Europe." *The Economic History Review* 60, no. 4: 649–684.

Ogilvie S., Küpke M., and Maegraith J. 2012. "Household Debt in Early Modern Germany: Evidence from Personal Inventories." The Journal of Economic History 72, no. 1: 134–167.

Reyerson K. 2002. *The Art of the Deal. Intermediaries of Trade in Medieval Montpellier.* Leiden, Boston, and Cologne: Brill.

Schlumbohm J. 2007. "Zur Einführung." In *Soziale Praxis des Kredits. 16.–20. Jahrhundert* [= Veröffentlichungen der Historischen Kommission für Niedersachsen und Bremen 238], edited by J. Schlumbohm, 7–14. Hannover: Hahnsche Buchhandlung Hannover.

Schuster P. 2008. "The Age of Debt? Private Schulden in der spätmittelalterlichen Gesellschaft." In *Schuldenlast und Schuldenwert. Kreditnetzwerke in der europäischen Geschichte 1300–1900,* edited by G. Clemens, 37–52. Trier: Kliomedia.

Shaw J. E. 2018. "The Informal Economy of Credit in Early Modern Venice." *The Historical Journal* 61, no 3: 623–642.

Signori G. 2015. "Einleitung." In *Prekäre Ökonomien. Schulden in Spätmittelalter und Früher Neuzeit,* edited by G. Signori, 7–16. Constance and Munich: UVK Verlagsgesellschaft.

Signori G. 2021. "Kleinkredite im städtischen Wirtschaftsleben des ausgehenden 15. Jahrhunderts." *Vierteljahrschrift für Sozial- und Wirtschaftsgeschichte* 108, no. 1: 30–56.

Skambraks T. 2021. *Monti di Pietà, franziskanische Wirtschaftsethik und städtische Sozialpolitik in Italien (15. und 16. Jahrhundert).* Unprinted habilitation thesis. University of Mannheim.

Skambraks T., Köhler S., Kehnel A., Kümper H., Gussone M., and Schniggendiller M. 2020. "Kleinkredit und Marktteilhabe in der Vormoderne: Projektdesign." *Mannheim Working Papers in Premodern Economic History* 1: 1–12.

Spufford P. 1988. *Money and its use in Medieval Europe.* Cambridge: Cambridge University Press.

Stasavage D. 2011. States of Credit. Size, Power, and the Development of European Polities. Princeton and Oxford: Princeton University Press.

Tomkins A. and King S. (eds.) 2003. *The poor in England 1700–1850: An economy of makeshifts.* Manchester and New York: Manchester University Press.

Tracy J. D. 1985. *A Financial Revolution in the Habsburg Netherlands. Renten and Renteniers in the County of Holland, 1515–1565.* Berkeley: University of California Press.

Ucendo J. I. A. and Limberger M. 2012. "Introduction." In *Taxation and Debt in the Early Modern City,* edited by J. I. A. Ucendo and M. Limberger, 1–12. London and New York: Routledge.

Usher A. P. 1934. "The Origins of Banking: The Primitive Bank of Deposit, 1200–1600." *The Economic History Review* 4, no. 4: 399–428.

Van Bavel B. 2011 "Markets for Land, Labor, and Capital in Northern Italy and the Low Countries, Twelfth to Seventeenth Centuries." *The Journal of Interdisciplinary History* 41, no. 4: 503–531.

Van Bavel B. 2016. *The Invisible Hand? How Market Economies Have Emerged and Declined Since AD 500.* Oxford: Oxford University Press.

Van Schaik R. (ed.) 2015. *Economies, Public Finances, and the Impact of Institutional Changes in Interregional Perspective. The Low Countries and Neighbouring German Territories (14th–17th Centuries)* [= Studies in European Urban History (1100–1800) 36]. Turnhout: Brepols.

Van Zanden J., Zuijderduijn J., and De Moor T. 2012. "Small Is Beautiful: The Efficiency of Credit Markets in the Late Medieval Holland." *European Review of Economic History* 16: 3–22.

Vries P. 2020. Review: Alfani, Guido/Matteo Di Tullio, The Lion's Share. Inequality and the Rise of the Fiscal State in Preindustrial Europe (Cambridge Studies in Economic History), Cambridge [u.a.] 2019, Cambridge University Press, XII u. 232 S., £ 31,99. *Zeitschrift für Historische Forschung* 47, no. 4: 62–63.

Wickham C. 2021. "How did the Feudal Economy Work? The Economic Logic of Medieval Socities." *Past and Present* 251: 3–40.

Zuijderduijn J. 2009. *Medieval Capital Markets. Markets for renten, State Formation and Private Investment in Holland (1300–1550).* Leiden and Boston: Brill.

CHANGE AND TRANSFORMATION OF PREMODERN CREDIT MARKETS

The Importance of Small-Scale Credits

Gilles Postel-Vinay

A View from Beyond?

The question mark in the title signals uncertainty about my possible contribution to this conference as I am neither a specialist of pre-modern credits nor an expert in small-scale credits. The research I conducted with my co-authors on the workings of credit markets in France from the seventeenth to the beginning of the twentieth century encompasses small-scale and large-scale-credit. More precisely, the credit markets we studied had at first very large social coverage, but over time became less and less enmeshed with small-scale credits. As such, it may be somewhat out of step with the issues raised in this conference. Moreover, the conference proposes a broad time frame by wrapping into a long "premodern period" both its medieval and its early modern component. This suggests a clear contrast between a modern and a premodern period while the type of credit we have studied developed mostly between the seventeenth century and World War I, and thus straddled the early-modern and the modern period. And there is a second reason. As part of our research pertains to the modern period, the risk would be to take the future as the yardstick of the past or as a kind of benchmark for the past. Here, I will certainly not pretend to find the key to premodern credit markets in more recent credit markets as Marx thought that "human anatomy contains a key to the anatomy of the ape". Instead, I will limit myself to sketching some of our conclusions in order to raise questions about the uneven development and changing spatial scope of small-scale credit markets over time and to offer some tentative explanations.

Published in: Stephan Nicolussi-Köhler (Ed.), Change and Transformation of Premodern Credit Markets. The Importance of Small-Scale Credits. Heidelberg: heiBOOKS 2021, 23–38. DOI: https://doi.org/10.11588/heibooks.593.c12689

A preliminary question could be why the title of the conference refers to markets in the plural. One answer, backed by an abundant historiography, is well-known. In premodern Europe, credit markets were local and doomed to be local. The situation has often been described. A recent monograph on a sixteenth-century French local market is a good example: most loans, big and small, in Saint-Maixent—a small town in South Western France—were interpersonal and linked closely related people.[1] To a large extent, the situation we found in seventeenth-century Paris was similar. At the beginning of the reign of Louis XIV, roughly half of the loans that Parisian notaries recorded involved borrowers and lenders drawn from the same family, neighbourhood, or profession. This practice reflected the difficulties of observing a borrower's actions and of verifying his collateral, but the result was to restrict credit. Credit activity was not only local; it was limited. Or, to use the jargon of economists: it was "thin".

Our research arose out of the difficulties created by this historiography—a historiography built on the modern/premodern divide and its attendant preconceptions. In fact, we had to revisit it "against the grain". It is usual to represent growth in modern Europe as a finance-driven process, in which banks played a central role because they assembled the necessary resources; moreover, banks centralised these resources while traditional markets remained both weak and confined to their narrow horizons. The hypothesis seemed even more convincing because it could point to the English experience, characterised by the early development of banks, in a political context favourable to a reduction in interest rates. However, this long-held consensus raised many questions. In a first book—*Priceless markets* (2000)/*Des marchés sans prix* (2001)—we showed that in eighteenth-century Paris, there was a very rapid expansion in credit activity that was independent of the banks and, furthermore, in which the interest rate played no role.

But was Paris one of a kind or, on the contrary, did this model pulse with more general explanatory power? That was the question we sought to answer when we began the (long) enquiry that led to a new book which, this time, deals with credit in the whole of France from the eighteenth century to the beginning of the twentieth century—*Dark matter credit* (2019)[2]. Since we found a situation that closely resembled that of Paris in the eighteenth century, we thought for a while of naming the new book "Priceless Markets 2". Then, it seemed to us that we should first stress the volume of credit activity outside of banking credit in order to analyse how these different types of credit coexisted. From there, we arrived at the final

---

1 Legendre 2020.

2 Hoffman, Postel-Vinay, and Rosenthal 2001; Hoffman, Postel-Vinay, and Rosenthal 2019.

book title. To evoke the role of non-bank credit, we use the image of black matter: that which is not directly visible but is nevertheless a major part of the universe.

The two books have in common a double point of departure. The first comes, as is often the case, from historical experience. We have known for a long time about non-banking credit in preindustrial Europe, which was considered as an archaism (often harmful, but residual) whose existence must tend to disappear in the modern era. It seemed legitimate then to seek a better understanding by measuring it over the long period and to investigate how it functioned. Simultaneously, the available means for analysis were in the process of changing when we started our projects, and this was the second element to orient the beginning of our research. When we started working on it, the economics of information were opening a whole range of new approaches. So, we began with the anachronism inherent in the work of a historian who brings foreign categories into the past. In addition, our contemporary context played a role: the current functioning of IT platforms has no doubt helped us to understand the success of these unexpected intermediaries—notaries—whose central role we discovered in the introduction and spectacular development of a credit system that has been around for two centuries. We thus formulated and tested some hypotheses about the ways in which information asymmetries were overcome through modalities other than those available to the banks.

The case of Paris showed not only that credit activity had boomed since the eighteenth century but that this credit activity was linked to quite unusual intermediaries: the notaries who used the precise information that they had about their clients to put lenders in touch with borrowers seeking loans, people whose reliability they could guarantee. Expanding the study beyond the capital city might seem logical since it is common to link the development of financial markets with organisations that centralise their resources—big banks and stock exchanges. Instead, we could have also considered two scenarios suggested by economic geography: if transaction costs are high then the economic activity stays close to the consumer (the case of hairdressers); if not then it tends to concentrate in one place (the case of the automobile in Detroit) or in some places (stock exchanges). The credit that we observed, however, followed neither of these models. Contrary to stock exchange transactions, the loans were not concentrated in one place; and contrary to haircuts, they were not done on the corner of the street. We were talking about credit whose centralisation was partial or incomplete. Towards the middle of the eighteenth century for example, towns and cities certainly took the lion's share of the sums lent, but the large majority of the borrowers had access to numberless loans of medium and small size which were spread over the country: 80 per cent of borrowers lived in parishes of fewer than 5,000 inhabitants.

Three main characteristics stand out.

First, the credit activity was on a scale that we had not imagined. To gauge its importance, we needed relevant evidence that revealed how much private credit there was and how loans were arranged. The bulk of this evidence concerns 239,269 individual loans and the variables that affected lending in a sample of ninety-nine French credit markets. They ranged from Paris to small villages, and, for each of them, we gathered the data for six years (1740, 1780, 1807, 1840, 1865, and 1899). These markets were chosen to reflect the urban hierarchy. But we needed more: we also gathered evidence from seventy-three additional markets which were close to each other to study the way credit was organised spatially. In France as a whole, from the eighteenth century to World War I, the astounding total of notarised loans represented on average between one fifth and one quarter of GDP.

Table 1 An estimate of outstanding loans in France as a whole relative to GDP

	Years					
–	**1740**	**1780**	**1807**	**1840**	**1865**	**1899**
Stock of outstanding loans (million livres/francs)	1426	2398	1120	3650	4150	7690
Stock of debt to GDP (%)	15.8	22.9	9.6	27.2	19.9	23.6

To keep a long story short, notaries were the primary source of private capital until the late nineteenth century.

Second, the loans reached a very large part of the population. In the eighteenth century, our data suggests that no less than one third of French households were involved. The loans were of all sizes—except the very small ones. To give an order of magnitude, the smallest loans were for amounts on the order of a few months' salary. In other words, this type of loan affected a very large part of the population, but was not used to meet the day-to-day insurance needs of the population.

Third, the credit markets were not isolated. In the first cross-section—in 1740—our data is imperfect because we do not always know where borrowers and lenders lived. When this information is available, however, it shows that only half of lenders and borrowers lived in the same place. Many had thus to travel, particularly from small municipalities. Better data in the 19th century corroborates this conclusion: travel was common. It was especially common for big loans, and even more if you lived in small municipalities.

Table 2 Percentage of notarised loans in which the borrower and the lender lived in the same community (by community size)

Community size (population)	Years		
—	1807	1840	1899
< 500	22	13	20
500–999	27	21	16
1000–2499	35	29	29
2500–4999	49	37	37
5000–19999	72	66	52
20000–99999	90	78	64
100000–500000	91	89	62
Paris	92	73	63

In a way, credit markets in eighteenth- and nineteenth-century French villages were as outward looking as marriage markets of contemporary villages in the mountains of Northern Italy were inward looking[3]. While in the latter, to the great displeasure of the Church, all the inhabitants declared that they wanted to marry within the village and could not marry elsewhere even though they were all related to each other, a French villager who wanted to borrow usually had to travel.

As the majority of lenders and borrowers were not neighbours, they were less likely to rely on their own limited personal connections. This does not mean that the credit was impersonal because if borrowers and lenders did not know each other, they were known by an intermediary—their notary—who put them in contact. Moreover, whenever a notary could not find a match within his clientele, he could decide to refer to one of his colleagues any potential borrower or lender he deemed creditworthy. In other words, credit markets were not islands. As a result, we have to break with a tradition of treating local credit markets in the past as isolated from one another. This idea lies behind the local histories that many historians have undertaken. Such an approach certainly has a number of advantages, but what we find raises questions about the premise behind them: as our data shows, credit markets in different places were clearly linked.

3 Merzario 1981.

But if local markets were not isolated, how did lenders find creditworthy borrowers or valuable collateral? To be sure, information would have been safer if borrowers or lenders had not travelled and restricted their transactions to relatives and friends or consigners. In this case, however, credit activities would have been severely limited. But, in eighteenth- and nineteenth-century France at least, this was not what was happening.

Admittedly, big problems may arise if borrowers or lenders travelled because they were unlikely to know one another. In addition, collaterals by themselves were not a solution either: how do you tell what the collateral is worth or whether it is already mortgaged? In France, this issue had been hotly debated at least since the sixteenth century, and one has to keep in mind that no effective lien registry existed before the late 1800s. If borrowers and lenders could not all know one another, how was the problem of asymmetric information solved?

The transactions depended on information about the guarantees that only the notaries held. Loans were thus usually organised within the clientele of each notary, but information could also circulate among offices. In this case, information on potential borrowers or lenders did not circulate in an undifferentiated manner: each notary created a group whose members were at one and at the same time supervisors and partners. Again, what mattered was not the price of credit (the loans being generally subject to the same rate) but the capacity of the intermediary to provide certain information to the lenders, the borrowers and, where appropriate, the offices with which he collaborated.

For a long time, no-one had any competing information. While the state of the Ancien Regime dreamed of it and the Revolution set it as a goal, almost another century passed before a public information system about loans was properly established.

In the absence of this public information, notaries were in a very strong position. It may be tempting to consider that the survival of traditional intermediaries such as notaries was proof of institutional failure. But they may simply have had a cost advantage, such as private information, which new entrants had not. As a result, such newcomers could not outcompete the traditional intermediaries. Banks, for one, confined themselves to other, highly diverse credit activities, commercial and industrial, but principally short term and concentrated in towns.

This specialisation in short-term commercial credit implied in-depth knowledge of a limited clientele, the activity of which was continuously changing such that credit had to rely mostly on reputation or frequent interrelation.[4] On the contrary, notarial credit reached a much broader population, the creditworthiness of

4 For a classic example, see Lamoreaux 1994.

which notaries certified as they knew their clientele and the wealth they could pledge well. In other words, the former offered credit based mostly on the reputation of a small group, the latter offered credit based mostly on collaterals owned by the rather large population of those who owned some wealth and particularly some real estate. Notaries could do so because they possessed lengthy records of past business doing lending and arranging other property transactions, from sales and leases to inheritances. Banks lacked such information. Hence, notaries had nothing to fear from bankers, who dared not compete with notaries in their own specialty of mortgage lending. The bankers and notaries in fact focused on different corners of the credit market, and their businesses were complementary: they reinforced one another. They were thus not competing with each other—and, when they did so, it resulted in major failures. Perhaps unexpectedly, it is thus when we look beyond the premodern period that we are faced with the long-lasting coexistence of a premodern informational structure and a modern one which formed an almost stable equilibrium up to World War I.

If we look backward, by comparison, during the premodern period both intermediaries and credit instrument seem less stable.

Let us start with credit instruments. At first glance, in France as elsewhere in Western Europe, we find the same credit instruments since the medieval period. During the whole premodern period, besides oral contracts and the various forms of IOU, there were two well-established ways to make loans: annuities and obligations. Annuities specified a set of payments, and either no repayment date (perpetual annuities) or the payment stopped when a person named in the contract (the "life", who was often the lender) died (life annuities). If the lender was not willing to enter into these contracts, he could accept an obligation, a type of loan in which the borrower promised to return a certain sum of money at some specified time in the future. But each of these instruments did change.

Take as an example life annuities. In some places, they were already common in the medieval period. This was the case in Spain, in particular. These medieval Spanish life annuities seemed to recall the memory of Roman life annuities, but this was not the case. They did not rest on the precise logic of the Roman version of life annuities based on life expectancy (indeed Ulpian's life table appears to provide a rough outline of ancient Roman life expectancy). Instead, the duration of the contract was fixed at the death of a son of either the creditor or the debtor, or of a well-known public figure, the pope, the king, whose death would soon be known.[5] As such, they were very different from the life annuities which became more and more popular in the seventeenth and eighteenth century when

5 Furió Diego 1998.

they were based on the wave of research which produced the modern mortality tables.[6] The other credit instrument also underwent major changes. This was the case of mortgages in Great Britain where "the evolution of modern mortgage was the major development that led to the elimination of yeoman farming in the eighteenth century".[7] In France, annuities changed too, but the structure of obligations changed even more dramatically. In the seventeenth century, these contracts, often for small sums, usually lasted a few months or a year or two and were closely related to the privately drawn-up IOU that came to be prevalent in England. Over the course of the eighteenth century, they grew larger, lasted longer and became so common that in the nineteenth century, they had come to dominate the medium- and long-term credit markets.[8]

Intermediaries also changed across space and over time. In the French case, since the eighteenth century, notaries played a decisive role as credit intermediaries because they had special access to information on lenders and borrowers. But this was a recent phenomenon. Notaries had been well-established since the Middle Ages in the Mediterranean rim of Western Europe[9], but much less in the Northern part of the continent. In France in particular, the efforts of the monarchy to gradually standardise the regulation of their activities throughout the kingdom notwithstanding, the presence of notaries had remained less dense in the North than in the South, which gave rise to different credit practices.

More importantly, if in France notaries were major credit intermediaries, elsewhere, other intermediaries played the same role. In some regions, the cities and their administration were the major player—David Sabean's book on a German village could be taken as an example: "From the middle of the sixteenth century onward, the village (Neckarhausen) was ever more closely bound together with officials in the Amtstadt and in Stuttgart through chains of paper" concerning volumes of mortgages in particular.[10] In other regions, the Church—especially the secular clergy—played the main role as Cyril Milhaud's recent thesis on early-modern Spain demonstrates.[11] Later on, the European States took the lead when they became able to produce reliable liens registries; but, most often, this was not before the nineteenth century.[12]

---

6 Weir 1989; Süssmilch 1998 [1741].

7 Allen 1992.

8 Schnapper 1957. See also, Hoffman, Postel-Vinay, and Rosenthal 2019.

9 Menant and Redon 2004.

10 Sabean 1990.

11 Milhaud 2017. Milhaud analyses the financial development of eighteenth-century Spain and emphasises the role of ecclesiastical institutions in intermediation.

12 For a point of comparison in classical antiquity, see Lerouxel 2016.

Paradoxically, the role of credit intermediaries, in whatever form they intervened, is perhaps best understood if we consider the situations where these intermediaries were absent as in medieval Normandy. There, for a while, any contract that changed the wealth of someone living in a given parish was made public in a particular way. A land sale or a loan had to be read during the mass "coram parocchia" or "in plena parocchia": the two formulas each insist in their own way on the pooling of information. There was no such thing as a notary, but once the contract was read during the mass, no one in the village was unaware of it. "Coram" indeed means "in the presence of"; and "in plena parocchia" emphasises that the whole local population was gathered together as if in a plenary session. All the parishioners assembled for Sunday Mass then constituted a collective witness of great authority. This solution certainly had many advantages. A contract "coram parocchia" was written by the local priest who enjoyed recognised authority and provided contractors with an easily accessible instrument. But as these bilateral loans were arranged directly without the help of an intermediary who combined the preservation of records with the roles of lawyer, financial adviser, real estate broker, matchmaker, and scribe, they remained of limited scope.[13]

This medieval situation highlights, albeit negatively, the importance of credit intermediaries and the informational infrastructure underlying credit markets that they put in place. But it also shows that credit—large-scale credit, but small-scale credit as well—may develop without intermediaries.

The poor and the rich behaved differently in credit markets. They did not have the same demand for credit, and did not take out the same kind of loans. Those who owned something may have used their wealth as collateral, those who did not could only pledge their reputation—if they were able to borrow at all. Of course, there were many sorts of wealth. In premodern cities, many people could take any small item to a pawn shop. But the major form of wealth was real estate and it was by far the main collateral. As is well known, real estate was unevenly distributed. This was the case in general, but not to the same degree everywhere: wealth and particularly real estate was highly concentrated in the hands of a tiny minority in towns, but more widely distributed in the countryside.

In premodern (and modern) Europe, collateral was the dominant way to reduce a lender's anxiety about the potential borrower's willingness or ability to repay. But it was not the only way, even if the choice of collateral was limited. In particular, you could no longer enslave yourself. As a result, a borrower could not pledge himself as collateral: if he pledged collateral, he could only offer his wealth (especially the principal form of wealth, i.e. real estate). The borrower of-

---

13 Arnoux 1996.

fered his wealth as a hostage, and the lender could seize it, if he failed to repay on time. But someone who had no wealth could still borrow by relying on his reputation. It was certainly a serious commitment because in so doing, he put his future access to credit at risk. But reputational credit and collateral credit did not follow the same logic.

What matters thus was who owned wealth? And where? These questions cannot be precisely answered before the beginning of the nineteenth century, which is, of course, very late information for thinking about the wealth distribution of the pre-modern period. Let us admit, however, that it is still informative. The French situation in the nineteenth century could then provide a useful example because, in this case, we can rely on a representative sample of the distribution of wealth in the whole population.[14] In this period, the proportion of adults leaving some wealth at death varied between seventy and sixty percent on average and from eighty to seventy percent in the countryside. By contrast, it was only 50 per cent in cities if one excludes Paris where as few as thirty percent of the population left some wealth upon dying (see Figure 1). The difference would be even greater if one considers only the population who owned real estate.

If what mattered was collateral, moreover if what mattered most was collateral based on real estate, the implication was that many people were left behind. This was true everywhere, in towns as in the countryside, but those who were left behind were more numerous in towns—especially in large towns and cities. Hence two consequences. First, the proportion of those who could borrow credit via collateral was higher in the countryside. And since land was often divided into small plots, loans in the countryside could be rather modest. Yet notarised loans were costly, and as such they were seldom used for the petty sums that the poor needed to make ends meet day after day. In other words, even in the countryside, many people did not have access to collateral credit. But in towns, this was the case of many more people, and the demand for informal reputational credit or for credit institutions specialised in small-scale credit was thus higher in an urban setting.

This was particularly true in large towns and cities where reputational credit was crucial for the poor as they had little or no real estate that could be used for collateral and hardly any wealth that could be pawned. There, in addition to informal reputational credit, urban authorities often provided an array of credit institutions specialised in small-scale credit. Amsterdam in the "Golden Age" offers a good example.[15] But the case of Venice is perhaps the most striking[16]: in the

14 Bourdieu, Kesztenbaum, and Postel-Vinay 2014.
15 McCants 1997.
16 Pompermaier 2019.

Figure 1 Percentage of individuals leaving an estate on death.

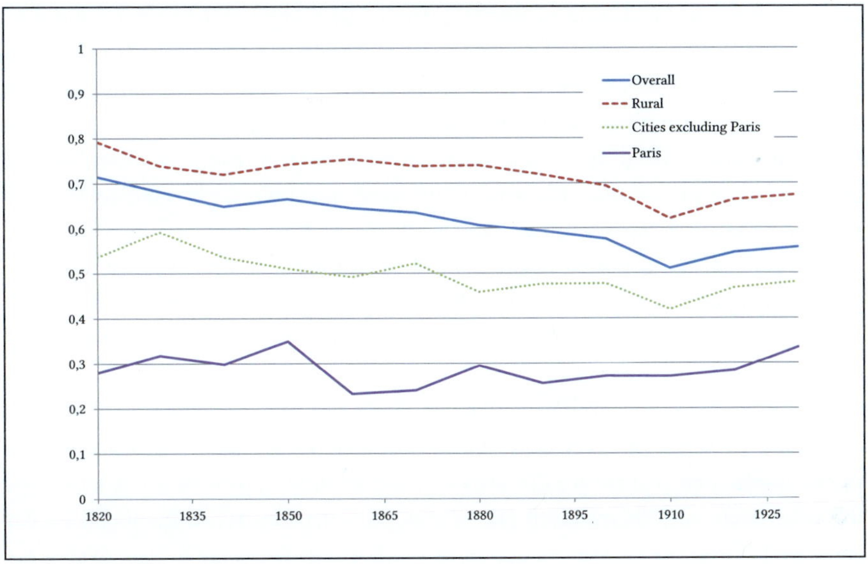

eighteenth century, a Venetian poor was able to borrow from no less than five sources of credit. As Pompermaier has shown, these different credit channels were not in competition with one another; rather they were positioned in a segmented market.

Informal reputational credit was also important in the countryside. European villages were part of tiny economies, in which inhabitants were inserted in a set of interlocking transactions which encompassed labour, rights to land, and loans.[17] For instance, landowners could offer insurance to their tenants by letting them fall behind in rent during "lean years". Then, arrears often soared: in effect, these were loans that the landowner made to tenant farmers. In such a context, a villager's reputation—in particular his past history of credit dealings—was enormously important. This type of credit was omnipresent in the "traditional society" of premodern European villages and, over time, it became even more so. Indeed, it is now generally agreed that inequality of wealth had been increasing in the countryside since the late Middle-Ages.[18] As a result, fewer villagers were able to offer real estate as collateral when they needed to borrow and informal reputational credit became more crucial.

17 Meuvret 1971; Hoffman 1996.
18 See Alfani and Di Tullio 2019.

One caveat remains, however. It would be misleading to estimate the importance of small-scale credits in isolation from other resources to which the poor could have access. Small-scale credit was tremendously important for the poor, but it was not the only resource they could rely on. This was particularly true for urbanites. Towns multiplied credit institutions (monts of piety, in particular)[19] but borrowing was one form of insurance among others. In the premodern as well as the modern period, the poor made ends meet not only with small-scale credit based on their private wealth or their reputation. They may have had access to the various forms of public resources available for social and welfare purposes, be they of religious origin—like the tithe—or part of the set of charitable institutions shouldered by local parishes or communities which provided poor-relief with more or less generosity.

In this respect, focusing on collateral credit—as my co-authors and I did—is unequally informative over time. Its importance varied since the frontiers between public and private wealth also varied and they indeed varied a lot during the premodern and the modern periods. In the Christian West, thanks to its patrimonial strategy, the Church held for more than a millennium a huge part of the property—rarely less than one tenth and up to one third. This heritage base made it possible to support not only an important clergy but also to finance a number of social services, the generosity of which could vary from place to place and over time, and as such could mitigate or amplify the very need of small-scale credit. Ecclesiastical wealth was far from stable. In many European countries "Fluctuat nec mergitur", in others "Fluctuat et mergitur". Its ebbs and flows affected its legitimacy and reshaped the division of roles between ecclesiastical wealth (which, in part, commanded assistance) and private wealth (which in part commanded access to credit), in particular since the sixteenth century.

For the poor, this changing balance of assistance and loans likely had a large impact on the forms and the role of small-scale credit. A late but telling example—telling as well for the "premodern" as the "modern" period—could be found in Victorian England. There, to be sure, the poor were vilified, especially after the "crusade against out-relief" of the mid-nineteenth century, and "shopkeepers and landlords viewed the application for poor relief as a clear signal of increased risk of default." As a result, poor households did strive as much as possible to remain off the Poor Law since to seek assistance was to give a negative signal. Someone who did so risked not being able to find a lender in case of need while the ability to obtain small-scale credits was "vitally important" for a majority of the population. Admittedly, the context had little in common with Italy in the Franciscan era.

19 See Mauro Carboni, this Conference.

Yet, in both cases, the uneasy complementarity of small-scale credit and assistance remained a basic feature of everyday life.[20]

Indeed, small scale credit was not the recourse of last resort for the poor; rather it was one resource among several others. With two consequences. Its use varied according to the availability of other resources. It was at times visible, at other times less visible, and sometimes altogether invisible when it left no trace. In the first half of the eighteenth century, small loans were often notarised in France even if they only represented a small part of the sums that passed through notarial credit. Decade after decade, however, they became less frequent. While notarised loan sizes were rising over time, the number of loans was falling, especially in the countryside. Rural notaries were drafting fewer and fewer small loans and it was not because they were swamped for business. Instead, it seems that demand for notarisation of small loans was shriveling up in the countryside. What, then, was the source of demand for these small rural loans? We should keep in mind that there was no legal requirement that debt contracts (including mortgages) be notarised. And although notarisation provided additional security of contract, it came at a cost: roughly one percent of the value of the debt. For the small rural loans, the reason the parties consulted a notary was probably not greater security; in all likelihood they did so because they were both illiterate and unfamiliar with the language of written debt contracts. This was indeed the case when contracts were in Latin, but it was still often the case when, from the sixteenth century onwards, they were written in French. That source of demand, however, was drying up in the eighteenth century and even more in the nineteenth century. The fraction of French men who could sign their names jumped eighteen percent between 1690 and 1790[21], and at the end of the nineteenth century almost everyone could read and write. In the eighteenth century, a majority of borrowers and lenders still needed to have notaries read their contracts out loud and attest that they had agreed to the terms of the loan. But over time, fewer and fewer borrowers and lenders did need their help. The effect would be felt primarily on small loans, for at a time when schooling was neither mandatory nor free, literacy was positively correlated with income, as was loan size. The illiterates would therefore have lower average incomes and borrow and lend smaller amounts. And as their numbers shrank, so would small (notarised) loans. But as the number of individuals who were able to read and write rose, more and more individuals could borrow or lend without the help of a notary, at least for small sums. All those who were literate enough would have likely opted for a private

20 Johnson 1985; Boyer 2019.
21 Furet and Ozouf 1977.

contract to spare them of the notary's fees. In this case, small-scale credit did not disappear, but it did not leave any trace anymore; except in private diaries (which seldom survive); except in post mortem inventories (which are far from general); or except in the archives of the legal system developed to ensure that debtors paid their dues.[22] Each of these potential alternative sources proved precious, but each suffered severe problems of selection.

Lucien Febvre famously wrote that historians ought to use "the texts but all the texts… The texts obviously, but not only the texts"[23], by which he meant all available sources. For small-scale credit, all texts and available sources are, in part, promising. But also, in part, elusive. Tantalus had to stand in a pool of water beneath a fruit tree with low branches, with the fruit ever eluding his grasp, and the water always receding before he could take a drink, and small-scale credit is a tantalising object. It shows up in many sources, but every one of them has serious limitations. Cities provide us with better observatories than the countryside, but in premodern Europe, cities housed a small part of the population. Post-mortem inventories provide particularly valuable information, but they only concern a minority of the people. When we studied notarial credit, we touched upon small-scale credit, and what we learned may also contribute to map how much terra incognita remains to be explored. But as the poor were poor in credit and as the credit they had access to was poorly documented, historians have to be particularly inventive. This conference shows that they are.

References

Alfani, G. and M. Di Tullio 2019. *The Lion's Share. Inequality and the Rise of the Fiscal State in preindustrial Europe.* Cambridge: Cambridge University Press.

Allen, R. C. 1992. *Enclosure and the Yeoman. The Agricultural Development of the South Midlands,* 1450–1850: Oxford: Oxford University Press.

Arnoux, M. 1996. "Essor et déclin d'une forme diplomatique: les actes coram parrochia (Normandie, XIIe–XIIIe siècle)". *Bibliothèque de l'École des Chartes,* 154, no. 2: 325–357.

Bourdieu J., L. Kesztenbaum, and G. Postel-Vinay 2014. "The TRA Project, a Historical Matrix". *Population* 69, no. 2: 191–220.

22 Sabean 1990; Claustre 2013; Smail 2016.

23 Febvre ²1992.

Boyer, G. 2019. *The Winding Road to the Welfare State. Economic Insecurity and Social Welfare Policy in Britain.* Princeton: Princeton University Press.

Claustre, J. 2013. "Vivre à crédit dans une ville sans banque. Paris XIVe–XVe siècle)". *Le Moyen Age,* 119 no. 3–4: 567–596.

Febvre, L. ²1992 "Combats pour l'histoire". Paris: Armand Colin.

Furet, F. and J. Ozouf 1977. *Lire et écrire: l'alphabétisation des Français de Calvin à Jules Ferry.* Paris: Minuit.

Furió Diego, A. 1998. "Endettement paysan et crédit dans la Péninsule Ibérique au Bas Moyen Âge". In *Endettement paysan et crédit rural dans l'Europe médiévale et moderne: actes des XVIIes Journées Internationales d'Histoire de l'Abbaye de Flaran, Septembre 1995,* edited by M. Berthe, S. 139–167. Toulouse: Presses universitaires du Midi.

Hoffman, P. T., G. Postel-Vinay, and J.-L. Rosenthal 2019. *Dark Matter Credit. The Development of Peer-to-peer Lending and Banking in France.* Princeton. Princeton University Press.

Hoffman P. T., G. Postel-Vinay, and J.-L. Rosenthal 2001. *Des marchés sans prix: Une économie politique du crédit à Paris, 1660–1870.* Paris: Ecole des Hautes études en sciences sociales.

Hoffman, P. T. 1996. *Growth in a Traditional Society. The French Countryside. 1450–1815.* Princeton: Princeton University Press.

Hoffman, P. T., G. Postel-Vinay, and J.-L. Rosenthal 2000. *Priceless markets: The Political Economy of Credit in Paris, 1662–1869.* Chicago: University of Chicago Press.

Johnson, P. 1985. *Saving and Spending: The Working-Class Economy in Britain 1870–1939.* Oxford: Clarendon.

Lamoreaux, N. 1994. *Insider Lending: Banks, Personal Connections, and Economic Development in Industrial New England.* Cambridge: Cambridge University Press

Legendre, R. 2020. *Confiance, épargne et notaires. Le marché du crédit à Saint-Maixent et dans sa région au XVIe siècle.* Paris: Ecole des chartes.

Lerouxel, F. 2016. *Le marché du crédit dans le monde romain (Egypte et Campanie).* Rome: École française de Rome.

McCants, A. E. C. 1997. *Civic Charity in a Golden Age: Orphan Care in Early Modern Amsterdam.* Urbana, IL: University of Illinois Press.

Menant, F. and O. Redon 2004. *Notaires et crédit dans l'Occident méditerranéen medieval.* Rome: Ecole Française de Rome.

Merzario, R. 1981. *Il Paese stretto. Strategie matrimoniali nella diocesi di Como. Secoli XVI–XVIII.* Turin: Einaudi.

Meuvret, J. 1971. "Circulation monétaire et utilisation économique de la monnaie dans la France du XVIe et du XVIIe siècle", *Études d'histoire économique.* Paris: Armand Colin.

Milhaud, C. 2017. *Sacré Crédit! The Rise and Fall of Ecclesiastical Credit in Early Modern Spain.* Phd thesis: EHESS.

Pompermaier, M. 2019. ""Wine and Cash": Osterie, Bastioni and the Venetian credit market (18th century)". Phd thesis: Université de Rouen, Universita degli Studi di Padova.

Sabean, D. W. 1990. *Property, production, and family in Neckarhausen 1700–1870.* Cambridge: Cambridge University Press.

Schnapper, B. 1957. *Les rentes au XVIe siècle: Histoire d'un instrument de crédit.* Paris: SEVPEN.

Smail, D. L. 2016. *Legal Plunder: Households and Debt Collection in Late Medieval Europe.* Cambridge, MA: Harvard University Press.

Süssmilch, J. P. 1998 [1741]. *L'ordre divin dans les changements de l'espèce humaine démontré par la naissance, la mort et la propagation de celle-ci,* French translation by J. M. Rohrbasser. Paris: INED.

Weir, D. R. 1989. "Tontines, Public Finance, and Revolution in France and England, 1688–1789". *Journal of Economic History* 49, no. 1: 95–124.

Picture Credits

Fig. 1 Bourdieu J., L. Kesztenbaum, and G. Postel-Vinay 2014. "The TRA Project, a Historical Matrix". *Population* 69, no. 2: 206.

COLONISATION AND CREDIT IN MEDIEVAL WALES

Matthew Frank Stevens

Abstract: This work surveys the roles played by credit in the conquest and colonisation of Wales. It outlines the Welsh native law of contract and surety, relating to debt, and analyses the new system of debt recovery set out in the 1284 Statute of Wales. The role of Jewish creditors will also be touched upon. Finally, a case study will be presented of debt-related litigation in the borough and commotal courts of the lordship of Dyffryn Clwyd, 1295–1391. It is concluded that an unavailability of credit hampered Welsh rulers' efforts to maintain their independence, that conquest brought about the modernisation of debt-recovery law in Wales, likely stimulating durable economic growth, and that Welsh persons were fully integrated into post-conquest local credit networks and debt recovery systems by the end of the fourteenth century

Keywords: Wales, credit, medieval, conquest, law

* Acknowledgements: I am grateful to Professor Phillipp Schofield, Aberystwyth University, for his comments on a previous draft of this article.
Funding: This work was supported by the British Academy under grant no. SG171150, "Jim Crow in Medieval Wales: a comparative approach to the long history of legal discrimination and segregation"; the National Science Centre, Poland (Narodowe Centrum Nauki) under grant no. UMO-2016/22/MHS3/00157; and the Polish National Agency for Academic Exchange (Narodowa Agencja Wymiany Akademickiej), Ulam Fellowship, under grant no. PPN/ULM/2019/1/00033.

Published in: Stephan Nicolussi-Köhler (Ed.), Change and Transformation of Premodern Credit Markets. The Importance of Small-Scale Credits. Heidelberg: heiBOOKS 2021, 39–63. DOI: https://doi.org/10.11588/heibooks.593.c12690

Virtually no research has sought to assess the continuity of key themes in the economy of medieval Wales, such as the growth of credit, throughout and beyond the era of English conquest, *c.*1067–1284. The economy of Wales has been subject to far less detailed study than the English economy. The main survey works of early twentieth century were the pathbreaking efforts of Edward Arthur Lewis (d.1942) on post-conquest industry, commerce and urbanisation, and William Rees (d.1978) on the economy of post-conquest agrarian south Wales.[1] Those of the mid- and later-twentieth century comprise, collectively, the nine chapters on pre- and post-conquest Wales within the first three volumes of *The Agrarian History of England and Wales*[2], plus two important surveys of the economic structure of native-controlled Wales and the Anglo-Welsh March by Rees Davies.[3] The first two decades of the twenty-first century have seen general studies by Antony Carr and Matthew Stevens, curating and advancing incrementally the findings of the previous century.[4] However, these works are bereft of any discussion of credit in medieval Wales (this author being among the guilty parties). Even among narrower, shorter-term studies, credit has barely been broached, excepting a short assessment of creditors in the early fourteenth-century borough of Ruthin (Denbighshire) and Llinos Beverly Smith's studies of deeds of gage of land and the late-medieval land market.[5]

In contrast, historians of medieval England have long recognised the centrality and importance of credit, at all levels of society, to the English economy. This has yielded several important volumes on medieval English credit in the twenty-first century, building on decades of prior research.[6] Historians of medieval Wales risk, by dint of the sin of omission, undervaluing the importance of credit. The growth and use of credit played an important role in the conquest and colonisation of Wales.

The Welsh economy, prior to 1067, was almost exclusively a subsistence economy. Coin finds suggest English and other monies were known and valued, but Welsh princes never minted coins, and "taxes" were collected as tribute in kind by rulers on progress.[7] Debt, and by extension credit, was considered in the medieval Welsh law of Hywel Dda. Associated symbolically with the eponymous tenth-century prince-king of Deheubarth, the law was compiled from an older oral tradi-

1 Lewis 1903, 1912, 1913; Rees, 1924.
2 Finberg 1972; Hallam 1988; Miller 1991.
3 Davis 1979, 392–456; 1991, 139–71.
4 Car 2003; Stevens 2020.
5 Stevens 2010, 99–109; Smith 1976, 1977.
6 For example, Schofield and Mayhew 2002; Briggs 2009; Goddard 2016.
7 Stevens 2020, 14–15.

tion from the late twelfth century and widely circulated in distinct, regionally influenced literary traditions, or redactions, by the mid-thirteenth century, when a number of the earliest surviving codices were produced. The various redactions of the Welsh laws differ in detail and come down to us both much amended and annotated, and accompanied by "tails" of ancillary information, making it challenging to discern older—that is, circa twelfth century—from newer content. Debt is best covered by the law of "surety and contract", present in all main redactions.[8]

The law of surety in the *Cyfnerth* redaction manuscripts—usually thought to be the oldest redaction, most closely associated with middle March of Wales—emphasises non-monetary obligation, that is, *neither* expressly commercial activity *nor* money lending, although these elements were later added.[9] It begins with a passage regarding the provision of surety for deadstock and livestock, and the potential for the surety who discharges a debtor to take compensation from the debtor in the form of the debtor's garments each time he should see him.[10] Early aspects of Welsh law present the surety, or *mach,* as formally validating an agreement through a ritual in which he clasped the hands of both contracting parties, as the chief witness of the transaction; he subsequently acted as the enforcer of the agreement.[11] It was assumed that the surety was a socially influential individual, such as the head of a kindred, who could compel the fulfilment of a contract or payment of a debt, and a creditor could neither give a debtor more time to pay nor make distraint against a debtor without the surety's permission.[12] This could not have been an efficient system for the widespread use of small credits, relying so heavily on social notables as witnesses to, and enforcers of, contracts. Little is said in the texts of how debts might come about, and the law was likely geared toward the provision of surety for non-commercial debts arising from dispute settlement before a judge. The law of Hywel Dda was a system of compensatory law in which every crime or liability had a compensation value, from killing—the blood price, or *galanas,* reckoned in cows—to trampling corn—to be replaced "a good sheaf for the bad".[13] Similarly, various tax-like tributes in kind, such as the *gwestfa* payment of a free township and its equivalent *dawnbwyd* from an unfree township, could be owed in part or in whole.[14] This is

8 For example, Jenkins 1986, 63–79; Roberts 2010, 121–123.

9 Roberts 2010, 2, 8–9; see below.

10 Roberts 2010, 121–123.

11 Chapman Stacey 1994, 147–148.

12 Chapman Stacey 1994, 147.

13 Chapman Stacey 1994, 97, 103.

14 Chapman Stacey 1994, 121, 183.

not to say that local exchange giving rise to small credits would have been absent, but that it was too insignificant to warrant formal legal remedies recorded in early Welsh law.

Interaction with Normans from 1067 led first to a "monetised economy", and later to a "money economy". As defined by Jim Bolton, a monetised economy is one in which goods and services are valued in notional currencies, but paid in goods of agreed values, especially fungibles like grain, emerging in England by *c.*1150.[15] A money economy is one in which "enough coin [is] in circulation to allow its use to be normal rather than occasional", sufficient literacy and numeracy exists in town and country to record accounts, standard weights and measures are regulated and there is a "widespread use of credit, with debt recovery enforceable by law"; this emerged in England by *c.*1300.[16] From the eleventh century, a monetised economy emerged in Wales as Norman conquerors arrived, imported an economic system based largely on grain cultivation and exchange in new towns, and initially introduced mints at Cardiff, St Davids, Abergavenny, Rhuddlan and Swansea that operated intermittently until at least 1158.[17] Influenced by colonisation, native princes streamlined old tribute payments in goods, for example, in Deheubarth, by reinventing them as new, more uniform *gwestfa* renders eventually commuted to uniform money values.[18] In David Stephenson's words, the nature of Welsh internal political competition shifted "from devastation to measured exploitation", that is, from plundering one's enemies to annexing their resources.[19]

Robin Chapman Stacey has argued that in this period the status of a surety in Welsh law transitioned "from enforcing to paying surety".[20] That is to say, the practical burden of enforcement moved from the surety to the purview of newly established courts, and sureties became fully liable for payment of the principal debt should the debtor default. This would have enabled the proliferation of credit, especially small interpersonal credits, as lower-status, non-enforcing sureties could more readily be had, and the strict liability of sureties mitigated the risk of non-repayment for creditors. Creditors were now afforded the option of suing either the debtor or his surety, although suing the debtor directly could release the surety of liability as it negated his lingering notional role as enforcer.[21] Moreover, curial developments gave rise to the designation of a person aware of

15 Bolton 2012, 132–133.
16 Bolton 2012, 133, 187–214.
17 Allen 2012, 23–26, 390–391.
18 Jones Pierce 1972, 318, 322–323.
19 Stephenson 2019, 47–54.
20 Chapman Stacey 1994, 149.
21 Chapman Stacey 1994, 159–161.

the nature of a disputed agreement as an *amodwr* (literally "contractor"), that is, a non-financially liable "designated witness" to transactions, offsetting the potential bias of the surety-*cum*-witness who was now co-liable with the debtor.[22]

Later content within surviving codices of the law of Hywel Dda, and their "tails", tellingly include detailed discussion of how one ought to claim from a debtor the gage used to secure a loan, should the debtor default, and instances in which debt litigation must be delayed—as when the surety or debtor is at war, or when related accusations of violence or theft were raised.[23] Moreover, the developed *Iorwerth* redaction includes phrases mentioning money, such as "it is right for him to be a surety for the last penny as for the first".[24] This is the growth and evolution of a law of debt—at least in the rarefied minds of lawyers and judges—suitable to a monetised economy and potentially a money economy. However, it was a money economy that could not come to maturity under the cash-strapped native princes who neither minted coins nor had access to credit allowing them to put more coins into circulation than they could first collect from their own subjects. Even in the 1270s–80s, in Gwynedd, the last bastion of native rule, attempts by prince Llywelyn ap Gruffydd both to raise revenues through "tribute" (as in 1273) and tax (as in 1275, 3 *d.* on every head of cattle), and, for a fee, to enforce the payment of debts secured by a surety, gave rise to discontent communicated to English royal officials at Bangor in 1283, immediately after conquest.[25]

There is no evidence of late medieval native princes themselves accessing credit, despite urgent needs to build castles, equip men, or hire mercenaries to fend off the English. Norman lords, alternatively, could and did employ credit to underwrite their Welsh campaigns and maintain their presence in Wales, accessing Jewish money lenders in England until their expulsion in 1290. Richard, son of Gilbert Fitz Richard, Lord of Cardigan, who had occupied much of Cardiganshire in the 1120s, found himself deeply in debt to English Jews by 1130–31.[26] Likewise Richard de Clare, "Strongbow", Earl of Pembroke and invader of Ireland died in 1176 in debt to the prolific Jewish lender Aaron of Lincoln, and an 1170 royal admonition against Jewish lending "to those who against the king's prohibition went to Ireland" leaves little doubt that similar credit would have been advanced to lesser adventurers in Wales.[27] Marcher lords of the early thirteenth century indebted to Jews included Walter de Lacey, lord of Ewias, indebted

22 Chapman Stacey 1994, 169–178.
23 Roberts 2007, 72–73.
24 Jenkins 1986, 68–69.
25 Given 1989, 11–45; Chapman Stacey 1994, 177; Smith 1984, 158–176.
26 Stephenson 2011, 11.
27 Hillaby 2003, 36.

to Hereford Jews, Walter de Baskerville of Eardisley, who owed at least £390 to Hereford and Warwick Jews, and Walter de Clifford, of Clifford, who owed at least 1,300 marks to Hereford, Oxford, York and Canterbury Jews.[28] Brock Holden has argued that such borrowing was connected with the increasing cost of defence, such as building fortified structures in stone, and that it extended equally to the knightly class of the March, citing the likely Jewish debts of the Devereux family of Lyonshall (Herefordshire) in the mid-thirteenth century, amounting to *c.*1,000 marks.[29]

Jewish communities existed in English cities on the southern March of Wales—and more generally in the south of England—at Worcester, Hereford, Gloucester and Bristol, until the expulsion of all English Jews in 1290. Urbanisation accompanied conquest in Wales. A wave of as many as 50 town foundations in areas conquered in south and east Wales in the twelfth century facilitated a growing "money economy" in English-controlled areas, as the introduction of markets at secure castellated sites and increasing silver specie circulation allowed commercialisation and the growth of credit. A second wave of urbanisation followed with about 50 post-1250 borough foundations primarily in north Wales.[30] Evidence suggests the late twelfth- or early thirteenth-century establishment of a small community of Jews in the new towns of Gwent, the first area of Wales to come under Norman control, focused in Caerleon and operating in Chepstow, Newport and Abergavenny until the mid-thirteenth century. Also, possible Jews are named in documents connecting them with Cardiff, Cardigan and Carmarthen.[31] This evidence emphasises that the reach of Jewish lending followed in the wake of the conqueror.

Stephenson has recently argued that a key aspect of the "fragility of the economic basis" of native rule was an inability to access borrowing in times of crisis.[32] Surveying native sources, he concluded that later Welsh princes were aware of the legal position of English Jews as enjoying Jewish law, but that the literate class of Wales was sufficiently unfamiliar with Jews so as readily to confuse them with Muslims.[33] Whatever their level of awareness of Jewish lenders, one acute difficulty that Welsh rulers would have faced in attaining credit was a lack of collateral against which to borrow, given their often fluid territorial possessions and weak powers of taxation; for the English crown, the assignment of customs rev-

28 Hillaby 2003, 36; Holden 2008, 118, 212–213.
29 Holden 2008, 118.
30 More on this below; Soulsby 1983, gazetteer.
31 Stephenson 2011, 8–11.
32 Stephenson 2019, 89–90.
33 Stephenson 2011, 17, 19–20.

enues was a key collateral when borrowing from Italian bankers (see below). It is notable that, in contrast to Welsh princes, ecclesiastical institutions in Wales did access Jewish credit. The Welshman, Bishop Gwion of Bangor (1177–*c.*1190), in the heartlands of Gwynedd, owed £45 to Aaron of Lincoln in 1186, likely contracted by he or his Welsh predecessor.[34] And by the 1250s, the abbots of Margam Abbey, in the Anglo-Norman lordship of Glamorgan, owed several marks to Bristol Jews.[35]

The greatest known creditor to any prince of Wales was the English crown. Henry III, at a time of domestic crisis in 1267, sold Prince of Gwynedd Llywelyn ap Gruffydd the homage and fealty of all the Welsh barons of Wales for 25,000 marks on a deferred payment basis of 5,000 marks in the first year and 3,000 marks each year thereafter, plus 5,000 marks for further dominions agreed in 1270.[36] From 1270–71, Llywelyn fell into arrears, and would eventually claim that he would not pay due to grievances with his marcher neighbours and the crown, but Beverly Smith has argued convincingly that he simply could not afford to pay, perhaps unsurprisingly given the low level of economic development in his principality, combined with a harvest failure in 1271.[37] Whatever the cause of non-payment, the arrears only added to a rapidly growing number of differences between Llywelyn and the cash-strapped new English king Edward I, crowned in 1272, that ultimately gave way to the Anglo-Welsh war of 1276–77. Although peace was established with the Treaty of Aberconwy in November 1277, and Llywelyn retained a diminished principality in northwest Wales, by the terms of the new treaty he "was required to pay 500 marks annually to the king in discharge of his outstanding debts" under the previous treaty.[38] This short-lived peace would be followed by the final Anglo-Welsh war of conquest in 1282–84 and subsequently—despite Welsh rebellions in 1287 and 1294–95—a very substantial overhaul of the economy, stimulating a growth in credit in north Wales commensurate with that which had long been underway in south Wales and the March.

Throughout this saga, Edward I, in stark contrast to the credit-starved native princes of Wales, was able to draw deeply upon the resources of the *Societas Ricciardorum de Luka* (Lucca), a company of Italian merchant-bankers, to finance his 1277, 1282–84, 1287 and 1294–95 campaigns. In the years 1272 to 1294, Edward borrowed a total of between £408,972 and £500,000 from the Riccardi, who ad-

34 Stephenson 2011, 11–12; Pryce 1999, 47, 55–56.
35 Stephenson 2011, 12.
36 Edwards 1940, 114; Smith 2014, 178–186, esp. 181.
37 Smith 2014, 363–366.
38 Davies 1991, 336.

vanced cash sums or made payments to third parties on behalf of the crown.[39] The crown's average annual borrowing in this period was about £23,000, or more than half of all wardrobe receipts, that is, all money coming into the government's hands (about £42,000 per annum). Edward borrowed about £40,000 in relation to the Welsh war of 1276–77 and £100,000 in relation to the Welsh war of 1282–84, plus monies associated with fighting the rebellions of 1287 and 1294–95 and an extended programme of castle construction to fortify his control over Wales.[40] This was, in effect, short-term acute deficit spending, secured against the collateral of customs revenue on wool exports, and, at least initially, it comprised "a rapid turnover of advances and repayments".[41] As Richard Kaeuper commented, over four decades ago, Edward's Italian bankers "were probably unknown to any Welshman, but it would be hard to overestimate their importance to the end of Welsh independence".[42]

As indicated above, a wave of town foundation and commercialisation followed the English conquest of north Wales, including more than a dozen boroughs and numerous fairs in the reformulated royal Principality of Wales.[43] Moreover, conquest was concomitant with what Bolton has called a "flood of silver" entering the economy as the total face value of circulating English coinage (silver pennies, half pennies and farthings) increased from as little as £30,000 in the twelfth century to around £2,000,000 by 1319.[44] The construction of castles and (often adjoining) walled towns in Wales stimulated the transformation to a money economy in which credit could play a greater role. For example, between 1277 and 1330 Edward I and his successors spent at least £93,346 on building works in Wales, raised from English taxes and loans from Italian bankers.[45] That was a sum equivalent to five per cent of all English coinage in existence in 1330, a proportion roughly equivalent to the Welsh population as a part of the combined English and Welsh population. In the royal Principality, circulation of this money was consciously stimulated by the blunt instrument of regulation. Post-conquest ordinances created prescribed market districts around the new towns of Conway, Beaumaris, Newborough, Caernarfon, Criccieth, Harlech and Bala, prohibited buying and selling outside markets anything other than necessities such milk, butter and cheese, and, until 1305, even required each Welsh household to send

39 Bell, Brooks, and Moore 2011, 101–104
40 Bell, Brooks, and Moore 2011, 104; Kaeuper 1973, 173–207.
41 Bell, Brooks, and Moore 2011, 104–105.
42 Kaeuper 1973, 207.
43 See below; Letters et al. 2003.
44 Bolton 2012, 141, 162.
45 Taylor 1986, 119.

someone to their local market once a week.[46] The use of credit was stimulated by the formulation of a novel process of debt litigation, incorporating recent innovations in English and Welsh law.

The 1284 Statute of Wales, by which the conquest of the native principality gave way to the new royal Principality of Wales—constitutionally settled as Anglesey, Merionethshire, Caernarfonshire and Flintshire in the north and Carmarthenshire and Cardiganshire in the South—allowed the continuation of Welsh law in civil disputes between Welsh persons, but mandated English legal procedure where at least one party was English. The Statute comprises, in Llinos Beverly Smith's words, an "outline schema for the governance of the king's lands in Wales", and dictates a discrete body of writs—formal written complaints by which litigation could be initiated—based upon, but more broadly and flexibly conceived than, writs in England.[47] The superior courts, presided over by a Justicier of North Wales and a Justicier of South Wales, heard debt litigation of a value of 40 *s.* or more initiated by writ (Flintshire disputes were heard before the King's Justicier of Chester, Cheshire being a county palatine); lesser disputes, of a value of 40 *s.* or less, brought by writ, bill or plaint, were dealt with in the county counts, presided over by a sheriff, or hundred and borough courts, to which we will return below.[48]

The "writ of debt" and attendant process was arguably superior to common law remedies for debt in England and may have been influenced by English law merchant. Process in debt cases in the Principality of Wales allowed judgement in default against recalcitrant debtors. In cases at the country court, "as well in pleas by writ as plaints without writ", should a defendant be summoned to three consecutive courts and not appear, then the plaintiff "shall recover their demands together with damages or amends".[49] In cases brought by writ before a justicier, an alleged debtor was to be summoned two times to answer the charge and if he neither appeared nor essoined himself at the second court, the creditor was to be awarded the alleged debt plus damages.[50] The royal courts of England generally did not allow judgement in default in actions of debt, although they did allow for levying amercement and/or distraint *in infinitum* against the debtor's sureties, and the customary law of some English manor courts allowed a creditor to sue a recalcitrant debtor's sureties for payment without first suing the debtor.[51]

46 Lewis 1912, 174–175.
47 Smith 1980, 146.
48 Bowen 1908, 3–7, 13–14, 20–21.
49 Bowen 1908, 4.
50 Bowen 1908, 21; Smith 1980, 146.
51 Smith 1980, 147; Briggs 2009, 92–93.

Moreover, in another departure from English common law, the statute allowed, at the request of "the people of Wales", for Welsh litigants to employ proof by the testimony of those "who saw and heard" in pleas of "contracts, debts, sureties, covenants, trespasses and chattels, and all other movables".[52] Such persons would include both the surety-witness and the *amodwr*, that is, the "contractor" or designated witness, of Welsh law. As per the statute: "When the plaintiff shall establish his case by those witnesses whose testimony cannot be disproved...then he ought to recover the thing in demand, and the adverse party to be condemned".[53] Witness testimony, like judgement in default, was allowed neither in English proceedings by write in the Principality nor in the royal courts of England. In Principality litigation involving an Englishman, only a written record of the debt bearing the defendant's seal, known as "specialty", could be admitted as evidence of a debt; the use of testimony in English manor courts remains little studied.[54] The capacity of a plaintiff to offer an additional form of evidence was important because evidence, be it specialty or—exclusively among Welshmen—testimony, barred a defendant from making the defence of "wager of law", or compurgation, whereby he exculpated himself by swearing an oath of denial, accompanied by eleven compurgators swearing with him. Wager of law was extremely common and effective in medieval ecclesiastical and secular courts, in civil and minor criminal actions.[55]

Llinos Beverly Smith has suggested that the 1284 Statute of Wales reflects "a spirit of reform and adaptation", being situated chronologically between the wide-ranging Edwardian reforms of the 1278 Statute of Gloucester and the 1285 Statute of Winchester.[56] While this is correct, the openness of the crown to judgement in default and the Welsh use of witnesses to prove debts for immediate recovery relates to an even tighter legislative chronology of mercantile law. Edward initiated the streamlining of debt recovery for merchants in England, issuing the Statute Acton Burnell in 1283, asserting that "because there is no speedy law provided for them [i.e. merchants] to have recovery of their debts...by reason hereof many merchants have withdrawn to come into this realm with their merchandise".[57] Acton Burnell allowed merchants to register commercial debts before mayors—initially those of London, Bristol, Lincoln, Winchester and Shrewsbury—who issued creditors a special bond with a royal seal that, in the event of non-

52 Bowen 1908, 26.
53 Bowen 1908, 26.
54 Briggs 2009, 93.
55 See, Helmholz 1983.
56 Smith 1980, 148.
57 Luders et al. 1810, 53.

payment, could be brought before the same mayor for immediate debt recovery (barring wager of law) and the imprisonment of the debtor until the debt should be paid. Edward, in 1285, after merchants "complained…that sheriffs…sometimes by male and false interpretation delayed the execution of the statute", issued the Statute of Merchants, clarifying aspects of Acton Burnell, including "in case… the debtor cannot be found", that the creditor may have the debtor's goods and hold his lands until the debt be paid by the sale of the goods and the revenues of those lands.[58] While recovery stemmed strictly from the creditor's claim on the bond, the effect was the same as judgement in default, in so far as recovery was now to be made against the debtor's goods and lands in the absence of the debtor, who might otherwise have offered the court a release or other exculpatory document under seal, something not made clear in Acton Burnell. Both statutes made provision for action to be taken against a defaulting debtor's sureties.

Edward's statutes of 1283 and 1285 paralleled the maturing of the English custom of law merchant, or *lex mercatoria,* a form of customary law employed in special courts held at some regular markets and periodic fairs in England to offer expedited process in disputes arising from market transactions—typically debt and contract—and occasional trespasses; James Davis has characterised the Statute of Acton Burnell and Statute of Merchants as "supplementary to merchant law".[59] Often called "piepowder" courts, such market courts were themselves supplementary to regularly held franchise courts, such as borough courts, and the right to hold them was likely "embedded in the royal grant of a market", as reflected in the *Quo Warranto* proceedings held under Edward I between 1272 and 1294 to investigate royal franchises and their upkeep.[60] Against the backdrop of *Quo Warranto* and the 1283 issuance of a copy of the Statute of Acton Burnell to the mayor of Bristol, the oldest known treatise on law merchant was composed sometime between 1272 and 1283, and preserved at Bristol.[61] The treatise's author states that law merchant differs from the common law of the realm in three ways: "it reaches decisions more quickly"; "whoever pledges for anyone to answer to a [plea of] trespass, covenant, debt or detinue of chattels pledges for the whole debt, damages and expenses sought"; and "it does not allow anyone to wager law on the negative side…it is for the plaintiff and not the defendant to make proof, whether by suit, or by deed or otherwise".[62] That is to say, under law merchant, as with process under Acton Burnell, the emphasis was on swift resolution. As in Welsh

58 Luders et al. 1810, 100.

59 Davies 2012, 208.

60 Davis 2016, 273.

61 Luders et al. 1810, 54; Teetor 1962, 179–180.

62 Teetor 1962, 182–183.

process, both by native law and under the Statute of Wales, witnesses—here proof by suit (i.e. persons testifying to the validity of the plaintiff's claim)—could prove a claim and bar the defendant from offering wager of law. As under Acton Burnell and Welsh native law, a debtor's pledges could ultimately be held liable for a debt. And, as in all debt process under the Statute of Wales, by writ, bill or plaint, as well as in prosecutions under Acton Burnell, a debtor could be adjudged liable in his absence; law merchant allowed judgement in default.[63]

The law merchant may also have influenced debt process in the Statute of Wales in that it suggests that tallies, like "writings", are sufficient evidence to prove a debt.[64] The Statute of Wales, in discussing the "trial of personal actions" brought on a writ of debt, names tallies, alongside the plaintiff's suit or a bond, as sufficient to affirm a plaintiff's plea at the stage of pleading; at common law it was the case that a bond must be produced or, if called upon, "good suit" must withstand examination, lest an action be dismissed upon first pleading.[65] The Statute of Wales did not, however, consider a tally sufficient to stop a defendant from waging law, and so embodies a middle way between law merchant's acceptance of bonds and tallies as evidence, and common law's acceptance only of bonds.

The elements of the Statute of Wales relating to credit and debt reflect Edward I's perception of post-conquest Wales as ripe for modernisation through urban colonisation and commercialisation. Almost all of his new castles in Wales were accompanied by new adjacent boroughs encircled by high stone walls, as at Rhuddlan, where the Statute was issued, and Caernarfon, Edward's administrative and judicial capital of north Wales. By the end of Edward's reign, he would create dozens of towns *de novo* in Wales, England and Gascony, going so far, in 1296–97, as to summon a commission of experts to advise on the task.[66] Wales was equipped with the most up-to-date debt recovery law and more than a dozen new royal boroughs with markets and courts founded after 1277. Additional piepowder courts applying law merchant were active in at least some of those boroughs around the turn of the fourteenth century, including Caernarfon, Beaumaris, Conwy and Newborough.[67] Excepting Newborough, discussed below, these were settlements populated largely by English colonists and designed to foster trade. The crown's observation in the preamble to the Statute of Acton Burnell that the absence of effective debt recovery mechanisms repelled trade, and

63 Teetor 1962, 185–190.

64 Teetor 1962, 188.

65 Bowen 1908, 21; Baker 2019, 339–346, esp. n. 43, on good suite and its fictionalisation from c.1300.

66 Beresford 1967, 3–13.

67 Lewis 1912, 300–304.

its corollary that their presence attracted trade, is difficult to assess. Certainly, use of the system of mercantile debt registration and recovery under Acton Burnell grew rapidly after 1283, indicating that the early fourteenth century experienced a "period of enormous credit provision".[68] Chris Briggs has demonstrated, in a study of some Cambridgeshire and Buckinghamshire manors, *c.*1290–1380, that manor courts with a reputation for strong debt recovery procedures influenced "the extent to which lending flourished within the local population" such that on at least one manor "curial 'reforms' there encouraged a fresh expansion in the overall number of transactions".[69] Conversely, in fifteenth-century London, creditors reacted to static institutions and economic crisis by rationing credit, and lending in ways to make recovery more tenable.[70]

Did colonisation lead to the proliferation of credit, and concomitant economic growth, in medieval Wales as a whole? The answer is unclear, as the various parts of Wales had differing economies, some likely earlier permeated by the widespread use of credit than others. The March was Anglicised progressively from the eleventh century, well before our earliest surviving records of local economic activity, and when it comes into view, its Welsh and English inhabitants already placed a greater emphasis on grain cultivation and market exchange than did native-dominated and more pastoral west and north Wales. Likewise, before and after the 1282–84 conquest of Gwynedd, the largest urban centres and highest concentrations of English immigrants—key catalysts of change—were in south Wales. In the first half fourteenth century, Cardiff had a population of about 2,000 and Carmarthen, considering together the royal "new" and ecclesiastical "old" boroughs, had a population of about 1,500 (estimated here and below as four to five times the number of burgages). Of the other seven towns in Wales with populations around 1,000 only one was in north Wales, Holt, on the west bank of the Dee, opposite Cheshire; the remaining six were Cowbridge, Glamorgan, Haverfordwest, Pembrokeshire, and the Monmouthshire towns of Chepstow, Usk, Newport and Monmouth.[71] However, the conquest and colonisation of Llywelyn's former principality, following the 1282–84 war, does provide an opportunity to gauge the impact of colonisation on the economy and the use of credit through a couple of suggestive proxies. These are income from perquisites, that is, profits of justice arising from regulatory fines and the operation of courts, and court records of interpersonal litigation.

68 Goddard 2016, 100–101.
69 Briggs 2006, 557.
70 Stevens 2016.
71 Stevens 2020, 62–64.

Income of the crown generated by the royal Principality rose dramatically in the first decades after conquest, in part because of an intensive new regime of revenue-raising. Across the first two decades after 1284, the crown employed a combination of commutation and rent increases to more than double receipts of cash dues from the free and unfree inhabitants of Anglesey, Caernarvonshire and Merionethshire.[72] It also enhanced revenues from *banalités,* such as fees to use the lord's mills, to be paid in cash. This strikingly increased levy of cash dues and fees was only possible in conjunction with the "flood of silver" discussed above, and the rapidly expanding liquidity likely stimulated both more intensive peasant exchange to meet cash demands and a growth of credit supported by relatively efficient post-conquest debt-recovery mechanisms; although, as in England, an extended regime of intensive taxation may have depleted liquidity and stifled credit towards the end of the century.[73] Briggs has argued for rural England that while it was possible for credit to be extended and repaid strictly in kind or by other non-monetary means, such transactions were rare.[74] Thus, one would expect increasing post-conquest liquidity in north Wales to have facilitated an expansion of credit, in turn reflected in litigation.

Records of debt litigation can only indicate the number of credit relationships-in-default considered by the creditor to be irreconcilable without recourse to a particular court, or courts. However, as amply illustrated by this volume, historians generally believe there to be a positive correlation between the number and value of credit transactions in a community and the number and value of debt-related lawsuits appearing before its courts. These lawsuits in turn contributed substantially to perquisites. Very broadly speaking then, higher royal revenues and higher perquisites are suggestive of a greater use of credit, but it is difficult to evidence a more substantive connection.

In the first two decades after conquest, perquisites of courts comprised around twenty-five per cent of all crown revenues (e.g. in 1305, £ 611 5 *s.* 11¾ *d.* of £ 2,400 3 *s.* 3¾ *d.*) from Anglesey, Caernarvonshire and Merionethshire, growing in parallel with overall revenue.[75] Research on court records from a variety of English manors has shown that, while local variation was significant, generally between twenty-five and thirty-nine per cent of the work of courts was inter-personal litigation, with much the same being true of Wales (Table 1, below); generally between a quarter and half of that interpersonal litigation was "debt-related", mainly

72 Given 1989, 24–26.

73 Briggs 2009, 203–205, 207–210.

74 Briggs 2015.

75 Given 1989, 29–30.

pleas of debt and unjust detention.[76] A handful of early account rolls survive from royal north-Wales boroughs, itemising different perquisite revenues.[77] Records of perquisites from the northwest counties begin from only *c.*1303–04 and so miss any first blush of new litigation in the twenty years immediately following conquest. They also sometimes sum the income of different categories of perquisites. Nevertheless, they indicate some growth of prerequisites arising specifically from courts available for interpersonal litigation, up to the Great Famine of 1315–22. At both Caernarfon and Conwy, each with a population of about 400, combined perquisites from the three-weekly borough court, piepowder court applying law merchant and "market and fair courts" grew from about £1 in 1304–05 to a little over £2 in 1312–13.[78] Later fourteenth-century court rolls form Caernarfon, 1361–1402, demonstrate debt-related disputes comprising about half of all interpersonal litigation and the application of both law merchant and legal procedures indicated in the Statute of Wales, such as judgement in default and Welsh plaintiffs' use of witnesses to bar wager of law by Welsh defendants.[79] These may have been favourably received by traders.

The accounts of Beaumaris, Criccieth and Harlech do not show any corresponding increase in perquisites in the first decade of the fourteenth century.[80] It is possible that some of the difference between these groups of towns relates to the differing capacity of boroughs to engage their overwhelmingly Welsh hinterlands in their new judicial and credit networks. Despite the existence of a patchily enforced 1295 prohibition against Welsh property ownership in the walled towns of the royal Principality—in 1298 all Caernarfon burgesses were English and in 1306 about ninety per cent of Conway burgesses were English—the later Caernarfon court rolls are replete with debt litigants bearing ethnically Welsh names.[81] Caernarfon was an administrative and tax-collection hub, and so could hardly be ignored by the Welsh, and, like Conwy, was on the coastal shipping route to Ireland. Beaumaris, with a population of about 350, was also on the route to Ireland. However, its foundation and habitation by new immigrant burgesses—in 1306 over ninety per cent were English—had been preceded by the dissolution of the fledging native mercantile settlement of Llanfaes.[82] Its occupants had been relocated

76 Schofield 2011, 119; Razi and Smith 1996, 46–49.
77 Lewis 1912, 300–304, summary accounts.
78 Lewis 1912, 300; Soulsby 1983, 88–91, 110–115.
79 Jones and Owen 1951: default 37 (piepowder court), 43 (default, borough court), et passim; witness testimony (Welsh litigants), 15–16 (piepowder court), 128–129 (probable, borough court).
80 Lewis 1912, 300–304.
81 Ellis 1838, 132; Stevens 2012, 141, 155–156.
82 Stevens 2012, 141, 155.

to a new site fifteen miles southwest, called Newborough. This led to a sort of de facto boycott in which many Welsh of Anglesey traded not in Beaumaris but in Newborough, compelling Beaumaris burgesses to petitioned Edward II and III for remedy.[83] Harlech and Criccieth may have attracted more Welsh participation, but both were small and geographically remote, with less than 150 residents throughout the Middle Ages.[84]

A much better proxy measure of credit usage is provided by records of debt litigation in the exceptional series of court rolls that survives from the lordship of Dyffryn Clwyd, formed by Edward I in 1282 from part of Llywelyn's former principality and granted to the king's Justicier of Chester, Reginald de Grey. The earliest court rolls—excepting one roll from June 1294—date to 1295, just after the destructive Welsh revolt of 1294–95; the rolls record litigation before the lordship's three rural commotes and borough of Ruthin, held at roughly three-weekly intervals, plus biannual "great courts" of the borough and lordship. Table 1 reflects the content of the court rolls of the three-weekly borough court and biennial "great court" of Ruthin, and of the commote of Llanerch, at increasing intervals from 1295 to 1390. The borough had been created in 1282 by reorganising a Welsh settlement as a colonial market town. In the early fourteenth century, roughly half of its about 500 inhabitants were Welsh and half English, the latter including most of the borough's office holders and wealthier inhabitants.[85] Llannerch was a predominately lowland commote with an upland, pastoral hinterland. It was the focus of a rural English settler community of no more than fifty families, recruited mostly from north-west and midland England, living alongside an older rural Welsh community.[86] At least fifteen English settler families had more than twenty acres of land, and some as much as 100 acres, typically in the best fertile lowlands, marking them out as conspicuously prosperous when compared to their Welsh neighbours.[87]

The data in Table 1 were collected by choosing and adjusting sample periods relative to the survival of court records. For example, the 1295–96 sample from Ruthin comprises records of ten courts; the patchy survival of early Llannerch court rolls necessitated expanding the sample to 1300 to encompass records of even seven courts. The "No. of court-roll entries" reflects essoins, fines to enforce lordship regulations, property transfers and interpersonal litigation. Interpersonal lawsuits often extended across several courts, giving rise to numerous

83 Ellis 1838, 223; Rees 1975, 469; Lewis 1912, 175–176.
84 Soulsby 1983, 116–117, 138–139.
85 Stevens 2010, 27–59, 109–114.
86 Barrell and Brown 1995, 333–336.
87 Barrell and Brown 1995, 338–339.

Table 1 Debt and unjust detention litigation in Dyffryn Clwyd, 1295–1391.

Place and sample years	No. of courts	No. of court-roll entries	No. of inter-personal lawsuit	No. of debts	Debts, per court-roll entry/per inter-personal lawsuits	Debts, creditor-plaintiff/s (PL) ethnicity			Debts, debtor-defendant/s (DEF) Ethnicity			Debts, PL and DEF have same ethnicity		Debts, PL and DEF have different ethnicity		Debts owed by a Welsh debtor per debt owed to a Welsh creditor
						English	Welsh	un-known	English	Welsh	Un-known	No. of debts	Per cent of debts	No. of debts	Per cent of debts	
Ruthin																
1295–1296	10	137	60	33	0.24/0.55	31	2	0	25	7	1	23	70%	9	27%	3.5
1315	6	178	123	53	0.30/0.43	38	15	0	21	30	2	29	55%	22	42%	2
1340–1341	13	565	231	106	0.19/0.46	53	52	1	41*	65*	1	65	61%	39*	34%	1.25
1390–1391	13	561	178	87	0.16/0.49	39	47	1	42*	46*	0	60	69%	26*	30%	0.98
Llannerch																
1294–1300	7	47	19	0	–	–	–	–	–	–	–	–	–	–	–	–
1315–1316	9	123	34	21	0.17/0.62	11	10	0	5	16	0	15	71%	6	29%	1.6
1340–1341	13	191	50	23	0.12/0.46	6	16	1†	9	13	1†	16†	70%	6†	26%	0.81
1390–1391	6	179	35	15	0.08/0.43	3	12	0	5	10	0	11	73%	4	27%	0.83

Source: The National Archives, SC 2/215/64–75 (1295–1316); SC 2/217/6 (1340–41); SC 2/220/9–10 (1390–91); All records, except Ruthin 1315, have been viewed in the database, Davies and Smith 1995.

* One case names Welsh and English co-debtors. Such cases are counted ONLY once, as a case in which "PL and DEF have different ethnicity".

† In one case, the ethnicity of both the creditor and debtor is unknown

entries. The "No. of interpersonal lawsuits" and "No. of debts" have been arrived at by tracking each lawsuit from its first entry to its last, to avoid double-counting. In the case of "No. of debts", this counts only initial credit agreements from which litigation sprang, and not secondary litigation such as separate actions against the pledges of defaulting debtors; again, this is to avoid double-counting. The ethnicity of litigants has been estimated based on personal-name data, with particular emphasis on the use of patronymic naming practice (e.g. Llywelyn ap Madog, meaning Llywelyn the son of Madog) as a marker of Welsh identity.

The numbers presented in Table 1 are necessarily "fuzzy", in the sense that they may be used to identify suggestive trends, but may never be taken as comprehensive or incontrovertible. Records of some courts, or parts of them, are missing from virtually every sample, and, as mentioned above, debt litigation reflects only defaults thought irresolvable without judicial aid, from an unknown total number of credit transactions. Further, assigning ethnicity to litigants based on name data inevitably leads to some misidentification given parents' personal choices in light of perceived social and political pressures, intermarriage, religious devotion or other factors. Close study of the English settler community of Llanerch has suggested that English adoption of Welsh Christian names remained the exception throughout the fourteenth century.[88] At the same time, the unequal legal status of English and Welsh in Dyffryn Clwyd, under which English litigants had small but important advantages over their Welsh neighbours when litigating, could have incentivised the adoption of English names among the Welsh. For example, Dyffryn Clwyd's courts disallowed essoins by Welsh defendants in inter-ethnic disputes; Welsh tenants' legal ethnicity was usually, but not always, dictated by Welsh land tenure.[89]

Even with these cautions, the Dyffryn Clwyd evidence provides our best indicators of credit usage in Wales during the first century after 1284. If one focuses on the sixth column from the left in Table 1, "Debts, per court-roll entry/per interpersonal lawsuit", it may be observed that in the borough of Ruthin, already in 1295–96, about one-in-two interpersonal lawsuits was debt-related, that is, actions of debt or unjust detention of goods. These were overwhelmingly small credits of less than 1 s. extended as loans or deferred-payment sales of foodstuffs or basic durables such as clothes or shoes. In Ruthin, the entry point of English immigration to the lordship and the location of a large castle, much improved and greatly expanded after 1284 by wage labour that would have increased the circulation of silver specie—similar works at Rhuddlan and Flint costing as much as £6,000 and £9,000—credit agreements leading to litigation were already

88 Barrell and Brown 1995, 352.
89 Phipps and Stevens 2020.

common.[90] However, in the rural commote of Dyffryn Clwyd, there are no debt-related lawsuits in the surviving seven sessions of the commotal court, from 1294 to 1300. It is possible, or even probable, that among the rural Welsh population at least, credit was being extended, and debts recovered, outside the purview of the court using Welsh law and the adjudication of Welsh judges, who were allowed to continue to operate in the lordship when disputants mutually agreed to use them. Their judgements, when not respected, sometimes gave rise to litigation in lordship courts.[91] In much the same way, it seems likely that the English of Llannerch were litigating in Ruthin's borough court, most Llannerch English having close ties to the borough community. For example, William le Serjeant was plaintiff in six actions of debts and unjust detention in the borough between 1312 and 1321, while Almary de Marreys acted as a surety in the borough court thirty-seven times in those same years.[92] However, by the famine years of 1315–16, and throughout the fourteenth century thereafter, about half of all interpersonal litigation before Llannerch's court was debt-related, initially mostly Welshmen indebted to their English neighbours (see below).

Both Ruthin and Llannerch litigants, over time, made increasingly sophisticated use of the courts. The use of delaying tactics in debt-related litigation, such as essoins and mutually agreed requests to move ongoing cases to a future court, is largely responsible for a marked change in the number of debt cases per court-roll entry (Table 1). At Ruthin, an early fourteenth-century ratio of one debt case to every three or four court-roll entries shifted to one debt case to every five or more court-roll entries by 1390–91. At Llannerch, the parallel shift was from around one debt to every five court-roll entries, to one debt to every ten or more court-roll entries. This shift took place despite the mid-century depopulation caused by the Black Death, and a reduction in strictly regulatory court-roll entries thereafter.

The final three columns at the right of Table 1 suggest the increasing participation of Welsh persons in credit agreements, especially as creditors. Throughout the fourteenth century, in both Ruthin and Llannerch, about seventy per cent of credit agreements were between two parties of the same ethnicity and thirty per cent were between parties of different ethnicities. The exception to this was Ruthin, during the famine year of 1315, when poorer Welsh persons borrowed more frequently from their wealthier English neighbours, pushing up the proportion of inter-ethnic transactions.[93] As mentioned above with respect to Llannerch,

---

90 Taylor 1974, 327–29, no. 1029.
91 For example, regarding suretyship, 1326 Llannerch; TNA, SC 2/216/6 m.11.
92 Barrell and Brown 1995, 337–338; Stevens 2010, 74–75, 103, 112.
93 On wealth and ethnicity see, Stevens 2010, 34–59, 99–109.

Welsh persons in the earliest surviving debt-related litigation records from the lordship tended to be debtors to English creditors. At Ruthin, in 1295–96, court records indicate 3.5 credit agreements featuring a Welsh debtor for every one credit agreement featuring a Welsh creditor, dropping to 2:1 in 1315, 1.25:1 in 1340–41 and 0.98:1 in 1390–91. The same can be observed at Llannerch, where in 1315 court records indicate 1.6 credit agreements with a Welsh debtor for every one credit agreement with a Welsh creditor, falling thereafter to about 0.8:1. As these latter ratios of less than one Welsh debtor for each Welsh creditor suggest, by the end of the century Welsh creditors of both Ruthin and Llannerch were occasionally lending the English debtors, for example: Dafydd ap Ieuan ap Iorwerth versus Walter le Barker in a plea of debt, Ruthin, 1390[94]; Gronowy ap Ieuan ap Gwilym versus Walter le Barker in a plea of debt, Ruthin, 1391[95]; Gruffydd ap Einion ap Ednyfed versus Thomas le Sowter in a plea of debt, Ruthin, 1391[96]; and Gwerful ferch Dafydd Gogh versus Thomas Passavaunt in a plea of debt, Llannerch, 1390[97], *et passim.*

In absolute numbers, at Ruthin, the 1294–95 sample contains thirty-one credit agreements with an English creditor and only two (six per cent) with a Welsh creditor, while the 1390–91 sample contains thirty-nine credit agreements with an English creditor and forty-seven (fifty-four per cent) with a Welsh creditor (Table 1, "Debts, creditor-plaintiff/s (PL) ethnicity"). At Llannerch, the growing relative importance of the court to Welsh litigants was even more pronounced. There, in 1315–16, the creditor was Welsh in ten of twenty-one credit agreements (forty-eight per cent), and in 1390–91 the creditor in twelve of fifteen credit arrangements (eighty per cent) was Welsh. That is to say, at both Ruthin and Llannerch, by the end of the fourteenth century, while lending and borrowing continued to take place mostly within ethnic communities, Welsh persons more frequently participated in debt-related litigation, and that litigation more frequently featured a Welsh creditor than a Welsh debtor.

These findings make sense in the context of prior research on the English settler community of Llannerch, in particular. Andrew Barrell and Michael Brown found that while the English of Llannerch consolidated their position through office holding, acting as surety for one another and intermarriage between 1294 and 1349, in the latter half of the fifteenth century, prominent old settler families died out and others likely fell into poverty.[98] The fate of the borough English after 1349

---

94 TNA, SC 2/220/9 m.2.
95 TNA, SC 2/220/9 m.4.
96 TNA, SC 2/220/9 m.4.
97 TNA, SC 2/220/10 m.2.
98 Barrell and Brown 1995, 340–350.

is yet to be studied. However, the data in Table 1 strongly suggests that the regular use both of credit and of the courts to recover debts had become a pervasive part of the economic and legal culture of Dyffryn Clwyd as much among the Welsh as the English. This is a story that was no doubt mirrored across Wales, as and when English conquest, colonisation, law and judicial practice reshaped native society.

The immediate and long-term impacts of conquest on virtually every aspect of Welsh society can hardly be overstated. The emergence of a money economy and the development of more sophisticated credit institutions, offering new potential for economic growth, must rank among the more important of these. The later Welsh princes' lack of access to credit placed them at a strategic disadvantage when faced by their better-financed enemies, from Norman adventurers to the English king. However, the conquest's legacies of a culture of credit usage and efficient debt-recovery law would help to nurture and to sustain urban life and economic activity in Wales at previously unknown levels, despite the vagaries of later medieval famine, plague and eventually Welsh revolt, from 1400–15. In this respect, the transformation wrought in Wales is not unique. As mentioned above, credit was extended to the conquers of Ireland, both great and small, where rural colonisation, urbanisation and economic transformation paralleled that seen in Wales.[99] Likewise, participants in the contemporaneous conquest, colonisation and urbanisation of the State of the Teutonic Order on the Baltic—including English participants—would both employ and create credit networks; in recent years, work on the credit market in the colonial towns of the Baltic has advanced substantially.[100] Evidence of the use of credit relating to medieval Wales is relatively abundant, warrants further research, and is of potential international significance as a comparator for other medieval colonial zones.

---

99 Frame 1981 (overview); Lydon 1972, 98–100; Murphy 2018, 385–414.
100 For example, Bell and Moore 2018; Kardasz 2013.

References

Archival References

TNA (The National Archives, Kew, London, UK), SC 2/215/64–SC 2/220/10.

Bibliographic References

Allen M. 2012. *Mints and Money in Medieval England.* Cambridge: Cambridge University Press.

Baker J.H. 2019. *An Introduction to English Legal History,* 5th edn. Oxford: Oxford University Press.

Barrell A.D.M. and M. Brown. 1995. "A settler community in Post-Conquest Rural Wales: the English of Dyffryn Clwyd, 1294–1399." *Welsh History Review* 17: 332–355.

Bell A.R., C. Brooks, and T.K. Moore. 2011. "Credit Finance in the Middle Ages: Edward I and the Ricciardi of Lucca." In *Thirteenth-Century England XIII,* edited by J. Burton, F. Lachaud, P. Schofield, K. Stöber, and B. Weiler, 101–116. Woodbridge: Boydell.

Bell A.R. and T.K. Moore. 2018. "The Organisation and Financing of English Expeditions to the Baltic During the Later Middle Ages." In *Military Communities in Late Medieval England: Essays in Honour of Andrew Ayton,* edited by G. Baker, C. Lambert, and D. Simpkin, 181–212. Woodbridge: Boydell.

Beresford M. 1967. *New Towns of the Middle Ages.* New York: Frederick A. Praeger.

Bowen I. (ed.) 1908. *The Statutes of Wales.* London: T. Fisher Unwin.

Briggs C. 2006. "Manor Court Procedures, Debt Litigation Levels, and Rural Credit Provision in England, *c.*1290–*c.*1380." *Law and History Review* 24: 519–558.

Briggs C. 2009. *Credit and Village Society in Fourteenth-Century England.* Oxford: Oxford University Press.

Briggs C. 2015. "Money and Rural Credit in the Later Middle Ages Revisited." In *Money, Prices and Wages: Essays in Honour of Professor Nicholas Mayhew,* edited by M. Allen and D. Coffman, 129–142. Houndmills: Palgrave Macmillan.

Bolton J. 2012. *Money in the Medieval English Economy, 973–1489.* Manchester: Manchester University Press.

Carr A. D. 2003. "Wales: Economy and Society". In *A Companion to Britain in the Later Middle Ages,* edited by S. H. Rigby, 125–141. Chichester: Wiley-Blackwell.

Chapman Stacey, R. 1994. *The Road to Judgement: From Custom to Court in Medieval Ireland and Wales.* Philadelphia: University of Pennsylvania Press.

Davis J. 2012. *Medieval Market Morality: Life, Law and Ethnics in the English Marketplace, 1200–1500.* Cambridge: Cambridge University Press.

Davis J. 2016. "Market Courts and *Lex Mercata* in Late Medieval England." In *Medieval Merchants and Money: Essays in Honour of James L. Bolton,* edited by M. Allen and M. Davies, 271–90. London: University of London Press.

Davies R. R. 1978. *Lordship and Society in the March of Wales, 1282–1400.* Oxford: Clarendon Press.

Davies R. R. 1991. *The Age of Conquest: Wales, 1063–1415.* Oxford: Oxford University Press.

Davies R. R. and Ll. B. Smith (eds.) 1995. Machine readable database. *The Dyffryn Clwyd Court Roll Database, 1294–1422.* Aberystwyth: University of Wales, Aberystwyth. Available from the UK Data Archive. Accessed 19 May 2020. https://www.data-archive.ac.uk.

Edwards J. G. (ed.) 1940. *Littere Wallie.* Cardiff: University of Wales Press.

Ellis, H. (ed.) 1838. *Registrum Vulgariter Nuncupatum: The Record of Caernarvon.* London: G. Eyre and A. Spottiswoode.

Finberg H. P. R. (ed.) 1972. *The Agrarian History of England and Wales, Volume I-ii: A. D. 43–1042.* Cambridge: Cambridge University Press.

Frame R. 1981. *Colonial Ireland.* Dublin: Helicon Limited.

Given J. 1989. "The Economic Consequences of the English Conquest of Gwynedd." *Speculum* 64: 11–45.

Goddard R. 2016. *Credit and Trade in Later Medieval England, 1353–1532.* London: Palgrave Macmillan.

Hallam H. E. (ed.) 1988. *The Agrarian History of England and Wales, Volume II: 1042–1350.* Cambridge: Cambridge University Press.

Helmholz R. H. 1983. "Crime, Compurgation and the Courts of the Medieval Church." *Law and History Review* 1: 1–26.

Hillaby J. 2003. "Jewish Colonization in the Twelfth Century." In *The Jews in Medieval Britain,* edited by P. Skinner, 15–40. Woodbridge: Boydell.

Holden B. 2008. *Lords of the Central Marches: English Aristocracy and Frontier Society, 1087–1265.* Oxford: Oxford University Press.

Jenkins D. (ed.) 1986. *The Law of Hywell Dda: Law Texts from Medieval Wales Translated and Edited.* Llandysul: Gomer Press.

Jones G.P. and H. Owen (eds.) 1951. *Caernarvon Court Rolls, 1361–1402.* Caernarvon: Gwenlyn Evans.

Jones Pierce T. 1972. "Medieval Cardiganshire—A Study in Social Origins". In *Medieval Welsh Society: Selected Essays by T. Jones Pierce,* edited by B. Smith, 309–27. Cardiff: University of Wales Press.

Kaeuper R. 1973. *Bankers to the Crown: The Riccardi of Lucca and Edward I.* Princeton: Princeton University Press.

Kardasz C. 2013. *Rynek Kredytu Pieniężnego w Miastach Południowego Pobrzeża Bałtyku w Późnym Średniowieczu: Greifswald, Gdańsk, Elbląg, Toruń, Rewel.* Toruń: Towarzystwo Naukowe w Toruniu.

Letters S., M. Fernandes, D. Keene, and O. Myhill (eds.) 2003. *Gazetteer of Markets and Fairs in England and Wales to 1516,* 2 volumes. Kew: List and Index Society.

Lewis E.A. 1903. "The Development of Industry and Commerce in Wales During the Middle Ages." *Transactions of the Royal Historical Society* 17: 121–73.

Lewis E.A. 1912. *The Medieval Boroughs of Snowdonia.* London: Henry Sotheran and Co.

Lewis E.A. 1913. "A contribution to the Commercial History of Medieval Wales." *Y Cymmrodor* 24: 86–188.

Luders A., T.E. Tomlins, J. France, W.E. Taunton, and J. Raithby (eds.) 1810. *Statutes of the Realm: Volume the First.* London: Great Britain Record Commission.

Miller E. (ed.) 1991. *The Agrarian History of England and Wales, Volume II: 1348–1500.* Cambridge: Cambridge University Press.

Murphy. M. 2018. "The Economy." In *The Cambridge History of Ireland, Volume 1: 600–1550,* edited by B. Smith, 385–414. Cambridge: Cambridge University Press.

Phipps T. and M.F. Stevens 2020. "Towards a Characterisation of 'Race Law' in Medieval Wales." *The Journal of Legal History* 41: forthcoming.

Pryce H. 1999. "Esgobaeth Bangor yn Oes y Tywysogion." In *"Ysbryd Dealltwrus ac Enaid Anfarwol": Ysgrifau Ar Hanes Crefydd Yng Ngwynedd,* edited by W.P. Griffith, 37–57. Bangor: Cyhoeddiadau'r Gair.

Razi Z. and R. Smith. 1996. "The Origins of the English Manorial Court Rolls as a Written Record: a Puzzle." In *Medieval Society and the Manor Court,* edited by Z. Razi and R. Smith, 36–68. Oxford: Oxford University Press.

Rees W. 1924. *South Wales and the March, 1284–1415: A Social and Agrarian Study.* Oxford: Oxford University Press.

Rees W. (ed.) 1975. *Calendar of Ancient Petitions Relating to Wales (Thirteenth to Sixteenth Century).* Cardiff: University of Wales Press.

Roberts S.E. 2007. *The Legal Triads of Medieval Wales.* Cardiff: University of Wales Press.

Roberts S.E. (ed.) 2010. *Llawysgrif Pomffred: An Edition and Study of Peniarth MS 259B.* Leiden: Brill.

Schofield P.R. and N.J. Mayhew (eds.) 2002. *Credit and Debt in Medieval England, c.1180–c.1350.* Oxford: Oxbow Books.

Schofield P.R. 2011. "English Law and Welsh Marcher Courts in the Late Thirteenth and Early Fourteenth Centuries." In *Wales and the Welsh in the Middle Ages: Essays Presented to J. Beverly Smith,* edited by R.A. Griffiths and P.R. Schofield, 108–125. Cardiff: University of Wales Press.

Smith J.B. 2014. *Llywelyn ap Gruffydd: Prince of Wales,* new edition. Cardiff: University of Wales Press.

Smith Ll.B. 1976. "The Gage and the Land Market in Late Medieval Wales." *The Economic History Review* 29: 537–550.

Smith Ll.B. 1977. "Tir Prid: Deeds of Gage of Land in Late Medieval Wales." *Bulletin of the Board of Celtic Studies* 27: 263–277.

Smith Ll.B. 1980. "The Statute of Wales, 1284." *Welsh History Review* 10: 127–154.

Smith Ll.B. 1984. "The Gravamina of the Community of Gwynedd Against Llywelyn ap Gruffydd." *Bulletin of the Board of Celtic Studies* 31: 158–176.

Soulsby I. 1983. *The Towns of Medieval Wales.* Chichester: Phillimore.

Stephenson D. 2011. "Jewish Presence in, and Absence from, Wales in the Twelfth and Thirteenth Centuries." *Jewish Historical Studies* 43:7–20.

Stephenson D. 2019. *Medieval Wales, c.1050–1332: Centuries of Ambiguity.* Cardiff: University of Wales Press.

Stevens M.F. 2010. *Urban Assimilation in Post-Conquest Wales: Ethnicity, Gender and Economy in Ruthin, 1282–1348.* Cardiff: University of Wales Press.

Stevens M.F. 2012. "Anglo-Welsh Towns of the Early Fourteenth Century: a Survey of Urban Origins, Property-Holding and Ethnicity." In *Urban Culture in Medieval Wales,* edited by H. Fulton, 137–162. Cardiff: University of Wales Press.

Stevens M.F. 2016. "London Creditors and the Fifteenth-Century Depression." *The Economic History Review* 69: 1083–1107

Stevens M.F. 2020. The Economy of Medieval Wales, 1067–1536. Cardiff: University of Wales Press.

Taylor A.J. 1947. *The King's Works in Wales, 1277–1330.* London: H.M. Stationary Office.

Teetor P.R. 1962. "England's Earliest Treatise on the Law Merchant." *The American Journal of Legal History* 6: 178–210.

SMALL CREDIT IN A SMALL TOWN: CLERICAL INSTITUTIONS AND THE CREDIT MARKET IN KAUFBEUREN IN THE FIFTEENTH CENTURY

Sven Rabeler

Abstract: In 1438, on the occasion of construction works on the parish church of St Martin in Kaufbeuren, a register of redeemed small interest rates ("*clain zins*") was made. These 318 annuities amounting from 1 to 24 haller belonged to St Martin and various other clerical institutions in the town. The about 180 debtors made up a large part of the citizenship. The case study outlines the structure of this source and analyses some economic and social aspects of the function of clerical institutions, especially the parish church, within the credit market of a rather small town.

Keywords: annuities, small towns, parish churches, foundations, *fabrica ecclesiae*

1 Introduction

In the first half of the fifteenth century, there were a lot of building sites in the imperial city of Kaufbeuren. Indications of the remarkable construction activity was the new steeple of the parish church of St Martin (in 1403 under construction),[1] the town fortification (work on the wall around 1420),[2] the *Kaufhaus* (con-

1 The earliest documents concerning the work on the new steeple date from 1403, e.g. Lausser 2008, vol. 1, no. 7. Cf. Lausser 2018, 86–88; Lausser 1994, 13–14; Breuer and Brenner 2001, 20.—I sincerely thank Lisa Leiber M.Ed. (Kiel) for reading an earlier version of this text.

2 Biller ^{2}2016, vol. 2, 83; Breuer and Brenner 2001, 39; Dieter 1999, 59.

Published in: Stephan Nicolussi-Köhler (Ed.), Change and Transformation of Premodern Credit Markets. The Importance of Small-Scale Credits. Heidelberg: heiBOOKS 2021, 65–88. DOI: https://doi.org/10.11588/heibooks.593.c12691

struction work mentioned in 1420)[3] and the house of the weavers' guild (1425)[4] at the market place, perhaps also the town hall (mentioned for the first time in 1412),[5] certainly the chancel of St Blasius (completed in accordance with several building inscriptions in 1436).[6] In the year 1438, the town council decided to replace also the chancel and the nave of the parish church of St Martin with a new construction.[7] According to an inscription at the portal on the south side of the nave, the building work started on 6 April 1438.[8] Some weeks later, on 1 May, the members of the town council took a resolution in order to cover a part of the expenses:[9] They made those who owed St Martin or other clerical institutions in the town small interest rates (*"clain zins"* as it is called in the source) the offer to redeem these annuities. The debtors had to pay 25 pfennige per 1 pfennig interest, and the offer was limited to interest rates of up to 1 schilling pfennige (that is 12 pfennige or 24 haller).[10] The payments were inscribed into a register, which has been preserved until today, now belonging to the holdings of the State Archives in Augsburg.[11] This source, also published in a transcription by Helmut Lausser

3 Dertsch 1955, no. 501; Lausser 2011, no. 158. Cf. Dieter 1999, 59.

4 Dieter 1999, 59.

5 Dertsch 1955, no. 427. Cf. Breuer and Brenner 2001, 40 (first mention 1423); Dieter 1999, 59.

6 Guggemos, 1989, 23; Lausser 2008, vol. 1, no. 257. Cf. Dieter 1999, 54; Breuer and Brenner 2001, 25. In mid-fifteenth century, the hospital's church was also rebuilt. Breuer and Brenner 2001, 41.

7 For the church of St Martin, see in general Lausser 2018; Lausser 1994; Breuer and Brenner 2001, 20–25; for its building history during the fifteenth century, Lausser 2018, 86–88, 96–107; Lausser 1994, 13–17.

8 *"Anno · dm̄ · m · / ccccº · xxxviiiº · Am · / sechstē · tag · aberel/lēs · hůb · man · / an · die · kirchen · // do · galt · ain · / metz · rogg · / lx · dn̄ · cůn/rat · speng/ler · pfleger."*—"In the year of the Lord 1438 on 6 April, there was the start of the construction of the church. 1 metzen of rye cost 60 pfennige. Konrad Spengler was church warden." The text is inscribed in two plates, a larger one (up to *"kirchen"*) and a smaller one below (reproduced in Lausser 2018, 97). It is printed (with minor differences) in Guggemos 1989, 72; also in Lausser 2008, vol. 1, no. 9. For the church warden Konrad (Kunz) Spengler, cf. below, notes 65–70.

9 StAA, Reichsstadt Kaufbeuren, MüB Lit. 9/1, fol. 1r; cf. Lausser 2013, 154.

10 For currencies used in the following, see below, note 25.

11 StAA, Reichsstadt Kaufbeuren, MüB Lit. 9/1, fol. 1r–25v.

in 2013,[12] gives us an unusual insight into the market of small loans in a rather small town.[13]

At this time Kaufbeuren, located about 60 kilometres southwest of the Swabian metropolis Augsburg, probably had about 2,500 inhabitants.[14] Since the thirteenth century, it had been an imperial city.[15] Besides the primarily regional character of its trade, the Upper Swabian town participated in long-distance trade in some degree.[16] Its fundamental manufacturing sector was weaving (linen, fustian), to a lesser extent also the fabrication of iron and other metal products.[17] The topographical structure (Fig. 1) was dominated by rather regular streets in east-west and north-south direction, disturbed significantly only in the settlement's northeast quarter. St Martin, by far the town's largest church,[18] lay in the centre, a little off the elongated market place. Within the wall with its three gates, there were a few smaller churches and the so-called *Maierhof*, a convent formed by women living in accordance with the "Regula Francisci", as well.[19] The northeast corner of the town was occupied by the hospital's building complex.[20]

The register of repaid small loans from 1438 immediately takes us into this rather confined urban world. On the basis of this source, I will outline a short case study on some economic and social aspects of the function of clerical institutions, especially the parish church, within an urban credit market.[21] My following con-

12 Lausser 2013, 153–176. Lausser's useful transcription is trustworthy, with only a few exceptions: Lausser 2013, 158 (line 24: only *"schůster"* instead of *"schüster weber"*), 161 (line 9: 7 instead of 12 d), 168 (line 31: 5 instead of 7 h), 171 (line 1: 6 instead of 11 d; line 3: 5 instead of 4.5 lb). Cf. StAA, Reichsstadt Kaufbeuren, MüB Lit. 9/1, fol. 5r, 7r, 17v, 19v. Besides, there are some minor errors without substantial content-related relevance, e.g. Lausser 2013, 156 (line 10: Hanns instead of Haintz), 157 (line 24: Cuntz instead of Cunrat), 163 (line 9: Cuntz instead of Cunrat). Cf. StAA, Reichsstadt Kaufbeuren, MüB Lit. 9/1, fol. 2v, 4r, 8v. In general, the study presented here is based on the archival source, but the pages of Lausser's transcription are indicated in addition.

13 Compared to larger cities, research on premodern credit markets in small towns is still underrepresented. Only as an example of a recent study, though of limited dimensions, cf. Rabeler 2020, 134–140; see also below, note 84.

14 On the basis of the tax register from 1479/83 (Dertsch 1955, 515–522; Lausser 2013, 179–194), Junginger 1965, 127, 129, calculates 2,497 inhabitants. Certainly, this is only a rough approach to the population.

15 For the history of Kaufbeuren, especially in the Middle Ages, see in general Kraus, Dieter, Fischer, and Westerburg 1999–2006; Simm 2012; Fischer 2016.

16 Dieter 2006a, 35–36; Dieter 1999, 51.

17 Dieter 2006a, 33–34; Dieter 1999, 50–51.

18 Cf. above, note 7.

19 For the *Maierhof*, see Dieter 1999, 56–57; Breuer and Brenner 2001, 33–35.

20 For the hospital, see Breuer and Brenner 2001, 41.

21 Instead of a literature survey, which must be all too short at this point, cf. the numerous references in Kypta, Bruch, and Skambraks 2019, 146–173.

Figure 1 Map of Kaufbeuren in the Late Middle Ages.

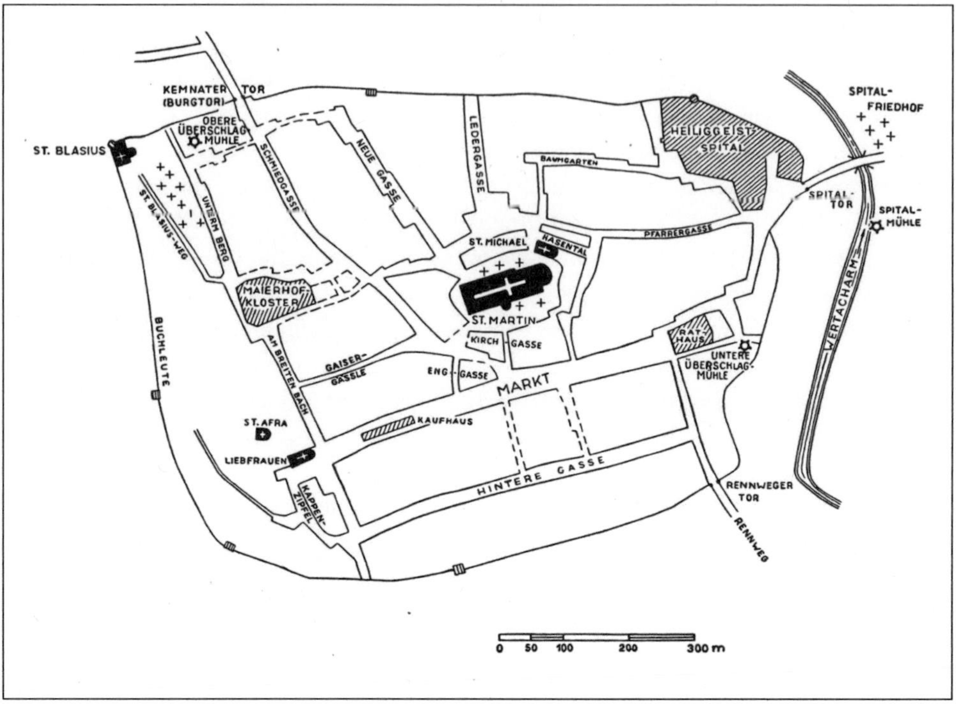

siderations will concern three points: first of all, the contents and the structure of the register from 1438; subsequently, a partial analysis of the debtors' characteristics by means of prosopography and social topography; finally, some structural issues regarding the significance of clerical institutions and of annuities in general for the market of small loans in urban society.

2 Clerical Creditors and Small Loans in Kaufbeuren

The register, preserved as a fair copy,[22] is written by an anonymous scribe without any discernible interruption, presumably in that same year 1438 that is given right at the beginning of the text.[23] On twenty-five leaves, it contains 297 entries[24] sorted by clerical institutions as creditors (the first section concerning St Martin by far the most extensive). In each case, the debtor's name, the annual interest rate, the repayment sum[25], and the estate (house or garden) encumbered with the former annuity are noted, sometimes also the debtor's profession.[26] Some entries comprise several transfers relating to the same person so that 318 transactions are noted in total.[27] There is no date of the initial credit transaction given, and likewise, we cannot learn from the source whether the mentioned person is the

---

22 There are a very few corrections like cancellations and insertions in the handwritten text, e.g. StAA, Reichsstadt Kaufbeuren, MüB Lit. 9/1, fol. 12r, 19r, 23v.

23 StAA, Reichsstadt Kaufbeuren, MüB Lit. 9/1, fol. 1r; cf. Lausser 2013, 154. There are a few later entries dated 1447, 1449 and 1450 respectively, StAA, Reichsstadt Kaufbeuren, MüB Lit. 9/1, fol. 9r, 25v; cf. Lausser 2013, 163, 176. All data given hereafter do not consider these entries, which prove that the manuscript was very sporadically in use for some time.

24 This number does not contain three later entries (cf. above, note 23) nor does it contain one incomplete entry (cf. Table 1, note 1).

25 Generally, the source gives money amounts (annuities and repayments) on the basis of *Haller* (h) and *Pfennig* (d), using also *Schilling* (ß) and *Pfund* (lb): 1 d = 2 h; 1 lb h = 20 ß h = 240 h. Only in four cases are other currencies used: *Groschen* (also Bohemian *Groschen*) as well as *Kreuzer*, the value of which is deduced from the other information given at the actual passage. StAA, Reichsstadt Kaufbeuren, MüB Lit. 9/1, fol. 8v, 12v, 14r, 17r; cf. Lausser 2013, 163, 165, 168. In the following, money amounts are usually given in *Haller* (h), notwithstanding the specification of the source.

26 The basic form of the entries is: "[Debtor's name] has bought [amount of annuity] burdening [real estate encumbered with the annuity]; for this he has paid [amount of the repayment]", e.g.: *"Item Partlin Nortwanger hat abkaufft 3 h uß sinem hẅse an der Schmidgasse by dem rörbrunnen am Spilman, darfur hat er geben 6 ß 3 h"*, or: *"Item Cuntz Anshalm hat abkaufft 2 d* [= 4 h] *zinses uß sinem garten vor dem Renntor by der becken garten, hat darfur geben 8 ß 4 h* [= 100 h]*"*. StAA, Reichsstadt Kaufbeuren, MüB Lit. 9/1, fol. 1v, 2r; cf. Lausser 2013, 154, 155.

27 For example, Hans Linsin repaid four debts concerning two houses and two garden plots: *"Item Hanns Linsin hat abgelöset 13 haller uß sinem hẅse an der Nuwengassen und 11 d* [= 22 h] *uß dem garten vor Kämpnater Tor, der des Clammers was, gelegen an der Hadergasse, stoßt uff des spitalz anger, und hat mer abkoufft ain d* [= 2 h] *zinses uß sinem hẅse an der Schmidgassen, daz Hwgen Freyings was, und mer hat er abkaufft 12 d* [= 24 h] *zinses uß dem garten am Espan gegen dem Mulbach, und hat fur daz alles geben 6 lb 7 ß 1 haller* [= 1,525 h]*."* StAA, Reichsstadt Kaufbeuren, MüB Lit. 9/1, fol. 2r; cf. Lausser 2013, 155.

original debtor or his legal successor.[28] So the register represents a snapshot lacking a deeper chronological dimension. The annuities cannot be verified by other sources, in particular there are no corresponding charters (annuity letters).[29] Furthermore, we have no information about annuities and loans which were not repaid at this time.

Actually, the register does not indicate the kind and conditions of the annuities.[30] Considering the source on its own and the ambiguity of the term *"zins"*, one could also assume that the register contains some kind of ground rents (*Grundzinse*) or tithes (*Zehnten*) not based on credit secured by real estate but on the transfer of real estate itself. However, this would mean that within the town wall (besides the gardening land in the district) a huge number of plots had been in the possession of clerical institutions, especially the parish church, at some time in the past so that the annuities could be the remains of those former manorial relationships. In Kaufbeuren, which emerged as a Staufer city in the thirteenth century,[31] such a wide-ranging clerical influence on real estate seems rather implausible. Furthermore, some houses were connected with at least two annuities.[32] Finally, these *"clain zins"* are not mentioned in other medieval sources from Kaufbeuren:[33] this is understandable, however, in the case of small loans for which

28 Some entries contain the name of a former owner of the real estate encumbered with the annuity, e.g.: *"Item Stöcklin hat abgelöset 1 d uß sinem hẘse uff dem kirchhof, daz ettwenn hern Hannsen Schäfflers säligen was, hat darfur geben 25 d"*, or: *"Item Endres Fries der kursner hat auch abkaufft 8 pfennige zinses, giengen uß ainem lußgartens, stoßt uff die Wyergassen, der vor zyten siner schwiger der Urßingerin was, darfur hat er geben 33 ß 4 haller."* StAA, Reichsstadt Kaufbeuren, MüB Lit. 9/1, fol. 10v, 18r; cf. Lausser 2013, 164, 169. Perhaps that means that the already existing annuity had been also transferred with the house or garden in question.

29 For different source types relating to annuities, cf. Huang 2019.

30 Perhaps, in one case, at the very beginning of the list, a connection with a foundation is indicated because an annuity of 2 d is intended for *"kirchprot järlich ze geben"*, i.e. a donation to the poor in the form of bread (cf. DRW 1983, 850, s.v. *"Kirch(en)brot"* II).

31 Lausser 2016a, 39–52; Simm 2012, 44; Lausser 1999, 25–26.

32 Examples: The grocer Cunrat Emich had to pay three annuities (3 h St Blasius' light, 9 h the *Täfelein-Almosen,* 3 h the leprosarium) connected with *"tanderlayes huse"*, which was in *Hintere Gasse* as one of the entries indicates, StAA, Reichsstadt Kaufbeuren, MüB Lit. 9/1, fol. 17v, 20v, 23v; cf. Lausser 2013, 168, 172, 175. Probably, *"tanderlayes huse"* means a junk shop *(Trödelladen),* cf. Fischer 1908, 48, s.v. *"Tand—Tändler/ Tand(el)-lade"*. The house which Hans Abel had received from a person named Hägnenberg was connected with two annuities (1 ß h St Blasius' light, 1 ß h the leprosarium), StAA, Reichsstadt Kaufbeuren, MüB Lit. 9/1, fol. 15v, 23r; cf. Lausser 2013, 166, 173. Some further entries concern a person's house situated in the same street.

33 When in 1546 a register of revenues claimed by the parish church St Martin was written *("Sandt Martins vnd seiner pfarrkirchen zů Kauffbewrn rent, zins, güllt, güeter, eewig vnd ablesig"),* one section was entitled: *"Hernach volgend die kleine zins aus den heusern vnd*

drawing up a charter may have been by far too expensive. So, the register's annuities very probably were based on credit in the form of *Ewigrenten* (perpetual annuities), which (at this time) could be terminated by the debtor repaying the loan sum, but normally not by the creditor.[34]

The 318 annuities amount to a sum of 3,374 haller or 1,687 pfennige (just over 14 pounds haller) per year (Table 1). Almost 45 percent of the entries concern St Martin,[35] but there are also annuities of other clerical institutions: specified foundations in the St Blasius church concerning a mass and the maintenance of light,[36] the hospital (*Spital*)[37], the so-called *Täfelein-Almosen* (a foundation connected with the hospital), the leprosarium (*Sondersiechenhaus*) administrated by the hospital,[38] and St Michael in Tabratshofen, a church incorporated into the hospital in a deserted village near Kaufbeuren.[39] Since there are no contemporary accounts or other registers preserved, we have no further insight into the revenues of St Martin or the other institutions at this time. Considering the low level of the individual annual payments, it is not surprising that this sum does not seem exceptionally large if it is compared, for example, with the regular interest income of the hospital (*Heilig-Geist-Spital*) in Pforzheim, a town in Baden about 40 kilo-

---

gertten in der stat, geuallen auff Martini, inhalt der allten büecher", Lausser 2008, vol. 1, no. 416 (quotations 93, 95). In the following, annual obligations ranging from 26 h to 144 h (besides two entries over 8 h and 216 h respectively) are listed, including the encumbered houses or gardens but without any further information about these annuities' character.

34 Helmut Lausser, who is very well informed about the sources of late medieval Kaufbeuren and has published, besides an enormous number of other sources, a transcription of the register from 1438 (see above, note 12), comments in a similar way: *"Ich vermute, dass es sich bei den genannten Zahlungen eher um die Zinsen von kleineren Krediten, sog, Ewigzinsen, handelt als um Zehntanteile. Belegen kann ich Ihnen das, da der angesprochene Text der einzige mit solchen Zahlungen ist, jedoch nicht"*. I thank Helmut Lausser for this email message from 24 June 2020.

35 Only in a few cases can annuities be assigned to special parts of the *fabrica*, e.g. in two cases the text indicates that annuities of the parish church belonged to St Martin's and St Michael's lights respectively (8 d *"gehorten an sanct Martins und sanct Michelz liechter"* and 14 d *"gehorten an sanct Martins liecht 8 und an sanct Michelz liecht 6 d"*, StAA, Reichsstadt Kaufbeuren, MüB Lit. 9/1, fol. 5r, 5v; cf. Lausser 2013, 158, 159).

36 For the St Blasius church, see Dieter 1999, 54; Breuer and Brenner 2001, 25–28. The mass which could be meant here was founded by the mayor, the council, and the commune in 1383, cf. Dertsch 1955, no. 295–296; Lausser 2008, vol. 1, no. 249–250.

37 For the hospital, see Dieter 1999, 54, 57–58; Breuer and Brenner 2001, 41.

38 For the leprosarium, see Dieter 1999, 54–55, 58.

39 For the village Tabratshofen, which became deserted in the early fifteenth century at the latest, cf. Dertsch 1960, 76–77; in addition, Dieter 1999, 53. For the incorporation of the church into the Kaufbeuren hospital (1350), see also Dertsch 1955, no. 185–186, 188–189; Lausser 2009, no. 23–26.

Table 1 Distribution of entries in the register of *"clain zins"* (1438)

Clerical institution	Number of annuities	Value	Average	Repayment
St Martin	142 (44.7 %)	1,469 h (43.5 %)	10.3 h	37,540 h
St Blasius (mass)	14 (4.4 %)	205 h (6.1 %)	14.6 h	5,141 h
St Blasius (light)	62 (19.5 %)	514 h (15.2 %)	8.3 h	13,237 h
Hospital (*Spital*)[1]	8 (2.5 %)	67 h (2.0 %)	8.4 h	1,675 h
Täfelein-Almosen	52 (16.4 %)	799 h (23.7 %)	15.4 h	20,367 h
Leprosarium (*Sondersiechen*)	36 (11.3 %)	270 h (8.0 %)	7.5 h	6,904 h
St Michael in Tabratshofen	4 (1.3 %)	50 h (1.5 %)	12.5 h	1,298 h
	318 (100.0 %)	3,374 h (100.0 %)	10.6 h	86,162 h

1 At the end of the section concerning the hospital, there is a ninth entry which does not give any information about the annuity itself because it breaks off in mid-sentence: *"Item Hanns Herman, beck, hat abkaufft."* StAA, Reichsstadt Kaufbeuren, MüB Lit. 9/1, fol. 19v; cf. Lausser 2013, 164. This entry is not considered in the following.

metres northwest of Stuttgart with a number of inhabitants not much lower than that of Kaufbeuren: according to a register from 1517, this hospital claimed annuities (*Gülten,* without payments in kind) of more than 190,000 haller, 49 percent of them lower than 1 rheingulden or 336 haller[40] (problems of exchange rates neglected).

As already stated, the offer towards the debtors was limited to annuities of up to 1 schilling pfennige (12 pfennige or 24 haller). The average annuity accounts for 10.6 haller. Almost 54 percent of the registered annuities amount to 4 pfennige or 8 haller (redeemed with 200 haller) or less (Table 2). However, these represent not even 26 percent of the annuities' total value. On the contrary, annuities ranging from 17 to 24 haller make up 22 percent by number, but about 46 percent by value. In order to accelerate the process, there was a benefit granted to all those who made the repayment before St Jacob's day (25 July) because in this case, the annuity of the current year was remitted. The repayment sums reveal that about half of the annuities were not redeemed until after this date.[41]

40 Rabeler 2004, 103, 121 (Table 3), for the conversion of rheingulden, pfennige and heller (haller) 101–102 (1 rheingulden = 168 pfennige = 336 heller).

41 Only in a few cases is it expressed explicitly that the annuity of the current year was also paid, e.g. StAA, Reichsstadt Kaufbeuren, MüB Lit. 9/1, fol. 23r: "[...] *hat darfur* [sc. an annuity of 12 h] *geben 1 lb 6 ß h* [= 312 h] *mit dem zins.* [...] *hat darfur* [sc. an annuity of 4 h] *geben 8 ß 8 h* [= 104 h] *fur zins und gelt*"; cf. Lausser 2013, 173. In many other cases, however, this can be gathered from the repayment sum.

Table 2 Distribution of interest rates in the register of *"clain zins"* (1438)

Interest rate	Number of annuities	Value
1 up to 8 h	170 (53.5 %)	852 h (25.3 %)
9 up to 16 h	78 (24.5 %)	978 h (29.0 %)
17 up to 24 h	70 (22.0 %)	1,544 h (45.8 %)
	318 (100.0 %)	3,374 h (100.0 %)

As already stated, too, the debtors had to pay 25 pfennige per 1 pfennig interest. Since the current year's annuities were included if applicable, they did not pay 42,175 pfennige (84,350 haller) but 43,081 pfennige (86,162 haller) altogether, a little more than 359 pounds haller. We do not know the original loan amounts. In the first half of the fifteenth century, annuity letters concerning larger amounts present a mixed picture. The hospital's *Täfelein-Almosen,* for example, purchased a perpetual annuity (*Ewigzins*) of 5 schillinge haller for 5 pounds haller in 1405 (interest rate 5 percent), but two years later another of 10 schillinge haller for 10.5 pounds haller (4.76 percent).[42] A perpetual annuity of 1 pound haller was sold for 23 pounds haller to the hospital in 1433 (4.35 percent), one of 2 gulden for 48 gulden to the citizen Peter Albrecht in 1440 (4.17 percent), another of 1 pound haller for 25 pounds haller to Konrad Spengler in the same year (4 percent).[43] Perhaps the debtors had to repay the original loan amounts when the annuities were multiplied by twenty-five in 1438. Thus, the only financial incentive for them would have been the prospect of saving the regular payment in that year, but many of them did not make use of this offer. It seems that supporting the church building for the community's benefit was a significant motive for redeeming these small annuities at that time.

Under the condition that the sum required in 1438 corresponds to the original loan amount, the annuities amounting from 1 to 24 haller correspond to loan amounts from 25 to 600 haller or from 12.5 to 300 pfennige. On the basis of examples from Nuremberg or Constance[44], we can roughly estimate that a day labourer's wage was 14 to 20 pfennige in the building trade (problems of exchange

42 Dertsch 1955, no. 369, 379.

43 Dertsch 1955, no. 661, 739, 742. It seems that annuities of 5 percent became more customary in Kaufbeuren in the second half of the fifteenth century, see e.g. Dertsch 1955, no. 982, 1113, 1115, 1133, 1173, 1188, 1195, 1198, 1209, 1219, 1228, 1233, 1256, 1271, 1292.

44 Nuremberg (16 d in the winter, 20 d in the summer, plus some minor extra payments): Lexer 1862, 40. Constance (14–16 d): Hagen 2018, 48, note 27.

rates neglected once again). In consequence, more than 50 percent of the original loan amounts, ranging up to 100 pfennige, correspond to a maximum of approximately a week's wages of this kind. Another opportunity to put the interest amounts into context is the comparison with real estate prices, which are, however, rarely documented so far as the town of Kaufbeuren itself and the cultivated land immediately before its gates are concerned. In the year 1431, Greta, Ulrich Wideman's widow, sold two garden plots (*Gartenlüsse*), situated before the *Kemnater Tor*, to her cousin Adelheid, Heinrich Ammunsun's wife, and her children. The buyer did not pay a specified purchase sum but was bound to pay 18 schillinge haller each year until the seller's death.[45] This interest rate of 9 schillinge haller seems to indicate the equivalent value of one garden (in form of a more expensive life annuity, however) whereas in the register from 1438, perpetual annuities connected with gardens only amount to little more than 1 schilling haller on average.

3 The Debtors: Prosopography and Social Topography

Who were the debtors mentioned in the register from 1438? A comprehensive prosopographical analysis of the records is not possible at this point, but some insights into social status as well as economic capabilities will be given in the following.

For certain, the about 180 debtors listed in the register (some of them more than once) do not form a cross section of the urban society as a whole since they all had one thing in common: they were real estate owners. Credit in the form of annuities excluded all other inhabitants, and thus, we cannot expect to find the actual lower social strata among our group of debtors. Those inhabitants are absent who occur seldom in sources from Kaufbeuren (and many other towns) anyway.

The value of the properties mentioned in the register as the basis of the liquidated annuities is not specified, but there is one distinction in quality: that between houses and gardens.[46] Could there perhaps be a tendency that wealthy

45 Dertsch 1955, no. 629.

46 313 annuities out of 318 were secured by houses or gardens. Furthermore, there were one *"badstube"* (annuity of 8 h), three *"acker"* (24 h, 24 h, 2 h), and one *"grasplatz"* (8 h), StAA, Reichsstadt Kaufbeuren, MüB Lit. 9/1, fol. 2v, 8r, 19r, 25r; cf. Lausser 2013, 156, 162, 163, 170, 176.

Table 3 Houses and gardens in the register of *"clain zins"* (1438)

Interest rate	Number of annuities based on		Value of annuities based on	
	houses	gardens	houses	gardens
1 up to 8 h	94 (56.3 %)	73 (43.7 %)	438 h (52.5 %)	396 h (47.5 %)
9 up to 16 h	45 (57.7 %)	33 (42.3 %)	545 h (55.7 %)	433 h (44.3 %)
17 up to 24 h	22 (32.4 %)	46 (67.6 %)	472 h (31.6 %)	1,024 h (68.4 %)
	161 (51.4 %)	152 (48.6 %)	1,455 h (44.0 %)	1,853 h (56.0 %)

citizens taking out a loan in this way encumbered their houses and that their less prosperous fellow citizens, who perhaps even had to rent a dwelling, made use of their gardens? The data do not verify such a connection (Table 3). On the contrary, higher annuities are much more often based on garden plots than on houses. In these cases, gardens may appear as additional property of the wealthy so that the differentiation between houses and gardens on its own does not allow any general conclusions regarding the debtors' stratification.

Conversely, the dispersion of the houses within the town is quite revealing (Table 4). The average amount of the annuities ranges significantly from 13.7 haller at the *Markt* (market place) to 7.4 haller at *Schmiedgasse* (Smiths' Alley). This range is even larger, from 17.6 haller (*Markt*) to 8.2 haller (*Unterm Berg*), when we refer to the number of houses, which are sometimes mentioned more than once. For comparison, we can look at the results of research on the house owners' guild membership in the late sixteenth century, about one and a half centuries later, but probably without fundamental changes in the town's social and economic structures in the meantime.[47] First of all, the different size of plots stands out: at the *Markt* and in the area around St Martin, but also at *Hintere Gasse,* there were comparatively large properties whereas especially the northwest of the town was dominated by much smaller plots. This concerned *Neue Gasse, Schmiedgasse* and the alley *Unterm Berg* in particular. At the *Markt* and in its immediate surroundings, many members of the *Herrenzunft,* the most prestigious guild in Kaufbeuren with numerous holders of the mayor's and the *Ammann's* offices among its ranks,

47 For the following, see the map of Kaufbeuren presenting the house owners' membership in the guilds in Kraus, Dieter, Fischer, and Westerburg 1999–2006, vol. 3, pl. iii; cf. Dieter 2006b, 60–62. Concerning the relations between social and spatial structures in late medieval Kaufbeuren, see Dieter 2006a, 36–38.

Table 4 Location of houses in the register of *"clain zins"* (1438)

Street	Number of annuities (houses)[1]	Value	Average
Markt	9 (7)	123 h	13.7 h (17.6 h)
Hasental	9 (8)	108 h	12.0 h (13.5 h)
Baumgarten	6 (6)	66 h	11.0 h (11.0 h)
Hintere Gasse	11 (9)	99 h	9.0 h (11.0 h)
Ledergasse	8 (6)	72 h	9.0 h (12.0 h)
Unterm Berg	11 (11)	90 h	8.2 h (8.2 h)
Neue Gasse	10 (8)	80 h	8.0 h (10.0 h)
Schmiedgasse	31 (27)	228 h	7.4 h (8.4 h)

1 Some houses are encumbered with more than one annuity (for examples, cf. above, note 32). Cases in which this is only indicated by the same owner are taken into account here, too.

had settled.[48] In the same area, there also lived some members of the *Krämerzunft,* the Grocers' Guild, ranking after the *Herrenzunft* regarding wealth and municipal offices,[49] whereas various members of the *Metzgerzunft,* the Butchers' Guild, a comparatively wealthy craft guild, too,[50] possessed plots at *Hintere Gasse,* located south of the *Markt.* In contrast, the northwest quarter of the town was settled by more or less small artisans: in particular weavers, smiths, and shoemakers,[51] whose houses lined up along the alleys between *Ledergasse* and *Unterm Berg.* This is just the area where the register from 1438 shows rather small annuities while most of the higher annuities are connected with houses at the *Markt.* By and large, this corresponds to the topographical distribution of wealth presented by the oldest tax register of Kaufbeuren, created in the years 1479 to 1483.[52] So our source mirrors the town's social topography quite accurately.

In the register, the profession of 44 persons is mentioned (Table 5). Several of them occur more than once, so 80 annuities are concerned. The ranking of pro-

---

48 For the *Herrenzunft,* see Dieter 2006a, 28–30 (also concerning the upper class's residential area); Dieter 1999, 48. For the mayor, see Dieter 1999, 46; for the *Ammann,* in earlier times the town ruler's representative but since 1424 a completely municipal official, see Dieter 1999, 45–46.

49 Dieter 2006a, 29; Dieter 1999, 48.

50 Dieter 1999, 48.

51 In Kaufbeuren, weavers and shoemakers were the poorest guilds. Dieter 2006a, 33; Dieter 1999, 48.

52 Cf. Dieter 2006a, 38, Fig. 4 (average assets in various streets, 1479/83).

Table 5 Professions mentioned in the register of *"clain zins"* (1438)

Profession	Number of persons	Number of annuities	Average value of annuities
weaver[1]	13	15	8.6 h
shoemaker[2]	6	9	12.9 h
grocer	5	18	10.7 h
mason[3]	4	7	11.4 h
smith[4]	4	9	11.2 h
baker[5]	2	3	14.7 h
butcher[6]	2	6	7.8 h
tanner	2	3	11.3 h
bleacher	1	1	9.0 h
cooper	1	3	4.7 h
furrier	1	4	8.0 h
pewterer	1	1	1.0 h
tailor	1	1	18.0 h
gatekeeper	1	1	3.0 h
town clerk	1	1	22.0 h
	44[7]	80	10.3 h

1 Two annuities of 11 h and 12 h were paid by Cunrat Schnyder/Schneider, who is characterised as a shoemaker and weaver in both cases so that these entries are relevant for both professions here, StAA, Reichsstadt Kaufbeuren, MüB Lit. 9/1, fol. 5r, 20r; cf. Lausser 2013, 158, 171.

2 See Table 5, note 1.

3 One annuity of 6 h had to be given by the mason Hans Nachtgall together with Jörg Hüter whose profession is unknown, StAA, Reichsstadt Kaufbeuren, MüB Lit. 9/1, fol. 19r; cf. Lausser 2013, 170.

4 Three entries concern the widow Adelhait Werner (*"Wernherin"*), the *"schmiedin"* (female smith), who obviously had taken over her late husband's workshop, StAA, Reichsstadt Kaufbeuren, MüB Lit. 9/1, fol. 1r, 18r, 22r; cf. Lausser 2013, 154, 169, 172. Cf. also Lausser 2016b, 395.

5 There is a further entry for the baker Hans Herman, but without any information about the annuity itself, cf. Table 1, note 1.

6 It is assumed that the butcher Cunrat Anshalm, mentioned only once, and Cunz Anshalm, mentioned three times without indicating his profession, are the same person, StAA, Reichsstadt Kaufbeuren, MüB Lit. 9/1, fol. 2r, 14r, 18v, 22r; cf. Lausser 2013, 155, 165, 169, 172.

7 For the sums, the two annuities of 11 h and 12 h which were paid by the shoemaker and weaver Cunrat Schnyder/Schneider (cf. Table 5, note 1) are taken into account only once.

fessions is led by 13 weavers, members of the particularly numerous and most export-oriented craft in Kaufbeuren. Shoemakers, grocers, smiths, and masons are represented six, five or four times respectively. One or two persons belong to eight other crafts in the fields of textile, metal, and food production. Finally, there are also two municipal officials among the debtors, the town clerk Ulrich Manseerder and the gatekeeper called Menhofer. The average value of the recorded annuities varies strongly from one craft to the other—to some degree this could correspond to the economic capabilities of the different crafts although a statistical interpretation is difficult.

At least eighteen councillors were among the debtors (Table 6),[53] so they make up about 10 percent of the total number of persons. We can assign 71 annuities with a value of 767 haller to them—or in other words: about 22 percent of the annuities, regarding number as well as value, were connected with councillors. For example, the mayor Ulrich Honold (Hanold) redeemed seven annuities with a value of 51 haller in total. They varied between 3 and 24 haller. Besides several garden plots, he had encumbered three houses: one at the *Markt* (probably his own home), one at the *Kemnater Tor* in the northern town, and one in the alley *Unterm Berg*, not far from that gate.[54]

Finally, let us take a closer look at another group of debtors: those who redeemed annuities of only 1 or 2 haller (Table 7).[55] There are nineteen annuities of this value, which make up about 6 percent of the total number. Twelve debtors encumbered a house, six a garden plot, and one—an exception among the whole data—a field (*"acker"*). The sixteen relevant persons demonstrate the wide social range of the debtors—and some problems of the prosopography as well. First, there are the councillors Konrad Endorfer the Elder, Hans Linsin and Kunz Weiß. Endorfer is documented as a member of the town council in 1422.[56] In 1443, he was dead because in this year his son of the same name issued a charter about his father's memorial foundation in St Martin.[57] Hans Linsin is mentioned as a

53 Hardly any of these persons is marked as a member of the town council in the register, with the exception of the mayor Ulrich Hanold, StAA, Reichsstadt Kaufbeuren, MüB Lit. 9/1, fol. 7r: *"Item Ulrich Hanold, an der zit burgermeister* [...]*"*; cf. Lausser 2013, 161. For references, cf. Dertsch 1955, 532–641 (index). Several times the name "Hans Mair" is mentioned in the register, obviously indicating different persons, but it is not clear whether the councillor Hans Mair, who is mentioned in other sources, is one of them. For the council of Kaufbeuren in the fifteenth century, see in general Dieter 1999, 46.

54 StAA, Reichsstadt Kaufbeuren, MüB Lit. 9/1, fol. 7r–7v (four entries), 17r, 19v, 23v; cf. Lausser 2013, 161, 168, 171, 175. For Ulrich Honold, cf. Lausser 2016b, 98–100.

55 Concerning the mentioned families, cf. in general Lausser 2016b.

56 Dertsch 1955, no. 516, p. 163. For Konrad Endorfer the Elder, cf. Lausser 2016b, 48.

57 Dertsch 1955, no. 780, pp. 236–237. For Konrad Endorfer the Younger, cf. Lausser 2016b, 49.

Table 6 Councillors in the register of *"clain zins"* (1438)

Name	Number of annuities	Value	Average
Peter Albrecht	1	16 h	16.0 h
Hans Angrer	2	42 h	21.0 h
Konrad Emich	6	43 h	7.2 h
Konrad Endorfer	4	24 h	6.0 h
Endres Fries	4	32 h	8.0 h
Ulrich Honold (Hanold)	7	51 h	7.3 h
Hans Linsin	7	127 h	18.1 h
Kunz Müller	7	84 h	12.0 h
Hans Pruggschlegel	3	38 h	12.7 h
Peter Pruggschlegel	1	24 h	24.0 h
Jos Scheuhenpog	2	32 h	16.0 h
Hans Schnyder	2	31 h	15.5 h
Heinz Segenschmid	1	6 h	6.0 h
Kunz (Konrad) Spengler (Spängler)	7	64 h	9.1 h
Hans von Ulm	4	26 h	6.5 h
Konrad Wälsch	5	64 h	12.8 h
Kunz Weiß (Wyß)	5	31 h	6.2 h
Konrad Weißerer (Wysirher)[1]	3	32 h	10.7 h
	71	767 h	10.8 h

1 One annuity of 8 h had to be paid by Konrad Wysirher and his brother-in-law Hans Ruscher together.

Table 7 Annuities of 1 haller (*) or 2 haller in the register of *"clain zins"* (1438)

Name	**Estate**	**Creditor**
Lienhart Burger	Garden	St Blasius (light)
Konrad Endorfer the Elder	Garden	St Martin
Kunz Häfelin	Garden	*Sondersiechen*
Daman Koler (tanner)	House (*Ledergasse*)	St Martin
Hans Linsin	House (*Schmiedgasse*)	St Martin
Franz Machenschalk*	House (*Kirchhof*)	St Martin
Hans Ott (the Mangöldin's husband)	House (*Ledergasse*)	St Martin
Klaus Pfnogner	House (*Hasental*)	St Martin
Klaus Pfnogner	House (*Baumgarten*)	St Martin
Heinz Prun	House	*Täfelein-Almosen*
Kunz Spengler	Garden	St Martin
Kunz Spengler	Garden	*Sondersiechen*
Stöcklin	House (*Kirchhof*)	Hospital
Wernlin Stöcklin's sun	House	St Blasius (light)
Kunz vom Weg (pewterer)*	House	St Martin
the old Weihermüllerin	House (*Kemnater Tor*)	St Martin
Kunz Weiß (Wyß)	House (*Hintere Gasse*)	Hospital
Kunz Weiß (Wyß)	Garden	St Blasius (light)
Ulrich Weißerer (Wyßirher) the Younger	Field (*"acker"*)	St Michael in Tabratshofen

member of the council between 1428 and 1448.[58] In 1445, he was a hospital warden, too.[59] He died in the year 1464 at the latest.[60] The third man in this group, Kunz Weiß, is documented as councillor in the years 1423 and 1431.[61] He died before 1446.[62] His uncle was the weaver Hans Oswalt.[63] Other information about him is scarce.[64]

Measured by assets and functions, at least two other persons also belong to the town's social leading groups though they were not councillors: The grocer[65] Kunz (Konrad) Spengler is mentioned in connection with a memorial foundation in St Martin[66] and with the foundation of a procession[67]. He was a warden of the *Liebfrauenkapelle* (chapel of Our Lady),[68] later of the parish church St Martin.[69] His economic capabilities become apparent in the purchase of 1 pound haller *Ewigzins* for 25 pounds haller in 1440 and in the acquisition of grassland in 1446 and 1451.[70] Another Kunz Spengler, probably his son, was councillor in 1485.[71] Ulrich Weißerer (Wyßirher) the Younger, related to the mayor Konrad Weißerer,[72] was in office as *Ammann* between 1424 and 1429.[73]

---

58 Dertsch 1955, no. 590, 772, 774, 776, 777, 779, 803, 808, 826, 832. For Hans Linsin, cf. Lausser 2016b, 171–172.

59 Dertsch 1955, no. 803, 808.

60 Dertsch 1955, no. 997.

61 Dertsch 1955, no. 537, 620. For Kunz (Konrad) Weiß, cf. Lausser 2016b, 382.

62 Dertsch 1955, no. 818.

63 Dertsch 1955, no. 478.

64 Dertsch 1955, no. 480, 742.

65 Dertsch 1955, no. 859, 864, 970. For Konrad Spengler, cf. Lausser 2018, 97–98; Lausser 2016b, 311–312.

66 Dertsch 1955, no. 840.

67 Dertsch 1955, no. 864, 970.

68 Dertsch 1955, no. 562, 580, 603, 605.

69 Dertsch 1955, no. 914, 946; see also no. 895, 922 (*Zechmeister* of St Martin).

70 Dertsch 1955, no. 742, 818, 859.

71 Dertsch 1955, no. 1342; see also no. 1392 (councillor and warden of St Blasius, 1487) and p. 519, 521 (tax register, 1479/83). Cf. Lausser 2016b, 312.—The older Konrad Spengler is mentioned as mayor in 1439–1440 in Lausser, Dieter, and Pfundner 2006, 334, which seems to be wrong according to Lausser 2018, 97; cf. also Lausser 2011, no. 23.

72 Cf. Lausser 2016b, 388–390.

73 Dertsch 1955, no. 544, 545, 547, 548, 552, 553, 556, 557, 558, 559a, 560, 561, 564, 567, 570, 574, 575, 577, 579, 580, 583, 584, 585, 590, 592, 599, 600; Lausser 2018, vol. 2, no. 405–418. Cf. Lausser, Dieter, and Pfundner 2006, 337; Lausser 2011, no. 24. For Ulrich Weißerer, cf. also Lausser 2016b, 387–388. For the *Ammann* office, see above, note 48.—In 1413, Ulrich Weißerer (Wyßirher) the Elder (perhaps the father?) is mentioned, too (Dertsch 1955, no. 439), so that confusion concerning the attribution of information to both persons is not excluded.

Furthermore, three of the debtors of annuities of 1 or 2 haller appear only sporadically in charters issued between 1422 and 1461: Klaus Pfnogner,[74] Heinz Prun,[75] and Kunz vom Weg.[76] Only for the latter do we know his profession: he was a pewterer (*Kannengießer*).[77] But we can assume that the other two belonged to the craftmen's milieu, too. This also applies to the remaining eight persons, for which no closer information is available yet.

4 Credit Market, Annuities, and Clerical Institutions: Some Structural Issues

Sources give us only limited information about the credit market in late medieval Kaufbeuren.[78] The register from 1438, however, allows us at least a fragmentary glimpse at the segment of small-scale credit. On the basis of the previous explanations, I want to turn towards three points.

(1) First, the omnipresence of (small) loans in urban society. According to the well-known words by Bruno Kuske, the medieval world was *"allseitig vom Kreditprinzip durchdrungen"*[79] ("permeated by the principle of credit on all sides"). The register from Kaufbeuren presented here verifies this thesis in a quite remarkable way, I think. In the town's oldest tax register from 1479/83, the names of 620 tax payers are listed,[80] and so we can conclude that the records of annuities redeemed in 1438 by about 180 persons concerned nearly one third of the town's

74 Dertsch 1955, no. 951 (the same person?).

75 Dertsch 1955, no. 621.

76 Dertsch 1955, no. 523. See also the following note.

77 Dertsch 1955, no. 690, 763.

78 For example, we have hardly any information about Jewish credit activities. Anyway, sources concerning Jews settled in late medieval Kaufbeuren are very sparse. In the first half of the fourteenth century, there was a Jewish community, which was destroyed in 1348. Shortly before, King Karl IV, confirming the rights of Kaufbeuren in 1348, had waived the Jews' tax (Dertsch 1955, no. 173). Obviously, Jews settled again in the town in the course of the following decades, but we do not hear anything specific before 1405 when Utz Harder and his mother Anna borrowed 38 rheingulden from the Jew Lazarus, citizen of Kaufbeuren (Dertsch 1955, no. 368a; Lausser 2011, no. 235; cf. also Pfister 1993, 883, 889). Later sources are seldom, too. Cf. Oelsner 1968, 392; Ledermann 1904, 721–722.

79 Kuske 1956, 52. Cf. also Skambraks and Köhler 2019, 146.

80 The tax register from 1479/83 is published in Dertsch 1955, 515–522, and in Lauser 2013, 180–194. In this list, the taxpayers are sorted according to the guilds: *Herrenzunft* 33 persons, *Metzgerzunft* 73, *Bäckerzunft* 79, *Schusterzunft* 89, *Schmiedezunft* 103, *Krä-*

taxable households. This corresponds quite well to the number of 161 annuities secured by houses (some houses mentioned more than once)[81]. For in 1588 there were 411 houses owned by citizens within the town wall (without outbuildings). This dimension is verified by the allocation of house numbers in 1800 (450 houses within, 50 outside the wall).[82] Indeed, small credit of this kind was an omnipresent phenomenon in this confined urban world. The social range within the debtors' group documented in 1438 was significant, from the town's leading families up to artisans with limited economic resources.

(2) Second, the significance of annuities for the market of small credit. Whereas annuities as a medieval form of credit (and also regarding the real estate market) are well-known in general, sometimes the research seems still to underestimate annuities as an instrument of small credit. In particular, this is a problem of the sources because as a rule, there are no sealed charters documenting annuities of this sort, so we depend on registers, ledgers, and similar sources. The example outlined here shows that eternal annuities (*Ewigrenten*) of low value could be a widespread phenomenon although they do not seem to be a very suitable instrument for short-term credits. But it is a difficult question as to what extent this can be generalised with regard to other towns. One limitation must be emphasised: annuities only allowed real estate owners the raising of capital, thus generally excluding considerable parts of urban society.

(3) Third, the *fabrica ecclesiae* as credit institution. In 1987, Gerd Wunder published a short paper under the title *"Die Stadt als Spar- und Darlehenskasse"* ("The town as savings and loan bank"), summarising his results as follows: *"Was der Rat oder die Stadtkasse im Zinsgeldgeschäft unternimmt, entspricht durchaus der Tätigkeit der späteren Spar- und Darlehenskassen"*[83] ("what is done by the council or the town treasury in the field of interest transactions correlates with the activity

---

merzunft 86, *Weberzunft* 157, together 620 persons (plus nine *Ausleut*, i.e. persons like noblemen and clerical groups with the status of citizens but living outside the town). There are minor differences between the two published versions because Lauser seems to have omitted three names mentioned by Dertsch: Othmar Ott *(Metzgerzunft)*, Hans Titelin *(Bäckerzunft)*, and Pauls Heller *(Weberzunft)*. Without consulting the archival source, preserved only in an eighteenth-century copy, the question of the right text version cannot be answered definitively. Some figures given in the literature have very slight divergences, cf. Dieter 2006a, 33; Dieter 1999, 49; Eitel 1970, 143, 146; Junginger 1965, table between 102 and 103.

81 Cf. above, note 32.

82 Simm 2012, 222.

83 Wunder 1987, 120.

of the later savings and loan banks"). But one significant point Gerd Wunder did not have in mind explicitly were the clerical institutions and foundations which were financially controlled by the *fabrica* led by the church wardens. As a rule, the latter were members of the town council themselves or they were accountable to the councillors. In Kaufbeuren, the dependence of the *fabricae ecclesiae* on the town council is shown just by the fact that in 1438, the latter decided upon the use of the churches' funds for the construction of St Martin. Until today, the research has not taken the parish churches' significance as credit institutions sufficiently into consideration.[84]

References

Archival References

StAA: State Archives/Staatsarchiv Augsburg, Reichsstadt Kaufbeuren, MüB Lit. 9/1.

Bibliographic References

Biller T. ²2016. *Die mittelalterliche Stadtbefestigung im deutschsprachigen Raum. Ein Handbuch,* 2 vol. Darmstadt: Wissenschaftliche Buchgesellschaft.

Breuer T. and A. Brenner 2001. "Die urbane Überlieferung. Kaufbeurer Baudenkmale und ihre Besonderheiten." In *Die Stadt Kaufbeuren,* vol. 2: *Kunstgeschichte, Bürgerkultur und religiöses Leben,* edited by J. Kraus and S. Dieter, 20–63. Thalhofen: Bauer-Verlag. [Reprint of the passages concerning Kaufbeuren in T. Breuer. 1960. *Stadt und Landkreis Kaufbeuren* [= Bayerische Kunstdenkmale 9]. Munich: Deutscher Kunstverlag, updated by A. Brenner.]

84 Cf. Bünz 2016, who gives a considerable number of examples for (in this case especially rural) parish churches as creditors. Besides other results, he concludes (66): *"Die Kirche hat im späten Mittelalter als Kreditgeber eine wichtige Rolle gespielt. Neben Klöstern und Stiften sind dabei die zahlreichen Weltgeistlichen von Bedeutung, die vielfach mehrere Pfründen in ihrer Person vereinigten, darüber hinaus aber vor allem die Pfarrei."* Examples for the activity of urban parish churches (i.e. the *fabricae ecclesiae*) as credit institutions are given e.g. in Leng 2009, 151–169 (Volkach); Kahleyß 2013, 189–191 (Zwickau). For the purchase and divestment of annuities by the *fabricae ecclesiae,* cf. also Reitemeier 2005, 398–403.

Bünz E. 2016. "Kredit bei den Heiligen. Die Dorfkirche als Geldinstitut in Spätmittelalter und Frühneuzeit." In *Zins und Gült. Strukturen des ländlichen Kreditwesens in Spätmittelalter und Frühneuzeit* [= Kraichtaler Kolloquien 10], edited by K. Andermann and G. Fouquet, 41–67. Epfendorf: bibliotheca academica Verlag.

Dertsch R. (ed.) 1955. *Die Urkunden der Stadt Kaufbeuren (Stadt, Spital, Pfarrei, Kloster): 1240–1500* [= Veröffentlichungen der Schwäbischen Forschungsgemeinschaft bei der Kommission für bayerische Landesgeschichte IIa, 3]. Augsburg: Verlag der Schwäbischen Forschungsgemeinschaft.

Dertsch R. 1960. *Stadt- und Landkreis Kaufbeuren* [= Historisches Ortsnamenbuch von Bayern, Schwaben 3]. Munich: Kommission für bayerische Landesgeschichte.

Dieter S. 1999. "Die urbane Prägung. Kaufbeuren im späten Mittelalter (1315 bis 1525)." In *Die Stadt Kaufbeuren,* vol. 1: *Politische Geschichte und Gegenwart einer Stadt,* edited by J. Kraus, S. Fischer, and S. Dieter, 42–63. Thalhofen: Bauer-Verlag.

Dieter S. 2006a. "Die Formierung der reichsstädtischen Gesellschaft und Wirtschaft: Die Sozial- und Gewerbestruktur im spätmittelalterlichen Kaufbeuren (1280 bis 1500)." In *Die Stadt Kaufbeuren,* vol. 3: *Sozialgeschichte, Wirtschaftsentwicklung und Bevölkerungsstruktur,* edited by J. Kraus, S. Dieter, and J. Westerburg, 26–45. Thalhofen: Bauer-Verlag.

Dieter S. 2006b. "Die reichsstädtische Gesellschaft und Wirtschaft in den Umbrüchen des konfessionellen Zeitalters. Die Sozial und Gewerbestruktur im frühneuzeitlichen Kaufbeuren bis zum Dreißigjährigen Krieg (1500 bis 1630)." In *Die Stadt Kaufbeuren,* vol. 3: *Sozialgeschichte, Wirtschaftsentwicklung und Bevölkerungsstruktur,* edited by J. Kraus, S. Dieter, and J. Westerburg, 46–71. Thalhofen: Bauer-Verlag.

DRW. 1983. *Deutsches Rechtswörterbuch. Wörterbuch der älteren deutschen Rechtssprache,* vol. 7. Weimar: Böhlau.

Eitel P. 1970. *Die oberschwäbischen Reichsstädte im Zeitalter der Zunftherrschaft. Untersuchungen zu ihrer politischen und sozialen Struktur unter besonderer Berücksichtigung der Städte Lindau, Memmingen, Ravensburg und Überlingen* [= Schriften zur südwestdeutschen Landeskunde 8]. Stuttgart: Müller & Gräff.

Fischer H. 1908. Schwäbisches Wörterbuch, vol. 2. Tübingen: Verlag der H. Laupp'schen Buchhandlung.

Fischer S. (ed.) 2016. *Kaufbeuren. Anfänge, Umbrüche, Traditionen: 900 Jahre Stadtgeschichte 1116–2016.* Neustadt an der Aisch: Verlag Ph. C. W. Schmidt.

Guggemos E. (ed.) 1989. *Inschriften im Stadtgebiet Kaufbeuren* [= Kaufbeurer Geschichtsblätter, Sonderhefte 4]. Kaufbeuren: Heimatverein Kaufbeuren.

Hagen C. 2018. "Das Konstanzer Ammanngerichtsbuch (1423–1434) als Quelle für christlich-jüdische Kreditgeschäfte. Ein Projektbericht." In *Ökonomische Glaubensfragen. Strukturen und Praktiken jüdischen und christlichen Kleinkredits im Spätmittelalter* [= Vierteljahrschrift für Sozial- und Wirtschaftsgeschichte, Beihefte, 242], edited by G. Fouquet and S. Rabeler, 43–62. Stuttgart: Franz Steiner Verlag.

Huang A. 2019. "Annuities (Letters—Ledgers—Urban Accounts)." In *Methods in Premodern Economic History. Case Studies from the Holy Roman Empire, c.1300–c.1600* [= Palgrave Studies in Economic History], edited by U. Kypta, J. Bruch, and T. Skambraks, 452–453. London: Palgrave Macmillan.

Junginger F. 1965. *Geschichte der Reichsstadt Kaufbeuren im 17. und 18. Jahrhundert.* Diss. phil. Munich.

Kahleyß J. 2013. *Die Bürger von Zwickau und ihre Kirche. Kirchliche Institutionen und städtische Frömmigkeit im späten Mittelalter* [= Schriften zur sächsischen Geschichte und Volkskunde 45]. Leipzig: Leipziger Universitätsverlag.

Kraus J., S. Dieter, S. Fischer, and J. Westerburg (eds.) 1999–2006. *Die Stadt Kaufbeuren,* vol. 1–3. Thalhofen: Bauer-Verlag.

Kuske B. 1956. "Die Entstehung der Kreditwirtschaft und des Kapitalverkehrs." In B. Kuske. *Köln, der Rhein und das Reich. Beiträge aus fünf Jahrzehnten wirtschaftsgeschichtlicher Forschung,* 48–137. Cologne/Graz: Böhlau [published for the first time in F. Beckmann, K. Diehl, B. Kuske, A. Müller, and J. Schumpeter. 1927. *Die Kreditwirtschaft,* vol. 1 [= Kölner Vorträge 1], 1–79. Leipzig: Gloeckner].

Kypta U., J. Bruch, and T. Skambraks (eds.) 2019. *Methods in Premodern Economic History. Case Studies from the Holy Roman Empire, c.1300–c.1600* [= Palgrave Studies in Economic History]. London: Palgrave Macmillan.

Lausser H. 1994. *St. Martin in Kaufbeuren. Zur Geschichte einer reichsstädtischen Pfarrkirche* [= Kaufbeurer Geschichtsblätter, Sonderhefte 6]. Kaufbeuren: Heimatverein Kaufbeuren e.V.

Lausser H. 1999. "Die urbane Prägung. Vor- und Frühgeschichte Kaufbeurens." In *Die Stadt Kaufbeuren,* vol. 1: *Politische Geschichte und Gegenwart einer Stadt,* edited by J. Kraus, S. Fischer, and S. Dieter, 10–41. Thalhofen: Bauer-Verlag.

Lausser H. (ed.) 2008. *Pfarrer, Kirchen, Seelenmessen. Die Quellen zur Geschichte des Pfarr- und Glaubenslebens in der Stadt Kaufbeuren vom Mittelalter bis zur Einführung der Reformation,* 2 vol. [= Kompendium der Quellen zur Geschichte Kaufbeurens im Mittelalter 8]. Thalhofen: Bauer-Verlag.

Lausser H. (ed.) 2009. *Pfründner, Siechen, arme Dürftige. Die Quellen zur Geschichte der Hospitalstiftung zum Heiligen Geist zu Kaufbeuren im Mittelalter* [= Kompendium der Quellen zur Geschichte Kaufbeurens im Mittelalter 6]. Thalhofen: Bauer-Verlag.

Lausser H. (ed.) 2011. *Die Bürger in ihrer Stadt. Die Quellen zum bürgerlichen Alltag in der mittelalterlichen Stadt Kaufbeuren* [= Kompendium der Quellen zur Geschichte Kaufbeurens im Mittelalter 3]. Thalhofen: Bauer-Verlag.

Lausser H. (ed.) 2013. *Zinsen, Schulden, Seelgeräte: Quellen zur Einkünftesituation von Spital, Pfarrkirche und Steuerbürgern der Stadt Kaufbeuren im 14. und 15. Jahrhundert* [= Kompendium der Quellen zur Geschichte Kaufbeurens im Mittelalter 7]. Thalhofen: Bauer-Verlag.

Lausser H. 2016a. "Vom Kolonisationsstützpunkt zur Reichsstadt." In *Kaufbeuren. Anfänge, Umbrüche, Traditionen: 900 Jahre Stadtgeschichte 1116–2016,* edited by S. Fischer, 9–52. Neustadt an der Aisch: Verlag Ph. C. W. Schmidt.

Lausser H. 2016b. *Von Abele bis Zoller. 201 Kaufbeurer Familien im späten Mittelalter* [= Kaufbeurer Schriftenreihe 16]. Thalhofen: Bauer-Verlag.

Lausser H. 2018. *St. Martin zu Kaufbeuren. Zur Geschichte einer schwäbischen Pfarrkirche* [= Kaufbeurer Schriftenreihe 19]. Thalhofen: Bauer-Verlag.

Lausser H., S. Dieter, and T. Pfundner 2006. "Ämterlisten zur Geschichte der Stadt Kaufbeuren. Bürgermeister, Stadtammänner, Pfarrer (St. Martins-Kirche und Dreifaltigkeitskirche), Oberinnen (Franziskanerinnenkloster), Spitalmeister." In *Die Stadt Kaufbeuren,* vol. 3: *Sozialgeschichte, Wirtschaftsentwicklung und Bevölkerungsstruktur,* edited by J. Kraus, S. Dieter, and J. Westerburg, 334–341. Thalhofen: Bauer-Verlag.

Ledermann R. 1904. "Geschichte der Juden in der Reichsstadt Kaufbeuren. Nach lokalen Quellen bearbeitet." *Monatsschrift für Geschichte und Wissenschaft des Judentums* 48 = N.F. 12: 721–730.

Leng R. 2009. "Glaube und Geschäfte. Kirchenfabrik, Gotteshausmeister, Kreditgeschäfte und bürgerliche Eliten im Volkacher Salbuch." In *Das Volkacher Salbuch,* vol. 1: *Beiträge und Transkription,* edited by K. Arnold and U. Feuerbach, 125–169. Volkach: Stadt Volkach.

Lexer M. (ed.) 1862. *Endres Tuchers Baumeisterbuch der Stadt Nürnberg (1464–1475)* [= Bibliothek des Litterarischen Vereins in Stuttgart 64]. Stuttgart: Litterarischer Verein.

Oelsner T. 1968. "Kaufbeuren." In *Germania Judaica,* vol. 2: *Von 1238 bis zur Mitte des 14. Jahrhunderts,* part 1, edited by Zvi Avneri, 392–393. Tübingen: J. C. B. Mohr (Paul Siebeck).

Pfister D. 1993. *Dokumentation zur Geschichte und Kultur der Juden in Schwaben,* vol. 1: *Archivführer,* part 2, edited by P. Fassl. Augsburg: Bez. Schwaben.

Rabeler S. 2004. "*Benannt, gegeben und gemacht zu einem Spital armen und elenden Siechen.* Zur Sozial- und Wirtschaftsgeschichte des Pforzheimer Heilig-Geist-Spitals (14. bis 16. Jahrhundert)." In *Neues aus Pforzheims Mittelalter* [= Materialien zur Stadtgeschichte 19], edited by S. Pätzold, 87–122. Heidelberg, Ubstadt-Weiher, Basel: Verlag Regionalkultur.

Rabeler S. 2020. "Transformationen einer bischöflichen Residenzstadt. Eutin, 15.–16. Jahrhundert." In *Residenzstädte im Alten Reich (1300–1800). Ein Handbuch,* vol. 2: *Soziale Gruppen, Ökonomien und politische Strukturen in Residenzstädten,* part 1: *Exemplarische Studien (Norden)* [= Residenzenforschung, N.F.: Stadt und Hof, II,1], edited by J. Hirschbiegel, S. Rabeler, and S. Winter, 121–157. Ostfildern: Thorbecke.

Reitemeier A. 2005. *Pfarrkirchen in der Stadt des späten Mittelalters: Politik, Wirtschaft und Verwaltung* [= Vierteljahrschrift für Sozial- und Wirtschaftsgeschichte, Beihefte, 177]. Stuttgart: Franz Steiner Verlag.

Simm M. 2012. *Des Königs Stadt zu Buron: Kaufbeuren—eine stadtarchäologische Studie zu Genese, früher Entwicklung und Topographie* [= Kaufbeurer Schriftenreihe 11]. Thalhofen: Bauer-Verlag.

Skambraks T. and S. Köhler 2019. "What Is Credit?" In *Methods in Premodern Economic History. Case Studies from the Holy Roman Empire, c.1300–c.1600* [= Palgrave Studies in Economic History], edited by U. Kypta, J. Bruch, and T. Skambraks, 146–150. London: Palgrave Macmillan.

Wunder G. 1987. "Die Stadt als Spar- und Darlehenskasse am Beispiel der Reichsstadt Hall im 16. und 17. Jahrhundert." In *Stadt und wirtschaftliche Selbstverwaltung* [= Stadt in der Geschichte 12], edited by B. Kirchgässner and E. Naujoks, 115–120. Sigmaringen: Thorbecke.

Picture Credits

Fig. 1 Dertsch 1955, ix

BETWEEN CITY AND COUNTRYSIDE: MONEYLENDING AND SETTLING DEBTS IN AND AROUND MERAN (1388–1392)

Stephan Nicolussi-Köhler

Abstract: In this paper, two different sources for credit transactions are used to describe the credit market in Meran and its surroundings. Comparisons between the register (*imbreviatura*) of the notary Jakob of Laas (1390–1392) and records of court assemblies (*eleichtaidings,* territorial court; 1388–1391) show that the size of recorded credits was significantly higher in the notary registers compared to the credits and debts mentioned in court protocols. To further profile the 14th century credit market in South Tirol, an analysis of the credit transactions written down by notaries and the (defaulted) debts litigated before the territorial court is made. To what extent did the clientele differ (social group, place of residence)? Was there a difference in their borrowing behaviour? Moreover, what economic mechanisms were used as a repayment guarantee? Besides, it will be tested whether urban centres were of special importance for functioning credit markets.

The general picture that emerges from the study is that different credit practices and institutions (written evidence provided by notaries, pawn broking, legal courts, and practice of pledging) helped different social groups to gain access to the capital market.

Keywords: Small-Scale Credits, Notary Registers, Court Protocols, Middle Ages, Tirol

Published in: Stephan Nicolussi-Köhler (Ed.), Change and Transformation of Premodern Credit Markets. The Importance of Small-Scale Credits. Heidelberg: heiBOOKS 2021, 89–132. DOI: https://doi.org/10.11588/heibooks.593.c12692

1 Introduction

It is common sense that access to credit is important for economic activity or even sustained economic growth.[1] In particular, this is also true for the Middle Ages.[2] Although this is an undisputed fact, only recently were a growing number of studies carried out on premodern—or even medieval—credit markets.[3] Research into the credit operations of peasants, artisans, small landowners, and day labourers in particular has been restricted by the lack of empirical evidence.[4] However, all credit systems have in common that they relied, at least in part, on some sort of contract enforcement. Thus, much data on credit activities in medieval Tirol survived in different sources. Copies of private contracts were kept in notarial registers (*imbreviatura*); legal disputes, including those concerning oral agreements, were brought before the territorial court of Meran and written down in court protocols. The combination of these sources allows us to reconstruct the functioning of the credit market in this specific part of Tirol.

This paper asks to what extent small-scale credits existed in Meran and the Vinschgau Valley by using court records, and compares them with notarised debts.[5] I introduce and use a novel dataset, the so far unused court protocols of provincial courts from 1388 to 1391, and the already known register of the notary Jakob of Laas, covering the years 1390 and 1391.[6] The court transcripts contain information about court sessions from the city of Meran as well as from smaller towns in the Vinschgau Valley like Naturns, Partschins, Algund, Tirol, Riffian, Mais, and Veran (Vöran). Most of the contracts written down by the notary Jakob of Laas dealt with business activities in Laas itself or other towns of the Vinschgau Valley. Therefore, the dataset allows the drawing of general conclusions about the credit activities in both the city of Meran as well as in its hinterland in the Vinschgau Valley.

The paper is structured as follows. First, the economic setting of Tirol in the 14th century is described. The sections that follow will deal with the two datasets

---

1 Cipolla 1994, 160–1882; Zuijderduijn 2009, 1–13; Hoffman, Postel-Vinay, and Rosenthal 2019, 1 f.; Skambraks and Köhler 2019.

2 Kuske 1956; Clemens 2008; Zuijderduijn 2009, 5–13.

3 An overview of the recent research is given by Skambraks et al. 2020.

4 Signori 2015, 11. Important studies on this topic include Groebner 1993; Fontaine and Schlumbohm 2000; Briggs 2015; King and Tomkins 2003; Signori 2015, 11.

5 There is no strict definition of small-scale credit. Usually, this term refers to a small sum equating roughly three months' wages of an unskilled worker. Cf. Hagen 2018a, 48. However, one has to keep in mind that in pre-modern Europe, wages were only a part of the overall income.

6 StAM, NI 22 and StAM, GP 1.

in more detail, i.e. the register of Jakob of Laas and then the court protocols, with regard to credit transactions. In the following section, I will analyse the differences between the debts contracted by the notary in Laas and debts litigated before the provincial courts in the Vinschgau Valley and Meran. Finally, I will try to explain the differences between the debts mentioned in the notary register and in the court protocols.

At the beginning, I will evaluate the credit transactions recorded in the register of Jakob of Laas by showing that credit was widespread in the rural town of Laas. A large percentage of the local population was actively involved in credit transactions. Furthermore, I am able to identify different types of credits concerning the maturity of the credit, size of loan, and collateral used. In the village of Laas and the Vinschgau Valley, long-term credits collateralized with real estate dominated. Short-term and small-scale credits collateralized with pawns are almost negligible in the register of the notary. Most debtors and creditors, who recorded their business in front of the notary, came from the town of Laas or from one of the neighbouring communities. Second, I compare these findings with credit activities recorded in the territorial court protocols. In this case, the picture is quite different. The average amount of money owed is much smaller. The court protocols mention a few big loans, but also many small-scale loans and pawn broking contracts. While loans collateralized with real estate dominated in the notarial registers, the court protocols show evidence of a co-existing, orally stipulated credit system. Considering these findings, the results provide evidence for the existence of different, overlapping credit markets, indicating that small-scale loans were usually not written down or recorded by a notary to keep the transaction costs low. Third, I ask for the importance of urban centres for rural credit. The standard argument is that peer-to-peer money lending, meaning a direct credit transaction conducted between two individuals, was insignificant or that the countryside was permeated by intermediated credit that passed through urban centres. The volume of debt was said to be centralised in cities, although the credits themselves were given out to people in small towns and villages.[7] I will show that most of the creditors in the countryside were actually peasants or small landowners from minor towns. The only remarkable exceptions are short-term loans, which were often granted by citizens and merchants from Meran.

Only little empirical research has been done on rural areas in Europe. Most case studies only use one type of source or deal with either an urban or rural environment.[8] This article is a first step to filling this gap, providing detailed

---

7 Hoffman, Postel-Vinay, and Rosenthal 2019, 48 f.

8 Fontaine 1993; Rosenthal 1994, 288; Briggs 2009; Gilomen 2016; Andermann 2016; Briggs and Zuijderduijn 2018a.

information about the functioning of the credit market in medieval Tirol. By analysing both the urban and rural credit activities, the paper complements research about the economic connection between cities and their surroundings. Thomas Ertl worked with a rich data set of Tirolian notaries from the 13th century and reconstructed land transactions in and around Bozen.[9] In his paper, he describes the economic entanglement between the city of Bozen and the countryside. Several people there owned houses, vineyards or other properties in both the city and the countryside, and economic transactions did not stop at the border of the city. Thomas Ertl further shows that *"the property market was strongly connected to the capital market"* and that land was needed as a guarantee to get access to credit.[10] Other studies have confirmed this finding and stressed the importance of mortgage contracts and the use of land as security for premodern credit markets.[11]

This picture partly emerges because of a selection bias of the sources. Transactions dealing with real estate obviously had a greater chance of survival than small-sized loan contracts. Therefore, the majority of notary registers contain contract types covering bigger investments.[12] Nevertheless, a great deal of everyday business included small-scale loans and pawnbroking that was usually not recorded by a notary. Another strand of literature focuses on these small-scale credits. For example, Valentin Groebner focused on the strategies of survival of the poor in Nuremberg. He concluded that there were numerous forms of credit like pawn broking and orally conducted small-scale credits that are beyond our knowledge.[13] Here, this article can contribute new insights, such as the observation that in Tirol rural and urban credit markets have not differed fundamentally.

2 The Economic Context

The Vinschgau Valley extends along a much-used mule track from the Reschenpass in the north to the Meran basin in the south. The valley, consisting of several political entities, was united in the 13th century to form the administrative and

9 Ertl 2017.
10 Ertl 2017, 25–27.
11 Cf. Briggs and Zuijderduijn 2018a.
12 In the notary register of Jakob Haas from Bozen from 1237, the average value of a transaction was 30 pounds. Two pounds was the price for approximately 150 litres of wine. Ertl 2017, 9.
13 Groebner 1993.

Figure 1 The Vinschgau Valley located in South Tirol.

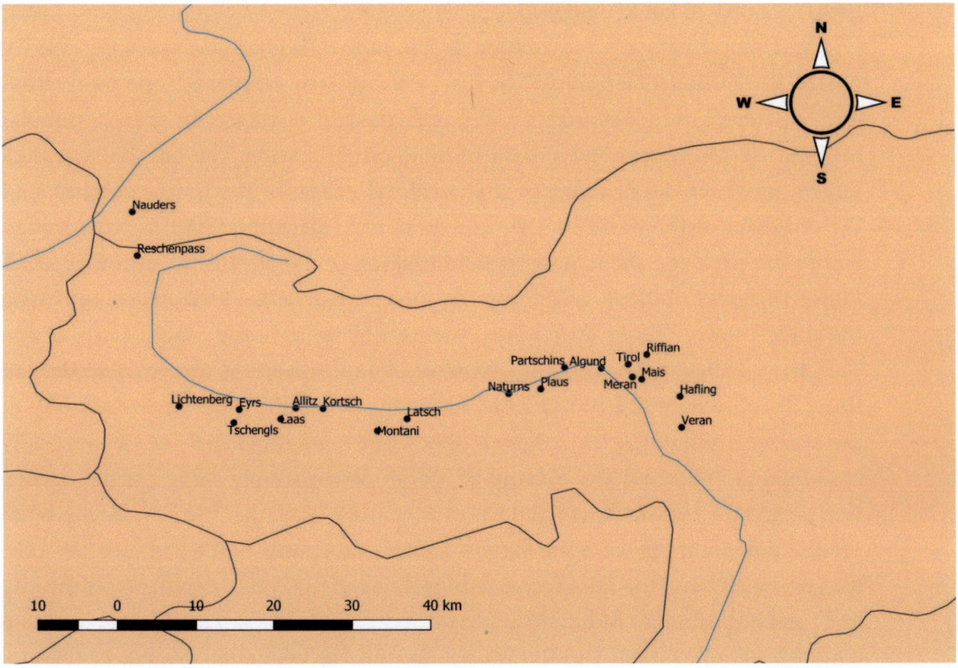

high court district Burggrafenamt or Landgericht (territorial court of) Meran respectively.[14]

In most of the villages of the Vinschgau Valley, like Naturns, Partschins, Plaus, Laas, and Kortsch, agriculture was predominant.[15] Manorial registers (*urbare*) from the late 13th and 14th century list agricultural goods like cereals (wheat, rye, oats, barley), wine, and animal products (meat, chicken, eggs, lambs, pigs and cheese) as levies.[16] The size of the individual farms in the countryside varied considerably, as the size of the levies to be paid suggests.[17] Most farmers held the land they cultivated as hereditary tenure, lease or fiefdom, for which they owed rents and other duties.[18] Throughout the region, landownership was spread

14 Stolz 1934, 7–16.

15 Wopfner 1997; Stamm 2007; Obermair and Stamm 2019.

16 Wopfner 1995, 477–485; Stamm 2008a, 192 f.

17 Wopfner 1995, 84–87; Loose 2008, 211.

18 Stamm 2008b; Stamm 2009; Stamm 2010.

among many noble and non-noble countrymen and city burghers and there was a great mobility of landownership.[19]

Tirol was already a winegrowing region in the Middle Ages and wine was exported to Southern Germany.[20] In the 13th and 14th centuries, vine cultivation was expanded and vineyards, usually measured in *manngraben,* were a popular investment. Many rents were paid in kind, often in wine. The notarial registers inform us about the dealings of the (wealthy) peasants, the minor nobility, and the burghers of the cities on the land market.[21] Agricultural goods were traded across the Alps and the commercial flourishing of the North-Italian towns accelerated this development. With growing trade, urban settlements developed along the trade routes.[22] Only little winegrowing was done in the higher parts of the Vinschgau Valley compared to the basin of Meran. The city of Meran, near the castle of Tyrol, where the counts held their court, was the most important city at the southern end of the Vinschgau Valley.[23] The market dates of the two annually held fairs at Pentecost and Martini of Meran demonstrably served as an orientation period for transactions from the 13th century onwards.[24] In Meran, artisanal production and trade were the biggest sources of income.[25] The commercial activities in the city and the fairs increased the demand for credit. Privileges of the city and the establishment of important institutions such as a mint and pawn broking bank (*casana*) in Meran laid the foundation for the economic growth of the city in the Middle Ages.[26]

The *casana* in Meran seems to have disappeared in 1346 or shortly after that time.[27] However, we have information about pawnbroking activities in Meran for the second half of the 14th century. In Meran, there was the public office of the *veiltraeger* or *feilträger,* who was responsible for the correct pledging and selling of pawned items.[28] In 1394, the comital *hauptmann an der Etsch* mediated disputes between the burghers of Meran and the usurers and pawnbrokers (*wucherer*), which tells us about the continuous existence of pawnbroking in the city.[29] The complex distribution of commercial activity in the Vinschgau Valley and the

---

19 Loose 2008, 212; Ertl 2017, 26.
20 Voltelini 1904, 4–25; Ertl 2017, 11; Kießling 2018, 435–440.
21 Loose 2008, 209–216; Ertl 2017, 25–28.
22 Demo 2018.
23 Stolz 1937, 125; Kießling 2018; Loose 2018.
24 Hagen 2015, 36–39; Kießling 2018, 436.
25 Kustatscher 2018, 194–202.
26 Rizzolli 2018.
27 Voltelini 1904, 40–42.
28 Pfeiffer 1848; Hagen 2015, 156 f.; Hagen 2018b, 143; Loose 2018, 269.
29 StAM, UU 98. Huter 1990, 30.

city of Meran created different demands for credit. On the one hand, landowners could pledge their property as security when asking for a loan. On the other, artisans, day labourers, and poor people would recourse to other means of securing a loan. The difference between these types of credit is visible in the sources.

3 The Dataset

Before describing the dataset, we must briefly discuss the difficulties of analysing credit activity in premodern times. The standard argument is that peer-to-peer money lending, meaning a direct credit transaction conducted between two individuals, was insignificant in the Middle Ages and that the countryside depended on urban centres for the supply of credit. This view rests on the idea that it would be logical to link the development of credit markets to institutions that centralise resources in one place (i.e. cities), as banks in modern times do.[30] This was not the case in medieval Tirol.

Tirol, with public notaries from the 12th century onwards, is a well-documented case for credit and land markets. These markets involved different social groups, living both in the city and the countryside.[31] The result is very heterogeneous source material and the danger of selection bias. If the contractors made use of a notary, the legal act was written down in a register. If, however, the parties conducted the transaction on their own, nothing was documented and registration was optional unless the contract became part of a legal process. Thus, the written contracts we have in the notaries and court protocols are only a subsample (approximate minimum) of all private agreements. Since not all contracts were registered, we have to tackle the question of sample selection.[32] Commercial credits, credits collateralized with real estate, credits intermediated by notaries, and loans with a bigger contract size are the most visible in the registers and have received most attention so far. On the other side, little is known about pawnbroking, small-scale, and peer-to-peer lending, which was usually orally conducted.[33] It will be argued that using different sources (i.e. the notary register, the court protocols) shows that there were multiple, coexisting credit markets in medieval

30 Cf. the contribution of Gilles Postel-Vinay in this volume. See also Hoffman, Postel-Vinay, and Rosenthal 2019, 48 f.

31 Ertl 2017, 9.

32 Cf. Rosenthal 1994, 291.

33 For the importance of oral traditions in Tirol see Johler 1999, 153.

Tirol. These credit markets are recorded with unequal accuracy. In the next step, I will show what kinds of data are available and how they were chosen.

We have many sources from Meran for the late 14th century.[34] There are 39 older notary registers in the city archive of Meran, covering the years 1328 to 1415.[35] Besides, there are several documents stemming from the city administration and court protocols. In this article, I am using one entire register of the notary Jakob of Laas and the oldest surviving court protocols. Both sources cover roughly the same period (1388–1391) and therefore offer the opportunity to analyse the credit market from different angles. The current dataset consists of 494 legal entries in total, stemming from the notary register of Jakob of Laas (95)[36] and from the court protocols of Meran (399).[37] Altogether, 198 out of 490 (40 percent) of these entries deal with credit operations. The sources cover the years from 1388 to 1392, with a focus on 1388/1389 and 1391. I tried to record as much information as possible from the different contracts (name, occupation, sex, and residence of creditors and debtors, size of loan, date, runtime, type of credit transaction, and interest rate). The collected data deals mostly with credit transactions of people from small towns and villages in the Vinschgau Valley and the Burggrafenamt (Naturns, Partschins, Algund, Tirol, Riffian, Mais, Hafling, Laas, Gschums, Kortsch, Laretz, Laas, Latsch, Martell, Montani, Nauders, Plaus, Schlanders, Schluderns) and Meran.[38]

4 Credit Activity in the Register of Jakob of Laas

The first set of data comes from a register of the notary of Jakob Mairjans of Laas.[39] Several *imbreviatura* of his are preserved in the city archives of Meran.[40] The present register (NI 22) is a paper codex, consisting of 45 sheets. There are altogether 95 entries (so-called *notulae*) written down in this *imbreviatura,* although some of them appear to be legal formulas and template designs. 22 out of

34 Cf. the edited volume about Meran with articles concerning various topics: Pfeifer 2018.

35 StAM, NI 1–39. For the notaries cf: Heuberger 1927; Stolz 1932, 89–92 and 162 f.; Fliri 2018.

36 StAM, NI 22. However, of the 95 entries eleven are fragments or were not completed.

37 StAM, GP 1.

38 Cf. Figure 1.

39 StAM, NI 22.

40 StAM, NI 22–28.

the 95 entries are written in German, but the overwhelming majority is in Latin. Most of the contracts (75) were written down between 21 February 1391 and 20 December 1391.[41] The busiest months for Jakob of Laas were May (10) and June (13) in the summer and November and December (twelve each) in the winter of 1391, when he recorded on average ten contracts per month. It appears that next to his notarial duties he was engaged in another activity. He was schoolmaster in his hometown of Laas.[42] Jakob of Laas recorded most of the contracts (75) in Laas, only occasionally do we encounter the notary doing business in the neighbouring villages of Glurns (1), Schlanders (3), and Tschengls (2). He was, at least from 1396 onwards, a citizen of Meran, but he had his office in the small town of Laas.[43] 24 contracts were concluded in the house of Jakob in Laas.[44]

Following a categorisation of notarial acts by Daniel Smail, I grouped the contracts into five groups: acts relating primarily to credit and debts (1), acts relating primarily to transfers or to investments (2), acts relating primarily to other rights and obligations (3), court-related activity (4), and other various (non-legally binding) entries (5).[45] 45 of the altogether 95 entries (approximately 49 percent) are concerned with debts or credit transactions. Various forms of credit transactions appear in the register. It is not always easy to distinguish credit contracts from land or house sales, since these two contract forms were often combined to use real estate as security or to disguise interest payments.[46] This was the case when real estate or an income (stemming from real estate) was sold for a certain amount of money with a limited or unlimited right of redemption. So what is basically and de jure a sale of land is supplemented by an additional entry at the bottom of the *notula*, that a charter for redemption (*carta redempcionis*) for aforementioned goods has been issued.[47] The seller (or debtor) could redeem his sold or mortgaged

41 The register is edited by Raffeiner 2008. The edition has some significant shortcomings as pointed out by Pfeifer 2008. Therefore, the current research rests on the use of the original documents in the city archive. For the sake of simplicity, the numbering of the entries of Raffeiner is followed.

42 StAM, NI 22, fol. 44v; Loose 2008, 207, 194, no. 5a.

43 Heuberger 1927, 84–98; Raffeiner 2008, 208 f.

44 *"in domo habitationis mei infrascripti notarii"*. Raffeiner 2008, no. 25, 28–31, 35–37, 39, 46–48, 560–56, 59, 61, 67, 75, 82.

45 Smail 1998, 36 f. The last group of entries in the cartulary includes legal formulas, a calendar and various forms of notes (for example a recipe against constipation). Cf. Table 1.

46 A similar observation was made by Ertl working on the land market in and around Bozen. Ertl 2017. Cf. Violante 1962; Briggs and Zuijderduijn 2018b, 3–7.

47 I.e. StAM, NI 22, fol. 16v: *"Carta redempcionis perpetualis pro dicta pecunia salvo iure colonia"*. For the sale of legal rights and rents connected to property in Tirol cf. Stamm 2009.

Table 1 Categories of acts in the register of Jakob of Laas, 1390–1392 (StAM, NI 22)

Category	**Name of contract**	**Description**	**Number of contracts**	**Share in %**
acts relating to debt	*accomodatum*	loan	1	1.05
	debitum (unspecified)	debt	4	4.21
	debitum cause emptionis	debt arising from a sale	5	5.26
	debitum cause thelonio	debt arising from unpaid toll	1	1.05
	emptio censi cum carta redimendi	purchase of rent with right of redemption	7	7.36
	emptio terre et iuris cum carta redimendi	purchase of land and rights with right of redemption	1	1.05
	emptio terre seu domo cum carta redimendi	purchase of land or house with right of redemption	17	17.89
	obligatio (moveable goods)	pawn	1	1.05
	obligatio (immoveable goods)	pawn	8	8.42
	–	subtotal	45	47.37
–	–	–	–	–
acts relating to transfer or investments	*cambium*	exchange	1	1.05
	divisio domus	division of property rights of a house	1	1.05
	donationis inter vivos	donation	1	1.05
	emptio terre et censi	purchase of a land and a rent	2	2.10
	emptio terre seu domo	purchase of land or house	12	12.63
	iure et nomine locationis investit	bestowal of a property or fief	5	5.26
	ratio	Rendering of account	1	1.05
	recognitio censi	acknowledgment of rent	2	2.10
	–	subtotal	25	26.31
–	–	–	–	–

Category	Name of contract	Description	Number of contracts	Share in %
acts relating to other rights and obligations	*abiuratio ludi*	promise to swear off gambling	1	1.05
	cessio iuris	cession of rights	1	1.05
	donationis ad antelectum	instrument of dowry	1	1.05
	inscriptio bona	inventory of goods	1	1.05
	inventorio	property inspection	1	1.05
	locatio opere	labour contract	1	1.05
	procuratio	nomination of procurer	1	1.05
	testamentum	testament	2	2.10
	–	subtotal	9	9.47
–	–	–	–	–
court-related activity	*causa mandamentum*	judicial mandament	3	3.15
	notarius publicus creetur	appointment of notary	1	1.05
	statuit arbitri	appointment of arbiters	1	1.05
	–	subtotal	5	5.26
–	–	–	–	–
miscellaneous entries	–	calendar	1	1.05
	–	legal formulas	7	7.36
	–	other entries	2	2.10
	–	register	1	1.05
	–	subtotal	11	12.63
–	–	–	–	–
–	–	total	95	100

Source: StAM, NI 22; Raffeiner 2008.

Notes: The categorisation follows the classification by Smail 1998, 36 f.

rent or property within the agreed period. In the meantime, the buyer (or creditor) would receive an interest payment in the form of the income or rent of the pledged or sold property.[48] That these were indeed credit transactions is proven by the fact that, if the land was not released on time, the buyer had to pay the seller the difference between the purchase price and the actual land price. Thus initially, the land was sold below its actual value and the full purchase price had to be paid only if it was not redeemed.[49] This was a common practice in Tirol as shown by entries from older notarial registers from Bozen and Meran.[50]

Who participated in this credit market? Nobles, such as the lords of Annenberg, were involved only in a small number of credit arrangements. Next to members of the nobility who bore the *dominus* title, there existed also a group of wealthy persons that could be given this title. The honorary title *dominus* (or *Herr*) and *domina* was also used for wealthy peasants, such as *her* Hans, son of Hans Mair Jansen, or the priest Johannes Aempfinger.[51] It is quite certain that they were not aristocrats but honourable people of the community.[52] Craftsmen, like cobblers (*calciatores*), turners (*tornatores*), carpenters (*carpentarii*), weavers (*textores*) or wheelwrights (*rotifici*), appear both as lenders and borrowers in the register.[53] Only two merchants appear in the contracts, Christlinus *specier* (*speciarus*, a spice merchant) from Latsch and Nikolaus *specier* from Meran.[54] The first one buys and sells rents and real estate, the second credits a large sale of wine.[55] The most important group were peasants, both as creditors and debtors. Although it is not directly mentioned that the persons involved are farmers, it is clear that the majority of the population earned their living mainly from agriculture.[56] Farmers

48 Voltelini 1899, C-CVII; Wopfner 1995, 552–555.

49 See for example the sale of a field with right of redemption in December 1391. The following was specified: *“Carta redimendi in tribus proximis annis super festo Zenonis pro 15 libris. Quod si non fecerit, tunc uterque pars debet eligere duos ydoneos. Quid tunc pecia magis valeret, hoc debet super addere. Et sic erit tunc perpetualis empcio.”* StAM; NI 22, fol. 37v.

50 The notaries Jakob Haas (1237) in Bozen and David of Meran (1328) already record sales with the right of repurchase, e.g. Voltelini 1899, 294, no. 698; Karner 1985, 81–85, no. 27–28; Ertl 2017, 23 f.

51 Pfeifer 2001. The title *domina* indicates a woman’s legal capacity without implying any nobility. Ibid., 54.

52 Raffeiner 2008, 214. Similarly, in the register of Jakob Haas from Bozen, nobles, burghers, and peasants were involved in transactions in the land market in the 13th century. Ertl 2017, 23.

53 Raffeiner 2008, 212 f, no. 23, 27, 28, 33, 50, 61, 63, 64, 67, 69, 87, 85, 87.

54 Nicolas Specier or Niklaw Spetziger also appears several times in the court protocols of Meran as creditor (see below).

55 Raffeiner 2008, no. 11, 35, 42, 43.

56 Raffeiner 2008, 211.

that directly—for example by hereditary tenure—owned land had particularly easy access to loans.[57] There were also intermediate social groups that could be called the sub-peasant strata, which included landless households or households with only small land ownership.[58]

Some individuals appear several times as creditors in the register. Jacobus Weigant, sometimes together with his wife Katherina, acquired rights and real estate worth 2,320 *grossi* (in the following abbreviated as gr) in six contracts.[59] In every case, they granted the seller a right of redemption, indicating that these acquisitions were probably credit transactions. Other persons were both lenders and creditors. For example, Nicolaus, *villicus* de Weingarten, sold real estate for 50 pounds on 21 June with a perpetual right of redemption.[60] Just eight days later, he bought an annual rent in kinds from Chuenradus Mairotten for 50 pounds.[61] Another interesting case is that of Ulricus of Turnell. He sold a rent from a field for six mark (720 gr.). Ulricus had the right to buy this rent back for the original amount of money within five years, and in the meantime, the rent in kind served as interest payment.[62] A few days later, Ulricus obtained a rent from Cristlinus Specier of Latsch, which stemmed from the farmstead of said Ulricus.[63] In other words: he freed himself from the proprietor's (that is Cristlinus Specier) levies.[64] These and other contracts suggest something of the purpose of the credit arrangements. Although the average size of most loans was rather small (equating to three months' wages of a skilled worker), they were in some cases invested in rents or (small parts of) real estate.[65] They were also of a size to buy tools, seeds or settle the accounts with merchants and thus probably served as working capital.

Five types of credit transactions appear in the register of Jakob of Laas: sales of land or rents with a repurchase agreement (1), mortgage contracts (2), loans and confessions of debts (3), sales on credit (4), and pawnbroking contracts with

57 The peasants had precarious usage rights on their farms, even if their land was only loaned to them by a landlord. Ertl 2017, 19; Beimrohr 2008.

58 Stamm 2010; Cerman and Mitterauer 2020.

59 Raffeiner 2008, no. 32, 48, 62, 72, 74, 81.

60 Raffeiner 2008, no. 54.

61 Raffeiner 2008, no. 55.

62 Raffeiner 2008, no. 37. For a similar use of the rent as interest rate, cf. Stolz 1998, 145–146; Hörmann-Thurn und Taxis 2010, 168; Ertl 2017, 16.

63 Raffeiner 2008, no. 35.

64 Stamm 2009, 39, describes this case.

65 There is little research done about investment patterns of the rural population in medieval societies. In the absence of further studies, reference is made here to Pfister's work on investment patterns in early modern Zurich and Zuijderduijn and de Moors work on asset management of poor households. Pfister 2007; Zuijderduijn and de Moor 2012.

movable goods (5). One finds both short-term loans (with a duration of 0.5 to 6 months) and long-term loans (6 to 60 months) in the register. Loans and sales on credit, i.e. credit for the acquisition of wine or drapery, usually had a short or medium runtime.[66] Loans secured with real estate usually had a much longer runtime and a duration of 8 to 72 months. The difference between a sale with the right of redemption and a loan, where land is pledged as security, lies in the direct right of disposal.[67] If a land is used as collateral and pledged to the creditor (as *pignus*), the debtor retains ownership and the creditor has no right to sell, pawn or dispose of it by other means. Only after it had passed into his possession could it be disposed of, whereas if real estate was sold, the creditor could freely use the property as soon as the land was transferred to his ownership.[68] However, the conditions of the pledging contracts varied.[69] In most cases notarised before Jakob of Laas, the possession of the pledged land was immediately transferred to the creditor.[70] The final category of contracts, pawnbroking, appears only once in the register of Jakob of Laas and is used for a short-term loan of three months. This leads to the conclusion that pawnbroking contracts were rarely written down by the notary Jakob of Laas and were rather documented in other ways.[71]

As Table 2 shows, roughly 70 percent of the overall credit volume was carried out as loans collateralized with real estate (including both mortgage and sales contracts with a charter of redemption). Short-term contracts were quite rare with only five loans, four sales on credit and one pawnbroking contract, accounting for only 26.5 percent of the total amount of credit. Land used as security was obviously the easiest way to obtain credit in a rural environment. The average

---

66 Very often wine was bought on credit. The payment was often due during one of the fairs of Meran. Cf. Raffeiner 2008, no. 11, 12, 20.

67 The terms used vary in the sources. A sale with the right of redemption is usually described as *emptio cum carta redimendi* (also *littera redemptionis*) or the German phrase *setzen, versetzen* of a property, which is to be redeemed (*losen*) at a certain time. A land pledged is indicated by the verb *obligare* (and the name of the property) or the German verb *versetzen, innsetzen, innegesetzt.* E.g. Raffeiner no. 2, 3, 4, 55, 67.

68 Ertl 2017, 14 f.; Briggs and Zuijderduijn 2018, 4 f.

69 Sometimes the *littera* or *carta redimendi* specified that the creditor was not allowed to sell the acquired land to anyone except the debtor during the term of the loan. Cf. Karner 1985, 85 f., no. 28, where the creditor was obliged to *"non vendatur obligetur aut alienetur, teneantur ei vel eis idem dominus B(erhtoldus) [= the debtor] emptor et sui heredes pro ipsa pecunia revendere et restituere".*

70 In the *imbreviatura* are two templates for such a resale contract, Raffeiner 2008, no. 14.

71 See below for lawsuits in the court of Meran concerning pawn broking. Several pawn broking contracts of the *casana* of Bozen are written down in the register of Jakob of Haas. Voltelini and Huter 1951, no. 608, 615, 651, 653, 681, 682, 688, 694, 704, 721, 723, 727, 739, 772.

Table 2 Size of debts and credits registered by Jakob of Laas (in *grossi*)

Type of credit contract	Number of contracts	Total amount	Share in %	Mean	Median	Coefficient of variation	Standard deviation	Duration in months	Duration in months (median)
accomodatum or *debitum* (loan and unspecified debts)	5	3912	17.99	782.4	720	70.41	550.91	27.66	18
debitum causa emptionis (sale on credit)	4	1728	794	432	456	32.47	140.28	4.87	6
debitum pro thelonio (debt for unpaid toll)	1	480	2.20	480	480				
emptio terre et censi cum carta redimendi (sale of land or rent with right of redemption)	26	13840	63.67	532.30	360	150.84	802.94	42.35	48
obligatio (mortgage)	8	1656	7.61	236.57	180	51.70	122.32	33.25	26.5
obligatio (pawnbroking)	1	120	0.55	120	120	–	–	3	3
Total	45	21736	100	–	–	–	–	–	–

Source: StAM, NI 22; Raffeiner 2008.

Notes: Only contracts where a concrete sum of money is mentioned were considered. Debts where no specific reason is stated were put together in a category with loans.

Table 3 Index of prices and wages in Laas, 1391

1 *marc* (m.) = 10 *libra* (lb.) = 120 *grossi* (gr.) = 200 *solidi* (sol.) = 2400 *denarii parvulorum* (den.)	
Cow	84 gr.
Rye (pro *modius*)	30 gr.
Barley (pro *modius*)	24 gr.
Wine (pro *carrata*)	180 gr.
Cheese (pro *schoett*)	6.8 gr.
Wage of an unskilled worker (per day)	4 gr.
Waged of a skilled worker, i.e. mason or carpenter (per day)	8–10 gr.
Wage per month (with assumed 20 working days)	80–200 gr.

Sources: Wages are taken from the accounting for the construction of a staircase. StAM, NI 22, fol. 11v; Raffeiner 2008, no. 22, 52–54. Prices are taken from sale of the specific products in the same register. A comparison with prices for food and wares from printed sources of the same time and region roughly confirms the findings. Cf. Sinnacher 1827; Ottenthal 1881; Lackner 1996.

Notes: One *modius* is approximately 37 to 45 litres. One *carrata* is approximately 622 litres. One *schoett* (of cheese) is approximately 8.9 kg. Cf. Rottleuthner 198.

amount of money borrowed by collateralizing land was 532 gr. (median 360 gr., for the sale of real estate or rents with the right of repurchase) and 237 gr. (median 180 gr., mortgage contracts) respectively, averaging about one or two months' wages for a skilled worker.[72] The biggest sum was the sale of a rent due in wine, sold by the noble *dominus* Hainricus de Annenberg (near Latsch) for 36 mark (4320 gr.). The noble debtor retained the right to repurchase this rent.[73] This extraordinary sum is unmatched by any other contract and represents an exception from the other loans registered by the notary.

Land sold and pledged as security for credits was rather cheap and was on average worth 29 pounds (348 gr.), compared to the average price of land sold on the land market of 67 pounds (804 gr.).[74] This might indicate that land used as collateral was sold below its actual value. In 13 cases, a meadow (Wiese) was pledged or sold as security, a field nine times, five times a farmstead, and once a garden and

72 Cf. Table 3. Prices and loans were gathered from an account from the *imbreviatura*. Raffeiner 2008, no. 22.

73 Raffeiner 2008, no. 59.

74 For land used as security for credit contracts, see Raffeiner 2008, no. 2, 3, 4, 12, 16, 31, 32, 33, 35, 40, 43, 45, 48, 49, 51, 54, 56, 61, 62, 63, 66, 67, 68, 72, 73, 74, 79, 80, 81, 82, 86. Land sold on the land market: Raffeiner 2008, no. 26, 27, 29, 30, 36, 42, 50, 64, 70, 76, 78, 84, 88.

half a house. Most of the properties sold and pledged were located in Laas and its surroundings (Latsch, Schlanders). In some cases, we are informed about the (hidden) interest rates, which are usually ten percent p.a. of the original sum. This is usually expressed by way of a rent that has to be paid in addition to the principal sum. Chunzli Hainrich granted a loan of 40 pounds (480 gr.) to Hanns Stadler, repayable in three years. In return, Hanns agreed to pay his creditor a rent of four pounds (48 gr.) per year. As security, he pledged his hereditary fief (*erblehen*), the Stadelhof in Tarnell (Laas). He could redeem his farmstead within three years by repaying the 40 pounds (480 gr.).[75] In another contract Jacob, son of the turner Merklinus, confessed that he had received 30 pounds (360 gr.) from Nicolaus, for which he had sold him three meadows. They agreed in a charter of redemption that Jacob could buy back the meadows within five years for the original amount of money. In the meantime, he had to pay a rent of three pounds (36 gr.) annually.[76] This confirms Stamm's observation that the land value was often based on the yield of the land, usually in a ratio of one to ten.[77] The rural credit system was obviously connected to the land market. Small pieces of fields, meadows or vineyards circulated in the rural area and were pledged or sold, offering even poorer peasants access to credits and capital. In one contract, a small meadow was sold for just five pounds (60 gr.) with the option to repurchase the property for the same price.[78]

The next group of credit transactions, loans and confessions of debts, were worth on average 782 gr. However, four out of five cases are concerned with outstanding payments and not loan contracts and thus it is not possible to reconstruct the maturity or underlying transaction of the debt.[79] The only "real" credit contract (*accomodatum*) in the register is a loan of 30 pounds (360 gr.), which was given from a father to his son. Once again, land was pledged as security.[80] Sales on credit were recorded four times by Jakob of Laas.[81] For example, Jaenlinus Mair Jans promised in June 1391 to pay the price for textiles on St. Andrew's Day.[82] More interesting is that in the other three sales on credit wares were exchanged against wares. Chuntz Mairotten sold a meadow to Weigant. He reduced the pur-

75 Raffeiner 2008, no. 3, 4.
76 Raffeiner 2008, no. 61.
77 Stamm 2009, 40.
78 Raffeiner 2008, 49.
79 Raffeiner 2008, no. 1, 11, 20, 58.
80 Raffeiner 2008, no. 60.
81 Raffeiner 2008, no. 12, 46, 65, 69.
82 The contract is actually a triangular business because a third party is involved to pay a part of the price for specific carriage services. Raffeiner 2008, 213, no. 46.

chase price by 1.5 florins (approximately 57 gr.), for which Chuntz Mairotten was to pay two oxen worth 48 pounds (576 gr.) and in return Mairotten promised to pay 24 pounds (288 gr.) in the form of two burdens (*purden*) of iron.[83] In the other two sales, wine was purchased on credit. In one contract, in exchange for the wine, the sellers agreed to receive two horses.

In both cases, the price for the wine, and the horses respectively, was determined by an amount of money or the usual market value. Chuentz Kaelb sold four *fuder* of wine for the usual market value and was to receive two horses within 14 days instead of circulating coins. The wine was to be delivered after the next vintage.[84] In another contract, Haertlinus Laimtaler of Latsch agreed to pay Petrus de Angaro at next Candlemas (meaning in five months) 39 pounds (468 gr.) in wine for four horses. He promised to deliver the specific amount of wine to Imst on the agreed date if he did not pay him before.[85] Apparently, it was usual in the Vinschgau Valley to conclude purchase contracts on the basis of exchange transactions.[86] However, in all cases the prices for the goods were determined by an amount of money or the usual market value. The exchange in goods might be a response to the shortage of coins in the rural areas.

Finally, there is one pawnbroking contract in the register. Margg Mesner pledged a cow for 10 pounds (120 gr.) to Gallen von Laretz.[87] Gallen should choose one of the cows in Margg's stable and should obtain all property rights of the cow until the ten pounds were returned. The loan had to be repaid within three months. The small size and short duration suggest that this loan was probably used to cover a shortage of money and to purchase food, seed or tools.

The absence of a bigger number of loan contracts (*mutuum, accomodatum*), sales on credit (*debitum cause emptionis*), and pawnbroking (*obligatio, depositum*) in the rural area is striking. Over the entire period, Jakob of Laas registered only eleven such contracts for the year 1391. For comparison, in the register of the notary Jakob Tugehenn from Bozen from the year 1295 there are 97 (from altogether 188) acts related to loans, pawnbroking, credit purchases or confessions of debts.[88] How can this difference be explained?

It seems as if collateral mattered a lot for the access to credit—and even more in the countryside. Since many people had some sort of ownership (hereditary

83 The second burden of iron could be replaced with twelve pound money or a corresponding amount of corn. Raffeiner 2008, no. 12.

84 Raffeiner 2008, no. 65.

85 Raffeiner 2008, no. 69

86 Raffeiner 2008, 213.

87 Raffeiner 2008, no. 5.

88 Voltelini/Huter 1951.

tenure, fief, ownership, leasehold contract) of the land they cultivated, they could borrow via collateral credit. The land in the countryside was often divided into small plots, or several family members shared the ownership. Because of that, many loans were rather small and rarely exceeded four months' wages of a skilled worker (800 gr.). Only in a few cases are we informed about credits that were conducted without collateral. This may have several reasons. For once, poor people without property had no access to collateral credit and turned to other means of credit like pawnbroking or reputational credit. Secondly, these transactions were usually not recorded by a notary. The fees for the registration of the loan together with the small sums and short runtime imply that contracting costs were a big component of the total borrowing cost.[89]

There were far more mortgage contracts notarised by Jakob of Laas than small-scale credits and short-term loans. This is indirectly confirmed when certain contracts in the register specify that no *instrumentum,* meaning a full charter, was dispatched, as one entry suggests.[90] Here, Hans Mair Jansen pledged one field for 13 pounds (156 gr.). However, it is stated that this *notula* is no legal contract like most of the others but a pro-memoria entry.[91] Obviously, Hainz Mair Jansen refrained from acquiring a full notarial instrument for financial reasons. Because of high transaction costs for notarising debts, people hesitated to demand legal instruments for loans small in size, averaging about two to three months' wages for a skilled worker. Only in a few cases do we have further information about the fees for the notary or about who had to pay for the contracting.[92] The contracting costs may explain the widespread absence of loans, sales on credit, and pawnbroking contracts in the *imbreviatura* of Jakob of Laas.

A further clue to the functioning of the rural credit market comes from a spatial analysis of the debtors and lenders. The majority of creditors came from the Vinschgau Valley or from small towns and villages there, like Laas and its neighbouring communes (see Figure 2). Local creditors, meaning people from Laas, Eyrs, Tschengls, Tarnell, and Allitz, lent 8368 gr. (38.5 percent) of the total amount of debt that was notarised before Jakob of Laas.[93] The same is true when looking

---

89 Rosenthal 1994, 293.

90 Raffeiner 2008, no. 66.

91 Ibid.; StAM, NI 22, fol. 30v. *"daz sol ain gedenkpriefli sein, kain nodersprief"*.

92 In one *notuale,* it is stated that the seller of the land had to bear the contracting costs: *"solucionem litere huius empcionis debet ipse Thomlinus dare"*. StAM, NI 22, fol. 37v. There are so far no studies on the transaction costs of notaries, although some registers mention fees for notaries. Karner 1985, 17; Gamper 1993, 11.

93 21 percent of the overall credit from Nauders came from one single contract. The Lord of Annenberg sold a huge rent of wine to one single creditor, Fridericus the Nauders. Raffeiner 2008, no. 59.

Figure 2 Loans by origins of creditors and debtors registered by Jakob of Laas

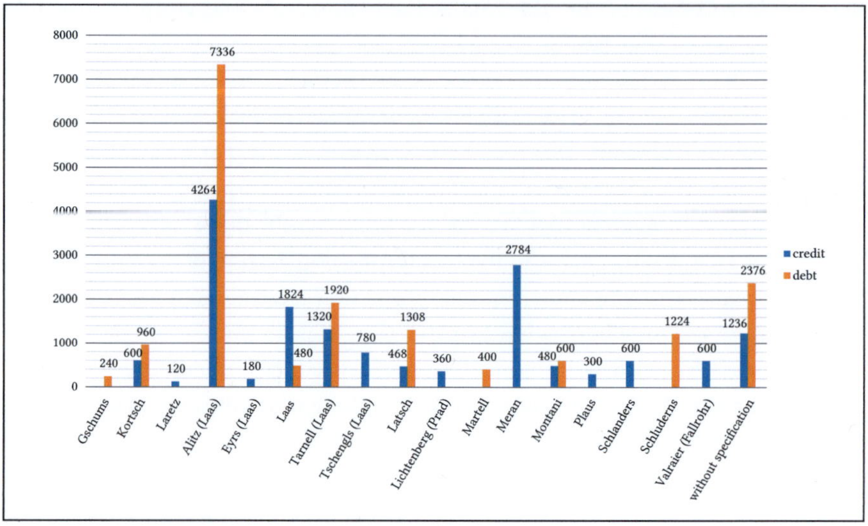

Source: StAM, NI 22; Raffeiner 2008.

Notes: Places of the origin of the borrowers and lenders and total amount of the loans taken or granted (in grossi).

at the debtors. People from Laas, Tarnell, and Eyrs incurred 46 percent of the debt volume notarised by Jakob of Laas. 20 different persons from Laas (8 creditors and 12 debtors) participated in the credit transactions, accounting for approximately 24 percent of the local population of roughly 80 in the late 14th century.[94] This is a very high number considering that a certain fraction of credit operations was not notarised at all and these are only the new contracts of 1391.

However, credit was not evenly spread by type of contract. Concerning short-term loans, merchants from Meran were predominantly lenders, accounting for 49 percent of the total loans given via sales on credit and short-term loans. Creditors from the Vinschgau Valley were less likely to give short-term loans. How can this difference be explained? One interpretation might be that it was more difficult to acquire loans not collateralized with real estate in the countryside. Besides, sales on credit for wine or clothes often involved merchants from bigger cities like Meran.[95] Finally, this is probably because of the bias of the source se-

94 A list of subjects from the counts of Tirol from 1427 mentions 80 such persons in Laas. The overall population was probably higher, since subjects of other feudal lords were not considered. Untertanenverzeichnis von Tirol, 1427: TLA, IC 12, fol. 177r–179v; cited after Stolz 1939, 188.

95 Raffeiner 2008, no. 11, 46.

lection. Obviously, contracts concerned with real estate were rather notarised than small-scale credits and short-term loans.[96] For comparison, another source, the court protocols from Meran, will be used to reconstruct the credit dealings in the Vinschgau Valley.

5 Credit Activity in the Court Protocols of Meran

The second source are the oldest existing court protocols from Meran (1388–1391), preserved in the municipal archives of Meran.[97] They consist of 140 sheets of paper in narrow folio (Schmalfolio) format. The court transcripts contain records of the actions, the persons involved, the subject matter, and settlement of the cases in a rather concise form. They are a unique source of the urban and rural Tirol since they include both the annual meetings of the rural court assemblies (*eleichtaidings*) as well as the territorial town and city courts of Meran. The book contains court sessions of the *taidings* taking place in Naturns (28 July 1388), Partschins (29 July 1388), Algund (30 July 1388), Tirol (3 August 1388), Riffian (4 August 1388), Mais (6 and 7 August 1388), Hafling (12 August 1388), and Veran and Rotenstain (12 August 1388). Afterwards, the complaints and judgments of the regular city and town court (*stadtrecht* and *dorfrecht*) in Meran are recorded with dates between April 1388 and May 1389.[98] The order continues in the following year, starting with Naturns (16 August 1388) followed by Partschins (17 August 1390), Algund (18 August 1390), Riffian (20 August 1388), Mais (30 August 1388), Hafling (1 September 1390), and Veran and Rotenstain (6 September 1390). The rest of the protocols cover the meetings of the city and town court between September 1390 and April 1391. The court protocols are entirely written in German.[99] The judicial district of the territorial court (*Landgericht*) of Meran included the parishes of Naturn, Algund, Partschins, Algund, Tirol (with Riffian and Kuens), Gratsch, and the city of Meran.[100] Local disputes were heard before the *taidings* in the aforementioned places or at the court in Meran. Lawsuits against citizens of Meran and

96 In some cities like Innsbruck and Hall, it was specified that charters relating to a legal business worth more than 10 pounds had to be sealed by the city or issued by an official scribe. Stolz 1998, 131.

97 StAM, GP 1. A few older judgements published as charters from the city court of Meran are printed by Stolz. Stolz 1932, 286–287, no. 50a; 288, no. 53.

98 The few entries concerning *gastrecht* and *bruckrecht* will not be discussed here.

99 Stolz 1932, 301–303, no. 76.

100 Stolz 1937, 131–133.

fines of over 50 pounds (600 gr.) had in some cases to be brought before the city court of Meran.[101] The ordinary city court (*stadtrecht*) met twice a week (Tuesday and Friday).[102] The town court (*dorfrecht*) met usually on Saturday.

The court protocols include information ranging from civil charges (*klagen*) and criminal charges (*ruegat*), the prorogation of these law cases to final verdicts. Fol. 1 to 48 include records of the *eleichtaidings*, fol. 49 to 103 include the charges of the *stadt-* and *dorfrecht* in Meran. This is followed in the same order by entries on the *eleichtaidings* of 1390 (fol. 111 to fol. 124) and *stadt-* and *dorfrecht* of 1390 and 1391 (fol. 126 to fol. 140). The court proceedings were public and held orally. The sessions were headed by the judge. The plaintiff presented his case himself or through a representative (*procurator*) in court and the defendant responded with his position and evidence was presented to the court. Then the judge addressed questions to the jurors, the so-called *aitsweren* (oath sworn), on the verdict (*volg und frag*). The lay assessors were appointed from the legal community for a fixed term. They passed judgements by majority vote.[103]

I analysed all 399 entries covering the period from 28 July 1388 to 7 April 1391.[104] These entries contain court cases from both the provincial *taidings* and the *dorfrecht* and *stadtrecht* of Meran. Three types of entries appear in the protocols: criminal charges from *aitsweren* acting as official prosecutors at the *taidings*, civil charges from everyone (both at the *taidings* and the courts of Meran), and announcements and verdicts in the court including the appointment of procurators, adjournments of cases or proclamations of penalties (fines, bans). The types of lawsuits brought before the courts are not easy to categorise. The lawsuits themselves were neither classified by the court nor the scribe of the court. Besides, many law cases refrain from a simple categorisation, since they deal with complex content. Most charges appear in a form where property, wares, obligations of some kind or money is claimed. To dissolve this huge group of claims of money or property, I followed Daniel Smail and created subcategories: acts related to money, credit and debts (1), acts related to property rights (2), acts related to in-

101 The cases worth over 50 pounds were tried in the province courts i.e. the *Weistum* of Naturns specifies which cases had to be heard before the court of Meran. Cf.: Zingerle and Egger 1888, 17–22; Stolz 1937, 121, 134.

102 Criminal trials were held every day. Stampfer 1889, 350, no. III.

103 Stolz 1932, 180; Stolz 1998, 124–132; Dopsch 2008, 74. The Tirolian customary laws (*Weistümer*) are printed by Zingerle and Egger 1888, 1–174. Cf. Obermair 2001, 189 and Stolz 1928, 271 f., no. 15 for a regulation of the customary law of Salurn (election of the jurors, holding of court meetings).

104 The few fragmentary entries were not considered in the analysis.

juries (3), acts related to family matters (4), and acts related to court activity (5).[105] Complaints about money and property together accounted for over half of all cases (62 percent). Criminal cases made up only seven percent. Family-related suits consisted mostly of cases concerning dowries (*heimstewr*) and inheritance disputes, making up four percent. Court related entries round off the list, making up 27 percent. These include the proclamation of several types of penalties (fines, bans) or notifications from the prosecutors (*aitsweren*) that they were not required to press charges. Unfortunately, when fines are proclaimed, there is no mention of the actual lawsuit, so in many cases it is not possible to categorise these entries.

Concerning credit practices, there are 156 entries involving unpaid debts or credits or the (re)claim of rents or wares (Table 6). The actual number of credit transactions is a little lower (108), since many cases are adjourned three or four times and thus appear more than once in the court protocols. Table 4 shows the average size of money in gr. and the value of goods respectively claimed in these

Table 4 Size of money debts registered by Jakob of Laas and claimed in the court of Tirol

–	Number of debts claimed	Total amount of money claimed	Mean	Median	Coefficient of variation	Standard deviation
Claims in court (1388–1391)	73* (156)**	43371	594	151	2.94	1747.38
Credits and debts registered by Jakob of Laas (1390–91)	44	21736	483	360	133.17	656.88

Sources: SAM, NI 22; SAM, GP 1.

Notes: *every lawsuit counted only once. If no sum is mentioned, the entry was skipped. ** In parentheses is the total number of observations given, including lawsuits that are dealt with for the second, third or fourth time.

cases, counting every lawsuit only once (and for the first time—cf. the number in the parentheses). Between July 1388 and April 1391 in 73 cases, financial claims worth 43,371 gr. were made.[106] The mean amount of money claimed was 594 gr. for unpaid debts, wares or rents. The median size was much lower with just 151 gr. The high mean figure is the result of the four lawsuits with the highest sums

105 Smail 2003, 37–42.

106 In several cases, the charge did not mention a specific sum but mentions unpaid debts, wares or rents. E.g. *"Item ez hat chlagt Minig der Neyer ab Plaban hintze Hainrich den Taler und hintz Fritzen den Nidenplatzer umb gült [...]."* StAM, GP 1, fol. 11r.

Figure 3 Distribution of the debt sums claimed in the court of Meran

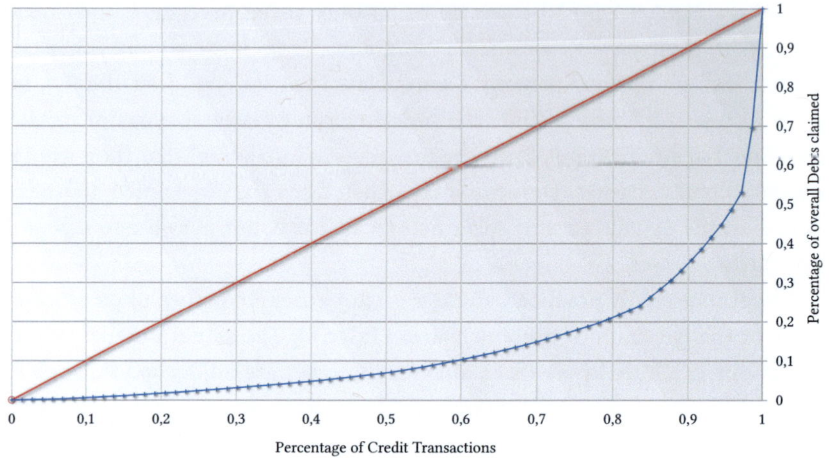

Source: StAM, GP 1.

Notes: Every lawsuit is counted only once, not considering any claims where no specific sum was mentioned. Number of observations is 73, total amount of the debt is 43371 gr. The red line represents an even distribution, the blue line shows the actual distribution of the debt sums among the individual claims.

claimed, which together amount to 24,000 gr., representing 55 percent of the total volume of debts and unpaid credits claimed before the court.[107] The remaining 69 claims were altogether worth just 19,371 gr. More than one third of them (26) were amounts of less than 100 gr (Table 5). Thus, 80 percent of the debtors owed roughly 20 percent of the overall money claimed in court, representing the sector of small-scale credit (Figure 3).

The small average size of the loans claimed in the court may indicate the purpose of these credits contracted. Most loans were worth just a month's wage of an unskilled worker, estimating roughly 80 gr. They were too small to acquire real estate but could be used as working capital of peasants and craftsmen to buy tools, seed, and livestock. In one case, it was written down that Albrecht Sneyder was to give Chuntzen dem Pretzler seven pound (84 gr.) for a pig.[108] Another suit dealt with the claim of Peter Schaffer of Forst, who sued Dietlein den Däumlein

107 These four are the only lawsuits involving sums over 1,500 gr. The biggest sum claimed was 60 mark (7,200 gr.) by the hospital of Bozen, which alone accounted for 30 percent of the overall total. StAM, GP 1, fol. 52r.

108 StAM, GP 1, fol. 55r.

Table 5 Class intervals of the debts claimed in the court of Meran

Class intervals	**Size of interval**	**Mid of interval**	**Number of observations (absolute)**	**Share of the specific observations (in %)**	**Share of observations summed up (in %)**	**Amount of money in each single interval (*grossi*)**	**Absolute product of the overall amount of money summed up (*grossi*)**	**Share of the amount of money of the intervals summed up (in %)**	**Percentage of the total product (column 7)**
1	2	3	4	5	6	7	8	9	10
1–100	100	50	26	35.62	35.62	1732	1732	3.99	3.99
101–200	100	150	14	19.18	54.0	1896	3628	8.36	4.37
201–300	100	250	11	15.07	69.86	2775	6403	14.76	6.4
301–400	100	350	6	8.22	78.08	2112	8515	19.63	4.87
401–500	100	450	4	5.48	83.56	1860	10375	23.92	4.29
501–1000	500	750	3	4.11	87.67	2880	13255	30.56	6.64
1001–2000	1000	1500	7	9.59	97.26	9716	22971	52.96	22.4
2001–8000	6000	5000	2	2.74	100	20400	43371	100	47.03
total	–	–	73	100	–	43371	–	–	100

Source: StAM, GP 1.

Table 6 Types of lawsuits in the court of Meran (July 1388–Janary 1389)

Category	Description	Number of entries	Share in %
credit and debts	claim of unpaid loan, sale or credit	130	32.58
	bankruptcy, right of lien	17	4.26
	claim of animals	1	0.25
	claims concerning pawns or pledged items	7	1.75
	subtotal	156	39.09
–	–	–	–
property	ownership	79	19.79
	rent or lease	6	1.5
	right of forest use	5	1.23
	subtotal	90	22.55
–	–	–	–
injuries	assault, injuries	25	6.26
	theft	3	0.75
	insults	1	0.25
	subtotal	29	7.27
–	–	–	–
family matters	inheritance dispute	12	3
	dowry, *heimstewer*	6	1.5
	subtotal	18	4.51
–	–	–	–
other court-related activities*	judgment	7	1.75
	procuration	24	6.01
	adjournments	7	1.75
	no prosecution	13	3.26
	ban	2	0.5
	fine	29	7.27
	other miscellaneous	24	6.01
	subtotal	106	26.56
–	–	–	–
–	total	399	100

Source: StAM, GP 1.

Notes: The number of entries refers to all entries in the court protocols. Since some cases are adjourned several times, the actual number of cases heard is significantly lower.

* In many cases, the true nature of the contest is not revealed. Punishments (fines, bans), for example, usually only refer to the amount of money paid and do not say anything about the original offense.

for two cattle and a calf.[109] In one case, the court granted Hansel Pekch, creditor of Chuntzen, a waggoner (*wagen man*), lien against his debtor for the small sum of just four pounds (48 gr.).[110] Other debts came from rent arrears.[111] A law case from 4 March 1391 shows that credit was not just a matter of monetary payments. Hainrich Stollz sued Hansen den Chesler, a tinkerer, for an old bowl, a soapstone basin and copper, which he gave him to make a big bowl out of.[112]

In contrast, some of the bigger loans might stem from the settling of long-running accounts with merchants. For example, a woman, called Grumserin, owed Niklaw Spetzinger, citizen of Meran, the huge sum of eleven mark (1,320 gr.) and five *fuder* of wood.[113] In July 1388, Jäkl an der Pankch, as procurator for Niklein den Pheyfferer, pressed charges against Haintzen dem Wirtlein for 33 pieces of wood (worth altogether 1,188 gr.), calculating three pound per piece.[114] Christan Rewpach, another merchant and citizen of Meran, claimed from a woman, Gesen, seven mark (840 gr.) and six *ellen* of cloth.[115] These few sales on credit differ highly from the average cases related to debts. However, with just a small timespan covered, it is hard to tell how money lending was affected by economic fluctuations. People might have borrowed to bridge shortcomings or bad harvests or just to improve their situation through investments. Without further information, it is hard to tell.

Unlike the credit transaction recorded in the register of the notary Jakob of Laas, these disputes relating to unpaid small-scale credits and debts were not collateralized with real estate. The small amounts of debt indicate that land as collateral was not a prerequisite for these small-scale loans. Instead, pawnbroking was often used to secure the credits. Some entries mention the practice of pledging items as collateral in court. A case from July and September 1388 involves the charge of the Mair of Gratsch to sell the goods of his debtor that were pledged in court. The case ended with the verdict that Diemlein, die Salthoferin, the debtor, should appear before the court and three or five persons should be appointed to value the pledged items. Moreover, if the selling of the pawns would not repay the debt then the Mair should receive a lien on all of her property.[116] Another case

---

109 StAM, GP 1, fol. 29r.

110 StAM, GP, fol. 57r.

111 StAM, GP 1, fol. 70v.

112 *"Ez hat chlagt Hainrich Stollz von Lanen hintz Hansen den Chesler [...] alz auf den ersten tag, umb ainen alten hafen und umb ein lafetsch und umb chuph, daz er im geben hat, daz er ainen grozzen hafen drawz solt machen [...]."* StAM, GP 1, fol. 135v.

113 StAM, GP 1, fol. 70v.

114 StAM, GP 1, fol. 62r., 64r–64v.

115 StAM, GP 1, fol. 69r., 73v.

116 StAM, GP 1, fol. 64r., 67r.

is that of Hanns Torkler, who claimed the return of his pawned property transferred to the court for a debt he owed to Niklaw Spetziger. As written in the court protocol, the judge, following an investigation, decided that the items were to be valued by three or five persons and then sold. Niklaw Spetziger should receive what Hanns Torkler owed him and the rest should be given to Hanns.[117] In both cases, we do not hear anything about the principal sum loaned.

Some entries report on the practice of seizure orders being filed in court if the debtor was unable to pay.[118] Small-scale credits, amounting only to one to three months' salary of an unskilled worker, were often collateralized with pawns. Either pawns were directly pledged when the credit was contracted or they were given on promises of payment in the court. This was the case in the court of Meran in July 1388. Heinrich der Rössel from Passeier settled with the notary Ulrich, procurator of Werbergerin, the payment of a debt of 40 pounds (480 gr.) for unpaid rents and damages on arears (*versezzens zins und für schäden*). They agreed that the debt should be repaid by two instalments of 20 pounds each. If he should fail to pay, the creditor or his procurator would retain a lien on his already pledged pawns and the rest of his property.[119] The majority of such loans were collateralized with pawns. In these cases, the borrower either pledged specific items or offered all his goods (his entire wealth) and the lender could seize it, if the borrower failed to repay on schedule. Most of the cases concerning unpaid credits and debts in the court of Meran belonged to this group.

The choice of collateral of the borrowers in Tirol was limited. They could either pledge property or their wealth (*alle hab*) as collateral. Alternatively, they could rely on their reputation. This was the case when borrowers presented guarantors in court for the repayment of unpaid credits and debts. A case from 29 July 1388 in the *eleichtaiding* of Partschins amply illustrates the degree to which guarantors served as security in credit transactions. Here, the guarantor had to repay the debts, but wanted to recover the payment from the original debtor. Prawn of Meran, the creditor, claimed 92 gr. from Marchlein (Märkchl) of Laim as a guarantor of the initial debtor, a woman called Tuesenichtin.[120] Simultaneously, Marchlein, the guarantor of Tuesenichtin, brought a case against said Tuesenichtin in court.[121] At the same time, she made a down payment of five pounds to Prawn in court.[122] Nevertheless, the judgment was adjourned until three days

117 StAM, GP 1, fol. 74r, 76r, 78v.
118 StAM, GP 1, fol. 27r, 28r, 57r, 80v, 81r, 93v, 94r, 95v, 133r, 138r, 138v.
119 StAM. GP 1, fol. 66r.
120 StAM. GP 1, fol. 11v.
121 StAM. GP 1, fol. 12r.
122 StAM, GP 1, fol. 16v.

later, when the case was closed with a final verdict. The debtor, Tuesenichtin, was sentenced to pay the initial principal of the sum and the resulting damages, which, as written down in the court protocols, went to a usurer.[123] If she failed to pay, Prawn should be granted lien on all her property.[124]

In most of the 57 cases dealing with property rights or rights of rent or lease in the *eleichtaidings* or the court of Meran, we do not know the reason the ownership of property was claimed or challenged. In many cases, the court protocol only state that the plaintiff claimed ownership of a house, meadow, vineyard or cellar as a charter he provided in court states.[125] In some cases, the real estate might have been sold, mortgaged or pledged as security. Without further information it is not possible to say how many claims of ownership were somehow connected with credit and loans and thus the claims of ownership of land will not be treated here in detail.

In twenty cases about unpaid debts and credits, the plaintiffs provided a charter or written document (*prief, zedl, urbar, previatur*) as proof in court.[126] In most of these cases, higher sums of between 15 pounds (180 gr.) and 60 mark (7,200 gr) were claimed.[127] This might indicate that for smaller loans, other means of credit security mechanisms, like oaths or oral testimonies, were used. The borrowers usually had to bear other costs besides the principal of the loan, like contract enforcement, which were covered by the interest rate. Small-scale credits were obviously more affected by these circumstances than bigger credit transactions, where the overhead costs of the loan made up only a small percentage of the principal.[128] To keep transaction costs of small-scale credits low, they might not have been recorded in notary registers. In most cases related to small-scale

123 The creditor went to a usurer and received the repayment of the original debt from him. The debtor then had to pay interest and damages for this loan, as stated on 30 July 1388 in court. *"Ez hat volg und frag bracht von der chlag wegen die der Prawn getan hat gen die Tuesenichtin alz gen ainen selb schaden und hintz Hainrich von Laim alz gen ainen bürgen umb .viii. libra perner minus .iiii. groschen und umb gangen schaden, der dar auf gangen ist an den wuchrer, daz der man dar umb den Prawn gewalt und gewer geben sol aus der Tuesenichtin hab."* StAM, GP 1, fol. 18r. One week later, on 7 August 1388, Marchlein received a penalty payment (*pen*) from Tuesinichtin. StAM, GP 1, fol. 32r.

124 StAM, GP 1, fol. 14v., 18r.

125 E.g. *"Ez hat chlagt der Mäusl von Ruffian alz ain chirchbräst [sic!] unser frawen ze Ruffian hintz Chuntzen den Huebber alz hintz ainen der ze der zeit dormaister an der gemaischaft geweswen ist, umb etliche güter, die unser frawen an gehörn, alz die priefe laut und sagt, den unser fraw dar umb hat [...]."* StAM, GP 1, fol. 23v.

126 StAM, GP 1, fol. 19r, 23r, 29v, 33v, 51r, 52r, 55v, 61v, 83v, 84r, 85r, 87v, 90v–91r, 96v, 98v, 118v, 120v, 122r, 127r, 129r–129v, 1303, 134v, 138r.

127 Only three times was a charter provided for rather small loans, twice for 84 gr. and once for 89 gr. StAM, GP 1, fol. 19r, 23r, 138r.

128 Van Zanden/Zuijderduijn/de Moor 2012, 4.

credits brought to the court, we do not hear anything about the burden of proof, although there was no unified line in this respect.[129] One case mentions a testimony of Chunrad, Zalner of Naturns, who testified under oath that Wirtl gave money to Pabenberger and further, that said Wirtl had never acted evil against his debtor.[130] This probably reflects the usual procedure of the court to read out written proofs or charters where applicable, hear testimonies and oaths in court, and then make a judgment.[131]

In contrast, sales on credit or credits granted by merchants were usually provided with a promissory note or a written charter. Niklaw Spetziger, citizen of Meran, whose name suggests that he was a merchant (*speciarius*), was one of the most active creditors. He had granted several big-sized loans, for which he claimed repayment in court. This, for example, was the case in his lawsuit against Fritz dem Gasser und his wife Mätzen. Troubles began for the married couple when Niklaw Spetziger reclaimed a debt of 89 gr. from them in the *eleichtaiding* of Tyrol on 3 August 1388. The sum, as is written down in the court protocols, should have been given to him long ago, as a charter (*prief*) that he presented in court stated.[132] The debtors were summoned to appear in court the next day at the *eleichtaiding* in Riffian. Once again, they did not appear in court and the case was adjourned for a final and third time to the next court meeting in Mais on 4 August 1388.[133] At the following court meeting in Mais, a final verdict was pronounced and the court granted Niklaw Spetziger a lien on all their property to the amount of the debt.[134] In another case, Niklaw Spetziger claimed 6 mark (720 gr.) from a woman, Tämerlerin. Once again, he provided a charter as proof. However, this time the debtor appeared in court at the third summons and voluntarily granted the creditor a lien on all her goods as well as the goods of her husband and her children.[135] A similar case happened on 7 August 1388. Niklaw Spetziger sued a certain Grumserin for the payment of the enormous sum of 11 mark (1,320gr.) and five *fuder* of wood.[136] He provided a charter as proof in court. This time it is stated that the debtor had

129 For example, a typical lawsuit in August 1388 over the small sum of 24 gr. mentions no proof. *"Aber hat der Mäusl chlat [sic!] alz auf den ersten tag hintz Haintzen den Tschauppen umb .ii. libra perner zu behalten minus oder mer; ist ertailt, daz ez ainen tag haben sol auf den phintztag gen Mais und sol an fur bot da, chumpt er und verantwortz, so bescheh, waz recht sey, chaem er aber nit, so sol doch beschehen, waz recht ist alz auf den andern tag".* StAM, GP 1, fol. 24r.

130 StAM, GP 1, fol. 11v.

131 Stolz 1998, 126 f.

132 StAM, GP 1, fol. 19r.

133 StAM, GP 1, fol. 23r.

134 StAM, GP 1, fol. 27r.

135 StAM, GP 1, fol. 30v, 33r.

136 StAM, GP 1, fol. 29v.

several guarantors (*bürgen*) to safeguard the payment. We do not hear about the final outcome of this case, but the successful repayment or settlement of the debt would be something not necessarily recorded in court. In other cases, penalty fees (*pen*) were paid because of arrear payments owed to Niklaw Spetziger.[137] Another indication of his activities as creditor is the lawsuit of Hanns Torkler against him, where said Hanns claimed the release of his pawns (see above).

People from the whole court district of the Burggrafenamt appeared in the court of Meran. However, the places of the court meetings (i.e. Naturns, Partschins, Algund, Meran, etc.) do not allow any conclusions about the persons involved. People would resort to the next court meeting wherever it took place. For example, Niklaw Spetziger from Meran sued Fritz den Gasser the first time in the *eleichtaiding* in Tyrol and later again in the court meeting in Mais because the next court meetings took place there. A clear identification of the origin of the creditors and debtors is only possible in some cases. As far as we can tell, citizens of Meran appear more frequently than average as creditors. Niklaw Spetziger appears seven times as creditor before the court, Cristan Rewpach of Meran two times and Nikl der Pheiffer of Meran four times. They partly dealt in trading goods like wine, wood, and cloth, but also extended cash loans.[138] In other cases, citizens of Meran, like Ulricus noder (Ulrich, the notary) or Öttlein Jaufner served as credit intermediaries and procurators in court.[139] Most of the creditors with identifiable place of origin who participated in more than one credit transaction came from Meran. Three of these people from Meran were big lenders, granting loans accumulating for over 5,180 gr. Other debtors and creditors are to be located among many different villages and towns like Algund, Auer, Bozen, Forst, Marling, Meran, Naturns, Partschins, Riffian, Passeier (the Passeier Valley), and Tirol. The actual number of people from Meran was probably much higher, but the source fails to provide further information. Nevertheless, nearly all the debtors and creditors came from towns in the court district of Meran, except for very few people from Bozen and some merchants from Germany (Nuremberg).

---

137 StAM, GP 1, fol. 22v. *"Item Geiger von Ruffian sol .xviii. groschen von Niklaw dez Spetzigers wegen. Item der Hold sol .xviii. groschen auch von Niklaws des Spetziger wegen."* No reason is given for these payments, although it is likely that they were for defaulted credits.

138 For Niklaw Spetziger see above, for Cristan Rewpach see StAM, GP 1, fol. 33v, 69r, 73v, 131r, 136v, 140v; for Nikl den Pheiffer see StAM,. GP 1, fol. 62r, 64r–64v, 65r, 88v, 90v–91r, 96v.

139 StAM, GP 1, fol. 54r, 61r, 66r. Öttlein Jaufner was later judge in Meran and judge in Mölten. That he was a citizen of Meran is stated in the register of the notary Christian of Meran. Mantoan 1999/2000, 91, no. 2; Huter 1990, 41.

Merchants appear among the most important creditors in the court protocols. Besides, wealthy citizens from Meran claimed credits in the court, like Peter Austrunk.[140] There were also some lenders who belonged to the church, like Hainrich, chaplain of the monastery in Stainach (Algund) and Chunrad, the minister of the parish Tyrol.[141] Church institutions like the church of St. Kathrein in Hafling or the hospital of Bozen, represented through the provost or other legal representatives, also sued for outstanding money claims.[142] Craftsmen are relatively rare plaintiffs in a monetary claim.[143] People of the lower social strata also asserted claims in court. On 28 February 1391, Haintz, servant (*chnecht*) of Rener, sued the tailor Haintz for a rent in wine (*umb 26 gr. wein gült*) worth 26 gr. The creditor received pawns from his debtor, which were to be sold to pay off the debt. If the sale cleared the debt then the debtor would not have to pay a penalty. Otherwise he was obliged to provide more pawns and pay a penalty of 18 gr.[144] In another case from 11 March 1391, Niklaw, a labourer (*ein arbaiter*), was granted a lien of 2 pounds against his debtor.[145] Debts were also created by outstanding wage claims. In one case, Seitz, servant of the deceased old Maretscher, sued the young Maretscher, heir of his former lord, for outstanding wages for the enormous sum of nine mark.[146] Among the debtors were craftsmen and labourers like cobblers, tailors, smiths, carpenters, and waggoners.[147] The sums they owed were rather low and between 20 gr. and 120 gr.

The central role of the territorial court of Meran, including both the *eleichtaidings* and the *dorfrecht* and *stadtrecht,* for the whole court district helped to reduce the uncertainty of credit contracting. Since all cases of bankruptcy, unpaid credits or debts had to be negotiated there, people could rely on the information

140 StAM, GP 1, fol. 127r–127v, 134v, 140v.

141 StAM, GP 1, fol. 61v, 85v, 89r.

142 StAM, GP 1, fol. 52r, 122r, 123r.

143 Kuntz der Schuester (cobbler) and Jäkl der Fleischächl (butcher) are among the few. StAM, GP 1, fol. 82v, 115v–116r.

144 *"Ez hat chlagt Haintz des Reners chnecht auf den ersten tag hintz Haintzen dem Pair, den sneider, umb .xxvi. groschen wein gült ze behalten waz, waz geleichew raitung bringt, do sprach der sneider er hiet gutew phant von im dar umb und wann pesser dan sovil geltz, alz er im schuldig belib, dar auf ist ertailt, daz der Haintz die phant verchaufen sol, wirt er seins geltz pezalt gar und gantz, so ist der Haintz umb den pan chomen umb .xviii. groschen, wurd er aber nicht pezalt, so sol der Haintz sneider mer phand geben und sol auch de pan auz richten .xviii. groschen."* StAM, GP 1, fol. 134r.

145 StAM, GP 1, fol. 138v.

146 StAM, GP 1, fol. 111r.

147 StAM, GP 1, fol. 57r (*Chuntz, der wagen man,* waggoner); fol. 84r and 98r (*Dorothen, die Smiedin,* smith); fol. 127r (*Oettlein der Schuester,* cobbler); fol. 134r (*Hainz der Pair, der sneider,* tailor), fol. 137r (*Chuntz der Zimmerman,* carpenter).

provided in court. Pledged property had to be sold, under threat of penalty, by the public official (*Feilträger*) appointed for this purpose.[148] People did not only pledge pawns, receive payments or verdicts there but were also officially acquitted from debts. On January 1389, Agnes, die Franklin, was acquitted of a charge and a debt of seven pounds (84 gr.) against her.[149] The institution was also used voluntarily, like several cases suggest. For example, on 8 August 1388 Tämerlerin appeared voluntarily (*willichleich*) at the court and granted her debtor, Niklaw Spetziger, the right of lien for an unpaid debt.[150] The court was one important place where unpaid debts were checked, disputed and paid off. It served as an evidence office for property and credit transactions, which later took the form of the *Verfachbücher*.[151] The court minutes also show that lawsuits could be processed rather quickly. In some cases, reaching a verdict was only a matter of days; in other cases, where the lawsuit was adjourned three or four times for a number of reasons, it took several months. When Christian Rewpach sued Gesen for six mark (960 gr.) and six *ellen* of cloth, the process was adjourned four times. The first hearing took place on 11 August 1388 and the final court meeting was 28 November 1388.[152] Three months seems to be a rather long time for a court case. Other lawsuits, like the charge of Hanns Torkler against Niklaw Spetziger, were solved within three days (see above). The passing of a judgment usually involved several people. Assessors were assigned to the judge, who were elected from local elites, providing a few checks on corruption.[153] Altogether, the court of Meran seems to have functioned well in practice.

6 Conclusion

Both the notary register and the court protocols show that the participation in the credit market was widespread among different social groups in Tirol. The fact that the credits registered by the notary Jakob of Laas and lawsuits related to credits in the court of Meran differ a lot in type and size forces us to confront the question of sample selection once again. The differences are most obvious in the case of the sizes of the debts. As Table 4 shows, the median size of

148 Huter 1990, 30; Pfeiffer 1848.

149 StAM, GP 1, fol. 79v.

150 StAM, GP 1, fol. 33r.

151 Huter 1990, 42–47.

152 StAM, GP 1, fol. 33v, 63v, 71r, 73v.

153 Huter 1990, 44. In the 15th century, the burghers of Meran were allowed to submit an election proposal for the judge of Meran.

debts contracted in the register of Jakob Laas (360 gr.) was more than two times that of debts (151 gr.) claimed in the territorial court of Meran. Individuals could borrow and lend money using different types of credit. In the notary register of Jakob of Laas, long-term debts collateralized with real estate (mortgage, selling of land with right of redemption) dominated the picture.[154] In the court protocols of Meran, the bulk of the negotiated debt consisted of small-scale lending, where pawns or guarantors served as security.

If collateral mattered to obtain access to capital and credit then it would be logical to assume that the situation was different in city and countryside. This would imply two consequences. Firstly, the proportion of those who could pledge land or property rights as security money was bigger in the rural areas than in the cities.[155] But still many people in the countryside had no access to mortgage credit. In the towns, the proportion of people who could pledge land as security was probably even smaller than in the countryside and many more people had demand for petty loans and small-scale credit. Secondly, if people had little or no wealth that could be used as collateral, they would resort to other means of credit.[156]

However, the findings of the notary register and court protocols allow other lessons to be drawn. Loans secured with collateral were the prevailing form of credit recorded in the notary register of Jakob of Laas. However, the absence of small-scale credit in Laas was not because of supposedly fundamental differences between urban and rural credit markets but rather because it was simply not common practice to have small loans recorded by a notary. There were other, more suitable, possibilities to gain access to credit and to ensure contract enforcement.[157] This acts as salutary reminder that simply because documentation exists for some types of credit in a source and does not exist for other types, we should be careful to draw conclusions for the entire credit market of Laas or even the whole of Tirol.

This can be seen from the court protocols of Meran. Pawnbroking and small-scale loans appear frequently in the court minutes. Here, other means to secure these credit transactions were in action, like social mechanisms (group solidarity, reputation) or contract enforcement in court.[158] The problem is that we can see when these credits are brought to court and debtors defaulted, but we do not

154 This finding corresponds with the land market of Bozen from 1295. Ertl 2017.

155 The distribution of house ownership in Meran can be estimated from the tax lists from 1438 onwards. Zeindl 2009, 54–60 and 89–118.

156 Cf. the contribution by Gilles Postel-Vinay in this volume.

157 For example, it was also possible to take out a loan from the community, as the example of Gries shows. Stamm 2013, 67.

158 Cf. Hoffman 1996, 69–80.

know how many were contracted and who participated in this credit market because the sources do not inform us about this. If a debt was reclaimed in court without the use of real estate as collateral, there could be several reasons. It could be that the debtor did not have any wealth to offer as security, that the transaction costs were too high in relation to the principal sum of the loan or that the creditor simply had no interest in real estate or property rights (because he would rather invest his wealth in something else).[159]

What we can learn from the results is that small-scale credits existed in both the city and the countryside, as is shown by various charges against debtors coming from rural areas. Thus, collateral was not the only determining factor to obtain access to credit in Tirol. The court protocols show various cases where people from rural areas received small-scale loans that were not secured with collateral and not notarised. Steger ab Labers (eastwards of Meran), Peter from Partschins, the Schneiderin (tailor) in dem Turm of Riffian or Tämerlerin from Mais were all sued for unpaid credits and debts of between 72 gr. and 132 gr.[160]

The key to explaining the use of different credit instruments in Meran and the Vinschgau Valley is the selection bias of the sources rather than the different economic settings. The pledging or transfer of property was usually registered by a notary. However, when no collateral was available or needed, individuals resorted to small-scale and short- and medium-term loans and pawnbroking. To reduce the (relatively high) transaction costs, these credits were usually not written down by a notary. This might explain the difference in the sizes of the loans tried in court between 1388 and 1391 and registered by the notary Jakob of Laas in 1391. Since Jakob of Laas registered mostly mortgage contracts where real estate served as collateral and land sales with a right of redemption, the average sum of loans was higher in Laas and the Vinschgau Valley than the sums claimed in the territorial court of Meran.

If differences between rural and urban areas did not matter, then, how important were urban centres like Meran for the credit market? The register of Jakob of Laas shows that individuals from Laas and the Vinschgau Valley seem to have preferred to borrow within the local community. Land was used as security for these loans, and the contracts were written down by a local notary. However, medium- and big-sized loans not collateralized with real estate were more often conducted with citizens of bigger cities like Meran—probably for a better risk pooling of the creditors. This is shown by the activities of citizens of Meran like Niklaw Spetziger or Christan Rewpach. In rural communities, credit availability was exposed to shocks to local agriculture, while merchant credit was rather in-

159 Van Zanden/Zuijderduijn/de Moor 2012, 13.
160 StAM, GP 1, fol. 27r, 28r, 28v, 76r.

dependent from these circumstances. Thus, merchant- and mortgage-credits were complimentary credit activities. The city of Meran was important in that the territorial court of justice provided information on borrowers and kept the costs of recovering debts and pawned items low. There were only a few places where debts, credits, and pawns of the entire Burggrafenamt could be claimed, checked, disputed or sold: the *eleichtaidings* and the court of Meran. Hence, nearly all debtors and creditors came from the same court district of Meran.

The differences in the use of credit instruments suggest that a further spatial comparative analysis of the credit activities in Tirol will be fruitful. In particular, one may ask if differences in credit contracting (i.e. court, notaries, and pawnbrokers) can explain differences in regional credit activity. The analysis of the two sources furthermore points to overlapping and complementary credit markets that deserve to be investigated in more depth.

References

Archival References

StAM = Stadtarchiv Meran NI 22; GP 1.

Bibliographic References

Andermann K. and Fouquet G. (eds.), 2016. *Zins und Gült. Strukturen des ländlichen Kreditwesens in Spätmittelalter und Frühneuzeit* [= Kraichtaler Kolloquien 10]. Epfendorf: Jan Thorbecke Verlag.

Beimrohr W. 2008. "Bäuerliche Besitzrechte und die ländliche Gemeinde in Tirol." In *Bauern zwischen Herrschaft und Genossenschaft/Peasant relations to Lords and Government: Scandinavia and the Alpine region 1000–1750*, edited by J.R. Myking, G. Thoma, T. Iversen, 85–108. Trondheim: Tapir academic press.

Briggs C. 2009. *Credit and Village Society in Fourteenth-Century England.* Oxford: Oxford University Press.

Briggs C. 2015. "Money and Rural Credit in the Later Middle Ages Revisited." In *Money, Prices and Wages: Essays in Honour of Professor Nicholas Mayhew*, edited by M. Allen and D. Coffman, 129–142. Houndmills: Palgrave Macmillan.

Briggs C. and Zuijderduijn J. (eds.) 2018a. *Land and Credit. Mortgages in the Medieval and Early Modern European Countryside.* eBook: Palgrave.

Briggs C. and Zuijderduijn J. (eds.) 2018b. "Introduction: Mortgages and Annuities in Historical Perspective", In *Land and Credit. Mortgages in the Medieval and EarlyModern European Countryside,* edited by C. Briggs and J. Zuijderduijn, 1–17. eBook: Palgrave.

Cerman M. and Mitterauer M. 2020. "The Sub-peasant Strata in the Late Medieval and Early Modern Eastern Alpine Region." In *Peasants, Lords, and State: Comparing Peasant Conditions in Scandinavia and the Eastern Alpine Region, 1000–1750* [= The Northern World 89], edited by T. Iversen, J.R. Myking, and S. Sonderegger, 269–291. Leiden: Brill.

Cipolla C.M. 1994 (3rd edition). *Before the Industrial Revolution: European Society and Economy, 1000–1700.* New York and London: Norton.

Clemens G.B. (ed.), 2008. *Schuldenlast und Schuldenwert. Kreditnetzwerke in der europäischen Geschichte 1300–1900* [= Trierer Historische Forschungen 65]. Trier: Kliomedia.

Demo E. 2018. "Il Ruolo di Merano nei Traffici Commerciali tra l'Area Tedesca e l'Italia settentrionale (secc. XIV–XVI). Nuovi Documenti e Spunti di Ricerca". In *1317: Eine Stadt und ihr Recht: Meran im Mittelalter: Bausteine zur Stadtgeschichte: Akten der Internationalen Tagung, Meran, Kurhaus und Kurmittelhaus, 22. bis 25. Februar 2017 = 1317: una città e il suo diritto: Merano nel Medioevo: materiali di storia cittadina: atti del convegno internazionale, Merano, Kurhaus e Vecchie Terme, 22–25 febbraio 2017,* edited by G. Pfeifer, 421–423. Bozen: Athesia.

Dopsch H. 2008. "Zwischen Herrschaft und Genossenschaft. Grundstrukturen bäuerlichen Lebens im Ostalpenraum" In *Bauern zwischen Herrschaft und Genossenschaft/Peasant relations to Lords and Government: Scandinavia and the Alpine region 1000–1750,* edited by J.R. Myking, G. Thoma, T. Iversen, 65–84. Trondheim: Tapir academic press.

Ertl T. 2017, "Small Landlords. Land Transactions in and around Bozen (South Tirol) in the Mid-Thirteenth Century." In *Vierteljahrschrift für Sozial- und Wirtschaftsgeschichte* 104, no. 1: 7–28.

Fontaine L. 1994. "Spaces, usages et dynamiques de la dette dans les hautes vallées dauphinoises (XVIIe–XVIIIe siècles)." In *Annales. Histoire, Sciences Sociales* 46:1375–1391.

Fontaine L. and Schlumbohm J. (eds.) 2000. *Household strategies for survival: 1600–2000. Fission, faction and cooperation.* Cambridge: Cambridge University Press.

Gamper M. 1993. *Die Tätigkeit des Notars David von Meran. Teiledition seiner Imbreviatur aus dem Jahre 1328,* Diplomarbeit zur Erlangung des Grades eines Magisters an der geisteswissenschaftlichen Fakultät der Leopold-Franzens-Universität Innsbruck. Innsbruck.

Gilomen H.-J. 2016. "Klöster und Spitäler als Kreditgeber der ländlichen Gesellschaft. Hilfe oder Ausbeutung." In *Zins und Gült. Strukturen des ländlichen Kreditwesens in Spätmittelalter und Frühneuzeit* [= Kraichtaler Kolloquien 10], edited by K. Andermann and G. Fouquet, 69–92. Epfendorf: Jan Thorbecke Verlag.

Groebner V. 1993. *Ökonomie ohne Haus. Zum Wirtschaften armer Leute in Nürnberg am Ende des 15. Jahrhunderts* [= Veröffentlichungen des Max-Planck-Instituts für Geschichte 108]. Göttingen: Vandenhoeck and Ruprecht.

Hagen C. 2015. *Fürstliche Herrschaft und kommunale Teilhabe. Die Städte der Grafschaft Tirol im Spätmittelalter.* Innsbruck: Universitätsverlag Wagner.

Hagen C. 2018a. "Das Konstanzer Ammanngerichtsbuch (1423–1434) als Quelle für christlich-jüdische Kreditgeschäfte. Ein Projektbericht." In *Ökonomische Glaubensfragen. Strukturen und Praktiken jüdischen und christlichen Kleinkredits im Spätmittelalter* [= Vierteljahrschrift für Sozial- und Wirtschaftsgeschichte, Beihefte, 242], edited by G. Fouquet and S. Rabeler, 43–62. Stuttgart: Franz Steiner Verlag.

Hagen C. 2018b. "Der Stadtherr und seine Bürger. Beobachtungen zur Interaktion zwischen Herzog Heinrich von Kärnten und der Stadt Meran unter besonderer Berücksichtigung des Stadtrechts von 1317." In In *1317: Eine Stadt und ihr Recht: Meran im Mittelalter: Bausteine zur Stadtgeschichte: Akten der Internationalen Tagung, Meran, Kurhaus und Kurmittelhaus, 22. bis 25. Februar 2017 = 1317: una città e il suo diritto: Merano nel Medioevo: materiali di storia cittadina: atti del convegno internazionale, Merano, Kurhaus e Vecchie Terme, 22–25 febbraio 2017,* edited by G. Pfeifer, 131–150. Bozen: Athesia.

Heuberger R. 1927. "Das deutschtiroler Notariat. Umrisse seiner mittelalterlichen Entwicklung." In *Veröffentlichungen des Museum Ferdinandeum* 6: 27–122.

Hoffman P. T. 1996. *Growth in a traditional Society. The french Countryside, 1450–1815.* Princeton: Princeton University Press.

Hoffman P. T., Postel-Vinay G., and Rosenthal J.-L., 2019. *Dark Matter Credit. The Development of peer to peer Lending and Banking in France.* Princeton: Princeton University Press.

Hörmann-Thurn und Taxis J. 2010. "Ein spätmittelalterliches Pfandverzeichnis (1309–1312) der Tiroler Landesfürsten. Edition und Kommentar." In *Päpste, Privilegien, Provinzen: Beiträge zur Kirchen-, Rechts- und Landesgeschichte; Festschrift für Werner Maleczek zum 65. Geburtstag* [= Mitteilungen des Instituts für Österreichische Geschichtsforschung. Ergänzungsband, 55], edited by J. Gießauf, 165–196. Wien: Böhlau.

Huter F. (ed.) 1990. *Das älteste Tiroler Verfachbuch (Landgericht Meran 1468–1471). Aus dem Nachlass von Karl Moeser* [= Schlern Schriften 282. Acta Tirolensia 5]. Innsbruck: Universitätsverlag Wagner.

Johler R. 1999. "Bäuerliches Kreditwesen im Alpenraum. Vorbemerkungen zu einer 'economic anthropology'." In *Historische Anthropologie: Kultur, Gesellschaft, Alltag* 7:146–153.

Karner H. 1985. *Die Tätigkeit des Notars David von Meran. Teiledition seiner Imbreviatur aus dem Jahre 1328,* Dissertation zur Erlangung des Doktorgrades an der Geisteswissenschaftlichen Fakultät der Leopold-Franzens-Universität Innsbruck. Innsbruck.

Kießling R. 2018. "Meran zwischen Reschen und Brenner. Spätmittelalterlicher Handel und Verkehr in Richtung Norden." In *1317: Eine Stadt und ihr Recht: Meran im Mittelalter: Bausteine zur Stadtgeschichte: Akten der Internationalen Tagung, Meran, Kurhaus und Kurmittelhaus, 22. bis 25. Februar 2017 = 1317: una città e il suo diritto: Merano nel Medioevo: materiali di storia cittadina: atti del convegno internazionale, Merano, Kurhaus e Vecchie Terme, 22–25 febbraio 2017,* edited by G. Pfeifer, 433–448. Bozen: Athesia.

King S. and Tomkins A. 2003. *The poor in England, 1700–1850. An economy of makeshifts.* Manchester and New York: Manchester University Press.

Köhler S. 2020. "Money Lending and Settling Debts in and around Meran (South Tirol) in the 14th Century" In *Mannheim Working Papers in Premodern Economic History* 1:13–45.

Kuske B. 1956. "Die Entstehung der Kreditwirtschaft und des Kapitalverkehrs." In Bruno Kuske. *Köln, der Rhein und das Reich. Beiträge aus fünf Jahrzehnten wirtschaftsgeschichtlicher Forschung.* Cologne/Graz: Böhlau, 48–137 [published for the first time in Fritz Beckmann, Karl Diehl, Bruno Kuske, Alfred Müller, and Joseph Schumpeter. 1927. *Die Kreditwirtschaft,* vol. 1 [= Kölner Vorträge 1], 1–79. Leipzig: Gloeckner].

Kustatscher E. 2018. "Bürger. Insasse. wohnhaft zu Meran. Eine Annäherung an die städtische Sozialstruktur auf der Grundlage ausgewählter Quellen (1300–1480)." In *1317: Eine Stadt und ihr Recht: Meran im Mittelalter: Bausteine zur Stadtgeschichte: Akten der Internationalen Tagung, Meran, Kurhaus und Kurmittelhaus, 22. bis 25. Februar 2017 = 1317: una città e il suo diritto: Merano nel Medioevo: materiali di storia cittadina: atti del convegno internazionale, Merano, Kurhaus e Vecchie Terme, 22–25 febbraio 2017,* edited by G. Pfeifer, 177–212. Bozen: Athesia.

Loose R. 2008. "Die Welt des Notars Jakob von Laas." In *Noderbuch. Notariatsimbreviaturen des Jakob von Laas 1390–1392. Mit einem Nachwort von Rainer Loose,* edited by H. Raffeiner, 204–218. Brixen: Provinz Verlag.

Mantoan D. 1999/2000. *Il Registro di Imbreviature del Notaio meranese Christanus q. Ulrici n. de Eppiano (1406–1407),* Università degli studi di Trento. Facoltà di Lettere e Filosifa. Corso di Laurea in Lettere (Indirizzo Moderno). Trento.

Obermair H. 2001. "Soziale Produktion von Recht? Das Weistum des Gerichts Salurn von 1403." In *Tiroler Heimat NF* 65: 5–24.

Obermair H. and Stamm V. 2019. "Alpine Ökonomie in Hoch- und Tieflagen—das Beispiel Tirol im Spätmittelalter und Früher Neuzeit. In: *Relire l'altitude: la terre et ses usages. Suisse et espaces avoisinants, XIIe–XXIe siècles,* edited by L. Lorenzetti, Y. Decorzant, and A.-L. Head-König, 29–56. Neuchâtel: Éditions Alphil-Presses universitaires suisses.

Pfeifer G. 2001. "'Nobis servire tenebitur in armis'. Formen des Aufstiegs und Übergangs in den niederen Adel im Tirol des 14. Jahrhunderts." In *Zwischen Nicht-Adel und Adel* [= Vorträge und Forschungen, 53], edited by K. Andermann and P. Johanek, 49–103. Stuttgart: Thorbecke.

Pfeifer G. 2008. "De arte edendi." In *Der Schlern* 82: 91–93.

Pfeifer G. 2018. "Die Zeichen der Stadt. Merans Siegel im Mittelalter." In *1317: Eine Stadt und ihr Recht: Meran im Mittelalter: Bausteine zur Stadtgeschichte: Akten der Internationalen Tagung, Meran, Kurhaus und Kurmittelhaus, 22. bis 25. Februar 2017 = 1317: una città e il suo diritto: Merano nel Medioevo: materiali di storia cittadina: atti del convegno internazionale, Merano, Kurhaus e Vecchie Terme, 22–25 febbraio 2017,* edited by G. Pfeifer, 401–420. Bozen: Athesia.

Pfeiffer F. 1848. "Das alte Stadtrecht von Meran." In *Zeitschrift für deutsches Altertum und deutsche Literatur,* 6:413–430.

Pfister U. 2007. "Rural land and credit markets, the permanent income hypothesis and proto-industry: evidence from early modern Zurich." In *Continuity and Change* 22, no. 3: 189–518.

Raffeiner H. (ed.), 2008. *Noderbuch. Notariatsimbreviaturen des Jakob von Laas 1390–1392. Mit einem Nachwort von Rainer Loose.* Brixen: Provenz Verlag.

Rizzolli H. 2018. "Die Münzstätte Meran im Lichte der Stadtordnung von 1317." In In *1317: Eine Stadt und ihr Recht: Meran im Mittelalter: Bausteine zur Stadtgeschichte: Akten der Internationalen Tagung, Meran, Kurhaus und Kurmittelhaus, 22. bis 25. Februar 2017 = 1317: una città e il suo diritto: Merano nel Medioevo: materiali di storia cittadina: atti del convegno internazionale, Merano, Kurhaus e Vecchie Terme, 22–25 febbraio 2017,* edited by G. Pfeifer, 449–460. Bozen: Athesia.

Rosenthal J.-L. 1994. "Rural Credit Markets and Aggregate Shocks. The Experience of Nutis St. Georges, 1756–1776." In *The Journal of Economic History* 54:288–306.

Signori G. 2015. *Schuldenwirtschaft. Konsumenten- und Hypothekarkredite im spätmittelalterlichen Basel.* Constance and Munich: UVK Verlagsgesellschaft Konstanz.

Skambraks T. and S. Köhler 2019. "What Is Credit?" In *Methods in Premodern Economic History. Case Studies from the Holy Roman Empire, c.1300–c.1600* [= Palgrave Studies in Economic History], edited by U. Kypta, J. Bruch, and T. Skambraks, 146–150. London: Palgrave Macmillan.

Skambraks T., Köhler S., Kehnel A., Kümper H., Gussone M., and Schniggendiller M. 2020. "Kleinkredit und Marktteilhabe in der Vormoderne. Projektdesign." In *Mannheim Working Papers in Premodern Economic History* 1:1–12.

Smail D.L. 1998. "Notaries. Courts and the Legal Culture of Late Medieval Marseille." In *Urban and Rural Communities in Medieval France. Provence and Languedoc 1000–1500,* edited by K. Reyerson and J. Drendel, 23–50. Leiden, Boston, and Cologne: Brill.

Smail D.L. 2003. *The Consumption of Justice. Emotions. Publicity and legal Culture in Marseille, 1264–1423.* Ithaca and London: Cornell University Press.

Stamm V. 2007. "Zur Bedeutung der Grundrente für die landesfürstlichen Einnahmen und bäuerlichen Abgaben in der Grafschaft Tirol (13./14. Jahrhundert)." In *Vierteljahrschrift für Sozial- und Wirtschaftsgeschichte* 94:47–56.

Stamm V. 2008a. "Daz ist der Gelt von Tyrol". Ein unveröffentlichtes Urbar aus dem Nahbereich einer weltlichen Grund- und Territorialherrschaft im 13. Jahrhundert." In *Zeitschrift für Historische Forschung* 35:189–205.

Stamm V. 2008b. "Lehnspraxis im spätmittelalterlichen Tirol." In *Tiroler Heimat NF* 72; 63–72.

Stamm V. 2009. "Kauf und Verkauf von Land und Grundrenten im hohen und späten Mittelalter. Eine Untersuchung zur historischen Wirtschaftsanthropologie." In *Vierteljahrschrift für Sozial- und Wirtschaftsgeschichte* 96: 33–43.

Stamm V. 2010. "Soziale Zwischengruppen in der mittelalterlichen Agrargesellschaft." In *Historische Zeitschrift* 291:1–22.

Stamm V. 2013. *Grundbesitz in einer spätmittelalterlichen Marktgemeinde: Land und Leute in Gries bei Bozen* [Vierteljahrschrift für Sozial- und Wirtschaftsgeschichte, Beihefte, 222]. Stuttgart: Steiner.

Stampfer C. 1889. *Geschichte von Meran von der ältesten Zeit bis zur Gegenwart.* Innsbruck: Universitätsverlag Wagner.

Stolz O. 1928. *Die Ausbreitung des Deutschtums in Südtirol im Lichte der Urkunden, vol. 2. Die Ausbreitung des Deutschtums im Bozner Unterland und Überetsch sowie in den deutschen Gemeinden im Nonsberg und Fleimstal.* Munich and Berlin: Oldenbourg.

Stolz O. 1932. *Die Ausbreitung des Deutschtums in Südtirol im Lichte der Urkunden, vol. 3. Die Ausbreitung des Deutschtums im Gebiete von Bozen und Meran, part 1: Darstellung.* Munich and Berlin: Oldenbourg.

Stolz O. 1934. *Die Ausbreitung des Deutschtums in Südtirol im Lichte der Urkunden, vol. 4. Die Ausbreitung des Deutschtums im Vintschgau und im Eisacktal und Pustertal.* Munich and Berlin: Oldenbourg.

Stolz O. 1932. *Die Ausbreitung des Deutschtums in Südtirol im Lichte der Urkunden, vol. 3. Die Ausbreitung des Deutschtums im Gebiete von Bozen und Meran, part 2: Urkundenbeilagen und Nachträge.* Munich and Berlin: Oldenbourg.

Stolz O. 1934. *Die Ausbreitung des Deutschtums in Südtirol im Lichte der Urkunden, vol. 4. Die Ausbreitung des Deutschtums im Vintschgau und im Eisacktal und Pustertal.* Munich and Berlin: Oldenbourg.

Stolz O. 1937. *Politisch-historische Landesbeschreibung von Südtirol* [= Schlern Schriften 40]. Innsbruck: Athesia.

Stolz O. 1939. "Das Verzeichnis der Untertanen der Tiroler Landesfürsten im Inntal und Vintschgau vom Jahre 1427. Text bearbeitet von H. Bachmann, L. von Berg, K. Dörrer, K. Finsterwalder, H. Kramer." In *Quellen zur Steuer-, Bevölkerungs- und Sippengeschichte des Landes Tirol im 13., 14. und 15. Jahrhundert, bearb. v. mehreren Innsbrucker Historikern. Festschrift zu Oswald Redlichs achtzigstem Lebensjahr 1938/1939*, 159–200. Innsbruck: Universitätsverlag Wagner.

Stolz O. 1998. *Geschichte der Verwaltung Tirols. Teilstück des 2. Bandes der Geschichte des Landes Tirol* [= Forschungen zur Rechts- und Kulturgeschichte, 13]. Für den Druck bearbeitet von D. Thaler. Mit einem Werkeverzeichnis von Otto Stolz, erstellt von F. Dörrer. Innsbruck: Universitätsverlag Wagner.

Van Zanden J.L., Zuijderduijn J., and de Moor T. 2012. "Small is beautiful. The Efficiency of Credit Markets in the late medieval Holland." In *European Review of Economic History* 16:3–22.

Violante C. 1962. "Les prêts sur gage foncier dans la vie économique et social de Milan au XI siècle." In *Cahiers de civilisation médiévale* 5: 147–168, 437–459.

Voltelini H. von (ed.) 1899. *Die Südtiroler Notariatsimbreviaturen des dreizehnten Jahrhunderts. Part 1. Mit der Benutzung der Abschriften Josef Durigs* [= Acta Tirolensia 2]. Innsbruck: Universitätsverlag Wagner.

Voltelini H. von 1904. "Die ältesten Pfandleihbanken und Lombarden-Privilegien Tirols." In *Beiträge zur Rechtsgeschichte Tirols: Festschrift,* edited by A. von Wretschko, 1–70. Innsbruck: Universitätsverlag Wagner.

Voltelini H. von and Huter F. (eds.) 1951. *Die Südtiroler Notariatsimbreviaturen des dreizehnten Jahrhunderts. Part 2* [= Acta Tirolensia 4]. Innsbruck: Universitätsverlag Wagner.

Wopfner H. 1995. *Bergbauernbuch: von Arbeit und Leben des Tiroler Bergbauern. Vol. 2: Kultur, Gemeinwesen und Niedergang* [= Tiroler Wirtschaftsstudien, 48]. Innsbruck: Universitätsverlag Wagner.

Wopfner H. 1997. *Bergbauernbuch: von Arbeit und Leben des Tiroler Bergbauern. Vol. 3: Wirtschaftliches Leben* [= Schlern-Schriften, 298]. Innsbruck: Universitätsverlag Wagner.

Zingerle I. and Egger J. (eds.) 1888. *Tirolische Weistümer. vol. 4, part 1: Burggrafenamt und Etschland.* Wien: Wilhelm Braumüller.

Zuijderduijn J. 2009. *Medieval Capital Markets. Markets for Renten. State Formation and private Investment in Holland (1300–1550)* [= Global Economic History Series 2]. Leiden and Boston: Brill.

Zuijderduijn J. and de Moor T. 2013. "Spending, saving, or investing? Risk management in Sixteenth-century Dutch households." In *Economic History Review* 66 no. 1: 38–56.

Picture Credits

Fig. 1 Map designed by S. Nicolussi-Köhler with the QGIS application.
Fig. 2 Figure designed by S. Nicolussi-Köhler.
Fig. 3 Figure designed by S. Nicolussi-Köhler.

CREDIT NETWORKS BETWEEN CITY AND COUNTRYSIDE IN LATE MEDIEVAL LUCCA

So Nakaya

Abstract: This paper considers small-scale credit relationships formed by the physician Maestro Iacopo di Coluccino Bonavia da Lucca to rural clients in late medieval Tuscany, especially the commune of Lucca, in the late fourteenth and early fifteenth centuries. His memorandum sheds light on informal credit practices that occurred amongst ordinary people and which were embedded in the context of their socio-economic relationships. Iacopo's lending activities, particularly those extended to his rural clients, coincided with the seasonal cycle of agriculture, frequently taking the form of lending in kind and sale on credit. Such loans were made to parties with whom Iacopo had shared interests, primarily tenant farmers on his rural estates. Yet while these loans had an assistive character in that Iacopo made loans available even to insolvent peasants who had faced repeated crises, he had no qualms taking legal action against those who were able but unwilling to repay. Maestro Iacopo's credit practices constitute part of a dense credit network established between city and countryside, as well as of a substantial sphere of local finance in late medieval Italy.

Keywords: small credit, city and countryside, memorandum, Lucca, Tuscany, Italy

Introduction

"On October 31, 1386, Andrea Pieri from Prato leased from me, Maestro Iacopo, five pieces of land in Santa Maria a Colle, and at the same time borrowed 1 florin and 10 *soldi* for one year. These contracts were drawn up under the notary *ser*

Published in: Stephan Nicolussi-Köhler (Ed.), Change and Transformation of Premodern Credit Markets. The Importance of Small-Scale Credits. Heidelberg: heiBOOKS 2021, 133–156. DOI: https://doi.org/10.11588/heibooks.593.c12693

Conte Puccini in his office". This passage is taken from a *memoriale,* or memorandum, kept by Maestro Iacopo di Coluccino Bonavia, a physician who was active in Lucca in the late fourteenth and early fifteenth centuries,[1] a source that has been much studied for the insights it offers into the activities of medieval physicians.[2] Moreover, in addition to his activities as a physician and apothecary, the memorandum also provides details concerning the large number of daily economic transactions in which he engaged in his capacity as a wealthy citizen, especially with regard to credit that he extended to his clients in cash and kind, as shown in the case of Andrea Pieri.

Entries in Iacopo's memorandum for the year following the above passage note nine loans to Andrea in both cash and kind, including a small loan of 2 *grossetti,* as well as 2 florins for the payment of a fine, 1 florin in lieu of an amount of straw, and two *staio* of wheat for sowing.[3]Even after that, Maestro Iacopo went on to rent a house to Andrea, consign livestock to him to raise, and provide him with five additional loans. That not all of these entries were struck out in the memorandum suggests that Iacopo continued to extend loans to Andrea on top of earlier loans that had not yet been repaid. Between 1389 and 1391, Iacopo took Andrea to court over the non-payment of his debts, and had the court sergeant (*messo*) place a provisional hold on Andrea's property. While the memorandum indicates that Andrea Pieri paid the land rent for 1392, his entry subsequently ends with the annotation "went out (*andosi via*)".

As noted by several recent studies, including those contained in this volume, lending was a vital part of the daily economy of pre-modern society.[4] In the cities of central Italy, the important role of providing consumer credit was initially played by local money changers and foreign pawnbrokers (*prestator*), who were followed in the fourteenth and fifteenth centuries by Jewish moneylenders, and then the Monte di Pietà (public institutional pawnbrokers) after the latter half of the fifteenth century.[5] The many account books left by the Monte, for example, provide a detailed illustration of the practice of small consumer loans in the medieval and early modern periods from the perspective of the pawnbroker's

1 Archivio di Stato di Lucca, *Ospedale di San Luca,* 180 (hereafter *San Luca*), fol. 31r, 45r, 50r. This source has been given editorial treatment by P. P. Calamari, ed. 1966. "Il memoriale di Iacopo di Coluccino Bonavia medico lucchese (1373–1416)". *Studi di filologia italiana. Bollettino annuale dell'accademia della Crusca* 24 (hereafter Calamari): 55–428, in particular 169, 222–224, 240–241.

2 Chiappelli 1921; Lazzareschi 1925; Mancini 1931.

3 Note that one florin was worth approximately 37.5 *grossetti,* which could purchase between three and four *staio* of wheat.

4 Fontaine 2014; Claustre 2013.

5 De Roover 1948; Goldthwaite 2011, 408–483; Muzzarelli 2007.

counter as a moneylending institution.[6] On the other hand, such professional lenders were not the only option available to medieval people; they could also seek loans from ordinary citizens who did not specialise in money lending.[7] The circulation of credit among ordinary people can be examined based on notarial documents.[8] Also, since creditors took their case to the courts when their debtors went into default, we should be able to find insolvent loans by perusing court records.[9] Such sources allow us to observe the credit practices that were diffused through the city and countryside from the official perspective of court clerks and notaries.

In contrast, the memorandum examined in this paper provides a glimpse of microcredit transactions from Iacopo's point of view as a wealthy citizen. Many of these transactions were not executed under notaries, and nor were they pursued in court when the debtors proved insolvent.[10] Furthermore, in addition to money lending, this source also describes details of land leases, livestock leases, and other commercial transactions that Iacopo entered into with borrowers. Considering these will allow us to discuss the social and economic relations between lenders and borrowers in which these credit practices were embedded, which are usually difficult to glean from other types of sources.

This paper considers the informal credit practices in which Iacopo engaged as a wealthy citizen, with a particular focus on his transactions with clients in the countryside. Urban-rural relationships in medieval Italy have elsewhere been studied in terms of the expropriation of rural lands by city residents and the urban migration of rural landowners: processes that were seen as a socio-economic expression of the domination of *contado* by city and city-state formation in the thirteenth and the first half of the fourteenth centuries.[11] It has been shown that the use of rural lands to secure loans by city residents to rural inhabitants led to insolvency among farmers and the accumulation of rural lands among urban citizens. Investment activities such as lending by these citizens to the inhabitants of rural areas has been characterised as avaricious usury, practices that contributed to the subsequent urban domination of the *contado* and a decline in rural autonomy.

---

6 Carboni and Muzzarelli 2008.
7 Carboni and Muzzarelli 2014.
8 Menant and Redon 2004; As for Lucca, Meyer 2000.
9 Smail 2016; Nakaya 2011; Gaulin 1997; Claustre 2006; Briggs ed. 2014, 3–142.
10 For the study of credit practices based on memoranda, see Muzzarelli 2014, 11–26; Claustre 2013.
11 A wealth of studies exists on this topic. For example, La Roncière 1973; Pinto 1982; Menant and Gaulin 1998.

As a city-based physician who provided loans to rural individuals that were secured by land and who acquired land as a result, Iacopo's situation is consistent with the account described above. As discussed below, however, a holistic view of his credit practices based on his own memorandum shows that his lending activities had a variety of features that do not fit the instrumental narrative of predatory land acquisition. Against the backdrop of the Tuscan countryside of the late fourteenth and early fifteenth century—a period of depopulation under a series of wars, famines, and pestilence—we will see how the credit extended by Iacopo constituted a supportive component of the rural peasant economy, nonetheless his relationships with his rural clients were often in crisis.

Credit Given by Maestro Iacopo

Let us begin by summarising an overall picture of the credit extended by Iacopo to each borrower. In total, his credit activities consisted of 957 loans to 176 individuals amounting to 10,485 florins between 1369 and 1411 (Table 1).[12]

Fourteen relatives and servants (*fante*) secured 346 individual loans from Iacopo worth a total of 6,082 florins. In particular, Iacopino (Iacopo's servant from 1383 to 1396) and Piero Brilla (the father of Iacopo's third wife, Giovanna) stand out in terms of the quality and quantity of the loans they received. Iacopino received 216 loans between 1383 and 1396, for a total of 167 florins.[13] Individually, these were usually for a small amount, often less than 1 florin. In contrast, one of Piero's loans amounted to 300 florins of a dowry that he had himself provided for Giovanna, and Iacopo also assumed existing debts on his father-in-law's behalf.[14] Over the 15 years from 1384 to 1398, Piero owed Iacopo a total 5,589 florins in 56 separate loans.

Beyond these two, 12 other members of Iacopo's household and extended family borrowed a total of 326 florins in 74 separate transactions. The cheesemaker Stefano Giuntori[15] and shoemaker Bartolomeo Masini, both listed as kinsmen (*cognato*) to Iacopo,[16] drew loans as large as 30 and 40 florins, while three

12 Maestro Iacopo would actually begin to use this memorandum only in 1373 and the last description was in 1416.

13 *San Luca,* fol. 2r, 11r, 17v, 22v, 25v–26r, 30v, 33v, 34v; Calamari, 68, 98–99, 120–122, 135–136, 146–147, 149–150, 168–169, 178–180, 183–184.

14 *San Luca,* fol. 38r, 52r, 56r–v, 60r; Calamari, 195–196, 249–251, 263–267, 280–281.

15 *San Luca,* fol. 1v, 10v, 29v, 34v–35r, 43v; Calamari, 66, 96–97, 163, 182–185, 217.

16 *San Luca,* fol. 29v, 33v, 37r, 39v, 44r, 64v; Calamari, 163–164, 177–178, 193, 201, 218–219, 295–296.

Table 1 Iacopo's clients

	persons	loans	amount (florins)
Relatives and Servants	14	346	6,082
Iacopino	1	216	167
Piero Brilla	1	56	5,589
Others	12	74	326
City residents	91	195	3,888
Merchants	13	43	2,597
Leading citizens	7	12	616
Medical Doctors	8	13	75
Notaries	8	10	33
Artisans and Shop Owners	23	35	188
Friars and Churchmen	5	17	110
Tenants of Iacopo	11	48	94
Others	16	17	175
Rural residents	71	409	512
Non-farmers	8	10	42
Farmers	63	399	470
Tenant farmers of Iacopo	36	298	330
Farmers leasing livestock from Iacopo	3	21	14
Other farmers	24	80	126
Uncertain	uncertain	7	3
TOTAL	176	957	10,485
TOTAL excluding loans to Piero Brilla and merchants	162	858	2,299

servants, Benedetta, Mante, and Perla, took out 20 small loans, ranging from 4.5 *grossetti* to 2 florins.[17]

Next, let us consider other borrowers by their place of residence, namely those who lived in cities and those who lived in the countryside. The former group, whom we may consider as Iacopo's neighbours, consisted of 91 individuals, who borrowed a total of 3,888 florins in 195 separate cases. Among them, 13 merchants, who traded pepper and textile with Iacopo, owed him a total of 2,597 florins in 43 separate transactions. We also find the seven prominent citizens as the members of the Anziani, the executive council, who in total received 12 loans amounting to 616 florins and numerous items; thus, each of the loans was large.[18] As for other wealthy people, eight notaries took out twelve loans totalling 33 florins, while eight medical colleagues borrowed 75 florins, and philosophy or other texts in 13 separate instances.[19]

23 artisans and shop owners—from weavers (both men and women, *tessitore* and *tessitrice*) to blacksmiths to haberdashers—borrowed a total of 188 florins in 35 transactions. Seven of these loans may be considered high-value (more than 5 florins), including for example 60 florins loaned to the haberdasher Michele Martini Locti[20] and 32 florins to the weavers Michele Leoni and Orso di Michele.[21] Iacopo's father, Coluccino, had been a blacksmith, and it is conceivable that loans extended to other blacksmiths in the early days of Iacopo's lending activities may have been those he took over from his father.[22]

Iacopo also provided credit to friars and churchmen. Two friars from the San Romano, one from San Ponziano, another from the *Ordine dei serviti,* and a priest from the church of San Alessandro borrowed relatively large sums ranging from 2 to 15 florins, totalling 110 florins in 17 separate instances.[23] These men often used books as collateral for their loans.

Eleven city residents who rented houses from Iacopo and one wet nurse approached him for loans, receiving a total of 94 florins in 48 separate transactions.

---

17 The servants also received salaries of between 7 to 8 florins per year. *San Luca,* fol. 42v, 64v, 90r; Calamari, 214, 296, 297, 373.

18 For example, Bartolomeo Angiorelli, a member of the executive council in 1377, 1379, and 1389, with his brother Angioro and Andrea together received 180 florins in 4 separate transactions. *San Luca,* fol. 30v, 32r, 35r, 46r; Calamari, 167, 173, 185, 227.

19 *San Luca,* fol. or, 12r, 30v, 38r, 45v, 61r, 65v, 79v, 81r, 91v; Calamari, 61, 101–102, 168, 195, 225, 286, 300, 349, 367–368.

20 *San Luca,* fol. 47v; Calamari, 231.

21 *San Luca,* fol. 35v; Calamari, 187.

22 *San Luca,* fol. 1r, 3v, 9v–10r, 26r, 49v, 61r; Calamari, 63–64, 74, 94–96, 149–150, 238–239, 286, 355.

23 *San Luca,* fol. 2v, 28r, 30v, 35v–36r, 45v, 66r; Calamari, 70, 73, 159–160, 167, 186–189, 225, 301.

These were individuals with whom Iacopo had a contractual relationship and shared interests.

Another 16 city residents whose occupation and contractual relationship with Iacopo are unclear received a total of 175 florins in 17 separate instances, of which a loan of 100 florins to Guglielmo Tolomei and his wife resulted in this larger amount.[24]

Incidentally, nine of these urban clients were outsiders who were only temporarily resident in Lucca. For example, Iacopo loaned 50 florins to Lodovico d'Agobio, a doctor from Florence, 25 florins to Giovanni Casini, a doctor from Siena, and 3 florins to a man named Arrigo di Francesco from San Gimignano, a town in Tuscany where Iacopo had once stayed.[25]

However, by far the most frequent loans provided by Iacopo were those extended to individuals who lived the countryside around Lucca. Overall, 71 rural inhabitants borrowed a total of 512 florins and other goods in 409 separate transactions. These included three blacksmiths from Compito and Saltocchio, two friars from Altopascio, the abbot of the monastery of S. Salvatore di Sesto in Capannore, a priest from Marlia, and a notary from Montecatini who solicited Iacopo for loans of cash and goods. For the most part, however, most of the other borrowers (63 people) were likely farmers, as no mention was made of their profession or status. The rest of this chapter focuses on the loans provided to these individuals.

Of this group, 36 are identified as tenant farmers who leased lands from Iacopo, three as farmers contracted to raise livestock owned by the doctor, and 24 as rural people with no further information as to their relationship with Iacopo, at least not in the details included in the memorandum. These farmers drew 399 separate loans totalling 470 florins, showing that Iacopo extended a significant number of loans to people in the countryside. These loans were provided in cash in small amounts and in kind, suggesting that a wealthy citizen like Iacopo fulfilled the peasants' daily demand for microcredit. In particular, a disproportionate number of these loans went to tenants leasing land and livestock from Iacopo, amounting to 319 loans totalling 344 florins. Iacopo did not take any collateral for these loans, likely because of the shared financial interest that his tenants had in managing his lands.

Interestingly, surveying the rest of the loans in this category (80 loans to 24 individual farmers) for those whose direct contractual relations are not apparent from the memorandum, many still bear a tangential relationship to Iacopo. This is because of the fact that 14 of these farmers (65 cases) lived in villages where

24 *San Luca*, fol. 34r, 68v; Calamari, 180–181, 309–310.

25 *San Luca*, fol. or, 12r, 45r; Calamari, 61, 101–102, 225.

Iacopo owned lands and thus had some economic interest. Presumably, Iacopo was personally or indirectly acquainted with these villagers. Only 15 loans totalling 16 florins were made to farmers (10 individuals) for whom no clues to their relationship to Iacopo can be confirmed. The relative absence of loans to complete strangers shows that Iacopo could not be counted as a professional money lender, one who would lend money impersonally to anyone offering collateral.

Citizen Iacopo and Rural Villages

Let us now turn our attention to the Lucchese countryside. Like other wealthy citizens, Iacopo, a physician, owned several properties in different villages. While the *Libro Grande* that he would have used for the management of his estates is no longer extant, it is still possible to reconstruct the distribution of his land properties from the entries concerning land sales and leases recorded in his memorandum.

To the west of Lucca, Iacopo owned lands at Santa Maria a Colle, Massarosa, Pieve a Erici, and Stiava. To the north, he had estates in the villages of Palmata, Valgiano, Sant'Ilario, and Ombreglio di Brancoli, located in the mountainous area facing the plain. This was also near Saltocchio, where his father-in-law Piero Brilla had estates on which Iacopo presumably held a mortgage. Furthermore, Iacopo also owned and leased several properties at Lammari, east of Lucca, and at Sorbano, to the southeast (Fig. 1).

Even though some of these estates were inherited from his father, Coluccino, as well as his mother, Iacopo invested in the lands to build up his assets. Those who sold lands to Iacopo are identified first as citizens. For example, between 1376 and 1381, Iacopo acquired from his business partner, Giovanni ser Cambi, also a famous chronicler, several lands and rent rights amounting to 386 florins in Valgiano, Sorbano, Pieve a Erici, and Massarosa, the last being in relation to Giovanni's ancestral lands.[26]

Iacopo also acquired lands from villagers. Instances of this can be confirmed for three cases in Massarosa (one of which was re-acquired by the farmer in question), three cases in Santa Maria a Colle, one case in Lammari, and one case in Sant'Ilario. Land sale agreements between Iacopo and such farmers often included a re-acquisition clause, and when a sale took place, the farmers signed a lease agreement with Iacopo to become tenant farmers. For example, Matheo

---

26 *San Luca,* fol. 15r, 22v, 27r, 31v; Calamari, 110–113, 134–135, 154–155, 171.

Figure 1 Localities of Iacopo's properties.

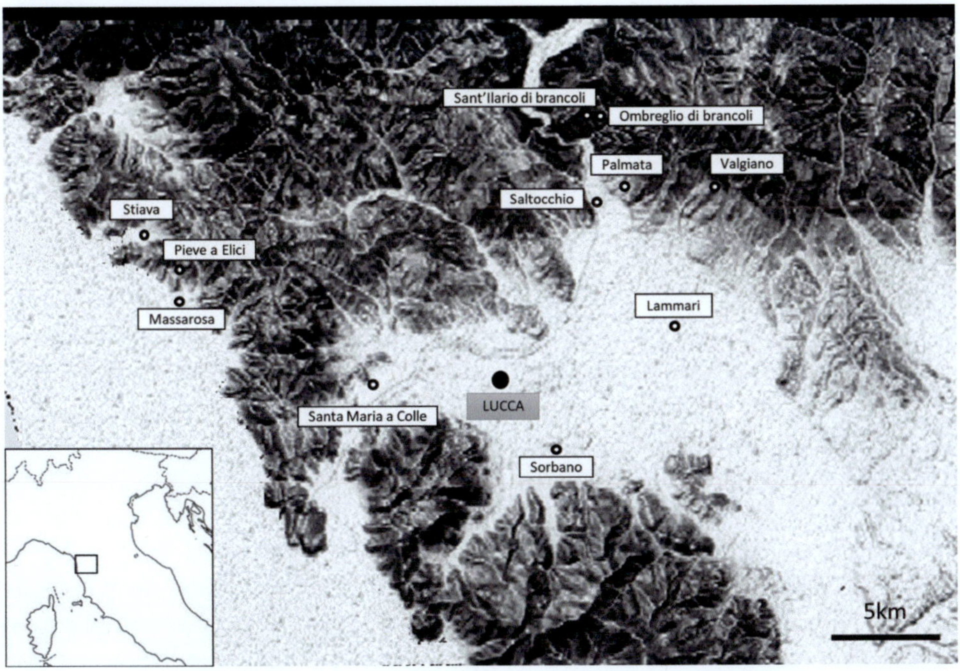

Giovanni, called Taulera, sold a farm with a house in Sant'Ilario di Brancoli to Iacopo on 10 January 1387 for 55 florins, with a provision that if Taulera should ever wish to repurchase the property, he could do so for the same amount, or else for half that price for half the land. On the day of the sale, Taulera leased the farm back from Iacopo and promised to pay the land rent for two *some* of the wine produced by the vineyard.[27] In effect, this amounted to a loan secured by land, which previous studies have pointed out as the means by which citizens acquired rural lands. In Iacopo's case, some farmers were successfully able to buy back the lands they had sold. Giovanni Bondacchi of Massarosa, for example, sold his lands to Iacopo on 20 June 1392 for 14 florins and then paid rent to occupy them until 25 February 1395, when he succeeded in repurchasing them for the same 14 florins.[28] In many other cases, after selling their lands, the previous owners stayed on as tenant farmers. Taulera, above, leased the farm he had sold and continued paying rent until 1410.

27 *San Luca,* fol. 44v; Calamari, 220–221

28 *San Luca,* fol. 58v; Calamari, 271–272.

What influence did Iacopo wield on the farmers in the villages where he owned lands? To answer this question, we will consider the *Estimo,* cadastral surveys undertaken to determine tax obligations, using the case of Massarosa, where Iacopo held comparatively larger estates than elsewhere.

The *Estimo* of Massarosa for 1386 lists 74 householders managing lands or other immovable property.[29] Of these, eight individuals bore some relation to Iacopo. Examining their holdings, we find firstly those farmers who were significant landowners, such as Ceccho Moni, who although he leased a piece of land from Iacopo with an assessed tax value of 36 *lire* 5 *soldi* in 1385, held 32 properties worth 424 *lire* 8 *soldi,* of which 23 (worth 261 *lire* 8 *soldi*) were his own property.[30] Giovanni Lemmi, who although not one of Iacopo's tenants was nevertheless indebted to him for four loans totalling 8 florins, managed 41 properties with a taxable valuation of 501 *lire* 10 *soldi,* with the share from properties that he owned in his own right amounting to 430 *lire* 10 *soldi.*[31]

In contrast, others were peasants owning little to no lands of their own. Petrus Chellini, called Zuccha, leased a piece of land from Iacopo with a taxable valuation of 16 *lire* 10 *soldi.* In total, he managed 13 pieces of land worth a total of 78 *lire,* none of which were his own property.[32] Giovanni Bondacchi, the farmer we saw above who sold and eventually repurchased his land also managed 16 estates, worth 170 *lire* 7 *soldi,* but no land of his own, at least as of 1387.[33]

Between these upper and lower village strata stood the brothers Lippo and Giovanni Damaschucci. The former managed 19 pieces of land worth 322 *lire* 9 *soldi,* of which he owned estates amounting to 64 *lire* 18 *soldi.* Among his leased properties was a farm (*podere*) with vineyards and olive groves, which had the relatively high assessed tax value of 120 *lire.*[34] Giovanni managed 17 properties with an assessed tax value of 175 *lire* 11 *soldi,* of which he owned four properties worth 22 *lire* 2 *soldi.* Four plots that he managed, worth 24 *lire,* were properties that he leased from Iacopo.[35]

The trend of the impoverishment of the countryside and the subordination of rural inhabitants to urban landowners is undoubtedly evident not only in the case of Iacopo's land acquisition but also by instances where the annotation "*propria*" in the margin of each land entry, indicating a farmer's ownership of his own property, has been struck out to be replaced by the name of an urban landowner.

29 Archivio di Stato di Lucca, *Estimo,* 95.
30 *Estimo,* 95, fol. 56r–57v.
31 *Estimo,* 95, fol. 33r–35r.
32 *Estimo,* 95, fol. 30r–v.
33 *Estimo,* 95, fol. 67r–v.
34 *Estimo,* 95, fol. 80r–81r.
35 *Estimo,* 95, fol. 62r–v.

Nevertheless, we can see that Iacopo's relationships with villagers in Massarosa spanned a diverse range of social classes, ranging from farmers who owned considerable estates to those who had no property of their own.

It is also apparent from the *Estimo* that Iacopo did not hold much influence in this village. Beyond the fact that Iacopo was only involved with 8 of 74 households, his properties did not necessarily account for a major interest among the landowners, even his tenant farmers. With the exception of Lippo Damaschucci, who leased a vineyard and olive farm from Iacopo that exceeded a third of the assessed tax value of the lands he managed, other farmers in Massarosa leased only a small percentage of their total holdings from Iacopo. Petrus Chellini, called Zuccha, leased from Iacopo about 20 per cent of the total land he managed (in terms of assessed tax value), a share that was 14 per cent for Giovanni Damaschucci, 8 per cent for Checco Monis, and only 2 per cent for Bartholomeus Puccini. Apart from their own properties, they also leased lands from other urban citizens, wealthy rural people, including notaries, and ecclesiastical institutions. For example, Lippo Damaschucci, in addition to his own lands and the farm he leased from Iacopo, also leased nine properties from *ser* Iacopo, a notary of Massarosa, three properties from a citizen Micuccio Cosci, and one property from the Lucchese cathedral chapter.

Peasants also leased lands from multiple landowners from different places, much in the way that Iacopo owned properties in multiple villages and leased various properties in a single village to multiple farmers. Unlike Florence and Siena, where farmers would often lease large integrated farms (*podere*) from individual landowners with whom they had an exclusive relationship, the structure of dispersed land ownership and the dispersal of patron-client relationships seen here was peculiar to the Lucchese region, and is evident from at least the twelfth century into the sixteenth century.[36] For the farmers of Massarosa, a village where Iacopo had a larger land investment than elsewhere, Iacopo was still only one landowner among many, and his influence was limited accordingly. Conversely, as we have seen, as one of many such patrons, even Iacopo was frequently called upon by villagers for loans.

36 Cherubini 1991; Wickham 1998, 136–137; Polica 1980; for the sixteenth century, Berengo 1965, 301–320.

Rural Credit and Materiality

How was Maestro Iacopo used by rural villagers as a provider of credit? They seem to have travelled to the city to secure loans. Such travel was not unusual, as a case study of Catalonia has shown.[37] From the following case, we can presume that Iacopo usually dispersed loans at his home or his place of business (*bottega*). On 17 June 1395, Iacopo arranged a loan of 20 *grossetti* to Giovanni Nucchi, a peasant from Valgiano, when "I was eating in the hall (*Io a desnare in sala*)."[38] Otherwise, as in the case of notarised credit agreements, Iacopo might disperse loans at a notary's office (*apotheca*),[39] or else at the house of colleagues such as Giovanni ser Cambi and Bartolomeo prete Vanni, an apothecary dealing in medical herbs.[40]

One reason why rural villagers travelled to the city was to discharge the monetary obligation, as seen in the case of Andrea Pieri, described at the start of this paper, who needed money to pay a fine.[41] Even so, the main reason for loans would be to purchase goods that were only available in Lucca, which served as a market hub for the surrounding countryside. For example, Marchesina, the wife of Paganuccio Giuntori of Lammari, borrowed 30 *grossetti* from Iacopo, which she said she would use to buy a pig.[42] Puccinello Francucci of Matraia received 8 *grossetti*, purportedly to buy shoes.[43]

The memorandum also shows that rural villagers often borrowed from Iacopo goods in kind (50 instances) or bought them on credit (88 instances). For example, between 1390 and 1393, Iacopo loaned Lippo Damaschucci of Massarosa a billhook (*pennato*) worth 6 *grossetti*, a bag (*sacco*) valued at 12 *grossetti*, as well as wheat, wine, and barrels. He also purchased 20 *grossetti* worth of cloth (*panno*) from

---

37 Soldevila Temporal 2014.

38 *San Luca*, fol. 49r; Calamari, 237.

39 For example, on 9 September 1385, Iacopo drew up land lease contracts and a loan agreement worth 3 florins with Giovanni Damaschucci under *ser* Conte Puccini in his apotheca, with Giovanni ser Cambi and Lippo, a priest of church of San Paulo as witnesses. *San Luca*, fol. 42r; Calamari, 210–211.

40 For example, on 14 November 1385, Gianni Parelli of Valgiano and his son signed a lease contract with Iacopo and borrowed 4 florins under *ser* Conte Puccini. These contracts were stipulated in the apotheca of Bartolomeo di prete Vanni, where Iacopo worked that same year. *San Luca*, fol. 41v, 43r; Calamari, 209–210, 214–215.

41 *San Luca*, fol. 45r; Calamari, 222: "tem prestaili a dì iii dicembre in 1388 fiorini ii in grossi 72, pagoe la condepnagione sua".

42 *San Luca*, fol. 5r; Calamari, 79: "Item prestaili a dì xvii aprile libre iiii et *soldi* x portòli Marchesuccia dice che volea comprare uno porco et funno grossetti xxx".

43 *San Luca*, fol. 8v; Calamari, 90: "Item ebbe a dì xxvi settembre grossetti viii dice volea comprare scarpe".

Francesco Berindelli's store, which he charged to Iacopo on credit.[44] Between 1394 and 1399, Piero della Vigna of Saltocchio, a tenant of Iacopo's father-in-law Piero Brilla (to whom Iacopo had extended credit on several occasions) also received wheat, wine, salt, and cups from Iacopo, as well as a sickle (*falce*) that he purchased from another after arranging for Iacopo to make the payment.[45]

Examining the goods that rural villagers got from Iacopo and others, it is immediately apparent that most are farm implements, such as sickles (*falce*), a billhook (*pennato*), hoes (*marella*), secateurs (*potatoio*), wooden tubs (*bigongia*), barrels (*botte*), a vat (*tino*), and bags (*sacco*). Iacopo, who inherited his father's blacksmith workshop, was able to lend such tools and ironware (e.g. *ferri sottigliati*) to villagers, or else to sell them on credit, especially in the early years of his activities.

Villagers who came to his *bottega* also obtained everyday items that Iacopo likely kept in stock at his *bottega*, such as a large pot (*paiolo*), a cup (*bicchiere*), shoes (*scarpe*), clogs (*soccoli*), and cloths (*panno*). Such transactions were sometimes described only in simple terms, as for example how Puccinello Fancucci of Matraia received 6.5 *soldi* for the "things in the shop" (*cose alla bottega*).[46] As the memorandum recorded only the transaction and repayment obligations, and since shop sales would have been recorded in a *Libro di Bottega*, no longer extant but referred to in the memorandum as being kept by Iacopo, there were undoubtedly other items that villagers who visited his shop acquired from Iacopo in the form of direct sales.[47]

Farmers were also provided with livestock such as a pig (*porco*), turtledoves (*tortora*), and a donkey (*ascina*). Bartolomeo Pardini of Massarosa, for example, arranged to purchase black-haired livestock from Iacopo as beasts of burden (*somiera*) at the end of a six-year lease, leaving 3 florins as the balance, which became a financial loan agreement under a notarial contract.[48]

---

44 *San Luca*, fol. 41r; Calamari, 207–208: "Item a dì iii ottobre in 1390 stetti per lui a Francesco Berindelli per i canna di panno albagio grossetti xx": "Item per i pennato del mese di gennaio 1392 grossetti vi": "Item a dì xi dicembre in 1393 per i sacco da oglio disse grossi xii".

45 *San Luca*, fol. 61r, 65v, 70v; Calamari, 286–287, 298–301, 317–318: "Item de dare lo ss.to Piero a dì xiiii giugno 1399, li comprai una falce da Iohanni Cettini, grossetti vi".

46 *San Luca*, fol. 6v; Calamari, 86: "Item ebbe per cose alla bottecha contòsi a me *soldi* vi 1/2."

47 Claustre has noted how credit was regularly generated from shop transactions in Paris, Claustre 2013, 576–582.

48 *San Luca*, fol. 18r; Calamari, 123: "Bartholomeo Pardini ss.to da Massaglogia mi de dare per carta facta da ser Conte Puccini a dì xxii gennaio in 1383 fiorini tre d'oro di qui a

Iacopo also provided villagers with wheat (*grano*) and other grains, as well as foodstuffs, including flour (*farina*), cheese (*formaggio*), wine, olive oil, salt, and likely also turtledoves and pigs for slaughter. Wheat was not only used for food but also for sowing. Bino, a peasant of Santa Maria a Colle, borrowed three *staio* of wheat in February 1394, two in June 1395, three more "for sowing" in October 1395.[49] Seed wheat was lent to the rural farmers in at least nine other cases, always during the sowing season in October or November, as also seen in the case of Andrea Pieri.

Loans to farmers corresponded to the seasonal cycle, as evident from the need for seed grain in autumn. Repayment dates were also linked to the harvest, often during the autumn grape harvest. Pasquino of Saltocchio, who borrowed 2 florins in July 1401, attested that he would repay it the following October.[50] Bontuccoro, from the same village, took out a loan of 24 *grossetti* in September 1394 that he promised to repay in October.[51] Bartolomeo Pardini, mentioned above, was to repay the balance of 3 florins for the livestock by the first day of the following November.[52]

Farmers often repaid cash loans with crops. Iacopo often received olive oil in January or February, wheat and grain between July and September, and wine in October or November. For example, Giovanni Nucchi, called Pentola, a peasant of Valgiano, who had borrowed 4 florins and 10 *grossetti* from November 1389, repaid Iacopo in October 1391 with 4.5 *some* of wine, which was equivalent in value to the borrowed sum, on top of the wine with which he made land rent payment.[53] The following October, he repaid a total of 5 florins borrowed over three loans, again with wine in addition to his land rent payment, which was also paid in wine. Thus, Iacopo took delivery of a considerable amount of agricultural production, in addition to land rent paid in kind. Such products were certainly more than Iacopo

---

kalende novembre proximo che viene, li quali denari mi rimase a dare per lo resto delle somiere ch'elli comproe da me." This contract can also be found in the notarial register, Archivio di Stato di Lucca, *Archivio dei Notari*, 187, fol. 13r.

49 *San Luca*, fol. 58r; Calamari, 269–270: "Item li prestai a dì xxv octobre in 1395 per seminatura grano staia iii".

50 *San Luca*, fol. 78v; Calamari, 342: "Prestai contanti a Pasquino da Saltocchio lo quale tiene et oe allogato lo podere nostro da Rabboli, fiorini due. Demeli rendere per tutto octobre che viene prossimamente".

51 *San Luca*, fol. 61r; Calamari, 286–287: "sale a dì xxvi settembre in 1394 a Bontuccoro da Saltocchio, demeli dare per tucto octobre che viene."

52 See note 47.

53 *San Luca*, fol. 49r; Calamari, 237: "Ebbi dal predicto Pentola di vendemmia del mese d'octobre del 1391 some di vino iiii 1/2 oltra l'affícto che mi diede contaimelo fiorini iiii grosetti x, et cosi sono pagato da lui et elli da me infine a qui."

would have been able to consume himself, and would easily have been sold for cash as market commodities.

Assistive Credit

Credit given in the form of small unsecured loans, mainly of goods, given in accordance with the agricultural cycle, would have been beneficial and essential for peasants who had exhausted any reserves until the next harvest. For his own part, however, it is doubtful that Iacopo expected significant economic benefits from such loans to rural villagers. The actual profits obtained from lending are unclear because Iacopo's memorandum does not provide details of the interest he charged. He earned a great deal as a physician, as a merchant, and as a landowner,[54] this last being a capacity that gave a particular significance to the loans he provided to his tenants. Namely, his lending had an assistive character for peasants, enabling them to make steady payments on their land rent.

As in the case of Andrea Pieri, many peasants received loans when they became Iacopo's tenants upon the signing of a lease contract. This means that Iacopo financed the initial costs that tenant farmers would normally accrue when beginning to farm a new property. For example, when Boncino Tuci began farming a vineyard at Palmata that had fallen into disuse, with its vines untied, Iacopo provided him with a loan of 4 florins so that he would work on the farm and maintain it well.[55] Providing a supply of seed wheat likewise gave assistance to farmers who shared interests with Iacopo in operating a successful farm.

Iacopo extended loans to his tenants on terms that compared favourably with what he offered other villagers, a distinction that is most evident in the setting of repayment dates. In a few cases, particularly loans arranged under a notary, Iacopo's memorandum contains notes about repayment deadlines. Loans to non-tenants had relatively short repayment periods. For example, Matteo Giuntini of Moriano, who borrowed 4 florins, and Giovanni Lemmi of Massarosa, who borrowed 5, both promised repayment within three months.[56] Giovanni Andriotti of

---

54 For example, Iacopo's annual income from medical activities often ranged between 300 and 500 florins, with approximately 100 more florins per year from commercial activities undertaken in partnership with Giovanni ser Cambi (from 1379 to 1383). *San Luca,* fol. 0v, 27v; Calamari, 62–63, 155.

55 *San Luca,* fol. 60r; Calamari, 280: "prestai contanti fiorini iiii a Boncino predicto perché lavorasse et ben conciasse il predicto podere".

56 *San Luca,* fol. 10r, 27r; Calamari, 94, 153.

Saltocchio agreed to repay a loan of 1 florin obtained within three weeks.[57] Bontuccorso and Piero della Vigna, also both of Saltocchio, were required to attest that they would repay loans of 24 *grossetti* and 1 florin, respectively, within a month.[58]

In contrast, Iacopo allowed his tenants a comparatively relaxed repayment period. We can find 12 loans, ranging in substance from 1 florin to 15 florins, with specified repayment dates. Of these, one was set to be repaid within three months, three within six months, and two within eight or nine months, while six others allowed terms of more than a year. For example, Iacopo gave Cettone Guido of Pieve a Erici two years to repay a loan of 2 florins and Giuntoro Parducci, called Giuntasso, five years to repay 4 florins.[59]

The favourable terms on loans that Iacopo extended to his tenant farmers were no doubt beneficial to borrowers, and we certainly find instances of those who both paid their land rent and repaid all debts they owed in cash and kind. For example, the entries in Iacopo's memorandum for the 21 loans taken out by Petro Chellini of Massarosa, called Zuccha, were all struck out, indicating that the debt had been cleared.[60] According to the *Estimo,* Zuccha did not own any land in his own right, and his holdings were small, with an assessed tax value of 81 *lire.*[61] As one of Zuccha's landlords, Iacopo's loans would have cushioned the peasant's farming activities enough and enabled him to pay his land rent and repay every loan.

Even so, peasant debts to Iacopo usually ended in arrears, or default. Examining the rates of loan repayment, we find that loans to villagers were repaid in only 58 per cent of cases (236/409 cases). By comparison, the clearance rate for loans to relatives was 75 per cent (259/346 cases), while that of urban residents was 93 per cent (181/195 cases). The overall repayment rate for Iacopo's tenant farmers was only 50 per cent (149/298 cases).

When Iacopo gave loans to his tenants, he undoubtedly did so with the empirical knowledge that they might not be repaid. Andrea Pieri received a loan of 1 florin and 18 *grossetti* when he leased property from Iacopo in 1386 and went on to receive an additional fourteen loans until 1391, none of which were struck out, and so presumably remained in default. Another example is the case of Matteo Giovanni of Sant'Ilario, called Taulera, who leased a vineyard from Iacopo in 1373.[62] While he was able to repay thirteen loans that he took out until 1387, he

57 *San Luca,* fol. 61r; Calamari, 283.
58 *San Luca,* fol. 61r; Calamari, 286–287.
59 *San Luca,* fol. 23v, 31r; Calamari, 140, 170.
60 *San Luca,* fol. 19r; Calamari, 125–126.
61 *Estimo,* 95, fol. 30r–v.
62 *San Luca,* fol. 4v, 44v, 46v, 67v, 68r; Calamari, 76–77, 219–222, 228–229, 304–309.

was unable to repay loans taken out after August 1388. Even during this period of insolvency, Iacopo extended five more loans until 1403 and renewed his lease contract in 1397. Taulera continued to pay land rent until 1410, albeit with occasional delays. During this period, Taulera was placed under a *bannum* as a criminal in 1398, and then captured and imprisoned by the *capitano del popolo* ("Captain of the People"), an officer of the law. Although his fine was as high as 20 florins, Iacopo arranged to loan Taulera the necessary funds, helping to free him from prison and return him to the farm.

Iacopo's motivations and intentions when extending loans varied in each case, and it is surely possible that there was an element of usury when lending money at interest to his commercial counterparts and other wealthy citizens. However, in the second half of the fourteenth century, when the working population was low after the ravages of plague, Iacopo's loans to the tenant farmers who worked his rural properties, at least, appear to have been less interested in profit than in helping his tenants remain sufficiently productive to be able to pay their rent. Such support by landowners was a daily necessity for farmers, and it must be remembered that rural farmers would have had several patrons, and thus been able to receive such loans from other landowners, city-based as well as local. In fact, when Taulera sold his land to Iacopo in January 1387, 20 of the 55 florins from the sale were paid to Giovanni Barettani, an urban citizen, and a further 18 florins to the weaver Luca Pellegrini, indicating that Taulera had also been indebted to those two men.[63] Furthermore, Iacopo sometimes consolidated his tenant's debt by repaying their loans to others on their behalf. For example, in October 1390, Iacopo paid debts that Lippo Damaschucci had incurred with Francesco Berindelli for coarse cloth to the amount of 20 *grossetti* and 20 *bolognini*.[64] Six months later, Iacopo also promised to cover a debt that Lippo owed to Bartolomeo del Grinta for 1 florin.[65]

Insolvency and Legal Action

As we saw above, many of Iacopo's loans to his tenants were never struck from the memorandum. Their presumed insolvency can be linked to the deterioration of conditions in Lucca and the surrounding territory in the late fourteenth and early fifteenth centuries. In Tuscany throughout the fourteenth century, famine,

---

63 *San Luca*, fol. 44v; Calamari, 220.
64 *San Luca*, fol. 41r; Calamari, 207–208.
65 *San Luca*, fol. 41r; Calamari, 208.

war, and pestilence, including the Black Death, tormented the countryside, and Lucca's situation proved a burden for villagers in its territory, especially after the 1380s. Agricultural production declined significantly due to the major plagues that occurred in 1383–84, 1390, 1399–1400, frequent invasions into Lucca's territory by the Pisan army, and terrible weather in the 1390s.[66] These catastrophes compounded the already tenuous economic situation of Iacopo's tenants, and left them unable to pay back their loans or keep up with their rents. An examination of the repayment of loans by Iacopo's tenants in different periods shows that the rate of repayment declined steadily from 96 per cent in the 1370s (25/26 cases) to 59 per cent in the 1380s (48/82 cases), to 47 per cent in the 1390s (63/133 cases), and 23 per cent in the 1400s (13/57 cases).

In addition to deteriorated circumstances, other possible reasons for tenants to fail to repay their debts include the relative premium on agricultural labour brought on by the devastation of the rural population in the second half of the fourteenth century, as well as increased mobility among the people. Leverotti has shown how many agricultural workers from other cities' territories were drawn to Lucca by virtue of the government's tax exemption policy, which sought to compensate for the declining population. For example, in the 1411–13 survey, 392 of 1874 households in the Lucchese territory were listed as having come from elsewhere.[67] Likewise, about a quarter of Iacopo's tenants (9 of 35) were outsiders. In Santa Maria a Colle, Iacopo leased lands to five peasants, including Andrea Pieri, who came from Prato, and Filippo di Simone, called Mancino, who came from San Miniato.[68] In Palmata and Fogliano, all of Iacopo's tenants were from other territories. In Palmata, Boncino Tuci hailed from Monte Rappoli in the Florentine territory, Giovanni Nardi from Asciano in the Sienese territory, Giovanni di Piero from Brescia, whilst Andrea and Ciullo, who worked in Fogliano, came from the Florentine states.[69] Also, Angioro, who leased lands in Pieve a Erici, was from Capua near Naples, while Antonio came from Genova and worked in Ombreglio.[70]

It is interesting to note here that with the exception of Ciullo in Fogliano, all those who came from other urban territories remained delinquent on their loans. This is all the more striking given that 11 of the 26 native peasants did repay their loans. For example, Iacopo's tenants in Massarosa, who we examined based on the Estimo, were all native to their village. Many, in fact, owned land, and were thus

66 Leverotti 1992, 76–86.

67 Leverotti 1992, 86–97. As for the foreigners in communal Italy, Forestieri e stranieri nelle città basso-medievali. Atti del Seminario Internazionale di Studio Bagno a Ripoli (Firenze), 4–8 giugno 1984, Florencefirneze 1988.

68 San Luca, fol. 31r, 45r, 50r, 58r; Calamari, 169, 222–224, 240–241, 268–269.

69 San Luca, fol. 60r–v, 80r; Calamari, 280–284, 348.

70 San Luca, fol. 24v, 47v–48r, 79r–v; Calamari, 143, 231–233, 344–347.

deeply rooted in their community, which conceivably provided them with different aid networks they could call on beyond Iacopo. In contrast, workers who had arrived from other territories did not own land, and their position was thus more likely to be socio-economically unstable. Citizens like Iacopo would have had little choice but to lease lands to such people in such precarious situations, and to forgo collateral when loaning them money with which to improve their farms. It is against this background that the widespread instances of delinquent loans in the late fourteenth century can be understood.

What steps, if any, did Iacopo take against such defaulters? As noted above, Iacopo's motivation when providing loans was likely to improve and secure the potential for the steady payment of rental income from his properties. Accordingly, as long as the land rent was paid, Iacopo was patient with loans that fell into arrears, and would even make new loans to secure his tenants' cash flow. But when tenants stopped paying their land rent, he did not hesitate to take legal action. The memorandum lists seven cases in which Iacopo took defaulters to court, all of whom were tenants. The case of Giuntoro Parducci, called Giuntasso, offers a characteristic example. Giuntasso leased a plot of land in Santa Maria a Colle from Iacopo in October 1376, contracting to make an annual rent payment of eight *staio* of wheat, which he continued to pay, while also receiving loans, until he renewed the lease contract in July 1381. At the time of renewal, he obtained a loan of 4 florins to be repaid within a five-year term. At the same time, he was also required to pay outstanding rent of five *staio* within the year. From the entries in the memorandum, it seems that Giuntasso might have then failed to make this payment. The lower margin of the entries for the lease and loan contracts contain notations indicating that, on 20 June 1383, Iacopo paid 18 *soldi* to the sergeant of the court of Podestà to seize (*intesire*) Giuntasso's hay, barley, wheat, and paid 9 *soldi* to the rural commune's officials as the cost of holding the assets in custody.[71] Afterwards, Giuntasso managed to resume payment of his land rent and loan obligations with deliveries of his crops to Iacopo until 1390.

Thus, while Iacopo exercised a degree of tolerance with regard to deferring the repayment of loans, he was relatively quick to ask the courts to seize assets when land rent payments became delinquent. This alacrity would have been his means of attempting to secure repayment ahead of other possible creditors to whom his tenant was indebted. Legal action does not seem to have been decisive enough to sever the relationship, and was in common use to force compliance from farmers who may have been reluctant to pay loans and land rents that had come due. As we saw in the case of Giuntasso, it was not uncommon for peasants to resume

71 *San Luca*, fol. 31r; Calamari, 170.

payment after such judicial action. Taulera, whose situation we examined in the previous section, also had his house seized after Iacopo brought a formal complaint before the court in June 1396 due to delinquency on loans and land rent, and he, too, subsequently resumed paying his land rent. Andrea Pieri, after falling into arrears on loans and land rent, had his movables seized in November 1391, or earlier, but had resumed paying land rent with wine by 1392.

Those against whom Iacopo was able to bring suits and arrange seizures of property were those farmers who, at the time of legal action at least, would have had some assets but were nonetheless reluctant to pay. Taulera owned a house that was mortgaged. Masseo Dominici of Santa Maria a Colle, who sold properties to Iacopo in 1391, 1395, 1396, and who became Iacopo's tenant, was seized by the court sergeant for claims brought against him by Iacopo in 1401 and 1402. Assets seized from Masseo in June 1401 included 40 *staio* of wheat, nine barrels (*botte*), and three vats (*tino*), with a wagon (*carro*) of wine seized in October of the same year, along with another 18 *staio* of wheat and 12.5 *staio* of millet.[72] This suggests that Masseo could have paid his debts, but had elected not to.

Iacopo had to cover the costs of the court himself when he appealed to the court to make the seizure. Therefore, in cases where he assumed that the court sergeant would find no goods to seize in a tenant's house or, even find the farm abandoned, Iacopo would not bother to sue. This is presumably why only seven of those whose payments became delinquent were seized, of the total of 35 farmers whose debts remained unpaid in the record. Some peasants were able to repay their loans in the beginning, only to become insolvent later, especially after the turn of the fifteenth century. These defaulters were those who had nothing with which to pay, or else who had abandoned Iacopo's properties to flee elsewhere. Such an eventuality was more likely to occur with especially those from other territories. Angioro from Capua, who leased land in Pieve a Erici, made some wine payments after having his assets seized, leaving 8 *grossetti* as the balance of the payment, but there is no further record of him after August 1393, and in fact, his name is not listed in the *Estimo* for the years 1394–96.[73] Also, as mentioned at the

---

72 *San Luca,* fol. 51v, 71v; Calamari, 245–248, 322–323. For example *intesimento* in June 1401: "Feci richiamo et intesimento del grano che è in sulle terre mie contra lo ss.to Masseo, et delle infrascritte massaritie etc., a dì 10 giugno 1401 per a dì 18 giugno per Nanni Bartolo messo, testimonio Masseo dicto Magnano, acomandate le cose intesite a Iohanni Andrucci officiale del dicto comune credo di Sancta Maria a Colle, notaio a la corte ser Raffaello; in somma di staia xxxx di grano lo quale è in sulle terre miei et sopra altre terre, item botti viiii di tenere carra iii in tucto, item tina iii di tenere carra iii".

73 *Estimo,* 70.

beginning, Andrea Pieri from Prato was explicitly noted to have fled (*andosi via*) following his payment of land rent in 1392.[74]

Conclusion

The ubiquity of credit and debts incurred in cash and kind between ordinary (i.e., non-professional) people in late medieval Europe has been suggested based on notarial documents and court records. However, Maestro Iacopo's *memoriale* shows us that many small loans were extended without the official involvement of notaries or court clerks, suggesting that these officially documented loans were just the tip of the iceberg. Out of the vast number of loans that presumably took place, this paper has focused on credit relationships that were formed in the network between city and countryside in the fourteenth and fifteenth centuries.

Previous studies have considered credit extended by urban citizens to farmers in the countryside as a strategic means of land acquisition that contributed to the decline of the rural society and economy and the formation of centralised city states. Indeed, Iacopo was one such citizen, making loans to rural farmers that were secured with their lands and then acquiring these properties when his debtors fell into insolvency. Nevertheless, Iacopo's memorandum also documents a considerable number of smaller loans, the greater part of which were *not* secured with lands, and were extended without the official preparation of notarial contracts. These loans were often assistive, based on shared interests between lender and borrower, and collaborative relations between landowners and farmers. Iacopo provided loans to cover the initial costs incurred when his tenants would begin to manage his properties. He also provided seed wheat, paid off their debts to others on their behalf, covered fines to prevent incarceration, deferred repayment until the next harvest, and offered additional loans even when repayment was not immediately forthcoming. These loans would be repaid in the form of land rents as the farmers became more profitable.

Such was not always the case, of course. Among the delinquent cases, if farmers who were defaulting on rent were rooted into local social networks and had some ability to repay, loans and arrears in rental payments could be recovered forcibly by arranging the seizure of assets through the city court. However, Iacopo faced more difficulty recovering his loans from those who came from other territories. Without any strong local ties or ability to draw on other sources of

74 *San Luca,* fol. 50r; Calamari, 241.

credit, it was relatively easy for them to take flight and seek other patrons. In such cases, Iacopo bargained with the peasants, appeasing them with loans on generous terms so that they would be remain incentivised to earn revenue from the land. This was one aspect of the small credit relationships connecting city and countryside in the late fourteenth and early fifteenth centuries, when the rural labour population had fallen into decline and become more mobile, and when famines and plagues were frequent.

Iacopo's credit activities were far from exceptional. Many other citizens also extended loans to tenant farmers as frequently as Iacopo, often more so. Rural producers also created a safety net for themselves by forming credit ties with multiple urban patrons. This was seen in the case of Massarosa, where Iacopo's tenants also leased lands from other landowners, in the case of Taulera, whose money from the sale of land to Iacopo was immediately used to pay off two of his creditors, and in the example of Iacopo's practice of consolidating his tenants' debts to other creditors by paying their debts on their behalf. This physician's notebook offers a glimpse of the myriad relationships within the dense credit network established between urban and rural areas on the basis of personal and mutual interests, as well as of the dynamic movement of credit in the movement of goods and money.

References

Archival References

Archivio di Stato di Lucca, *Archivio dei Notari,* 187.
Estimo: Archivio di Stato di Lucca, *Estimo,* 70, 95
San Luca: Archivio di Stato di Lucca, *Ospedale di San Luca,* 180.

Bibliographic References

Berengo M. 1965. *Nobili e mercanti nella Lucca del Cinquecento.* Turin: Einaudi.
Briggs C. (ed.) 2014. "Law courts, contracts and rural society in Europe 1200–1600". *Continuity and Change* 29, no. 1: 3–18.
Calamari P.P. (ed.) 1966. "Il memoriale di Iacopo di Coluccino Bonavia medico lucchese (1373–1416)". In *Studi di filologia italiana. Bollettino annuale dell'accademia della Crusca* 24, 55–428.

Carboni M. and M. G. Muzzarelli, eds. 2008. *I conti dei Monti. Teoria e pratica amministrativa nei Monti di Pietà fra Medioevo ed Età Moderna.* Venice: Marsilio.

Carboni M. and M. G. Muzzarelli, eds. 2014. *Reti di credito. Circuiti informali, impropri, nascosti (secoli XIII–XIX).* Bologna: Il Mulino.

Cherubini G. 1991. *Scritti toscani. L'urbanesimo e la mezzadria.* Florence: Salimbeni.

Chiappelli A. 1921. "Maestro Iacopo di Coluccino da Lucca medico ed il Giornale delle sue ricordanze (1364–1402)". *Rivista di Storia delle scienze mediche e naturali* 12: 121–133.

Claustre J. 2013. "Vivre à crédit dans une ville sans banque (Paris, XIVe–XVe siècle)". *Le Moyen Age* 109: 567–596.

Claustre J. (ed.) 2006. *La dette et le juge. Juridiction gracieuse et juridiction contentieuse du XIIIe au XVe siècle (France, Italie, Espagne, Angleterre, Empire).* Paris: Publications de la Sorbonne.

La Roncière C.-M. de 1973. *Un changeur florentin du Trecento, Lippo di Fede del Sega (vers 1290–vers 1362).* Paris: Ecole pratique des hautes etudes.

De Roover R. 1948. *Money, Banking and Credit in Medieval Bruges. Italian Merchant-Bankers, Lombards, and Money-Changers. A Study in the Origins of Banking.* Cambridge: Medieval Academy of America.

Fontaine L. 2014. *The Moral Economy. Poverty, Credit, and Trust in Early Modern Europe.* Cambridge: Cambridge University Press.

Forestieri e stranieri nelle città basso-medievali. Atti del Seminario Internazionale di Studio Bagno a Ripoli (Firenze), 4–8 giugno 1984, Florence 1988.

Gaulin J.-L. (ed.) 1997. "Le bannissement pour dettes à Bologne au XIIIe siècle" *Mélanges de l'Ecole française de Rome. Moyen-Age* 109, no. 2: 477–567.

Goldthwaite, R. A. 2011. *The Economy of Renaissance Florence.* Baltimore: Johns Hopkins University Press.

Lazzareschi E. 1925. "Le ricchezze di due medici lucchesi della Rinascenza". *Rivista di scenze mediche e naturali* 16: 12–139.

Leverotti F. 1992. *Popolazione, famiglie, insediamento: le Sei Miglia lucchesi nel XIV e XV secolo.* Pisa: Pacini.

Smail D. L. 2016. *Legal Plunder. Households and Debt Collection in Late Medieval Europe.* Harvard: Harvard University Press

Mancini A. 1931. "Il libro memoriale di medico Iacopo. Medico lucchese del Trecento". *Atti della reale accademia lucchese di scienze, lettere ed arti,* nuova serie I: 97–121.

Menant F. and J.-L. Gaulin 1998. “Crédit rural et endettement paysan dans l’Italie communale” In *Endettement Paysan and Crédit rural dans l’Europe médiévale et moderne,* edited by M. Berthe, 35–67. Toulouse: Presses universitaires du Midi.

Menant F. and O. Redon, (eds.) 2004, *Notaires et crédit dans l’Occident méditerranéen médiéval.* Rome: École française de Rome.

Meyer A. 2000, *Felix et inclitus notarius. Studien zum italienischen Notariat vom 7. bis zum 13. Jahrhundert.* Tübingen: De Gruyter.

Muzzarelli M. G. 2014. “Per ussire de affanno”: il credito informale, improprio, nascosto”. In *Reti di credito. Circuiti informali, impropri, nascosti (secoli XIII–XIX),* edited by M. Carboni, M. G. Muzzarelli, 11–26. Bologna: Il Mulino.

Muzzarelli M. G. 2007. “I banchi ebraici, il Monte Pio e i mercati del denaro a Bologna tra XIII e XVI secolo”. In Bologna nel medioevo [= Storia di Bologna 2], edited by O. Capitani, 977–1016. Bologna: Bononia University Press.

Nakaya S. 2011. “La giustizia civile a Lucca nella prima metà del XIV secolo”. *Archivio storico italiano* 630, no. 4: 635–678.

Pinto G. 1982: “Aspetti dell’indebitamento e della crisi della proprietà contadina” In *La Toscana nel tardo Medioevo. Ambiente, economia rurale, società,* edited by G. Pinto, 207–223. Florence: Sansoni.

Polica S. 1980. “An Attempted “Reconversion” of Wealth in XVth Century Lucca: the Lands of Michele di Giovanni Guinigi”, *Journal of European Economic History* 9, no. 3: 655–707.

Soldevila Temporal X. 2014. “Rural courts, notaries and credit in the county of Empúries, 1290–1348”. *Continuity and Change* 29, no. 1: 83–114.

Wickham C. 1998. *Community and Clientele in Twelfth-century Tuscany. The Origins of the Rural Commune in the Plain of Lucca.* Oxford: Oxford University Press.

Picture Credits

Fig. 1: Map created by So Nakaya.

WEBS OF CREDIT AND USES OF CIVIL JUSTICE

The Case of 15th-Century Basel

Benjamin Hitz

Abstract: This article discusses the contribution that quantitative methods such as network analysis and spatial analysis can make to the study of late medieval credit relations. Using the example of a civil court in Basel, the so-called *Schultheissengericht,* questions of access to justice as well as its use, network structures and the influence of various attributes are presented. The study is based on two samples of court records in the middle and at the end of the fifteenth century. On a further level, reflections will be made on the possibilities of presenting the results of quantitative and spatial analyses. The article describes asymmetries in the access to court and in the ways defaulted credit is negotiated in court, and discusses the topographies of debt within the city of Basel and in its hinterland.

Keywords: credit, network analysis, civil justice, use of justice, Basel

Introduction

The ubiquity of credit in premodern societies has become a commonplace observation, in long-distance trade as well as in local urban economy.[1] Credit in local settings was generally less formalised and consequently harder to observe;

1 As Daniel Lord Smail has put it, "For medieval historians, the matter is settled: credit was everywhere." (Smail 2016, 90). With regard to urban economy, see for example Schuster 2008; Schuster 2014; Signori 2015; Gilomen 2007; Gilomen 2011; Gilomen 2014; Gilomen 2018.

Published in: Stephan Nicolussi-Köhler (Ed.), Change and Transformation of Premodern Credit Markets. The Importance of Small-Scale Credits. Heidelberg: heiBOOKS 2021, 157–191. DOI: https://doi.org/10.11588/heibooks.593.c12694

quite often only disputed debts that have been the subject of legal proceedings left traces one can analyse today. This paper presents the main results of my research project on credit networks and the use of urban civil justice in late medieval Basel.[2] It covers three areas of interest. First, the people involved: Who used courts and what kind of procedure? What constellations of people could be observed? How did individual cases connect with others, thus creating network structures? The second perspective is one of court usage: What was the role of the court as an offer to litigate over credit? How did the court staff perform their function as arbitrators of conflicts? The last area of interest is the characteristics of credit as a relationship. Was credit merely an economic relation or was there more behind it, in concrete terms a social relation? What indications of long-lasting economic relationships do we have? What can be said about the moment when a transaction or a chain of transactions turn into credit?

My project tried to answer these questions with a combination of qualitative and quantitative approaches, the focus here being more on the quantitative analysis, in particular network analysis.[3] Credit relations have been described and analysed as networks,[4] stating that credit was based on networks and created networks at the same time.[5] Formal network analyses, however, were only carried out on 19th century credit relations.[6] Studies on premodern credit quite generally use the term *network*, but mostly in a metaphoric way.[7] Thus, formal network analysis of medieval credit economy remains a desideratum.[8]

---

2 The research was conducted as a habilitation project; the manuscript titled "Ein Netz von Schulden. Schuldbeziehungen und Gerichtsnutzung im spätmittelalterlichen Basel" contains more details on the methodology and literature used.

3 For an overview of historical network analysis, see Bixler 2015; Düring, Eumann and Stark 2016; Düring and Stark 2011; Graham, Milligan and Weingart 2016; Lemercier 2012; Nitschke 2016.

4 A selection of literature: Bolton 2011; Chilosi, Schulze and Volckart 2016; Clemens 2008; Von Doosselaere 2009; Gestrich and Stark 2015; Lipp 2007; Reupke and Stark 2015; Stark 2015; Vogel 2015; Wirtz 2010.

5 Crowston 2013, 12.

6 For examples, see Stark 2015; Reupke and Stark 2015; Vogel 2015. The statement is also based on a review of the collaborative bibliography on Zotero called "Historical Network Analysis", https://www.zotero.org/groups/209983/historical_network_research (accessed on 10 February 2021).

7 Most prominently Muldrew 1998a, for ex. 95. To the metaphoric use of the term *network*, Ruggiu 2009, 73; Burkhardt 2014, 13; Düring and Kerschbaumer 2016, 31; Bixler 2015, 54.

8 Lipp 2007, 27.

Credit or Debt?

From a modern point of view, the terms *credit* and *debt* do not necessarily mean the same thing. The corresponding German terms[9] suggest a distinction between a more contractual (*credit*) and a less restricted form (*debt*). But this distinction is rather hazy—especially since the use of legal procedures could serve as a means to actually formalise debts.[10] While the German *Schuld* opens the semantic field of guilt,[11] the English and French term *credit* has a second meaning besides the material aspect, namely the dimension of a person's reputation that went beyond the knowledge about the person's financial situation.[12] Craig Muldrew claims that the two dimensions of the term could not be separated in premodern societies; thus, credit and reputation were in constant circulation.[13] The sources of the civil justice in the city of Basel use mainly the term *debt* (*schuld sein*) to describe all sorts of situations of indebtedness.[14] Aspects of reputation and trust are nonetheless present in these sources, as some examples show.[15] While the sources do not distinguish forms of credit or debt by the use of specified expressions, it is still necessary to contextualise the choice of wording in this paper. In light of these considerations, I decided to use the term *credit.*[16] It stands here for all sorts of situations where one person owes something—money, things, or work force—to another person. Credit is generally measured in terms of monetary value and always involves time as a crucial factor.[17]

The credit relations examined in this paper are quite manifold—but in general, the credit only appears in the records after a longer preliminary period, only when the debtor failed to pay his due. Mostly, the court records do not mention how the credit first came into existence. One type of source can help out here. Testimonies recorded in court for the use as evidence in lawsuits tell stories from the perspective of people present in various transactions. In my study, I examined such stories in detail. Here, it seems necessary at least to note that actual moneylending was relatively rare compared to the numerous sales of consumer and pro-

---

9 *Kredit* and *Schuld.*

10 Reifner 2015, 380–382.

11 As does the French *dette,* see Fontaine 2008a, 19.

12 Crowston 2011, 11; Fontaine 2008a, 20.

13 Muldrew 2008b, 75.

14 This is similar to the situation in France as described by Claustre 2014, 39.

15 StABS, Gerichtsarchiv D 6, fol. 93v; StABS, Gerichtsarchiv D 6, fol, 62v.

16 In German, I prefer *Schuld/Schulden.*

17 See the definition of *dette* by Claustre 2014, 37–38.

duction goods. In such situations, sale transactions turned into credit where the creditor was not always willing to extend credit.[18]

Sources and Approaches

The records of the court in question comprise about 160 volumes, a mass of sources that can never be handled by any research project, let alone by one person alone.[19] Thus, I decided to work with two samples of one year each, namely 1455 and 1497 AD. The samples were chosen for their proximity to tax rolls which allowed to identify many individuals and obtain additional data on their wealth, address within Basel, and profession.[20] For each sample, I coded approximately 900 credit relations, further split up into various court procedures.

The data of these two samples can cover two areas of research. The first mentioned here is the use of the courts, where data on wealth, place of origin, and sex can help to describe a differentiated use of the court and the procedures it offered as one means of collecting debts. The second area is of course credit itself. One has to consider, though, that only a minor part of all credits were negotiated in court. Only if the debtor failed to pay back and if the creditor subsequently chose to go to court (among other options) was a trace of the debt handed down. It is impossible to know what proportion of the total volume of credit these court records represent, but probably it was only a small part.[21] For a credit-based economy to function, a sufficiently large proportion of credits should be paid back more or less on time, and given the social embeddedness of credit,[22] other, less escalating ways of debt recollection were probably quite common. The object of my research is therefore not credit in general but conflictual credit brought to court—an observation that ties the two aspects together.

---

18 Smail 2003, 144–145.

19 Hagemann 1987, 6; Signori 2015, 20; see more generally about the problem of the mass of serial sources Piant 2007.

20 See Schönberg 1879, 594–689; Degler-Spengler 1974. Localisation was only possible for the 1497 sample and the (larger) part of Basel south of the Rhine river. I am very thankful to my colleague Andreas Gehringer for digitising and georeferencing the 1497 tax roll.

21 Gilomen 2011, 122, compared a list of about 200 debtors to a deceased merchant in Basel with the debt recognitions in the court records of the era and found only one coincidence. See Muldrew 1998a, 117 and 178, for some speculations as to the proportion of "desparate debts" and the total number of credit transactions in an early modern English town. Muldrew estimates the proportion of credit transactions reaches up to 90 per cent, with 5 to 7 per cent credit failures.

22 Crowston 2011, 15.

This paper not only presents results from a quantitative analysis but it tries at the same time to evaluate the possibilities of representation. The data I collected is relational (ties of credit between individuals), georeferenced (villages and cities outside Basel for both samples, address-level in Basel for the 1497 sample), and contains attributes like sex and wealth (for those individuals identified on a tax roll) as well as information about the type of court procedure. For each hypothesis in the two domains of research mentioned above, I propose the analysis and representation that in my opinion suits the data best—in the sense that they allow a solid reflection on the hypotheses I made.[23] This paper thus contains a selection of the most speaking graphs, tables, and maps that resulted from my research project on the networks of credit in late medieval Basel. It is important to note here that a beautiful image does not represent a result of research in itself. In the process of research, I created many more visual representations which will never appear in a publication—but even the discarded visualisations were of great help for formulating questions and enhancing the design of my research.[24]

Using Civil Justice

The so-called *Schultheissengericht*[25] where cases of credit were negotiated was a lay court. A number of well-to-do citizens formed a jury, the role of the judge was limited to conducting the trial. Jurors only received a minor attendance fee, but profited from the high prestige of the function—many of them ended up in high political positions. The court offered various procedures of debt recollection. The most accessible option consisted of the recording of debt recognitions. If the debtor agreed, the entry in the court book was free of charge. Seizures were a bit more conflictual. The court records distinguish two forms. Seizures of movables were nearly as frequent as debt recognitions and quite widely used, seizures of real estate were used more restrictedly, mainly for failure to pay interest on annuities or feudal duties. Seizures were to be confirmed by the creditor on three occasions, only after the last time could the goods actually be sold. The most conflict-prone form were the actual lawsuits, where the debtor tried to worm out of

23 Cf. Düring and Kerschbaumer 2016, 36–37.

24 To the role of visualisations in the domain of historical network research see Eumann 2016, 127; Reupke and Volk 2013, 310; Düring and Kerschbaumer 2016, 43; Bixler 2015, 61.

25 Hagemann 1987, 18-68; Signori 2015.

any obligation to pay immediately. The different forms of procedures were recorded in particular series of codices.[26]

Differentiated Access to Justice

At a first glance, the *Schultheissengericht* was easily accessible. It convened locally on a nearly daily basis, and costs of procedures were comparatively low.[27] And indeed, one can find people from all social strata, men and women, from poor domestic servants to rich patricians! But the quantitative analysis of the samples allows for a more differentiated perspective. The comparison of the number of households for each category of wealth to the number of people actually represented in court records shows that not all people could make use of the court in the same ways (see Figure 1). The richer the people, the larger the proportion of people found in court. The data for the 1497 sample are a bit less distinctive, due to the fact that only three categories of wealth could be formed. But the overall tendency is the same. Considering that the jury was formed by the (future) political elite of the city, it can be argued that the court was above all an institution for the economic and social elite, populated by the elite.

A second characteristic to analyse is sex. Approximately 15 per cent of all people found in the court records were women. They appear a bit more frequently in the role of a creditor. But this percentage misrepresents the role of women in the credit economy. When real estate served as a collateral and was threatened with seizure, women were often involved without being mentioned. Property deeds regularly mention the buyer's or seller's wife, though often without a name.[28] Joint liability probably existed in many cases where only men appeared in court. When a husband was absent, on the other hand, their wives could step in and negotiate the couple's or the husband's debts in court.[29] Among the women

26 For example StABS, Gerichtsarchiv A (*Urteilsbücher,* i.e. verdicts); StABS, Gerichtsarchiv C (*Vergichtbücher,* i.e. debt recognitions); StABS, Gerichtsarchiv E (*Frönungen und Verbote,* i.e. seizures).

27 Hagemann 1987, 104–105. Unfortunately, the exact cost of a procedure cannot be evaluated. The court seemed relatively inexpensive in comparison with the ecclesiastical courts (see Albert 1998, 77 and 85).

28 StABS, Gerichtsarchiv B (the so-called *Fertigungsbücher* recorded property deeds). The number of mentions is quite high in the 1455 sample and somewhat lower in the later sample. But at this time, a new legislation had been imposed, according to which real estate was generally common property of husband and wife (Signori 2015, 71).

29 StABS, Gerichtsarchiv C 6, fol. 37v; StABS, Gerichtsarchiv C 16, fol. 47v; see also Fontaine 2008a, 150–151.

Figure 1 Participation in court procedures according to wealth category, 1455 sample.

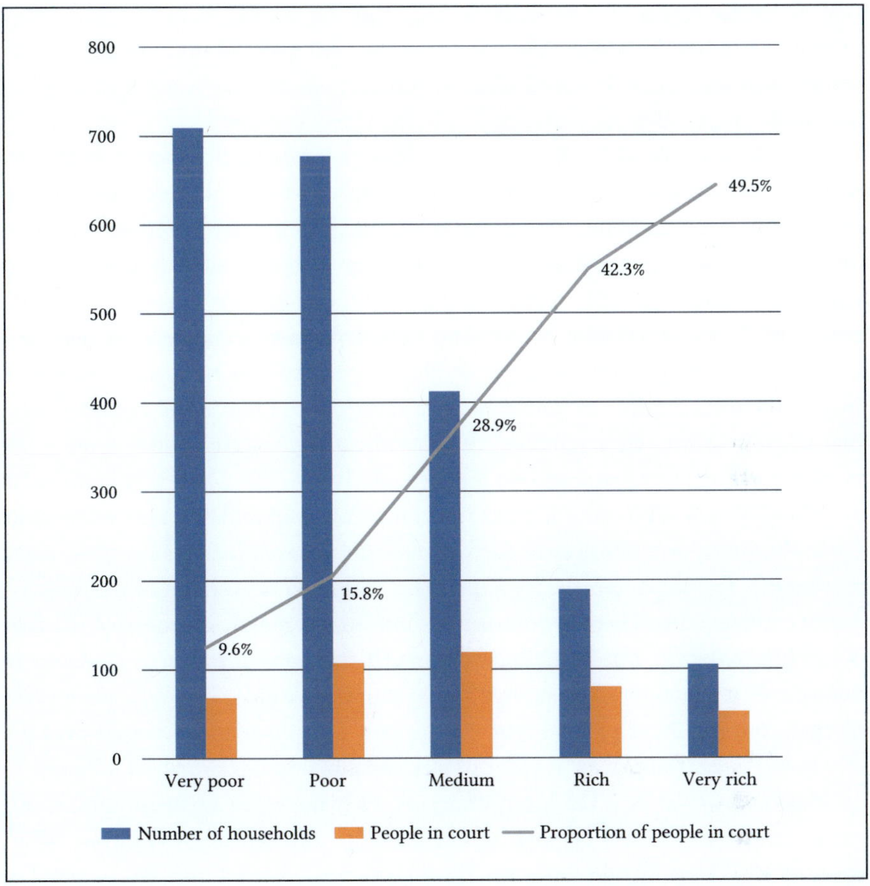

who appeared in court, widows were well represented. They could pursue their affairs without legal representation.[30] But not all cases of the use of justice by women could be explained by such particular circumstances. In many situations, women could go to court just like men. Thus, I would describe the difference between sexes as a quantitative rather than a qualitative matter. To obtain a better understanding of the underrepresentation of women in the court records, the pro-

30 I will not go into detail here as the impact of the obligation to be represented legally is highly unclear (see for Basel Hagemann 1987, 144; Gilomen 2014, 117; Signori 1999). It seems to me that there was a considerable gap between quite rigid norms and manifold ways of handling representation in practice (see Schneider 2000).

portions mentioned above can be compared to the proportion of households in the tax rolls that have female heads of household. For both samples, the proportion of female heads of household is higher in the tax roll than the proportion of female users of justice. As has been observed with regard to criminal justice,[31] women had less access to civil justice. Court records, therefore, seem to be a bad means to measure female participation in the urban economy.

The 1497 data allows for the analysis of the geographical distribution in the city of Basel. When looking at categories like wealth and sex, I did consider the actual role in court in detail. Certainly, it did make a decisive difference whether one was in the role of a debtor or creditor. For the geographical analysis presented here, I take that difference into account. In order to represent the participation in justice as a debtor or creditor, I divided the city map into squares and calculated the proportion of people in court in one role or the other in comparison to the total number of households in the square. Figure 2 and Figure 3 show that while creditors were much more concentrated in the city centre around the market place, debtors are scattered more regularly over the whole city, with some peripheral places with quite high proportions (coloured red), but also many debtors in the city centre. This result corroborates the observations made above, since it is known for Basel that the wealthy were mainly concentrated in the centre.[32] And it confirms that it is their role as a creditor that is mostly responsible for their over-representation. But how can we interpret this concentration of creditors in the centre? Knowing that economic transactions took place in public places like markets, but also in private houses, we can now imagine people from all over the city going to central places in order to buy consumer goods or obtain a loan.

How can we know if the interpretations we make based on geographical representations are valid? I claimed in the introduction that representations often serve as a base for further analysis. This was the case here: I used the concept of spatial autocorrelation (LISA),[33] which detects patterns of geographical structures that have similar values for a variable (here the proportion of creditors). Each grid square with a significant result is assigned to one of four possible categories and coloured accordingly (see Figure 4). Bright red stands for squares with a high proportion with similar neighbours, faint red for squares with a high proportion but with different neighbours. Bright blue stands for low proportion and similar neighbours, and faint blue finally for low proportion and different neighbours. The result confirms mainly the strong concentration in the city centre, while the low proportion in the periphery is less distinct. The same analysis for debtors is

31 Burghartz 1991.
32 Simon-Muscheid 1988, 199.
33 The concept goes back to Anselin 1995.

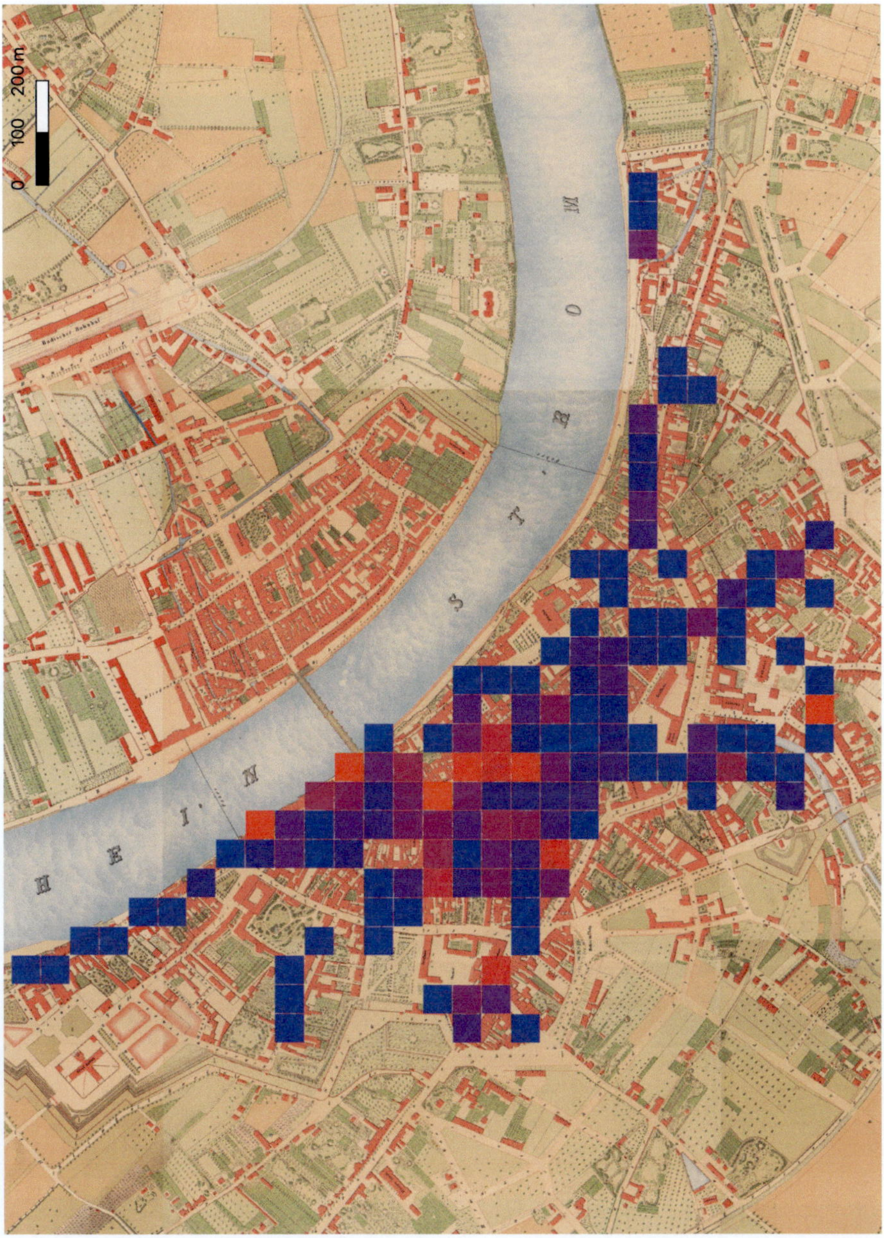

Figure 2 Densities of participation in credit relations as a creditor (the redder the square, the more frequent the participation as a creditor), 1497 sample.

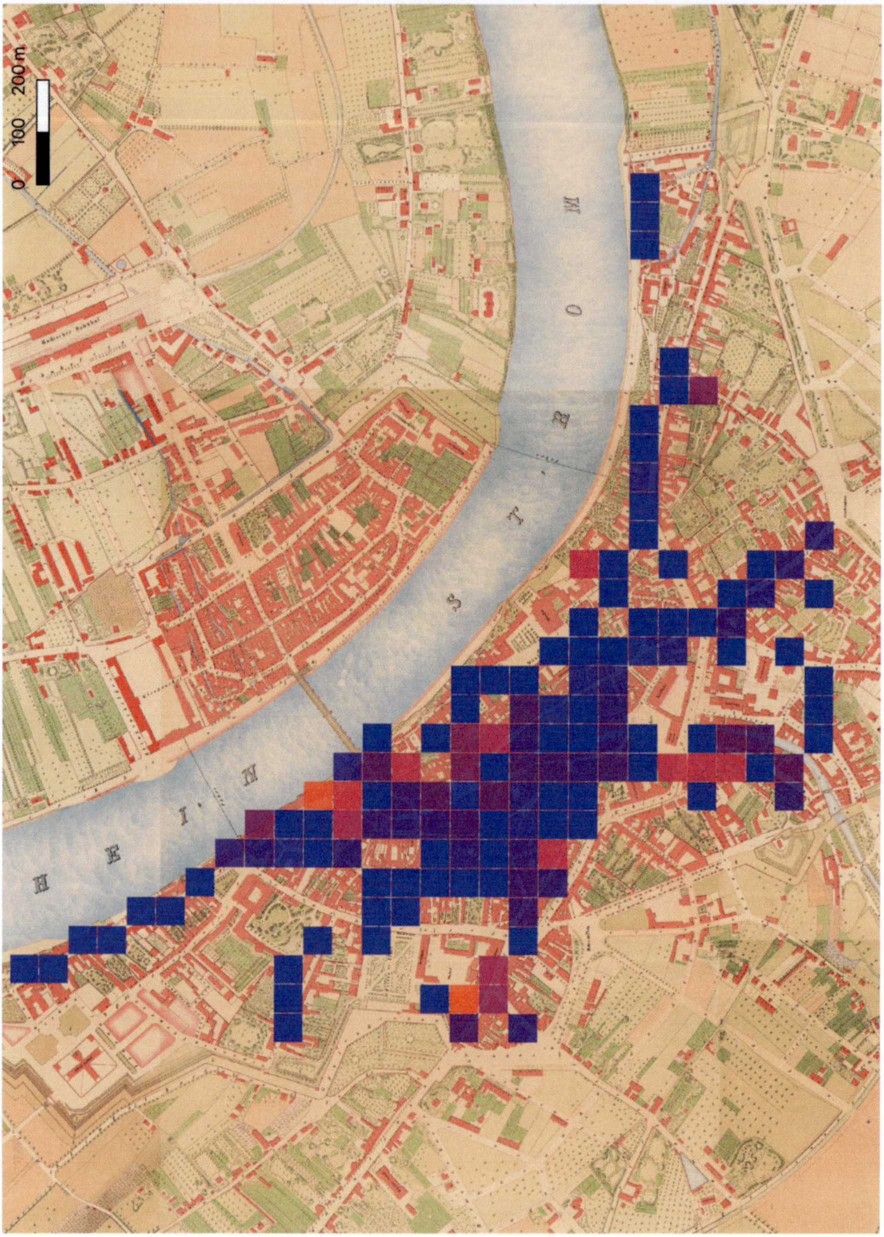

Figure 3 Densities of participation in credit relations as debtor (the redder the square, the more frequent the participation as a debtor), 1497 sample.

Figure 4 Spatial autocorrelation (LISA), squares with significant patterns of autocorrelation. The chart shows a massive concentration of frequent creditors in the city centre.

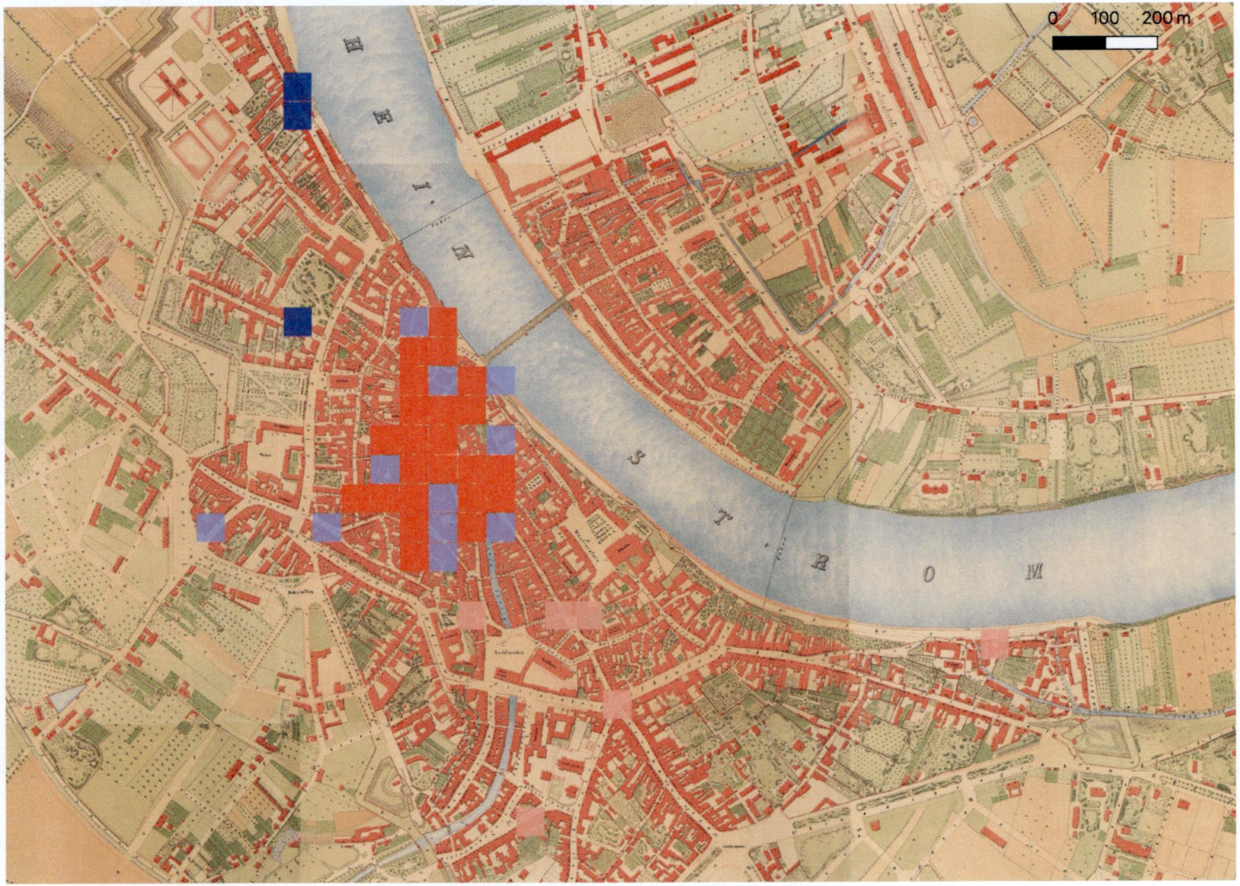

less clear and therefore not shown here—but in accordance with the observation of a more regular distribution over the city. In light of this additional analysis, the interpretations made above based on visual observation are confirmed by statistical means.

Apart from the important distinction between the use of justice as a creditor and the much less voluntary apparition in court as a debtor, the use of different court procedures present an interesting object of research. The choice of procedure varied with different aspects, of which I pick two, firstly the sum at stake, and secondly the category of wealth of the people involved. Table 1 shows the mean and median sum at stake for the four most frequent types of procedure in the 1497 sample.[34] The difference between the two indicators of central tendency

Table 1 Mean and median of the amount owed in the 1497 sample.

Procedure	Mean amount	Median Amount	Number of Values	Percentage of cases
Debt recognition	7.6	2.8	190	66.2 %
Seizure of moveable goods	15.1	2.7	124	55.6 %
Seizure of real estate	24.6	3.5	21	58.3 %
Lawsuit	85.2	10.0	55	34.0 %

indicates an unequal distribution. Whatever the procedure, a large number of rather small amounts that lead to a low median value is combined with a few high amounts that are responsible for a higher mean value. The more conflictual the procedure, the higher the difference between mean and median. Only the actual lawsuits involved distinctly higher amounts—although this observation is somewhat put into perspective by the many cases without a known amount of debt. All in all, this is what one would expect—the more money at stake, the higher the willingness to pursue the case against all resistance. By the way, statistical methods indicate that the differences observed were not accidental.[35]

The second observation is that the choice of procedure is not only linked to the sum at stake but also to the wealth of the people involved. Interestingly, the

34 The 1455 sample allows less detailed analyses, since the records mentioned debt amounts less frequently.

35 Both analysis of variance (ANOVA) and mood's median test proved significant at a 5 per cent level.

wealth of the creditor made less difference than the wealth of the debtor. The former had a slightly higher inclination to sue and to use debt recognitions at the expense of seizure when they were richer—the tendency of this is unclear as it combines the most conflictual with the least conflictual procedure. As debtors, on the other hand, rich people were virtually not subject to (voluntary) debt recognitions but to lawsuits (see Figure 5). Surprisingly, seizures of real estate

Figure 5 Frequency of court procedures for wealth categories, 1455 sample.

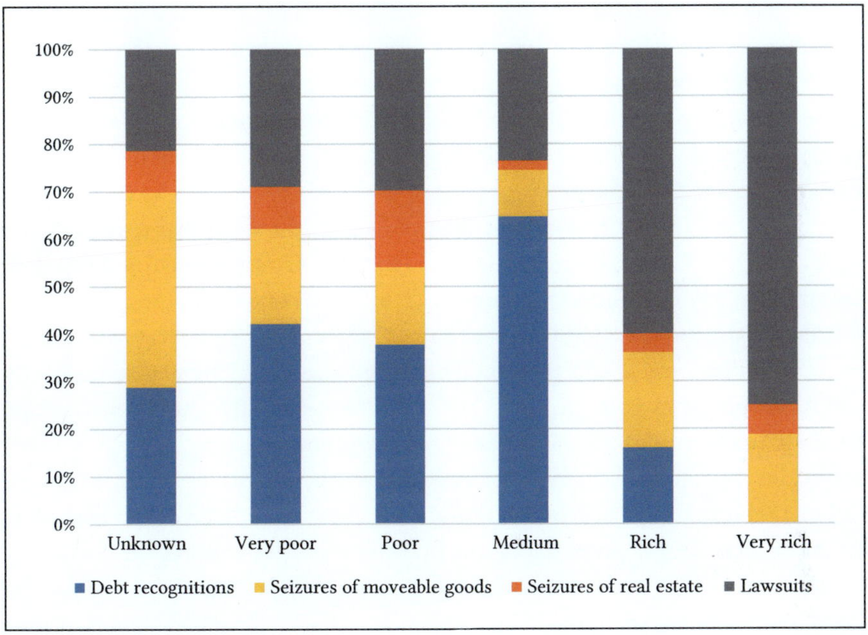

affected the poorer people much more frequently. This indicates that the poorest were probably completely absent (as seen above, richer people were proportionally more involved in justice). While poorer debtors were either subject to the threat of seizure or trying to uphold their obligations by promising to pay back their credits, richer people were involved in more conflictual cases—the omnipresent question for poorer people, if and how they could pay their due, receded behind conflicts over whether there was any debt at all. This observation leads to questions about the role of the court in the urban credit economy of Basel. Therefore, the next chapter tries to describe the court as an institution.

The Court as an Institution

Taking a case of unpaid credit to court certainly meant escalation.[36] As we have seen, the choice of procedure depended on factors like the sum at stake or the wealth of the people involved. Other factors rather prevented people from going to court. In both samples, cases of dispute within families or among neighbours[37] were quite rare. People who were socially close tended to use other means for resolving their conflicts. It was only when all other means had failed that people resorted to the courts. Accordingly, the cases where family or neighbours were involved look like stories of formerly good relations going "bad". The data on usage of justice as well as the relational data discussed below suggest that the court played an important role for all those credit relations that were not based on other, social relations. As a relatively low-threshold service, the court facilitated the extension of credit—in case of default, it gave creditors efficient means to recover debt. But how did this happen?

The analysis of debt recognitions that often took the form of promises of payment speaks in favour of their efficiency. People generally seemed to keep their promise and pay more or less within the given timeframe.[38] The promises of payment often mentioned additional securities. Only a minor and decreasing part of those securities were pawns that could be turned into money immediately. Mostly, people promised to come to town and stay there until the matter was settled (when they were not residents of Basel), or they promised to pay all at once if they missed one instalment (when such a payment was arranged), or simply to pay additional costs arising from the pursuit of their debts. In a majority of cases, thus, creditors were simply given the means to take the case to court again.

Cases of seizure were similar in the sense that the opening of proceedings did not allow direct access to the debtor's property. The creditor had to wait at least six weeks and repeat his claims thrice to obtain permission to actually access the assets. Even so, several judgements show that the debtors could raise objection, forcing the creditor to further proceedings. In the 1455 sample, the clerks noted the three dates regularly in the court book.[39] Implying that the creditor did not reappear when no further dates are noted, I could estimate a (maximum) number of abandoned cases. Only half of the cases contained the three dates—and consid-

36 Smail 2003, 87.

37 Neighbourhood was measured by distance between people in the 1497 sample. As I could not locate people this precisely for the 1455 sample, I looked at cases within one street (the tax roll being grouped by street).

38 Generally, one month, but other arrangements could be made, often giving the debtor more time. See Signori 2015, 138, concerning the efficiency of debt recognitions.

39 StABS, Gerichtsarchiv E 4, fol 5r–22v.

erably more frequently when a dead person's debt was at stake. So while seizures could lead to actual confiscation of goods and public auctions, engaging a procedure mostly forced debtors to negotiate their debts (hence the higher proportion of actual seizures when the debtor was dead—he could no longer negotiate). Taking a case to court did not necessarily mean to bring it to a judgement—rather on the contrary. Actual verdicts were seldom, it seems that the court served as a means of leverage in an attempt to negotiate a solution outside the court.[40]

The entries of the so-called verdicts book (*Urteilsbuch*) show best how the court saw its own role as an arbitrator rather than a judge. One of the most frequent decisions of the court consisted of adjourning cases in order to give the parties time for further negotiations or to produce evidence. The jurors could also simply refuse to decide a case, admonishing the parties to solve their problem otherwise.[41] Sometimes the court would propose possible arbitraries. Such verdicts generally offered to look into the matter again if the arbitration outside the court failed. The court records often mention arbitration, either in verdicts that were necessary because it had failed, or in the series of debt recognitions, where the repayment arrangement was presented as a result of arbitration. Quite often, court clerks were at the origin of such arbitration. The court even went so far as to present their own verdicts as arbitration![42]

All in all, the court tried to prevent conflicts from escalation. The abrupt disappearance of cases from the court records serves as an indicator of a finally successful to and fro between court procedures and out-of-court negotiations.[43] Only a minority of cases dragged on for a long time, forcing the court to utter a final verdict. If one only looked at these exceptional cases, one would have a completely wrong idea of the functioning of the court and the use people made of it. Mostly, people could find arrangements—combining the patience of the creditors with the obligation of the debtor to finally pay, if not with cash, then with their possessions or their work force.

---

40 This is no particularity of Basel, see for example Smail 2003.

41 There are numerous examples in StABS, Gerichtsarchiv A 26; StABS, Gerichtsarchiv A 41.

42 StABS, Gerichtsarchiv A 26, fol. 74r; StABS, Gerichtsarchiv A 26, fol. 83r; StABS, Gerichtsarchiv C 16, fol. 48r.

43 This observation is in line with research on the so-called *infrajudiciaire* (Garnot 1996; Loetz 2000; Piant 2006, 208).

Topography of Credit

Since the proclamation of the so-called *spatial turn*,[44] historians have turned their attention to spatial aspects. The geo-referencing of households in Basel thanks to tax rolls and the identification of villages and towns in the surroundings of Basel allowed spatial analysis of credit relations. In this section, I look at representations of those aspects.

Credit in the Surroundings of Basel

Many of the places from which people came to Basel to negotiate their debts could be identified and thus represented using GIS technology.[45] But what data should be used for such a representation? I very much wanted to avoid showing modern boundaries and transportation like motorways and railways, as would have been the case when using modern, freely accessible maps.[46] There are no contemporary maps of sufficient precision to use with GIS, so I had to combine the data that seemed to make sense myself. I decided to focus on topographic aspects, combing elevation data with waters and forest data.[47] The first are obviously very stable over time, the latter considerably less so, but still useful to identify places with a high level of forest vegetation. To complete the picture, I added larger places—based on current data, as contemporary data is not available in an edited form.[48] Figure 6 and Figure 7 show the area around Basel (represented as a bright blue circle), representing creditors as green and debtors as red dots. The size of the dots indicates the number of credit relations in connection with a place (the green dots are a bit bigger in general, but in the background, allowing better visibility in case there were creditors and debtors at one place).

The representations are quite similar for both samples: the immediate vicinity of Basel shows a dense pattern; more remote regions show less density. The role of debtor predominates, but with increasing distance from Basel, the propor-

---

44 Rau 2013; Schwerhoff 2011, 11.

45 I worked with QGIS, an open source GIS program (https://qgis.org, accessed on 10 February 2021). For the field of historical GIS, see for example Geddes, Gregory 2014; Lilley, Porter 2016.

46 Like for example open street map (https://www.openstreetmap.org, accessed on 10 February 2021).

47 https://data.europa.eu/euodp/data/dataset/data_eu-dem; http://www.naturalearthdata.com/downloads/110m-physical-vectors; https://forest.jrc.ec.europa.eu/en/past-activities/forest-mapping/#Downloadforestmaps (all links accessed on 10 February 2021).

48 www.mapcruzin.com (accessed on 10 February 202).

Figure 6 Geographical distribution of creditors (green) and debtors (red) in the surroundings of Basel, 1455 sample. Larger points mean a larger number of debt relationships and/or persons.

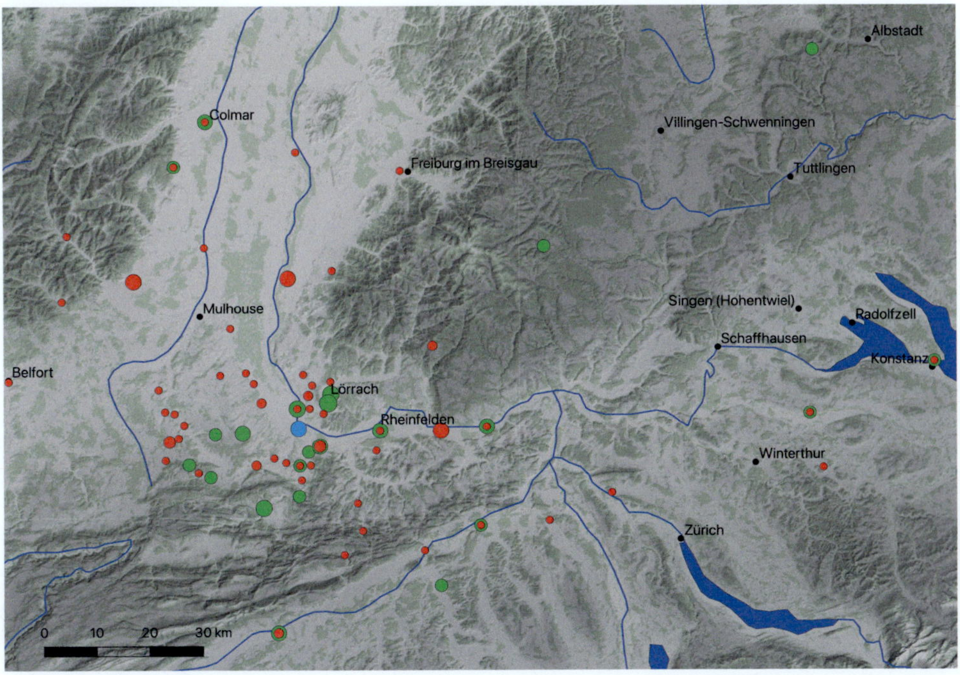

tion of creditors increases—in the more distant regions not represented here, the ratio is even inverted. It seems that not only the roles change with increasing distance but also the distribution over space. To test this hypothesis, I calculated the centres of gravity for the patterns of debtors and creditors. The centre of gravity serves as a kind of average location.[49] One calculation was made only with people within a 40 km radius from Basel; the other calculation included all persons. The result is presented in Figure 8; the centres of gravity for the immediate environment are shown as rhombuses, the others as circles.

The short distance of the diamond symbols from the city of Basel indicates that in the urban hinterland, creditors as well as debtors were found regularly. The less populated, hilly and forested areas north and south of Basel occur less frequently as places of origin, but the effects cancel each other out. In the overall perspective, on the other hand, one can see more marked differences. While the debtors' cen-

49 It is actually calculated as an average of longitude and latitude.

Figure 7 Geographical distribution of creditors (green) and debtors (red) in the surroundings of Basel, 1497 sample. Larger points mean a larger number of debt relationships and/or persons.

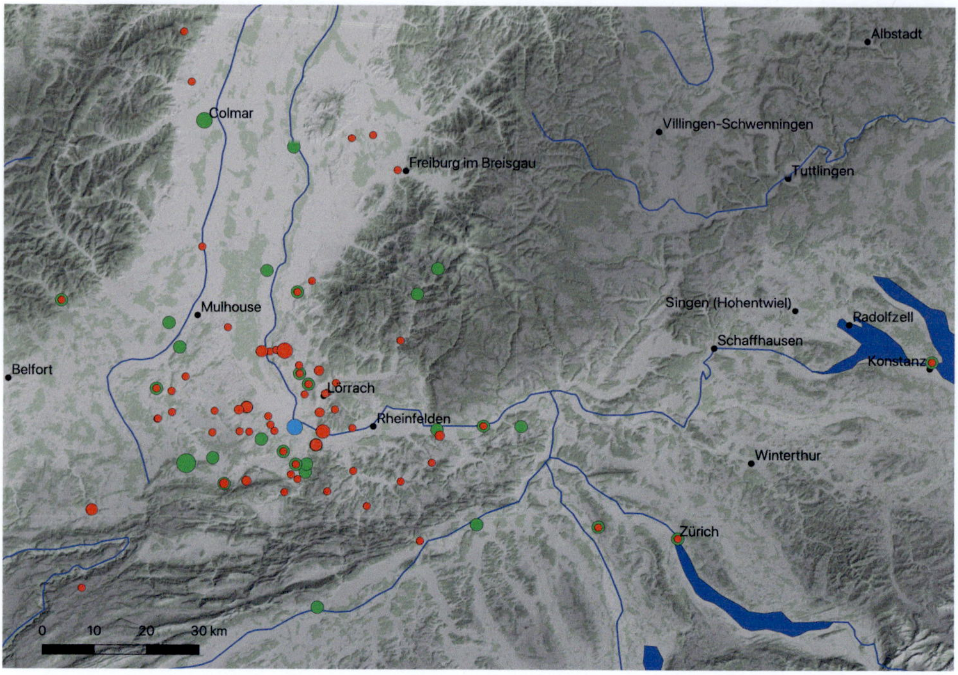

tres of gravity deviate only slightly to the north, the creditors' deviation to the North-East is striking. These observations point to different types of economic interdependence. Basel can be perceived as an urban economic centre with a rural hinterland whose credit needs are met in the city. This confirms quite traditional views,[50] but the presence of creditors in this area should not be neglected. The economic integration with the hinterland was not one-sided. In a wider regional context, the distribution of (mainly) creditors shows the integration into the empire's economy.[51]

As in the case of the network representations, it is evident that topographic representations are often only the starting point for further considerations and

50 Rippmann 1990, 132; Steinbrink 2007, 74; Gilomen 1998.

51 Basel was not yet part of the Swiss Confederation—it would be interesting to compare the patterns fifty years later to see to what extent the membership in the Confederation changed the economic integration.

Figure 8 Centres of gravity of the distribution of creditors (green) and debtors (red) from outside Basel, both samples.

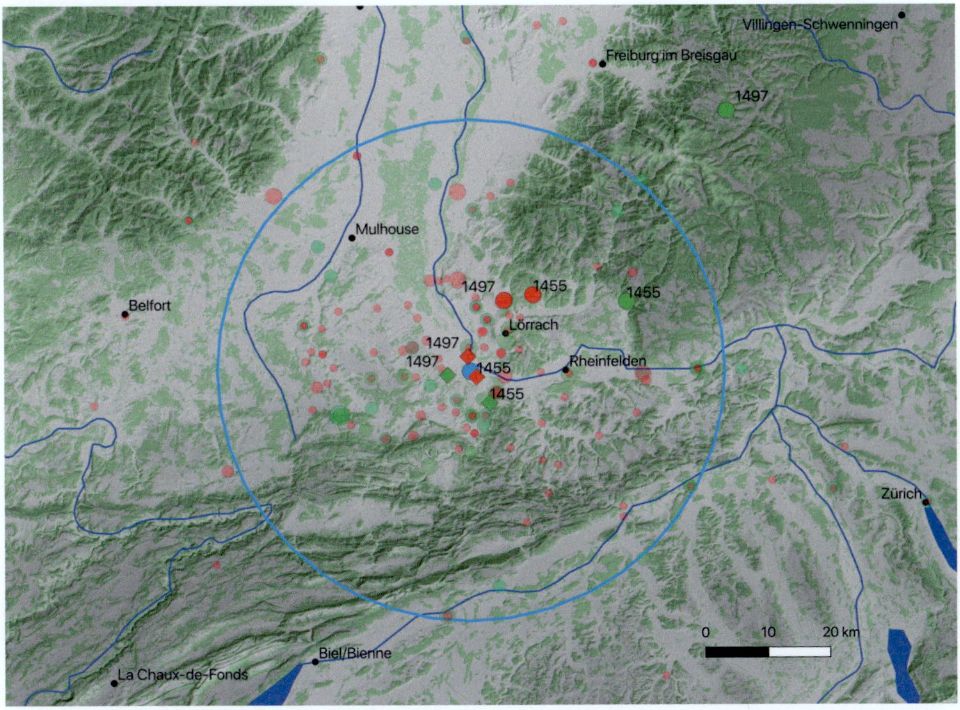

analyses. In this case, the hypotheses concerning the differentiated dispersion of individuals could be tested by means of calculations of the centre of gravity.

Credit in the City of Basel

For the representation of credit relationships within the city of Basel, I chose a city map established in the nineteenth century, one of the first to be geometrically precise enough to allow easy integration into GIS software.[52] The relative stability of the city's topography since the late Middle Ages justifies this choice, although one must consider city growth. Not all the suburbs visible on the map were actually populated around 1500. Figure 9 shows a possible representation of credit relations in the city. As usual for the representations in this paper, debtors

52 Source: Geodata of the Canton of Basel, https://shop.geo.bs.ch (accessed on 10 February 2021).

Figure 9 Topography of credit relations in the city of Basel, 1497 sample.

are marked as red, creditors as green circles. The size of the circle stands for the number of incoming credit relations of a person (in network terms: the indegree). As the tax rolls do not allow a precise localisation of people from the part of the city north of the Rhine, they are not represented here.[53]

The observations made above, concerning the distribution of creditors and debtors over the city perimeter, are confirmed. The resulting pattern of credit relations—every relation is drawn as a blue or red line, the red lines standing for credit relations with a distance of less than 100 metres—shows a clear hub-and-spoke structure. With the exception of one suburb (the *Spalenvorstadt,* inhabited by relatively rich people occupied in the transportation business[54]), the short-distance credit relations were concentrated in the city centre around the market-place and in a second centre at the bridge head of the only Rhine bridge. Although creditors were also present in the suburbs (albeit much less frequently), they were generally in connection with debtors from relatively distant places.

For further analysis, I calculated the distance of credit relationships, which averaged 310 metres. This distance can be put in perspective by calculating the average distance between all people found in the sample, which amounted to approximately 400 metres. Given the concentration of creditors in the centre—which suggests short distances—the difference is small, indicating widely spread credit relations and confirming the hub-and-spoke structure.

Networks of Credit

Let us now look at the results of the network analysis of the two samples of my study. Both networks are composed of a relatively large main component of interconnected people and other parts of lesser density. Formal analysis was made difficult by the fact that approximately 70 per cent of all people appeared in only one record. So the overall density of both networks was low, which prevented meaningful results of analyses like clustering (forming groups of strongly interconnected people) or blockmodelling (identifying people in similar structural positions).[55] I could use some network measures, though, to compare the two sample

53 The court was actually jurisdictional for the southern part of the city, but people from the northern part appeared quite often.

54 Simon-Muscheid 1988, 137 and 213.

55 See for these concepts general introductions like Jansen 2012; Prell 2012. Van Doosselaere 2009, 148, describes the same problem. For a classic historical blockmodel analysis, see Ansell and Padgett 1993.

Figure 10 Network representation, main component, 1455 sample. The credit relationships are coloured according to time criteria (always two months combined).

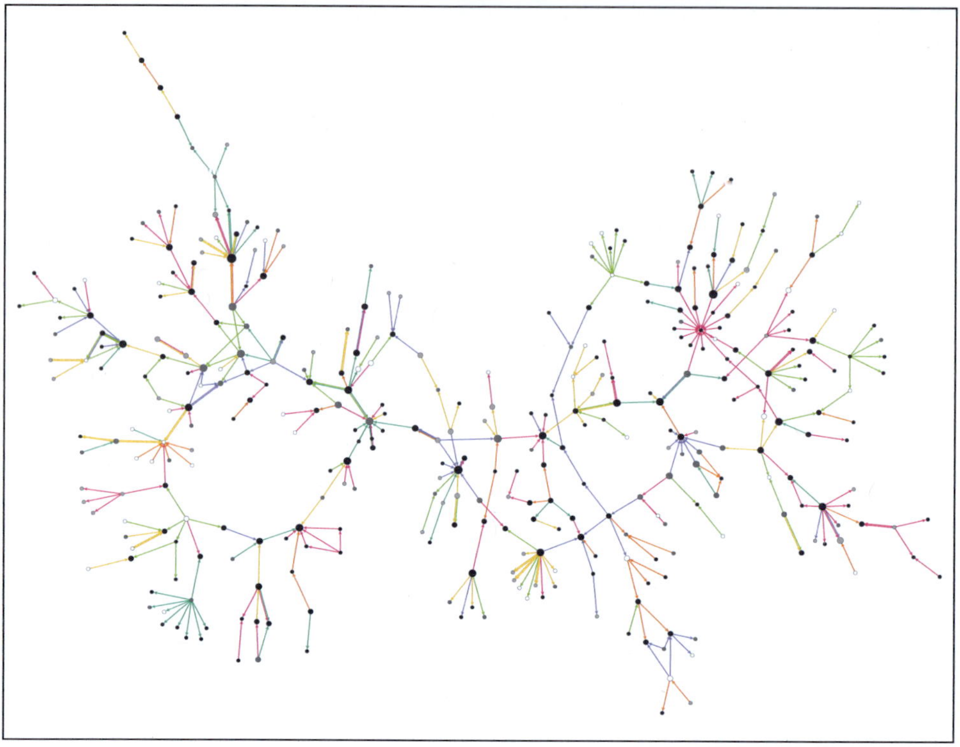

networks and note that they had a similar structure (see Figure 10 and Figure 11). The most striking difference was due to several cases of bankruptcy in the 1497 sample. Those cases caused a rush of creditors trying to obtain their share of the bankruptcy assets, resulting in dense star-shaped sections of the network.

For both networks, measures of centrality were meaningful.[56] Obviously, bankrupts had high centrality values, but creditors seemed more interesting to me. Using the Indegree (the number of incoming credit relations) centrality measure, I identified important creditors and noted that they were important nodes of the network for holding it together. Those creditors turned out to be well-to-do citizens of Basel, mostly merchants, but also craftsmen, who seemed to have been engaged in money lending as an ancillary activity.

56 Stark 2016, section IV.

Figure 11 Network representation, main component, 1497 sample. People who are creditors as well as debtors (pivots of credit chains) are marked in orange.

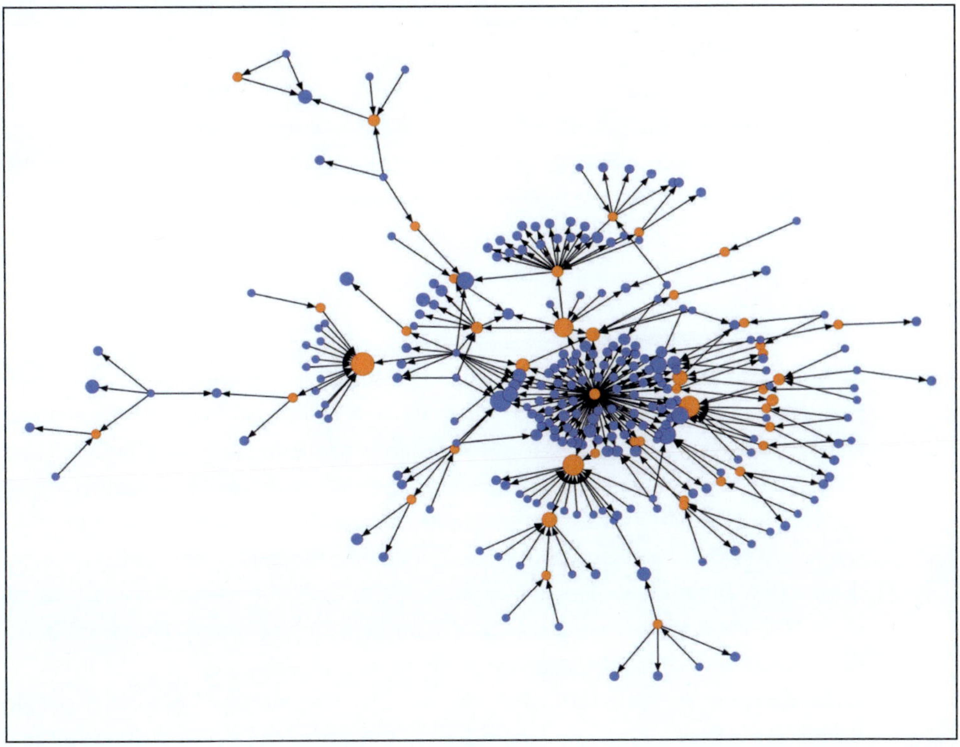

The two examples of network representations show ways of further exploration of the data beyond the simple network structure. For the 1455 sample (see Figure 10), I coloured the links according to temporal criteria, trying to evaluate the distribution of cases over the year. A colour represents a time frame of two months. What this shows is not seasonal variation[57] but how individuals were present. Debtors tended to be confronted with debt claims in a temporally concentrated manner, whereas creditors' use of justice was much more regularly distributed. The representation of the 1497 sample (see Figure 11) anticipates the question of credit chains (see below) by colouring individuals who were creditors as well as debtors. This shows that many of those people were in quite central positions in the network and that it is worth looking closely at credit chains.

57 This could be observed too, showing peaks of amounts in spring and autumn, and a peak in the number of cases only in autumn.

From the many network representations I made in the course of my research, I only retained a few. Mostly, they served as inspiration for new questions and deeper analysis. Network representations do not speak for themselves, nor can they be easily interpreted. Often, other forms of representation serve the purpose of analysis and visualisation of results much better. It turned out that the aggregation of actors according to attributes like wealth, sex, and origin was an important track of investigation, but aggregated network representations were of little use to present results. Thus the following section on density matrices.

Density Matrices

In light of the lack of clear results on a single-actor level of the network, it seemed promising to group individuals by attribute, and observe structures between and within those groups. The aggregation of data has been proposed before[58] and proved interesting here. For each constellation of attributes, the number of observed credit relations was set in relation to the theoretically possible number. The resulting densities are used to colour a matrix; the darker the field, the higher the density. The role as a debtor is represented in rows, the role as a creditor in columns. The most interesting attribute is again wealth (see above). Figure 12 shows the density matrix for the 1455 sample with five wealth categories. As many individuals could not be identified on the tax rolls (this obviously applies to people from outside Basel, but many inhabitants of the city could not be assigned either),

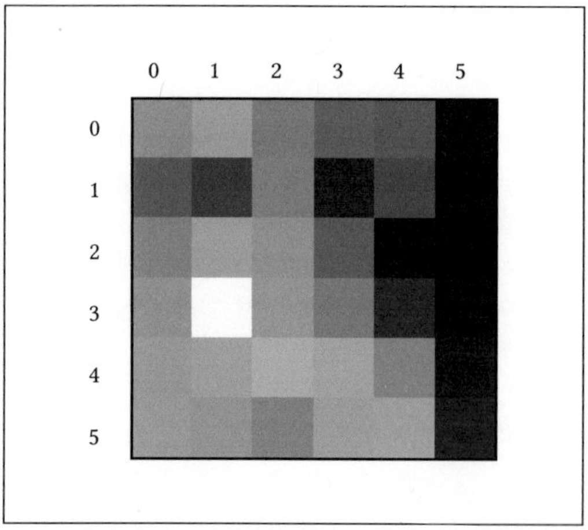

Figure 12 Density matrix of credit relations between categories of wealth, 1455 sample (0: unknown, 1: very poor, 2: poor, 3: medium, 4: rich, 5: very rich).

58 Jullien 2013.

I included the category *unknown* to detect additional patterns.[59] The first observation is in line with what was said above about the uses of justice. Richer strata, and especially the richest, were clearly more frequently found in the role of a creditor (see the column to the right). The second, not less striking observation is that the lower left corner shows significantly[60] lower densities. Credit negotiated in court tended to be asymmetric in nature. Although almost every constellation actually occurred, situations with a wealthier creditor of a poorer debtor outnumbered other situations. Credit within people of similar standing was not very frequent, but slightly more frequent than poor creditors trying to obtain payment from richer creditors.

As seen above, it is promising to look at the different procedures the court offered. Figure 13 shows the density matrices for wealth categories of the 1497 samples for two types of procedure, namely lawsuits and debt recognitions. The

Figure 13 Density matrices of credit relations for lawsuits, debt recognitions, and seizures of movables (from left to right), 1497 sample (k.a.: unknown, 0: poor, 1: medium, 2: rich).

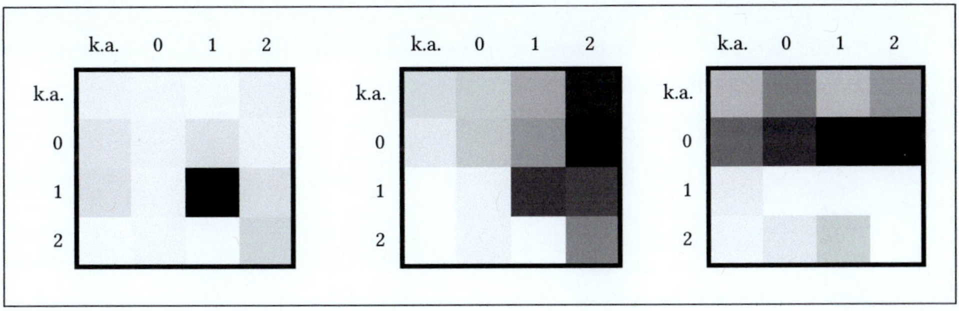

debt recognitions show a pattern similar to the matrix for the 1455 sample shown above, with a dense top right corner. In comparison, lawsuits were much less evenly distributed. The richer strata were even more involved, especially the medium category (which corresponds more or less to the second richest category of

59 Since the proportion of unclear classifications was regularly quite high, I kept comparing the *unknown* category to check for systematic bias. As a general observation, bias seemed rather low.

60 I used a homophily analysis to check the overall tendency of the sample to form relations within or between groups. A significant result served as indication that the observed patterns were not just accidental.

the 1544 sample). The poorer people were less involved, not even as debtors, and lawsuits quite often took place within categories, thus on a horizontal level. This confirms the conflictual character of the procedure, much more oriented towards the question of whether any credit was due than other procedures more occupied with the negotiation of payment in cash or in nature. Payment in nature was enforced with the procedure of seizure, which was mainly a tool used by richer people against debtors of the poorer strata.

These differences make it clear that using the court or being confronted with a court procedure did not mean the same thing for all people. Poorer people were more frequently in a passive role, being forced to sell their goods, whereas richer people hardly ever felt pressure on their possessions. If all debtors seem unwilling to pay to a certain degree, they did so for different reasons: the poor because they did not want to pay with their goods,[61] the rich because they could afford to stall the case hoping to outlast the suing creditor.

The representation of network data in an aggregated matrix[62] was extremely helpful for interpretation as patterns are easily recognisable. Although it might not be obvious at first glance, the data represented in density matrices is still relational data, but actual network graphs—aggregating data or not—could not show the structures with the same clarity. On the methodological level, I therefore advocate the use of such forms of representation for network analysis wherever categorical attributes are present.

Credit Chains

The notion of credit chains is a second metaphor mentioned with some regularity when looking at structures of credit relations.[63] As with the network metaphor, it has never been subject to an actual formal analysis. The formation of chains is based on the fact that some people appeared as creditors as well as debtors in the samples. Formally, credit chains are paths[64] through the network, following the directed edges. In my samples, I could identify hundreds of such paths with a maximal length of seven credit relations. The redundancy is high, as many paths pass through the same links. When looking at credit chains, I focussed on patterns suggesting the presence of a hierarchy in the chain, based on increasing amounts of credit or increasing socio-economic status of the people involved. If such pat-

61 On goods as stores of value, see Smail 2016, 61; Smail 2013, 367; Fontaine 2008b.
62 I thank Claire Lemercier for the very precious advice on this matter.
63 Muldrew 1998a, 3; Ago 1999, 195. Maybe today these authors would speak of networks.
64 See Jansen 2012, 96; Stark 2016, 163–164.

terns are not found, credit chains could just be accidental combinations of relatively independent credit situations. An obvious starting point were the people at the end of the chains. But they proved to be of little interest, many of them from outside Basel claiming small sums of money on only one occasion. Instead of trying to construct a structure that obviously had little meaning, I decided to look at the frequent creditors of both samples (see above). And here, I could identify hierarchical structures, as the example of the rich merchant Ludman Meltinger from the 1455 sample shows (see Figure 14). The credit chains are represented as a network graph excluding all people who are not part of the chains, in concrete terms, several direct debtors of Meltinger.

Figure 14 Example of credit chains (Ludmann Meltinger in the middle), 1455 sample. The size of the nodes is based on the category of wealth (the larger, the richer).

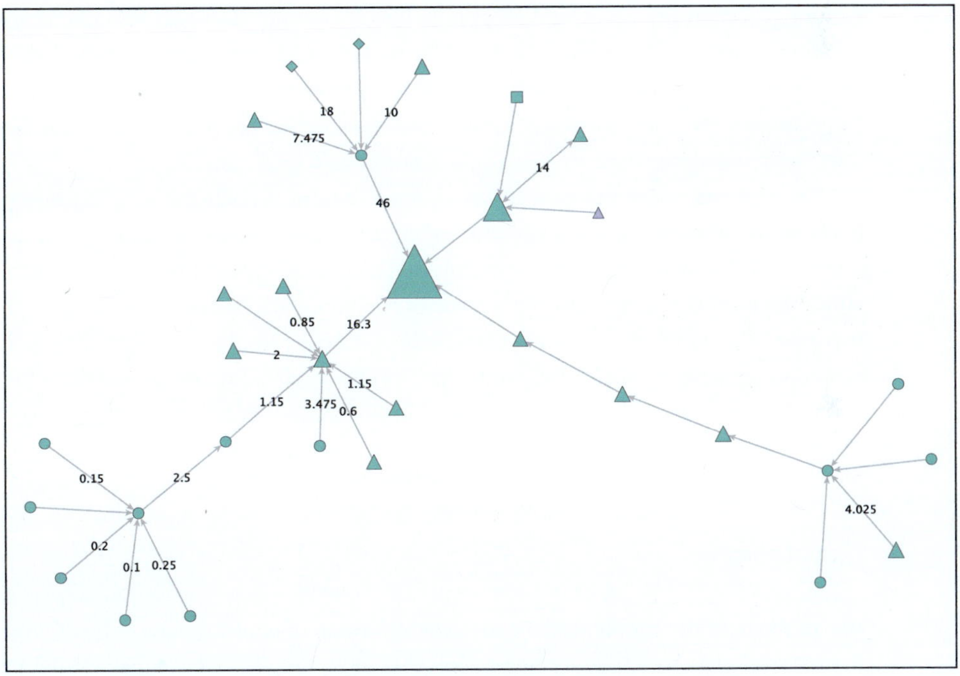

The representation of the credit chains leading to Meltinger repeatedly show the same pattern of several debtors grouped around one creditor, who himself is debtor to another person (Meltinger, but also two other individuals). In two cases, enough data on credit amounts is known and one can see that this last credit relation involves a higher sum than the star-shaped patterns at the beginning of the chain. The Meltinger example is not the only one showing such structures. The same observation of hierarchical structures could not be made for the longer chains—the Meltinger example shows that, too. I conclude that only patterns involving two credit relations—and in consequence three people—can be interpreted meaningfully. All other structures were more or less accidental and where the people involved were not necessarily aware of the other relationships. When looking closely at some cases of the Meltinger sample, one can see that the suing creditors were aware of their debtor's debtor. The seizures they sought concerned the credits of their debtor's debtors. This quite common proceeding actually forced the person in the middle to pass on any payment received. Here again, the awareness of credit chains did not go beyond the length of three linked people.

These observations show that the interpretation of computationally found data and structures is important. If one interpreted all credit chains found as a meaningful pattern, one would most certainly be wrong. However, the randomly appearing debt chains were contrasted by hierarchical structures. Although it is not possible to calculate an exact proportion of the various forms, the considerations on how the participating actors perceived structures appears to be an important key. I will come back to this point in the concluding remarks.

The analysis of credit chains is an example where it made sense to represent parts of the network graphically. The relatively small number of individuals involved and the focus on certain structural effects made it possible to form conclusions based on the analysis of the networks, including attribute data on the people involved and additional data on the credit relations like the amounts. This permitted comparisons (which I cannot carry out here) and targeted research in the source material about conspicuous points in the credit chains.

Conclusion

The analysis of the access to the court, the relations of creditors and debtors, and the networks created thereby points out that most credit relations negotiated in court were characterised by asymmetry. Socially, economically, and also geographically, aspects of distance prevail over aspects of closeness. This can be seen as an expression of strong economic integration, as people from all over the city and the hinterlands had access to credit. But at the same time, this vision should not obscure the fact that poorer people faced many more problems in case of default, being forced to sell their possessions, sometimes even being evicted from their homes. But was credit consequentially purely economic? I would argue that a credit relationship was always more than just an economic relation, in a society that did not know economy as a separate sphere. Sources I could not mention here indicate that credit often developed from longstanding business relations and was based if not on trust, then at least on knowing one's partner quite well. Furthermore, most credit in everyday transactions was neither initially nor at a later stage based on collateral like real estate or pawn, but on the options offered by the court to enforce payment. In the case of asymmetry, creditors probably tended more easily to use these options. But whatever the degree of escalation, going to court was a step that only exceptionally led to longer proceedings and a final verdict. The court actively encouraged arbitration outside the court and gladly recorded its results, thus trying to mitigate conflicts and integrate their resolution into the city's society as a whole.

To come to such conclusions, network analysis was used as a tool. I now want to consider to what extent contemporaries perceived their credit relations as part of a network—knowing that the term is of course anachronistic. I argued above that in general, people did not see more than two or three links of a network structure. Citizens of Basel thus did not dispose of actual knowledge of who owed whom (a partial reconstruction of which was made for this study), but they certainly had an idea of whom to ask for credit and thus a general perception of availability of credit—especially with regard to the moneylenders frequently occurring in the court records.[65] Although it would be wrong to claim the perception of a network, the contemporaries' awareness of interdependences makes network analysis appear a useful tool of analysis for today's historians.

References

Archival References

Staatsarchiv Basel-Stadt (StABS), Gerichtsarchiv A 26; A 41.
StABS, Gerichstarchiv B 7; B 14.
StABS, Gerichtsarchiv C 5; C 6; C 16.
StABS, Gerichtsarchiv D 6.
StABS, Gerichtsarchiv E 4; E 7.
StABS, Gerichtsarchiv G 1; G 9.

65 See for questions of information circulation, Hitz 2020.

Bibliographic References

Ago R. 1999. "Enforcing agreements. Notaries and courts in early modern Rome." *Continuity & Change* 14, no. 2: 191–206.

Albert T. 1998. *Der gemeine Mann vor dem geistlichen Richter. Kirchliche Rechtsprechung in den Diözesen Basel, Chur und Konstanz vor der Reformation.* Stuttgart: Lucius und Lucius.

Anselin L. 1995. "Local indicators of spatial association—LISA." *Geographical Analysis* 27, no. 2: 93–115.

Ansell C. and J. Padgett 1993. "Robust Actions and the Rise of the Medici, 1400–1434." *American Journal of Sociology* 98, no. 6: 1259–1319.

Bixler M. 2015. "Historical Network Research. Taking Stock". In *Debtors, Creditors, and their Networks. Social Dimensions of Monetary Dependence from the Seventeenth to the Twentieth Century,* edited by A. Gestrich and M. Stark, 43–67. London: German Historical Institute.

Bolton J. L. 2011. "London merchants and the Borromei Bank in the 1430s. The role of local credit networks." In *Parliament, personalities and power. Papers presented to Linda S. Clark,* edited by L. Clark and H. Kleineke, 53–73. Woodbridge: The Boydell Press.

Burghartz S. 1991. "Kein Ort für Frauen? Städtische Gerichte im Spätmittelalter." In *Auf der Suche nach der Frau im Mittelalter. Fragen, Quellen, Antworten,* edited by B. Lundt, 49–64. Munich: Wilhelm Fink.

Burkhardt M. 2014. "Networks as Social Structures in Late Medieval and Early Modern Towns. A Theoretical Approach to Historical Network Analysis." In *Commercial networks and European cities, 1400–1800,* edited by A. Caracausi and C. Jeggle, 13–43. London: Pickering & Chatto.

Chilosi D., M.-S. Schulze, and O. Volckart. 2016. "Benefits of Empire? Capital Market Integration North and South of the Alps, 1350–1800." *Economic History Working Papers* 236: 1–76.

Claustre J. 2014. "Vers une ethnographie des transactions de crédit. La relation de dette à Paris à la fin du Moyen Âge." In *Prekäre Ökonomien. Schulden in Spätmittelalter und Früher Neuzeit,* edited by G. Signori, 35–51. Constance: UVK.

Clemens G. B. (ed.) 2008. *Schuldenlast und Schuldenwert. Kreditnetzwerke in der europäischen Geschichte 1300–1900.* Trier: Kliomedia.

Crowston C. H. 2011. "Credit and the Metanarrative of Modernity." *French Historical Studies* 34, no. 1: 7–19.

Crowston C. H. 2013. *Credit, fashion, sex. Economies of regard in Old Regime France.* Durham: Duke University Press.

Degler-Spengler B. 1974. "Der gemeine Pfennig und seine Erhebung in Basel." *Basler Zeitschrift für Geschichte und Altertumskunde* 74, no. 1: 237–258.

Düring M.U. Eumann and M. Stark (eds.) 2016. *Handbuch historische Netzwerkforschung. Grundlagen und Anwendungen.* Berlin: LIT-Verlag.

Düring M. and F. Kerschbaumer 2016. "Quantifizierung und Visualisierung. Anknüpfungspunkte in den Geschichtswissenschaften." In *Handbuch historische Netzwerkforschung. Grundlagen und Anwendungen,* edited by M. Düring, U. Eumann and M. Stark, 31–43. Berlin: LIT-Verlag.

Düring M. and M. Stark 2011. "Historical Network Analysis." In *Encyclopedia of social networks,* edited by G.A. Barnett, 593–595. Los Angeles: SAGE Publications.

Eumann U. 2016. "Heuristik. Hypothesenentwicklung und Hypothesentest." In *Handbuch historische Netzwerkforschung. Grundlagen und Anwendungen,* edited by Marten Düring, Ulrich Eumann and Martin Stark, 123–138. Berlin: LIT-Verlag.

Fontaine L. 2008a. *L'économie morale. Pauvreté, crédit et confiance dans l'Europe préindustrielle.* Paris: Gallimard.

Fontaine L. (ed.) 2008b. *Alternative exchanges. Second-hand circulations from the sixteenth century to the present.* New York: Berghahn Books.

Garnot B. (ed.) 1996. *L'infrajudiciaire du Moyen Age à l'époque contemporaine. Actes du colloque de Dijon, 5–6 octobre 1995.* Dijon: EUD.

Geddes A. and I.N. Gregory (ed.) 2014. *Toward spatial humanities. Historical GIS & spatial history.* Bloomington/Indianapolis: Indiana University Press.

Gestrich A. and M. Stark (ed.) 2015. *Debtors, Creditors, and their Networks. Social Dimensions of Monetary Dependence from the Seventeenth to the Twentieth Century.* London: German Historical Institute London.

Gilomen H.-J. 1998. "Stadt-Land-Beziehungen in der Schweiz des Spätmittelalters." In *Stadt und Land in der Schweizer Geschichte. Abhängigkeiten, Spannungen, Komplementaritäten,* edited by U. Pfister and B. Witthöft, 10–48. Basel: Schwabe.

Gilomen H.-J. 2007. "Die ökonomischen Grundlagen des Kredits und die christlich-jüdische Konkurrenz im Spätmittelalter." In *Ein Thema—zwei Perspektiven. Juden und Christen in Mittelalter und Frühneuzeit,* edited by E. Brugger and B. Wiedl, 139–169. Innsbruck: Studien-Verlag.

Gilomen H.-J. 2011. "Der Kleinkredit in spätmittelalterlichen Städten. Basel und Zürich im Vergleich." In *Städtische Wirtschaft im Mittelalter. Festschrift für Franz Irsigler zum 70. Geburtstag,* edited by R. Holbach and M. Pauly, 109–148. Cologne: Böhlau Verlag.

Gilomen H.-J. 2014. "Frauen als Schuldnerinnen und Gläubigerinnen in der Stadt Basel in den 1420er-Jahren." In *Prekäre Ökonomien. Schulden in Spätmittelalter und Früher Neuzeit,* edited by Gabriela Signori, 103–137. Constance: UVK.

Gilomen H.-J. 2018. "Christlicher Glaube und Ökonomie des Kredits im Spätmittelalter." In *Ökonomische Glaubensfragen: Strukturen und Praktiken jüdischen und christlichen Kleinkredits im Spätmittelalter,* edited by G. Fouquet and S. Rabeler, 121–160. Stuttgart: Franz Steiner Verlag.

Graham S., I. Milligan and S. B. Weingart 2016. *Exploring big historical data. The historian's macroscope.* Hackensack, NJ: Imperial College Press.

Hagemann H.-R. 1987. *Basler Rechtsleben im Mittelalter. Zivilrechtspflege.* Basel: Helbing und Lichtenhahn.

Hitz B. 2020. "Informationszirkulation in der spätmittelalterlichen Justiz am Beispiel Basels." In *Informationsverarbeitung in der Stadt des 12.–16. Jahrhundert. Beiträge des interdisziplinären (Post-)Doc-Workshop des Trierer Zentrums für Mediävistik im November 2018,* edited by E. Burkart and V. Schwab. https://mittelalter.hypotheses.org/25525 consulted on 3 March 2021.

Jansen D. 2012. *Einführung in die Netzwerkanalyse. Grundlagen, Methoden, Forschungsbeispiele.* Wiesbaden: VS Verlag für Sozialwissenschaften.

Jullien E. 2013. "Netzwerkanalyse in der Mediävistik. Probleme und Perspektiven im Umgang mit mittelalterlichen Quellen." *Vierteljahrschrift für Sozial- und Wirtschaftsgeschichte* 100, no. 2: 135–153.

Lemercier C. 2012. "Formale Methoden der Netzwerkanalyse in den Geschichtswissenschaften. Warum und Wie?" *Österreichische Zeitschrift für Geschichtswissenschaften* 23, no. 1: 16–41.

Lilley K. and C. Porter 2016. "GIS, spatial technologies and digital mapping." In *Research methods for history,* edited by L. Faire and S. Gunn, 125–146. Edinburgh: Edinburgh University Press.

Lipp C. 2007. "Aspekte der mikrohistorischen und kulturanthropologischen Kreditforschung." In *Soziale Praxis des Kredits. 16.–20. Jahrhundert,* edited by J. Schlumbohm, 15–36. Hanover: Verlag Hahnsche Buchhandlung.

Loetz F. 2000. "L'infrajudiciaire. Facetten und Bedeutung des Konzepts." In *Kriminalitätsgeschichte. Beiträge zur Sozial- und Kulturgeschichte der Vormoderne,* edited by A. Blauert and G. Schwerhoff, 545–562. Constance: UVK.

Muldrew C. 1998a. *The Economy of Obligation. The Culture of Credit and Social Relations in Early Modern England.* New York: St. Martin's Press.

Muldrew C. 1998b. "The currency of credit and personality. Belief, trust, and the economics of reputation in early modern English society." In *Des personnes aux institutions. Réseaux et cultures du crédit du XVIe au XXe siècle en Europe,* edited by L. Fontaine, 58–79. Mons: Academia Bruylant.

Nitschke C. 2016. "Die Geschichte der Netzwerkanalyse." In *Handbuch historische Netzwerkforschung. Grundlagen und Anwendungen,* edited by M. Düring, U. Eumann and M. Stark, 11–29. Berlin: LIT-Verlag.

Piant H. 2006. *Une justice ordinaire. Justice civile et criminelle dans la prévôté royale de Vaucouleurs sous l'Ancien Régime.* Rennes: Presses Universitaires de Rennes.

Piant H. 2007. "Des procès innombrables. Éléments méthodologiques pour une histoire de la justice civile d'Ancien Régime." *Histoire & Mesure* 22, no. 2: 13–38.

Prell C. 2012. *Social network analysis. history, theory and methodology.* Los Angeles: Sage.

Rau S. 2013. *Räume. Konzepte, Wahrnehmungen, Nutzungen.* Frankfurt am Main: Campus Verlag.

Reifner U. 2015. "Thesen zur Dogmatik eines sozialen Nutzungsvertrages (Life Time Contract)." In *Zivilrecht im Wandel. Festschrift für Peter Derleder zum 75. Geburtstag,* edited by H.G. Bamberger, G. Hölzle and K.-O. Knops, 369–392. Berlin and Heidelberg: Springer.

Reupke D. and C. Volk 2013. "Von der Akte zum Netzwerk. Erfahrungsberichte aus der Werkstatt des Historikers." In *Visuelle Netzwerkforschung. Qualitative, quantitave und partizipative Zugänge,* edited by M. Gamper, M. Kronenwett and M. Schönhuth, 297–316. Bielefeld: Transcript.

Rippmann D. 1990. *Bauern und Städter. Stadt-Land-Beziehungen im 15. Jahrhundert. Das Beispiel Basel, unter besonderer Berücksichtigung der Nahmarktbeziehungen und der sozialen Verhältnisse im Umland.* Basel: Helbing & Lichtenhahn.

Ruggiu F.-J. 2009. "A Way out of the Crisis. Methodologies of Early Modern Social History in France." *Cultural & Social History* 6, no. 1: 65–85.

Schneider Z.A. 2000. "Women before the Bench. Female Litigants in Early Modern Normandy." *French Historical Studies* 23, no. 1: 1–32.

Schönberg G. 1879. *Finanzverhältnisse der Stadt Basel im 14. und 15. Jahrhundert.* Tübingen: Laupp'sche Buchhandlung.

Schuster P. 2008. "The Age of Debt? Private Schulden in der spätmittelalterlichen Gesellschaft." In *Schuldenlast und Schuldenwert. Kreditnetzwerke in der europäischen Geschichte 1300–1900,* edited by G.B. Clemens, 37–52. Trier: Kliomedia.

Schuster P. 2014. "Soziale und kulturelle Aspekte des Schuldenmachens im ausgehenden Mittelalter." In *Prekäre Ökonomien. Schulden in Spätmittelalter und Früher Neuzeit,* edited by G. Signori, 17–34. Constance: UVK.

Schwerhoff G. 2011. "Stadt und Öffentlichkeit in der Frühen Neuzeit—Perspektiven der Forschung." In *Stadt und Öffentlichkeit in der Frühen Neuzeit,* edited by G. Schwerhoff, 1–28. Cologne: Böhlau.

Signori G. 1999. "Geschlechtsvormundschaft und Gesellschaft. Die Basler 'Fertigungen' 1450–1500." *Zeitschrift der Savigny-Stiftung für Rechtsgeschichte* 116, no. 1: 120–151.

Signori G. 2015. *Schuldenwirtschaft. Konsumenten- und Hypothekarkredite im spätmittelalterlichen Basel.* Constance: UVK.

Simon-Muscheid K. 1988. *Basler Handwerkszünfte im Spätmittelalter. Zunftinterne Strukturen und innerstädtische Konflikte.* Bern: Lang.

Smail D.L. 2003. *The consumption of justice. Emotions, publicity, and legal culture in Marseille, 1264–1423.* Ithaca (N.Y.): Cornell University Press.

Smail D.L. 2013. "Les biens comme otages. Quelques aspects du processus de recouvrement des dettes à Lucques et à Marseille à la fin du Moyen Âge." In *Objets sous contrainte. Circulation des richesses et valeur des choses au Moyen Âge,* edited by L. Feller and A. Rodríguez, 365–383. Paris: Publications de la Sorbonne.

Smail D.L. 2016. *Legal plunder. Households and debt collection in late Medieval Europe.* Cambridge, Massachusetts: Harvard University Press.

Stark M. 2015. "Networks of Lenders and Borrowers. A Rural Credit Market in the Nineteenth Century." In *Debtors, Creditors, and their Networks. Social Dimensions of Monetary Dependence from the Seventeenth to the Twentieth Century,* edited by A. Gestrich and M. Stark, 99–118. London: German Historical Institute.

Stark M. 2016. "Netzwerkberechnungen. Anmerkungen zur Verwendung formaler Methoden." In *Handbuch historische Netzwerkforschung. Grundlagen und Anwendungen,* edited by M. Düring, U. Eumann and M. Stark, 155–171. Berlin: LIT-Verlag.

Steinbrink M. 2007. *Ulrich Meltinger. Ein Basler Kaufmann am Ende des 15. Jahrhunderts.* Stuttgart: Franz Steiner Verlag.

Van Doosselaere Q. 2009. *Commercial Agreements and Social Dynamics in Medieval Genoa.* Cambridge: Cambridge University Press.

Vogel A.-C. 2015. "Credit, Trust, and Social Networks. Mortgage Credit in the Industrializing Town of Esslingen (Württemberg, Germany)." In *Debtors, Creditors, and their Networks. Social Dimensions of Monetary Dependence from the Seventeenth to the Twentieth Century,* edited by A. Gestrich and M. Stark, 71–97. London: German Historical Institute.

Wirtz T. 2010. "Vertrauen und Kredit in der frühneuzeitlichen Stadt." In *Gläubiger, Schuldner, Arme. Netzwerke und die Rolle des Vertrauens,* edited by C. Hergenröder, 57–70. Wiesbaden: VS Verlag für Sozialwissenschaften.

Picture Credits

All graphics are made by the author. GIS Representations are based on freely available and usable GIS data (all links last accessed on 10 February 2021).

Data	**Source**
Digital Elevation Model over Europe (EU-DEM)	https://data.europa.eu/euodp/data/dataset/data_eu-dem
Vector data of waters	http://www.naturalearthdata.com/downloads/110m-physical-vectors
Places	www.mapcruzin.com
Pan-European Forest/Non-Forest Map 2000	https://forest.jrc.ec.europa.eu/en/past-activities/forest-mapping/#Downloadforestmaps
City map by L. H. Löffel, 1862	https://shop.geo.bs.ch

THE OTHER SIDE OF BANKING

Private Lending and the Role of Women in Early Modern Italy

Marcella Lorenzini

Abstract: This article examines the role of women in private capital markets in northern Italy in the seventeenth and eighteenth centuries. If bankers, financial dealers and major merchants were prevalent in the institutionalized credit markets, women proved crucial in private lending intermediated by notaries. The assets allowing them to participate in the credit market derived principally from their dowries, mainly consisting of cash but also including real estate. They used their properties as collateral for mortgages, which were employed to meet family needs or to fund their husbands' businesses, in some cases rescuing them from bankruptcy and safeguarding their reputation. The cash was invested in interest-rate loans: female capital was not mere "petty finance". Many widows coming from the aristocracy or the urban elite had large sums at their disposal which were channelled into the circuits of credit to finance manufacturing, trade and agriculture, boosting silk production in some regions, the opening of new shops and partnerships in others, and promoting local and international commerce. A portion of this capital was also lent to rural communities for paying taxes, funding current expenditures, and modernizing infrastructure.

Keywords: informal credit market, notaries, women, early modern age, Italy

1 Introduction

Far from the highest spheres of finance, where bankers, financial dealers and big merchants controlled large lending and borrowing transactions and engaged in long-distance trade, private credit markets—intermediated by non-specialised,

Published in: Stephan Nicolussi-Köhler (Ed.), Change and Transformation of Premodern Credit Markets. The Importance of Small-Scale Credits. Heidelberg: heiBOOKS 2021, 193–213. DOI: https://doi.org/10.11588/heibooks.593.c12695

"informal"[1] professionals, i.e., notaries—were spreading at local level and able to move significant amounts of capital. Their strength was reflected in their increasing expansion and density and in the shaping and development of new credit instruments able to meet the challenges of a transforming economic and financial world.[2] Women were a constant presence within these capital markets, both as creditors and as debtors.[3] While their participation—at least as autonomous actors—was limited to the above spheres of finance, dominated by specialised institutions and qualified agents[4], they were very active in peer-to-peer borrowing, where both small and substantial sums were exchanged. In some cases, conspicuously wealthy women were able to compete with seasoned players on the interest rates, collateral and deadlines. Ladies of different social rank and marital status were involved: widows, spinsters, married or unmarried women, young and old. They acted individually or alongside their husbands as business partners, or asset managers for their underage children. Loans were contracted with family members or neighbours, but most deeds were drawn up with "unknown" parties, individuals from other geographical areas, different social classes, and different professions. Transactions recorded by women show how their financial ties stretched well beyond the family circle, debunking the stereotype of women confined exclusively to family management and affairs.[5] Their financial behaviour did not differ so much from that of their male counterparts in this specific context, but this depended on the fact that notaries acted as brokers in both cases, advising on the most appropriate operation.

The aim of this study is to explore the role played by women in the capital markets intermediated by notaries, specifically their weight in terms of the cap-

1 By "informal" professionals we refer to individuals that in loan contracts operated as intermediaries, but whose main qualification was something other than finance or banking activities. In the early modern age, notaries mostly fulfilled this task. Conversely, by "formal" we refer to specialised financial institutions and agents working specifically as brokers (i.e., banks, money changers).

2 The reference is for instance to the contract of *emptio cum locatione,* used for mortgages in order to circumvent usury bans, see next chapter.

3 Fontaine pointed out the relevance of a female presence in informal credit networks, pawnbroking, and occasional markets (Fontaine 2011, 521).

4 Women were not totally absent from the "formal" financial markets, yet. In England, specifically, with the 18th century witnessing the Financial Revolution, women invested like men in joint-stock companies. In the Bank of England, they "made up 18 per cent…of unique sellers and 16.3 per cent…of unique buyers". Their presence was lower in the Royal African Company—perhaps considered riskier: there women made up 8.46 per cent of buyers and 7.37 per cent of sellers (Carlos, Neal 2009, 38, 41). See also Carlos, Neal 2004.

5 Ait, 2014, 780, 787

ital they mobilised, their approach to risk, and the destinations of the sums they borrowed or lent. The research focuses on certain cities in northern Italy in the seventeenth and eighteenth centuries, drawing upon notarial deeds.[6] The paper is organised as follows: Section II is devoted to the analysis of private capital markets brokered by notaries, including instruments, rules and mechanisms; Section III concentrates on the share of these markets covered by women, defining their role, their approach to risk, and the impact of their financial activities on the capital market and on the real economy. Section IV lays out the conclusions.

2 A Veiled Financial World

Alongside the formal financial markets, characterised by specialised institutions and operators such as banks, money dealers, and merchant bankers, a private credit network was taking shape and growing. While the former involved international markets and the presence of qualified agents and brokers, the latter developed simultaneously at local level among private individuals whose deals were brokered by notaries, who were not specialised in financial assets but operated informally as intermediaries. Recent studies have pointed out that considerable sums were exchanged within these markets, which were widespread yet fragmented and thus veiled from view, difficult to discern in their entirety, but nevertheless well-organised and effective.[7] When the first modern banks emerged in the mid-nineteenth century, notaries continued drawing up mortgage contracts. The new institutions in effect did not replace the "old" role of notaries, who proved competitive in this field, operating in a parallel channel. The information they had accumulated over generations of contract-writing and that allowed them to allocate credit, was something that the modern credit institutions could not quickly match.[8]

---

6 This research draws upon about 3,000 deeds of Milan, Verona, Trento, Rovereto. However, other cities of central and northern Italy have been used in the comparative analysis.

7 Hoffman, Postel-Vinay, and Rosenthal defined it "dark matter credit" in reference to the fact that, though invisible, the largest share of transactions took place within this framework. (Hoffman, Postel-Vinay, and Rosenthal 2019)

8 It is noteworthy that when modern finance institutions first appeared, they did not displace the notarial credit market, which continued to exist alongside them and operate in a complementary manner. The brokerage service provided by notaries in allocating credit remained competitive. France, for instance, which had more banks than any

In societies based on a civil code (Roman law), where the figure of the *notarious* was conceived, notaries played a brokerage role as far back as the Middle Ages.[9] According to Alberto Liva, it was in the twelfth century that notarial deeds were transformed, refined, and adapted to purposes other than that for which they were originally created. Notaries contrived instruments and means to satisfy the needs of businesses or the rapidly evolving money-lending market.[10] In effect, sales and rental contracts soon became one single deed—*emptio cum locatione* (literally sale followed by rent)—when they involved collateralised credit, in order to circumvent the anti-usury laws.

The voluminous protocols, where they registered all kind of contracts, have turned out to be archival goldmines. In his handbook for notaries, Giovanni Pedrinelli from Verona highlighted that "much of what happens in men's affairs, in life and in death, pass through the hands of notaries: in life by means of contracts, in death by means of wills".[11] The data and information that notaries gained during their career made them able to properly channel it into the capital market and match demand and supply of credit. They were able to connect someone looking for money with someone else with "idle" liquidity to invest. They provided their customers with details of price, collateral, risk, and reputation of debtors and creditors, reducing information asymmetries and transaction costs. Only if the latter two elements are moderated can mortgage markets evolve, and notaries as brokers, were able to limit them. They knew their clients, their economic and financial position, and also their reliability quite well. In the early period, much more significantly than now, trust was the pillar upholding credit markets; a bad reputation deriving from bankruptcy or insolvency would leave a borrower critically isolated from the financial community. For example, Valentino Isach, a glassblower in Trento, overburdened by arrears and vexed by his creditors, chose to sell his house, "the only real estate he owned", in order to get out of all his debts and "preserve his and his family's reputation".[12]

---

other European country, "should have made the shadow lending [notarial credit market] disappear. But it did not vanish. Indeed, it persisted [...] up to World War I and was only killed off by government intervention that tipped the scales in favour of banks" (Hoffman, Postel-Vinay, and Rosenthal 2019, 2).

9 According to some studies conducted by Silvana Collodo in medieval Padua, the *emptio cum locatione* was a masked sale—actually an interest rate loan—devised to bypass anti-usury laws (Collodo 1940, 196).

10 Liva 1979, 35.

11 Pedrinelli 1768, 6.

12 Archivio di Stato di Trento (henceforth Astn), Notarile, Notary A. F. Poli, f. IX, Trento, 7 January 1750.

Trustworthiness and respectability, along with assets and financial exposure, was information that the notary naturally collected about his clients in the normal course of his professional activity.[13] This gave him an overview of the players and their capital allocation needs. In his research on *livelli* (a term used for loans in northern Italian regions) in seventeenth-century Venice, Gigi Corazzol found out that almost 18 per cent of credit had been drawn up by one single notary, Gerolamo Luran[14], which led him to confirm his insight: "It is clear that some notaries were simultaneously technicians and *intermediaries* (italics added), and so well known as intermediaries as to function substantially as institutions".[15]

The concentration of lending activity in the hands of a small group of notaries is evident also in late seventeenth-century Verona where four notaries[16]—out of 62—accounted for *livelli* that amounted to 90 per cent of all credit transactions. Not only were they the most active and prominent notaries in Verona, they also controlled the city's largest capital flows.[17] Evidence of the notaries' knowledge of debtor reputations is seen in the qualifying title placed before their client's name, such as *prudente, degnissimo, legal debitore* (prudent, most honourable, legal debtor), to emphasise the debtor's respectability, and the low-risk operation.[18] The names of borrowers or lenders in the documents of certain professionals are those of merchants, wealthy individuals, or aristocratic households who generally had a *notaio di fiducia* (trusted notary) who attended to all steps in the evolution of the family's assets. Since he had to have a hand in the family's affairs—property transfers, financial assets, wills, marriages, etc.—he entered into an intimate and confidential relationship with his clients, becoming in some cases a sort of "confessor"[19], as well as advisor and broker. This was the case of Giuseppe Macchi, one of the most renowned notaries in eighteenth-century Milan, to whom his client Gio. Filippo Visconti addressed a private bill stating that he was in need of money

---

13 Hoffman, Postel-Vinay, and Rosenthal 2000.

14 Corazzol 1994; Similarly, Faggion maintained that intermediation work began before drawing up the deed, which was, in effect, just the final step in a process—often long and difficult as the two parties negotiated the most advantageous agreement—leading up to the contract. In this preparatory phase, the notary participated as advisor and mediator (Faggion 2008, 533).

15 Corazzol 1986, 17.

16 Specifically, notaries: Francesco Bernardi, Vincenzo Ferro, Antonio Trezio and Gio. Francesco Vidali (Lorenzini 2016, 122, 127).

17 Lorenzini 2016, 127.

18 Lorenzini 2016, 85.

19 Pedani Fabris 1996, 129; Berengo 1981, 28.

and explicitly asked him to arrange a loan of 2,000 *gigliati*.[20] Giuseppe Macchi, son of a notary, made finance intermediation his chief activity, gradually abandoning the other attributes of the notarial profession.[21]

2.1 Rules, Instruments, and Participants

Credit brokered by notaries was based on a contract that guaranteed safety to the transaction. Mortgages were backed by collateral, most commonly a plot of cultivated land, a workshop, a mill, or—in more advanced economies—also mobile assets. The more economically lively cities devised terms and strategies that proved to be pioneering in the use of financial instruments. The market was made more liquid by the use of credit or futures (prospective rent) as collateral. In Milan, for instance, *censi* (loans backed by a collateral) were used to back other loans.[22] In the much smaller city of Rovereto, in Trentino, at its apogee in the eighteenth century as a crossroads of European trade, collateral shifted from the traditional real estate towards moveable, future profits, like felled timber ready for the sawmill, foreshadowing modern leveraged buyouts.[23]

In northern Italy, interest rates ranged from 3 per cent to 8 per cent in the sixteenth and seventeenth centuries, with a median of 5 per cent, falling to 4 per cent in the eighteenth century. Variations of one percentage point higher or lower, within this range, were related to the riskiness of the transaction, which was affected not only by the size of loan, its duration, and the collateral but also by the debtor's trustworthiness. An interest rate of 6 per cent or 7 per cent was considered equitable, both for borrowers and for lenders. For those who had cash, interest-rate loans were an attractive form of investment: for a given level of risk, they were more profitable than land (which produced yields from 3 per cent to 5 per cent) and easier to manage. It was also more lucrative than investing in the Mint,

20 Which means 35,120 lire. In 1778, one *gigliato* equalled 17.56 lire (De Maddalena 1974, 421).

21 Archivio Policlinico di Milano, Causa Pia Macchi, Macchi 41, 1 June 1778. On Giuseppe Macchi, see M. Borgonovo 1992, 51–100.

22 See De Luca 1996. On *census consignativus* and its innovative characteristics see De Luca, Lorenzini 2018, 15–16.

23 Lorenzini 2018, 115; Rovereto, under the Habsburg Empire and with half the inhabitants of Trento, which conversely was the capital of the Prince-Bishops, proved to be a thriving economic hub thanks to its lively silk manufacturing and international trade; such a boom had significant repercussions in the financial markets, which were shaping more advanced financial instruments.

where deposits generated yields similar to land. Another alternative was deposits at Monti di Pietà, but they too generated yields of around 3 per cent.

The cap on interest rates was usually set by local authorities; the changes within the limits depended on different factors, such as the availability of capital, the level of demand, and—as mentioned above—the debtors' reliability. For 100 ducats (600 Venetian lire) supplied to Antonio Nascimbeni—borrowed for "very urgent needs"—Angelo Bertolini charged 8 per cent interest (the highest rate possible).[24] For twice that sum (200 ducats), issued to Geronimo, who needed the money to help his son start a bakery, Tommaso Canterio charged half that rate, 4 per cent.[25] Capital was employed for a wide range of purposes, from purchasing a wig to opening a spinning mill, from buying a pair of clogs to preventing a silk factory from going bankrupt or building and repairing infrastructure. For instance, in the late seventeenth century, the City Council of Verona borrowed 16,000 ducats (99,200 Venetian lire) to repair the banks of the Adige river, which had been destroyed by a flood in 1677.[26] The mayor of Cremona, near Milan, on the other hand, borrowed 2,000 *gigliati* (33,500 Milanese lire) from Francesco Sala for 6 years at 4.25 per cent to build the stretch of postal road that connected Cremona to Mantua.[27]

The precondition for participation in this market was ownership of assets, which could be either liquidity or properties. This allowed a large share of the population, from earls, marquises, and dukes to craftsman, manufacturers, professionals and small property-owners, to be the actors of peer-to-peer credit; only the indigent were excluded.[28] Notarised loans passed from hand to hand, crossing barriers of social status, occupation, and gender.

---

24 Verona State Archives (Archivio di Stato di Verona, henceforth Asvr), Notarile, Notary B. Bonumioli, fol. 1344, deed of 8 January 1691.

25 Asvr, Notarile, Notary D. Muttoni, fol. 6984–6985, deed of 30 June 1681.

26 Letter to the Captain of Verona, 4 July 1677 in Pregadi, document contained in Asvr, Notarile, Notary G. F. Vidali and D. Moretti, fol. 11295, deed of 10 February 1681.

27 Milan State Archives (Archivio di Stato di Milano—henceforth Asmi), Notarile, Notary C. A. Coquio, deed of 24 May 1780.

28 For the lower social classes, the Monti di Pietà (pawnshops) and pious institutions were created. They provided pawn loans which were originally short-term and involved small amounts (Carboni and Fornasari, 2019).

3 Women's participation

Women were a constant presence in the private capital market, their activity strengthening across the centuries in terms of both number of transactions and capital flow.[29] This increase was quantitative—and partly physiological since credit networks generally expanded when the economy was growing, bringing in more female agents—and also qualitative, with changes in the type of woman engaged in the mortgage market.[30] While female lenders in the past had been typically widows[31], single and married women now began to be involved in the credit market, creating a more complex and composite cluster. Finally, we may assume that their broader presence was also the result of the autonomy that women had slowly (and not without pain) achieved over the generations, as a consequence of their greater involvement in the labour market and consequently in economic production. This provided access to new sources of income, allowing them to accumulate wealth—through other means than inheritance—and to manage it by lending or borrowing.[32]

In eighteenth-century Milan, women drew up 17 per cent of total deeds and mobilised 11 per cent of global sums (both as debtors and as creditors).[33] The number of female creditors grew to exceed that of female borrowers, with a spe-

29 Studies on the participation of women in financial markets ("formal and informal" capital markets) have been growing in the last two decades; see, for brevity: Carlos, Neal 2004; Dermineur 2010; Fontaine 2011; Laurence A, J. Maltby, and J. Rutterford (eds.) 2012; Carlos, Maguire, and Neal 2012; Bellavitis 2012; Ait 2014; Dermineur 2014; Naymo 2017; Dermineur 2018. Though not focused specifically on women, some research on capital markets also pointed out the female presence and role, see De Luca 1996; Hoffman, Postel-Vinay, and Rosenthal 2000; Lorenzini 2016.

30 Despite this unequal distribution of wealth, the Roman law safeguarded women and their wealth more than common law (Licini 2011, 47).

31 In early seventeenth-century Milan, widows represented almost 86 per cent of operations in bills of exchange, where profits were produced by speculation on rates. Moreover, the Statutes of the Duchy of Milan fixed that in case of the husband's death, the wife could regained possession of the dowry and, if there were no children, also of the assets received by the family of origin or her husband's. This measure led widows to manage large assets in some cases. In addition, in some Milanese wills, in order to protect children, wives were nominated by their husbands' usufructuary of the entire patrimony. Their financial investments were also safeguarded by the laws, establishing that in case of a banker's failure, they were the first creditors to be reimbursed (De Luca 1996, 198–199).

32 A research study on notarial contracts drawn up in sixteenth-century Naples shows the "gradual reduction of male intervention in notarial deeds as a guarantee for women", especially spinsters and widows. (Naymo 2017, 449–452).

33 These figures come from the calculous of 800 contracts of Milanese notaries, active in the second half of the eighteenth century.

cific ratio of close to 60:40, and a similar proportion was seen in female credit v. female debt. The trend continued in the following century. Deeds signed by women rose from 15 per cent in the 1770s to 20 per cent in the 1830s, accelerating to 24 per cent in the 1840s. Milan represented an exceptional case since its financial market was one of the most advanced of the Italian peninsula. These figures are all the more striking when compared to those of other urban centres: in Imperia, (Liguria), for instance, female participation (in terms of mobilised capital) was much lower at 3.5 per cent (number of deeds, 34 per cent). However, in other developing cities, the share reflected the significant quota of women. In Pavia (Lombardy), 15 per cent of capital was mobilised by them (number of deeds, 26.3 per cent), in Forlì 28 per cent[34], and in Cesena one third[35].

The numbers of women in the eighteenth-century mortgage market in Milan did not differ greatly from the situation in Paris, where female lenders made up 27.6 per cent of the total at that time and mobilised 23.5 per cent of funds.[36] Similar percentages were seen in the French provinces. Specifically, female creditors provided 24 per cent of total exchanges in Florimont, while in Delle they accounted for 22 per cent.[37] In Rovereto, in the Italian Alpine region, with its booming economy in the eighteenth century thanks to rapidly growing industry and international commerce, the data are quite noteworthy. The share of capital mobilised by women rose from 11.7 per cent (1740) to 12.6 per cent (1780). The figures were slightly more modest in late-seventeenth-century Verona. Borrowed capital amounted to 9.8 per cent while lending was at 6.2 per cent. This may be partially explained by the fact that Verona was still recovering from the plague and economic crisis of the 1630s.

3.1 Women's wealth

Possessing wealth, real estate for those requesting a mortgage and cash for lenders, was, as mentioned above, the prerequisite for taking part in the borrowing market. In a society where the economic system was monopolised by men, ladies had fewer opportunities to obtain an income or to amass wealth. Their principal job options were crafts, the putting-out system (mainly textiles), and domestic service. If they did earn an income—when not in kind—they were paid much less than their male counterparts. Women's lower share of capital flow was influenced

34 Fantini 2019.

35 Campana 2014.

36 Hoffman, Postel-Vinay, and Rosenthal 2000, 67.

37 Dermineur 2010, 71.

by the very different initial conditions of men and women. Women's assets traded on the private capital market mostly derived from inheritance. But here too, inheritance tended to favour male heirs. As Licini maintains, except from the part of estate that they inherited, "women were bequeathed with land and financial resources mostly, if not only, when there were no other ways to preserve and transmit the family fortune. Roman law tradition actually protected women's rights to property better than Common law rules, but this was not enough to prevent gender inequality." Although this disparity did exist, women were far "from being completely divorced from ownership"[38].

The most common source of women's wealth was the dowry, i.e., the portion of assets they received before getting married or entering a convent.[39] Although women's rights to property were better safeguarded in civil-law societies than in common-law countries, where married women lost all rights to their patrimony[40], the use of the dowry had restrictions since it was exclusively aimed at the maintenance of the family, which essentially meant that the woman was not free to employ it for her own needs as she saw fit. After marriage, her assets were managed by her husband, although he was not allowed to sell, pawn, or divide them without his wife's approval.[41]

The dowry attracted increasing attention through the early modern age for its social implications. From a simple transfer of wealth from one household to another, it became an instrument for improving socioeconomic status, establishing political and business alliances, or consolidating intra-household sodality. Wealth bequeathed to daughters and sisters began to grow in the sixteenth century[42], and people often went into debt in order to create a respectable and hon-

38 Licini 2011, 47.

39 The case of the dowry that young women took with them once they entered the convent had a significant impact on the capital market since female convents used to invest that liquidity in interest-rate loans. For some of these religious institutions, the revenues yielded by credit constituted the main source of livelihood.

40 Bellavitis 2012, 264.

41 Garlati 2011, 6; Lanaro and Varanini 2009, 93.

42 From the late fifteenth to the seventeenth century in Venice, its value almost tripled, reaching a peak of several thousands of ducats. See Lanaro and Varanini 2009, 85; Chojnacky 1975, 571–572. See also Lanaro 2010, 759–769. In order to gauge the sum, the average annual expenditure of a family of four was about 50 ducats (310 Venetian lire), Pezzolo 2003, 158. A master craftsman earned around 120 ducats per year (Lorenzini 2016, 22). Anna Bellavitis, in her study on credit and trust of women in sixteenth-century Venice, maintained that, according to the words of the Venetian nun Arcangela Tarabotti—forced to the nunnery against her will—the constraints of marriage, the cause and effect of the uncontrollable increase in dowries, and the subsequent crowding of convents, was strictly connected to the necessity to limit births in order to maintain political power within a narrow elite (Bellavitis 2012, 265).

ourable dowry, regardless of their social position. After all, a good marriage was a lifelong investment. Hence, when the Veronese nobleman Domenico Zugno borrowed 600 ducats (3,720 Venetian lire), it was to "provide a dowry to his noble sister Angela, wife of the nobleman Mandricardo Mercanti".[43] Similarly, Vittoria Carzali, widow of Giacom'Antonio Guerra, borrowed 300 ducats (1,860 Venetian Lire) to make a dowry for her daughter. She was willing to pledge as collateral the workshop she possessed in the *contrada* of San Fermo e Rustico, to which she was entitled as "successor to her son, Ottavio".[44] In pre-industrial Italy, the dowry constituted one of the most widespread motives for going into debt.

This portion of wealth could be made of moveable or immoveable assets or a mixture thereof. In Venice for instance, liquidity (cash, financial instruments, jewellery, furniture) constituted 18 per cent of the dowry, with property making up the balance. For the middle class (craftsmen, merchants, professionals, small landowners), money represented between 13 and 30 per cent of the dowry, and real estate the rest. The moveable assets could be used for providing interest-rate loans, while the real estate—lands, villas in the countryside, palazzi in the city, workshops, mills, etc.—could be employed as collateral in order to obtain a loan.

Once married, the management of the wife's wealth was transferred to the hands of her husband, but he could not use it as collateral for a loan without her consent since she was a co-signer on the deed. When Antonio Sesia from Milan was looking for a loan of 500 Milanese lire, his wife, Giuseppa Sanpietro, also signed the deed, pledging her "dowry, for which she includes the authorisation from the Senate".[45] On the other hand, Gaetano Rusca lent 9,000 lire at 4 per cent interest rate to Giovanni Lampugnani, specifying that that money belonged to his wife Rosa Villa.

Women could use and manage their dowry independently only if their husband was absent—abroad, jailed, or deceased—, a situation which was not infrequent in a society where women enjoyed a lower mortality rate: they usually married men older than them, they did not go to war, and had a longer life expectancy.[46] Widows were the most active female agents in the informal credit market. They could use the portion of cash as interest-rate loans or the property as security for borrowing. In seventeenth-century Verona, the widow Chiara Stella Vigili used as collateral a house with "walls, roof, hayloft, walled courtyard and stall at

43 Asvr, Notarile, Notary D. Muttoni, fol. 6.992, deed of 3 September 1686.
44 Asvr, Notarile, Notary A. Trezio, fol. 10.910, deed of 21 January 1681.
45 Asmi, Notarile, Notary C. A. Coquio, fol. 45145, deed of 1 August 1752.
46 In sixteenth-century Venice, 75 per cent of women asked for the restitution of the dowry (Bellavitis 2012, 266).

the end of the vegetable garden" that she owned "as a dowry", in order to secure a loan of 220 ducats (1,364 Venetian lire).[47]

Women's transactions did not involve only petty finance; quite the opposite in numerous cases, making them prominent agents in peer-to-peer lending. The widow Paola Tartara issued total credit amounting to the considerable sum of 232,873 Milanese lire, spread over ten transactions.[48] The countess Maria Olgiati Perusati, on the other hand, borrowed 45,000 Milanese lire from the Duke Gian. Galeazzo Visconti at 3.5 per cent—a relatively low rate—for 5 years, in order to pay her sister's dowry.[49] To give an idea of how much the sum was, a bricklayer's income was 1.46 lire per day, and 1 *moggio* of wheat (approx. 146 litres) cost 32.10 lire.[50]

3.2 Women's role

Women were often represented by a male figure—their father, brother, husband or other "procurators"—operating on their behalf in legal and financial transactions. However, our research shows that it was not rare to find ladies signing contracts on behalf of others, mostly when their children were underage, but also when their husbands or brothers got themselves into financial straits.

Very often they were in charge of representing their children and, more importantly, managing their assets until the children came of age. Maria Caterina Caimi, representing her sons, issued two loan contracts, supplying in total the large amount of 333 *gigliati* (15,943 Milanese lire) at interest rates of 4–4.5 per cent.[51] The money was inherited from her sons' uncle, Antonio Maggi, and Maria invested it in profitable transactions. Likewise, the widow Paola Tartara issued a total of 232,873 Milanese lire, distributed in ten deeds, charging an interest rate ranging from 3.5 per cent to 5 per cent.[52]

Women were rarely owners or administrators of partnerships on their own, but they could co-partner with their husbands, which implied that they co-signed

---

47 Asvr, Notarile, Notary F. Bernardi, fol. 1.427, deed of 6 June 1676.

48 Asmi Notarile, Notary Gio. Agostino Gariboldi, fol. 2326, deed of 10 June 1779.

49 Asmi, Notarile, Notary G. A. Gariboldi, fol. 2326, deed of 10 June 1779.

50 De Maddalena 1974, 379.

51 Asmi Notarile, Notary C. A. Coquio, fol. 1712, deed of 6 May 1756. Male relatives made no resistance, also in those cases where the attribution of the protection of the widowed mother forces the division of the assets of the male mercantile partnership, which the father had founded with his brothers, and that allowed their mothers to manage the dead husband's fortune (Bellavitis 2012, 263).

52 Asmi, Notarile, Notary Gio. Agostino Gariboldi, fol. 2326.

borrowing contracts, participating in an entrepreneurial role. Mr. and Mrs. Guaita borrowed the significant amount of 60,000 Milanese lire at 4.75 per cent for three years from the count Stefano San Giuliani. To obtain the loan, they offered their wool-mill in Como and their jointly-owned business in Amsterdam as collateral.[53] Clara Ravizza, together with her husband Leonardo Savini, borrowed 7,000 Milanese lire (at 5 per cent for three years) from Silvestro Annoni in order to remodel their perfume shop.[54] Similarly in 1770 in Rovereto, home to flourishing silk manufacturing and trade since the mid-eighteenth century, ladies were frequently engaged in businesses along with their husbands and were next to them when they had to draw up contracts. Husband and wife Pietro and Virginia Manzoli turned to the nobleman Giacinto Cobelli for a five-year loan of 1,000 Florins (5,000 Venetian lire) at 5 per cent to pay off an outstanding debt owed to Cobelli himself for grain they had purchased in his shop.[55]

Women's signatures on mortgage contracts represented an additional guarantee, and also solidified the relationship between husband and wife. As argued by Elise Dermineur, a married woman "could decide to oppose the signature of a deed and, in theory, she could not be compelled to sign. If the deed became too risky, she had the option of withdrawing her lineage property and seeking a separation of property from her husband's". The fact that her lineage property and assets were "at stake did not represent a reinforcement of patriarchy but rather a breach in it".[56]

Women often went into debt to settle their husband's arrears. Antonia d'Este, for instance, asked for a loan of 10,000 Milanese lire in order to "pay off her husband's creditors, the brothers Bellinzago, owners of the Carlo Andrea Bellinzago partnership".[57] She obtained the loan at a 5 per cent interest rate for three years. Hence women and their assets turned out to be smart exit strategies to the entire families of husbands who were in financial difficulties, bringing unquestionable repercussions on gender hierarchies within the families.[58]

Reputation was a crucial factor in the credit market, but with credit in preindustrial economies highly "embedded in society", it had played a social function, a means through which values like trust and reliability were transmitted and the glue that held communities together.[59]

---

53 Asmi, Notarile, Notary M. A. Pizzigalli, fol. 3775, deed of 27 November 1786.

54 Asmi, Notarile, Notary C. A. Coquio, fol. 1712, deed of 28 February 1764.

55 Astn, Notarile, Notary G. Bettini, fol. XIV, 2721, deed of 3 October 1770.

56 Dermineur 2010, 68.

57 Asmi, Notarile, Notary G. A. Gariboldi, fol. 2326, deed of 1 March 1786.

58 M. R. De Rosa 2017, 27.

59 Muldrew 1998, 5; Fontaine, 156.

3.3 Motives for women's debts

When women drew up debt contracts on their own, it was mainly for meeting needs linked to family affairs such as house expenditures or management costs. Money was borrowed to cover everyday expenses or to be put into long-term investments, such as a daughter's dowry, which might imply very large sums in aristocratic households. The countess and widow Camilla Dugnani borrowed the considerable sum of 10,000 *gigliati* (16,750 Milanese lire) from the countess Giulia Lucini Borromeo in order to "pay off past family debts", such as the 4,000 Milanese lire that she received from the notary Carlo Francesco Saccabarozzi as a two-year loan at 4 per cent. However, she had previously secured two other loans—both three-year loans of 400 *gigliati* at 4 per cent—to create her daughter Maria's dowry.[60] Women also went into debt to make house repairs. In Verona, Toscana Leonardi negotiated a more modest loan of 100 ducats (620 Venetian lire) with Pietro Tregnani to "cover the many household expenses".[61] Women were often forced to borrow to save their husbands or sons from disgrace. The widow Orsola Bernardoni secured a mortgaged of 300 ducats (1,860 Venetian lire) to "free her son Gio. Giacomo Botti from prison, where he was serving a criminal sentence". In order to secure the loan, she offered a plot of land that was "part of her dowry" as collateral.[62] Similarly, Caterina Massarga asked for a more modest sum of 30 ducats (186 lire) in order to "free her husband from the prison in which he currently finds himself here in Verona because of a criminal offense".[63] Chiarastella turned to the count Marco Crema for a loan of 200 ducats (1,240 Venetian lire), necessary to "free from prison her husband Iseppo, who was banished from the state and thus not at home, and her son Alcide, both of them sentenced by the most excellent Consul and most excellent supreme municipal authority".[64]

60 Asmi, Notarile, Notary G.A. Gariboldi, fol. 2326, deeds of 1 October 1777; 2 October 1777; 7 January 1780; and 26 May 1780.

61 Asvr, Notarile, Notary F. Bernardi, fol. 1.444, deed of 8 October 1681, *creditum*.

62 Asvr, Notarile, Notary C. De Gasparo, fol. 3.139, deed of 22 January 1676.

63 Asvr, Notarile, Notary A. Trezio, fol. 10.910, deed of 8 February 1681.

64 Asvr, Notarile, Notary D. Moretti, fol. 7.035, deed of 11 January 1691.

3.4 The destination of women's credit

While the motives for taking out a debt were, as stated, usually limited to family needs, the money women lent went to satisfy a much broader array of purposes. It was invested in finance, trade, businesses, productive activities, as well as welfare in the form of loans to parishes, towns and villages, hospitals, helping nurture the economic and financial systems of their communities. As pointed out above, most female creditors were widows, such as Carlotta Pickler, who lent 2,000 Milanese lire for four years at 4.5 per cent to Clara Clerici and her husband Gio. Batta Ballioni, who used the money to "establish a linen and wool pinning mill in the town of Luino, Lombardy".[65] Similarly, the capital lent by Rosa Sturioni Solivetta to Marco Chiappone, amounting to 3,250 Milanese lire in a five-year 4 per cent loan, was employed to build silk workshop.[66] In another transaction, she provided a loan of 400 *gigliati* (8,700 Milanese lire) to the merchant Marco Antonio Chiappone, who used it to build a silk factory in Milan. Rosa Cagliati Mariani, on the other hand, signed a loan of 6,000 Milanese lire on behalf of her husband to expand his trade network. Sums were also invested in municipal debts. Over the course of a few months in Verona in 1676, the patrician Barbara Piatti provided 22,320 Venetian lire to the rural communities of Povegliano and Cerea, highly indebted.[67]

4 Concluding remarks

Poorly represented in the institutionalised financial world, mainly dominated by men and characterised by qualified financial dealers and organisations, women played a significant role in the private capital markets. Notaries, acting as informal brokers, played a crucial role in their involvement. If their participation in the system of production was limited to activities linked to manufacturing (mainly the textile putting-out system), domestic work, and sometimes partnerships with their husbands, peer-to-peer lending turned out to be a strategic alternative for investing their liquidity and guaranteeing a source of income. The precondition for participation in the mortgage market, both as lenders and as borrowers, was the possession of assets that chiefly comprised the dowry or their savings, if they had a paying job. An in-depth analysis of their financial behaviour shows that

---

65 Asmi, Notarile, Notary G. A. Gariboldi, fol. 2326, deed of 24 January 1784.

66 Asmi, Notarile, Notary M. A. Pizzigalli, fol. 3775, deed of 23 April 1771.

67 Asvr, Notarile, Notary V. Ferro, fol. 5.248, deed of 18 April 1676.

they differed little from their male counterparts and their propensity to taking risks. This kind of market was yet intrinsically low-risk, with loans always backed by collateral, and information asymmetries being overcome by the intermediation service provided by notaries. However, a gender gap existed in motivations and purposes. The money that they borrowed was always associated with household needs—day-to-day expenses and house management costs—or family issues, like creating the dowry to their daughter, paying off their husbands' arrears, saving them from possible bankruptcy and damage to their reputations. Conversely, the money that they lent was invested in a wider range of operations, including the financing of economic activities such as manufacturing, trade, or businesses, or funding towns and local communities, overburdened by taxes. They came to lend meaningful sums charging interests, 4–4.5 per cent, that were often below the market rate. They also favoured gold coins—*zecchini* or *gigliati* in Milan—because they were less subject to depreciation and in case of bankruptcy, they were the first creditors to be reimbursed. All these factors made women competitive financial agents, able to hold their own against the most qualified and specialised lenders. This trend would strengthen in the following century, the nineteenth century, when women were able to supply hundreds of thousands of lire in credit.

Throughout the early modern age, women's participation increased in both quantity and quality. The credit network expanded very rapidly and pervasively in the absence of modern financial institutions, and the number of woman-mediated transactions was not entirely a "physiological" response. This study shows that the type of woman taking part in the credit market, at least as regards marital status, changed, with more and more wives and single women becoming involved. We may suppose that their emancipation, very slow and not pain-free, came about partly via the informal financial markets. The possibility of gaining an independent income certainly contributed to strengthening their economic status. Within the family context, this would be reflected in greater bargaining power, which would slowly erode the rigid patriarchal structure, while in the greater economy, they would represent a fundamental source of financing for the productive system and the financial markets.

References

Archival References

Archivio Policlinico di Milano, Causa Pia Macchi, Macchi 41.

Asmi (Archivio di Stato di Milano), Notarile, Notaries: M. A. Pizzigalli; C. A. Coquio, G. A. Gariboldi; C. A. Aureggi.

Astn (Archivio di Stato di Trento), Rovereto, Notarile, Year 1750, Notaries: B. G. Battisti; G. A. Bellotti; M. B. Broilo; G. Candioli; B. Costa; C. G. Eccher; A. G. Giordani; D. A. Givanni C. A. Grasser; G. A. Mascotti; G. B. Prato; V. Rella; C. Rigotti; P. Trentoini; G. A. Valentini; G. A. Zanini.

Year 1760: G. A. Prato; B. G. Battisti; G. Bettini; G. Bonfioli de Cavalcabò; G. Candioli; B. Costa; D. A. Filippi; G. A. Forer; L. Garavetti; A. G. Giordani; D. A. Givanni; G. B. Grasser; G. C. Guarinoni; G. A. Mascotti; P. A. Rella; B. A. Valentini; G. A. Valentini; G. A. Zanini.

Year 1770: G. G. Battisti; G. Bettini; G. Bonfioli de Cavalcabò; F. A. Candioli; D. A. Filippi; L. Garavetti; A. G. Giordani; G. B. Grasser; G. A. Mascotti; D. F. Ponticello; G. A. Romani; G. Untersteiner; B. A. Valentini.

Year: 1780: A. A Prato; D. L. Battisti; G. G. Battisti; G. Bettini; F. A. Bissaldi; G. Bonfioli De Cavalcabò; F. A. Candioli; G. Candioli; G. B. Grasser; G. A. Mascotti; D. F. Ponticello; G. Untersteiner; B. A. Valentini; G. G. Valentini; G. A. Zanini.

Asvr (Archivio di Stato di Verona), Notarile, Year 1676, Notaries: A. Avanzini; N. Bajetta; P. P. de' Peregrini; G. B. Battistini; G. Bassan Gradenigo; G. Bernardelli; G. Badili; A. Bertini; B. Bonumioli; G. Bagatta; A. Bergamaschi; F. Bernardi; F. Bertoni; G. Borghetti; B. Bernardi; G. Brighignato; C. Corrubioli; C. de Gasperi; S. Cozza; D. Cristofori; F. Cristofori; P. Dalle Femmine; F. Dolobella; P. P. Dalla Costa; G. Emendatori; F. Ferro; G. F. Fasoli; F. Filippini; A. Fiorio; P. Fontana; V. Ferro; B. Franchini; A. Fracanzani; Gelmetti; G. F. Gianfilippi De' Parenti; C. Lavori; G. Fagioli; D. Muttoni; D. Moretti with G. Rossi; A. Montagna; A. Monte; V. Marconi; G. P. Passeri; D. Rinaldi; G. Rizzi; C. A. Sartori; A. Suttori; G. Squarzago; G. Simeoni; G. C. Tresana; C. Tombesani; A. Trezio; G. F. Vidali; G. Vanzonetto; A. Zannini; G. Zeni; G. Zambenetti; F. Zannini; N. Zeni Nicolò.

Year 1681: Notaries: A. Avanzini and S. Avanzini; D. Alessandri; P. P. Battistini de' Peregrini; G. B. Battistini de' Peregrini; G. Bassan Gradenigo; G. Badili; A. Bertini; B. Bonumioli; G. Bagatta; A. Bergamaschi; F. Bernardi; F. Bertoni; N. Bajetta; G. Badili; G. Borghetti; G. Brighignato; F. Battagin; B. Bruni; G. Brighignato; C. Corrubioli; G. Colombo de Gasperi; S. Cozza; D. Cristofori; F. Cristofori; P. Dalle femmine; P. P. Dalla

Costa; G. Emendatori; F. Filippini; A. Fiorio; P. Fontana; V. Ferro; F. Filippini; B. Franchini; A. Fracanzani; Gelmetti; G.F. Gianfilippi de Parenti; C. Libardi and A. Seriati; D. Muttoni; D. Moretti; A. Montagna; A. Monte; G. Maioli; V. Marconi; M. Marini; G. Meriggi Azzolini; G. Morlati; D. Rinaldi; G. Rizzi; C. Sartori; A. Suttori; R. Secondini; G. Squarzago; G. Simeoni; A. Sartori; G. Scarsi; G. Scanagatti; C. Tombesani; A. Trezio; G.F. Veniteo; G.F. Vidali and D. Moretti; G. Vanzonetti; A. Zannini; G. Zeni; G. Zambenetti; F. Zannini; N. Zeni.

Year 1686: Notaries: A. Avanzini; D. Alessandri; A. Alessandri; P.P. Battistini de' Peregrini; G.B. Battistini de' Peregrini; G. Badili; A. Bertini; B. Bonumioli; G. Bagatta; A. Bergamaschi; F. Bernardi; F. Bertoni; G. Badili; B. Bruni; G. Brighignato; G. Bernardi; C. Corrubioli; S. Cozza; Cristofori Donato; S. Cristofori; P. Dalle Femmine; A. Dalle Femmine; G. Emendatori; F. Ferro; F. Filippini; V. Ferro; F. Filippini; A. Fiorio; P. Fontana; B. Franchini; A. Fracanzani; G.F. Gianfilippi de Parenti; Gelmetti; C. Libardi; G. Meriggi D'Azzolini; V. Marconi; M. Marini; A. Maroldi; G. Maioli; M. Mantovani; D. Moretti; A. Monte; G. Monticali; D. Muttoni; G. Rizzi; G. Scarsi; G. Scanagatti; A. Sartori; G. Sartori; R. Secondini; A. Seriati; G. Simeoni; G. Squarzago; G. Suttori; A. Suttori; C. Tombesani; A. Trezio; L. Tavolini; G. Vanzonetto; G.F. Veniteo; B. Vidali and C. Libardi; A. Zannini; F. Zannini; G. Zeni; N. Zeni; G. Zambenetti.

Year 1691: Notaries: D. Alessandri; A. Alessandri; Battistini de' Peregrini; G. Badili; A. Bertini; B. Bonumioli; G. Bagatta; F. Bertoni; G. Badili; B. Bruni; G. Bighignato; G. Bernardi; S. Cozza; F. Cristofori; S. Cristofori; N. Cerù; P. Dalla Costa; A. Dalle Femmine; G.B. Dalla Via; G. Emendatori; A. Fiorio; P. Fontana; V. Ferro; F. Filippini; B. Franchini; A. Fracanzani; G.L. Franceschini; Gelmetti; Gianfilippi de Parenti; D. Muttoni; D. Moretti; A. Monte; G. Maioli; V. Marconi; G. Meriggi Azzolini; G. Morlati; G. Monticali; A. Maroldi; M. Mantovani; O. Majelli; L. Pontesani; G. Rizzi; A. Suttori; R. Secondini; G. Simeoni; A. Sartori; G.B. Scarsi; A. Seriati; G. Tommasini; C. Tombesani; A. Trezio; L. Tavolini; G. Veniteo; G. Vanzonetto; F. Zannini; N. Zeni.

Bibliographic References

Ait I. 2014. "Un valore aggiunto delle donne: il credito". *Studi storici* 55, no. 3: 779–787.

Bellavitis A. 2012. "Dare credito, fiducia e responsabilità alle donne (Venezia, secolo XVI)". In *Dare credito alle donne. Presenze femminili nell'economia tra medioevo ed età moderna. Convegno internazionale di studi Asti, 8–9 ottobre 2010. Atti di convegno, 6*, 259–267. Asti: Centro studi Renato Bordone sui Lombardi, sul credito e sulla banca.

Berengo M. 1981. "Africo Clementi, agronomo padovano del Cinquecento". In *Miscellanea Augusto Campana Medioevo e umanesimo 44*, edited by Rino Avesani, Mirella Ferrari, Giovanni Pozzi, 27–69. Padua: Il Mulino.

Borgonovo M. 1992. "Giuseppe Macchi: ascesa di un banchiere nella Milano del Settecento". *Il Risorgimento* 44, no. 1: 51–100.

Campana F. 2014. "Il mercato del credito tra privati: Cesena a metà Ottocento". *Romagna arte e storia* 44, no. 101: 45–60.

Carboni M. and M. Fornasari 2019. "The 'untimely' demise of a successful institution: the Italian Monti di pietà in the nineteenth century", *Financial History Review* 26, no. 2: 147–170.

Carlos A., K. Maguire, and L. Neal 2009. "Women in the city: financial acumen during the South Sea Bubble". In *Women and their Money 1700–1950, Essays on women and finance,* edited by A. Laurence, J. Maltby, and J. Rutterford, 33–45, London: Routledge International Studies in Business History.

Carlos A. and L. Neal 2004. "Women investors in early capital markets, 1720–1725". *Financial History Review* 11, no. 2: 197–224.

Chojnacky S. 1975. "Dowries and Kinsmen in Early Renaissance Venice", *The Journal of Interdisciplinary History* 5: 571–572.

Collodo S. 1940. *Una società in trasformazione. Padova tra XI e XV secolo.* Padua: Antenore.

Corazzol G. 1986. *Livelli stipulati a Venezia nel 1591.* Pisa: Giardini Editore.

Corazzol G 1994. "Varietà notarile: scorci di vita economica e sociale". In *Storia di Venezia,* vol. VI, 775–776, Rome: Treccani.

De Luca G. 1996. *Commercio del denaro e crescita economica a Milano tra Cinque e Seicento.* Milan: Il Polifilo.

De Luca G. and M. Lorenzini 2018. "Conflicts, Financial Innovations, and Economic Trends in the Italian States during the Thirty Years' War". In *Financial Innovation and Resilience. The Outstanding Achievements of the Public Banks of Naples (1462–1808),* edited by L. Costabile and L Neal, 165–185. London: Palgrave Macmillan.

De Maddalena A. 1974. *Prezzi e mercedi a Milano dal 1701 al 1860.* Milan: Banca Commerciale italiana.

De Rosa M. R. 2017. *A tempo debito. Donne, uomini, relazioni di credito a Napoli tra Ottocento e Novecento.* Roma: Viella.

Dermineur E. 2009. "Female Peasants, Patriarchy and the Credit Market in Eighteenth-Century France". *Proceedings of the Western Society for French History* 37: 61–84.

Dermineur E. 2014. "Single Women and the Rural Credit Market in Eighteenth-Century France". *Journal of Social History* 48, no. 1: 175–199.

Dermineur E. 2018. "Credit, strategies and female empowerment in early modern France". In *Women and credit in pre-industrial Europe,* edited by E. Dermineur, 253–280. Turnhout: Brepols.

Dermineur E. (ed.) 2018. *Women and credit in pre-industrial Europe.* Turnhout: Brepols.

Faggion L. 2008. "Il notaio, la società e la mediazione in età moderna nelle storiografie francese e italiana: un confronto". *Acta Histriae* 16: 527–544.

Fantini I. 2019. "Notai e reti creditizie a Forlì nel primo Ottocento". *Romagna, arte e storia* 113: 61–84.

Fontaine L. 2011. "Il posto delle donne nella piccola economia finanziaria in Europa, in età moderna". *Quaderni Storici* 46, no. 137 (2): 513–532.

Fontaine L. 2008. *L'économie morale. Pauvreté, crédit et confiance dans l'Europe préindustrielle.* Paris: Gallimard.

Garlati L. 2011. "La famiglia tra passato e presente". In *Diritto di famiglia,* edited by S. Patti and M. G. Cubeddu, 1–48. Milan: Giuffré.

Hoffman P. T., G. Postel-Vinay, and J.-L. Rosenthal 2019. *Dark Matter Credit: The Development of Peer-to-Peer Lending and Banking in France.* Princeton and Oxford: Princeton University Press.

Hoffman P. T., G. Postel-Vinay, and J.-L. Rosenthal 2000. Priceless Markets. The Political Economy of Credit in Paris 1660–1870. Chicago: University of Chicago Press.

Lanaro P. 2010. "La restituzione della dote. Il gioco ambiguo della stima tra beni mobili e beni immobili (Venezia tra Cinque e Settecento)". *Quaderni storici* 45, no. 135 (3): 753–778.

Lanaro P. and G. M. Varanini, 2009. "Funzioni economiche della dote nell'Italia centro-settentrionale (tardo medioevo/inizio età moderna)". In *La famiglia nell'economia europea,* secc. XIII–XVIII, edited by S. Cavaciocchi, 81–102. Florence: Florence University Press.

Laurence A, J. Maltby, and J. Rutterford (eds.) 2012. *Women and their Money 1700–1950* [= Routledge International Studies in Business History]. London: Routledge.

Licini S. 2011. "Assessing female wealth in nineteenth century Milan, Italy". *Accounting History* 16, no. 1: 35–54.

Lorenzini M. 2016. *Credito e notai. Capitali per l'economia veronese del secondo Seicento.* Bologna: Il Mulino.

Muldrew C. 1998, *The Economy of Obligation: The Culture of Credit and Social Relations in Early Modern England.* London: MacMillan.

Naymo V. 2017. "Donne e notai: la presenza e il ruolo femminile negli atti notarili del Regno di Napoli in età moderna". In *Scritti in onore di Giovanna da Molin. Popolazione, famiglia e società in età moderna,* edited by A. Carbone, 447–474. Bari: Cacucci

Pedrinelli G. 1768. *Il Notaio Istruito nel suo Ministero secondo le Leggi, e la Pratica della Serenissima Repubblica di Venezia. Opera Umiliata al Magistrato Gravissimo degl'Ill.mi, ed Ecc.mi Signori Conservatori ed Esecutori delle Leggi da Giovanni Pedrinelli Avvocato Fiscale del medesimo Magistrato.* Venice: Carlo Todero.

Pedani Fabris M. 1996. *Veneta Auctoritate Notarius. Storia del notariato veneziano (1514–1797).* Milan: Giuffrè.

Pezzolo L. 2003, *Il fisco dei veneziani. Finanza pubblica ed economia privata tra XV e XVII secolo.* Sommacampagna (VR): Cierre Edizioni.

Van Zanden J. L., J. Zuijderduijn, and T. De Moor 2012, "Small is beautiful: the efficiency of credit markets in the late medieval Holland". *European Review of Economic History* 16, no. 1: 3–22.

HIGH FINANCE, BANKING AND SMALL-SCALE MONEYLENDING: A NEW TRINITY OF FINANCIAL FUNCTIONS FOR LOMBARDS IN THE LATE-MEDIEVAL LOW COUNTRIES?

David Kusman

Abstract: In this paper, we argue that within the late medieval Low Countries Piedmontese moneylenders offered their clientele a "trinity" of financial services: a stake in high finance undertakings, banking facilities and small credit transactions. To demonstrate this thesis, we use two complementary methods. First, we study the commercial strategies of Piedmontese banking societies with respect to their lending patterns in various regions. Second, we analyse their position in the public finances of two major cities of the Low Countries—Mechelen and Mons. We show that they fulfilled an important function as capital providers in both the private and the public credit sectors, allowing for a steady credit supply and probably contributing, on a short-term basis, to money supply in times of silver scarcity or famine shocks. We argue finally that these banking societies' interest rates ought to be considered, not on a yearly basis, but rather on a weekly basis, which more accurately reflects medieval trade credit practices.

Keywords: Public finances, financial intermediaries, interest rates, banking, high finance

From De Roover's "Holy Trinity" of Financial Actors to a Trinity of Financial Services

More than sixty years have passed since the publication of De Roover's masterwork, *Money, banking and credit in mediaeval Bruges. Italian Merchant bankers, Lombards and Money-Changers. A Study in the Origins of Banking*. De Roover's harsh judgment on the modest economic functions of the so-called "Lombards"—

Published in: Stephan Nicolussi-Köhler (Ed.), Change and Transformation of Premodern Credit Markets. The Importance of Small-Scale Credits. Heidelberg: heiBOOKS 2021, 215–249. DOI: https://doi.org/10.11588/heibooks.593.c12696

in fact mainly Piedmontese—moneylenders natives from Asti and Chieri who, in his eyes, were only small-scale usurers operating within the tight regulations of the city of Bruges, has been revised in quite a number of features. De Roover argued that the big guns—if I may use this colloquial expression—of the financial system in Bruges were the moneychangers and the Tuscan merchant bankers. When the former offered financial services ranging from money changing to deposit banking and supplying the ducal mint with ingots, the latter could loan vast sums of money to the city elites and the Prince while at the same time participating in the cloth trade between Tuscany and the Low Countries. Florentine merchant bankers like the agents working for the Medici and the Portinari used frequently, of course, advanced financial techniques such as the bill of exchange. Only the Florentine super-companies such as the Bardi or the Peruzzi could afford to have partners in all major trading cities in North-Western Europe. Such was not the case, obviously, of small usurers lending at 43.3 per cent a year. De Roover's ideological framework remained ingrained in his accountant's educational background. He could not envision a world, the late medieval urban society of the Low Countries, where financial institutions and economic functions were less rigid and shakier than in the 1920ties, when Raymond de Roover had studied finance at a business school of Antwerp.[1]

That De Roover's views were seen as too rigid was already a fact in 1956 when the city archivist of Antwerp, Frans Blockmans, hinted at the pivotal function of Piedmontese financiers as providers of credit for merchants at the fairs of Antwerp, acting probably also as brokers between Köln wine merchants and local tradesmen from Antwerp. The recent doctorate of Federico Canelloni has shown how strong the integration of the Piedmontese family Asinari was in Antwerp at the beginning of the fifteenth century. Some members of this rich family had strong ties with the city moneychangers of Bruges and Antwerp, others kept an account with the Borromei Bank in London. In this instance, they could make use of letters of exchange for their business dealings between London and Bruges. Other studies have shown that Piedmontese financiers did not shy away from venturing into the cloth business, as Murray demonstrated for Bruges. I could prove that for the duchy of Brabant around the beginning of the fourteenth century, Piedmontese banking societies were in a strong if not overwhelming position with regard to high finance, loaning to the duke of Brabant huge sums that were on a par with the annual incomes of the ducal receipt. This was a confirmation of Bordone's thesis: as early as 1992, Renato Bordone could argue convincingly that so high were the profits derived from moneylending in the Low

1 De Roover 1948, 99–108, Aerts 1980 and Aerts 2018.

Countries that, back in Asti, the potent families Roero and Solaro could buy with this capital entire lordships and gain access to the nobility ranks from the beginning of the fourteenth century. All in all, in 2020 one can say, to quote the Belgian historian Camille Tihon, that the distinction between Tuscan merchant bankers, city moneychangers and the so-called "Lombards" is more akin to a curtain made of bamboo than to a watertight compartment.[2]

In this paper, I will try in a first part to reconstruct the "business plan" of some Piedmontese families whose partnerships were spread on a regional scale, aiming to identify typical business patterns among a number of these *societates*—business partnerships—that were lending their capital between roughly 1280 and 1330 in middle-sized and big cities of the Low Countries and the neighbouring regions: Gent, Köln, Leuven, Mechelen, Mons, Tournai, to name just a few of the most important cities where Piedmontese moneylenders expanded their business.[3] These partnerships were often family-based and offered their clientele a wide array of services, ranging from book transfers between accounts to money changing and investments in moneylending enterprises. Therefore, in the following pages, I will preferably refer to Piedmontese financial establishments as banks or lending houses rather than using the too restrictive term pawnshops to describe their activities. I will mainly focus on the case of Tournai, and draw a comparison with the *societas* of Mechelen. If you would like to tackle the topic of "everyday" credit transactions among various social layers of the society then assessing the business strategy of creditors is a prerequisite for such an approach.

In a second part, I will argue that having pooled funds and revenues kept and perceived by various formal and informal economic actors (moneychangers, brokers, courtiers, members of the high-nobility, etc...), Piedmontese financiers might well have contributed to the money supply available in some major cities of the Low Countries. Being able to accept bank deposits and to loan huge sums of money to the Prince, while at the same time operating on a small-scale level of moneylending, "Lombards", as they were dubbed in medieval sources, were in a crucial position to offer a "trinity" of financial services: high finance, banking and short-term small credits. To illustrate this thesis, I will draw upon quantitative

2 Blockmans 1956, 269–70; Tihon 1961, 335, n. 2; Aerts 1980, 35–36; Van Uytven 1987, 55–56; Bordone 1992, 482–493; Murray 2005, 138–148; Kusman 2012, 372–382 and Canelloni 2015, 134–151.

3 Piedmontese moneylenders defined their partnerships as *societates* and the partners of a given *societas* as *socios* each owning a fixed number of partnerships in the society. It took the form of an *ex commenda* commercial contract: Castellani 1998, 165–168. The publication of Reichert's atlas of Lombards highlights the wide supra-regional scope of Piedmontese credit undertakings (Reichert 2003, vol. 2, 6).

data from two case studies: the city of Mons in the county of Hainault and the city of Mechelen, a territorial enclave in the duchy of Brabant.

In this analysis, I shall strive to be as concise as possible, allowing for a broader view of the Piedmontese lending operations, shifting here and there from the micro-level, the city, to the macro level, the territorial state. In the concluding remarks, I will reflect upon the influence of Piedmontese finance on small-scale moneylending, even though this notion remains, in my opinion, difficult to grasp with respect to the late Middle Ages credit practices.[4]

First Approach, the Commercial Strategies of Piedmontese Bankers in the Low Countries

As Winfried Reichert showed in his paper of 1987 on Lombards between the Rhine and Maas regions during the late Middle Ages, if you aim to understand the credit networks of Piedmontese moneylenders then you need to pinpoint a single family in each instance.[5] You need also to find out how far these credit networks, based on kin connections, extended. In other words, you need to put on a map the circulation of capital and men. This is a necessary step because the vast majority of these financiers coming from Asti did not leave behind any commercial archives of the sort you would normally expect if you were studying Florentine merchant banker companies. No accounts, no merchant books, no letters, usually no *libro de riccordanze,* thus no family's chronicle and almost no wills remain today to help the historian of Piedmontese moneylenders. All the historian is left with, for the Low Countries, are mainly debt recognisances and some city accounts that mention, in passing, "Lombards". This scarcity of private business archives might explain why, too often Lombards were denied any sense of a commercial strategy. Obviously, debt recognisances belonged to the sort of legal records that would be, more often than not, drawn up before the local aldermen of the city where Piedmontese financiers were operating so that lenders could benefit from the legal guarantee of their city of residence for the enforcement of their creditor's rights. This means that the Piedmontese moneylenders were speaking through the al-

4 The concluding debate of the conference showed how blurry this concept may be for the late medieval economy: for instance, do we have to take into account a purely quantitative approach when we try to define a small-scale loan or do we have to take into account a geographical factor (local versus international credit) or the features and form of the credit instrument (pawnbroking vs. annuities)?

5 Reichert 1987, 198–199.

dermen's voice and therefore observed through the lens of the Prince or the local authorities[6]. Yet, this does not necessarily mean that they were not able to devise their own business strategy, adapting to the changing commercial opportunities of each region, similarly to the commercial site analysis used by Tuscan merchant bankers, whether it focused on the abundance of money flows or on the volume of the market[7].

Between, roughly said, 1250 and 1290, the Piedmontese moneylenders established their societies in a number of cities and "chatellenies": the word meaning in its most common acceptance a fortified borough or a medium-sized to big city where a toll station (See Fig. 1) existed with a tax being levied on transit trade (this was the case in Antoing, Audenarde, Aardenburg and Hulst, in the county of Flanders).[8]

Figure 1 Map of supra regional Piedmontese credit networks around 1292.

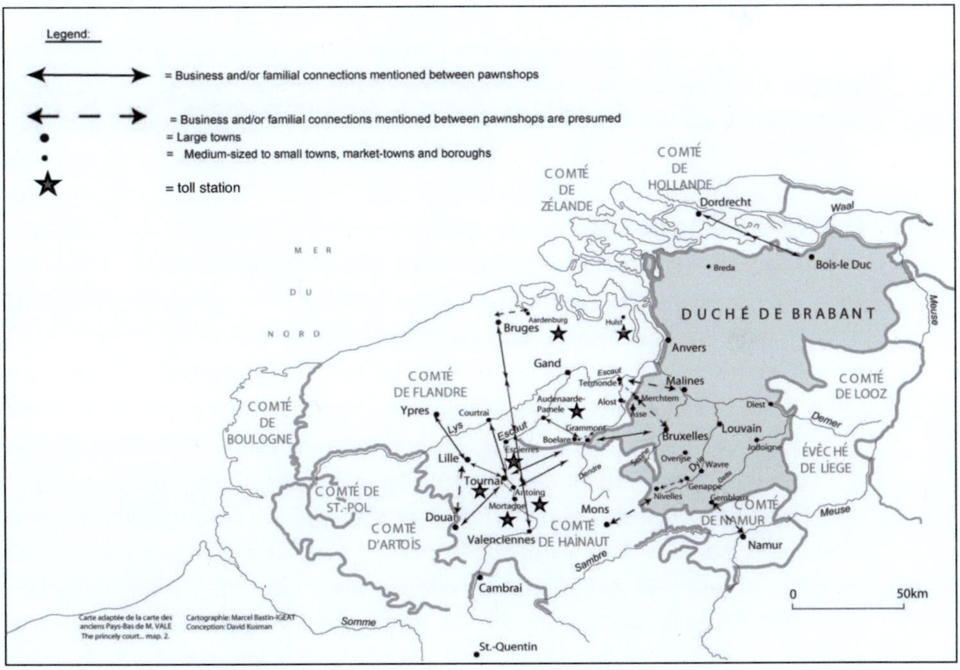

6 This perspective is particularly striking in Bautier 1979 and Van Uytven 1987.
7 I draw this approach from the stimulating considerations of Weissen 2002, 72–73.
8 For the financial dealings of the Piedmontese moneylenders in Tournai, see Kusman 2012, 67–82.

During the second half of the thirteenth century, the Scheldt basin became a vital commercial axis for the late medieval Southern Low Countries. The Picardy region exported grains and dyestuff products such as woad to the county of Flanders while Tournai exported building materials such as the notorious Tournai stone to the city of Ghent, an essential component of the prestigious houses of the Ghent top urban elite. Grains from Picardy transited the Tournai toll before flowing to Ghent via the toll stations of Esplerres and Audenarde; in Ghent, the grains had to be unloaded and sold prior to other cities, by virtue of this town's staple right on grains.[9] This institutional framework of tolls and staple rights had to rely on the services of middlemen, whether financiers or princely officers as the "châtellain".

The "châtellain" or castellan, while being a lord, performed jurisdictional and financial duties related to the management of the toll's income. Toll stations were of course of strategic interest to the Italians bankers and merchants. In these places, they could work as moneychangers, lenders and brokers and as translators if there were other Italian merchants. Lombards, as they were dubbed in the medieval sources, tended preferably to develop at first their activities in the estates of powerful manor lords belonging to the high nobility (as in Mortagne, Tournai and Audenarde). These lords had a strong interest in developing a local market and a fair so that they could derive profits from it in setting up a toll station.[10] This is illustrated by the case study of Tournai, a city that belonged to the French Crown, on the river Scheldt, where members of the families de Baeini, de Solaro and de Roero had managed a lending house on the right bank of the river since 1254, in an enclave within the city: the lordship of the manor lord, Arnould de Mortagne. Arnould de Mortagne had strong connections to the Flemish nobility and was also a vassal of the count of Flanders.[11] This powerful lord owned the lordship of le Bruille, not far from his fortress. Thanks to their privileges received from this local lord, the Piedmontese lenders benefited from a tax exemption from the *taille* (the direct income tax levied in the other part of the city). In addition, they enjoyed the legal status of bourgeois de Monseigneur de Mortagne, or lord of Mortagne's burghers. This statute of seigniorial burgher was in many ways similar to the statute of city burghers also offering tax exemptions for the navigation on the river Scheldt. In exchange for the lord's protection, they had to pay an annual fee to the lord for their *octroi* or license to lend at interest. The license was

9 Boone and Lecuppre-Desjardin 2007, 195–198.

10 Dyer 2005, 20–23 on manor lords and tolls and about the castellans in the Low Countries, see Nieuss 2006, vol. 1, 19 and 21–22 and vol. 2, 316.

11 On this family, see Warlop 1975–1976, vol. 1, 48, vol. 2, 310, vol. 3, 916 and 921–924 and vol. 4, no. 210, 1155 and more recently Buylaert 2011, 506–511.

subject to negotiation as pictured here in the charterbook of the rents of the lord of Audenarde, another powerful manor lord who possessed a toll station on the river Scheldt and relied on the Lombard credit (Fig. 2).

Figure 2 Lombards negotiating their license to lend at interest with the town magistrate of Audenarde.

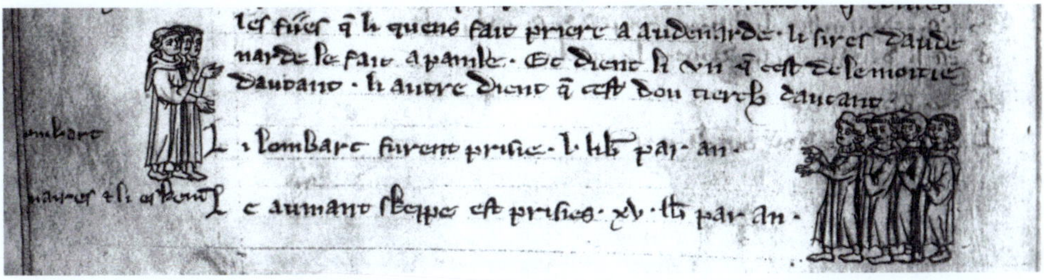

The taste of Piedmontese moneylenders for establishing their banking society in the vicinity of the lord's manor, offering them strong incentives to expand their business, the *Herschaftsnähe* as it is called in German, is something that Reichert also pointed out in 1987.[12]

Within the time span of twenty years or a generation in medieval terms, the de Baieni, de Solaro and Roero families from Asti expanded their lending business, becoming important providers of fresh capital in Tournai. Their clientele encompassed a wide cross section of the urban population ranging from the middling groups to the urban elite. The main features of their lending undertakings were the following:

- An average loaned amount of forty-seven pounds parisis, worth more than 600 times the daily wage of a skilled mason which equals more than two years of wages, clearly not a "lending for the poor" pattern[13]
- A strong presence of cloth merchants among the borrowers—some of them being traders in dyestuffs—which amounted to eight per cent of the clientele[14] (Table 1)

12 Reichert 1987, 194–195 and 213–216

13 Bernardi 2011, 110: a typical working year in the building sector would generally count 250 days.

14 In 1271, two Tournai entrepreneurs loaned Tommaso and Auberto de Solaro the sum of twelve pounds ten shillings parisis. One of them was an important investor in woad, an important dyestuff for clothes.

Table 1 The social status and occupations of the Tournai Lombard's borrowers and their co-debtors*

Food and drink trades	**Cloth trade**	**Cloth crafts**	**Metal workers**	**Leather workers**	**Wood merchants**	**Money-lenders**
4%	8%	4%	2%	4%	2%	3%
Urban Elites	Nobility	Town landlords	Burghers without further details	Traders without further details	Clerics	Peasants
20%	5%	8%	14%	2%	2%	5%

* A word of caution is indicated as the cloth crafts encompass a variety of occupations and incomes, going from the simple fuller to the cloth entrepreneur. Two examples will illustrate this disparity between social statutes. In the first one, Colars li Auwiers des Cauffours, coming from the industrial part of the city where the lime kilns *(cauffours)* were located (Billen and Heirwegh 1985, 253), loaned the Lombards the sum of sixteen pounds and two and a half shillings in 1273, together with his two co-debtors, Colars li Piniers and Theris Galais, a sum to be reimbursed sixty-three days later. Colars li Auwiers had been known as a linen clothier since 1256 (State Archives in Mons, Papiers Léo Verriest, classeur no. 2, 1250–1268 and Bigwood 1921–1922, vol. 2, 110, no. 76). In the second one, a Jakemes *li taitenier* (or teinturier: dyer) de Ramegnies (a village situated north-west of Tournai), a rich dyer entrepreneur loaned with his co-debtor, the big sum of eighty pounds tournois to Bonifacio de Baieni and his relatives in 1267, for days (Bigwood, 1921–1922, vol. 2, 104, no. 10), to be reimbursed forty days later. Those eighty pounds were on a par with roughly ten years of yearly wages of an unskilled worker in the building industry (see Verriest 1905, 37 for the wage).

Table 2 Terms of reimbursement of the Tournai Lombard's bank (1254–1289)

Term	**Number**	**Percentage of loan contracts**
Less than 3 months	71	57%
Between 3 and 6 months	33	27%
Between 6 and 9 months	15	12%
Between 9 and 12 months	4	3%
12 months	1	0,8%

- Their lending society provided a short-term credit mainly for commercial purposes, sometimes explicitly in connection with the cycle of the commercial fairs of Champagne and Flanders: a less than three-month term for reimbursement was set in fifty-seven per cent of the loans, which hinted at the importance of merchants among the clientele[15] (Table 2)
- The Piedmontese moneylenders resorted to a broad range of interest rates depending upon the trust they put in their debtor: e.g. between roughly five and thirty percent for a short-term loan (less than three months)[16]
- The debt registration was enforced before the town magistrate through the use of bonds called chirographs. This practice shows that Piedmontese moneylenders were keen on securing their creditor's rights even if that proved costly[17]

The 124 debt recognisances (whose maturity was mentioned) recorded by the Tournai aldermen, tell the tale of a credit relationship increasingly concerned with the refinancing needs of the upper strata of the middling groups: fourteen per cent, taking into account the crafts and the food and drink trades, and this figure is certainly an underestimation as we did not include the burghers without any mentioned occupation. This means that, probably, households on a median yearly income between hundred pounds parisis and 1,000 pounds parisis could have access to the loans of the Lombard lending house.[18] The fact that the debt recognisance instrument took the form of a chirograph or *charte-partie,* and was written in old French (Picard, the regional version of old French) certainly made the Lombard credit popular among middling groups: this tripartite bond

---

15 Two reimbursement terms are set at the next fairs of Lille and Lagny in Champagne.

16 In two loan contracts concluded in 1273 with associates of the Baieni, Roero and Solaro families of the Lombard pawnshop of Tournai, one of the wealthiest families of Tournai, the A le Take family benefited from preferential interest rates of about five per cent for loans whose maturity was inferior to sixty days: fifty-two and fifty-seven days respectively (Bigwood 1921–1922, vol. 2, no. 80–81, 110). This family drew its incomes from profitable investments in the cloth trade and in the wine trade (Kusman 2012, 76).

17 On these instruments and the costs of their use, see later in this paper.

18 In October 1280, for a call to arms, the urban magistrates make a distinction between those who can afford to have a horse and enough weapons suited for fighting on horseback, owning a fortune of 1,000 pounds parisis, and those who have less than those 1,000 pounds of fortune (*vaillant*), with enough weapons, but implicitly without horse, drawing a line between the urban elite groups and the other social groups (Verriest 1905, 127). For comparison's sake, it is interesting to underline that in Arras, around the same period (1305), a capital of 300 hundred pounds parisis is deemed as mandatory to be able to access to an alderman's seat with exactly the same term (*vaillant*): Billen and Boone 2020.

was written in three exemplars: one for the debtor, one for the creditor and one for the magistrate. Chirographs were authenticated before two *voir-jurés,* (literally "see-jurors"), urban officers testifying legally that the credit transaction actually happened; this legal framework reassured both creditors and debtors.[19] One estimate made by Léo Verriest, a great specialist of the legal history of Tournai in the late Middle Ages, gives a likely figure of 80,000 Tournai chirographs before the bombing of the city archives in 1940, of which "tens of thousands" would have dealt with credit matters. In Ypres, with the same chirographs being used by traders and crafts, about ninety per cent of these bonds dealt with credit for roughly the same period.[20]

During their more than thirty years of activity (1254–1289), the Piedmontese financiers of the Tournai bank society relied on a business model that would characterise all their future credit undertakings in the Low Countries. Their society had a strong commercial character with each partner owning a fixed number of partnerships, usually expressed on a fractional basis (i.e. the fourth part, the sixteenth part…). The more broken up the partnerships were, the likelier it was for the partners to expect a high risk for their investments. The fact that around 1320, Benedetto Roero had only the sixteenth part in the *domus Lombardorum* of Leuven, in the duchy of Brabant, whereas he owned three parts out of four in its counterpart of Valenciennes in the county of Hainault, suggests the existence of a kind of risk-management from the perspective of the main partners in the banks. In Hainault, the Prince had a stake in all positive—for the creditor—outcomes of trials between Piedmontese creditors and their debtors when it came to debt litigation.[21] When a partner left the society, all mutual debts were settled, and profits and loss were shared in proportion of each other's partnership. At the end of the thirteenth century, the average partnership in a society amounted to probably around 1,000 pounds petits tournois. For this reason alone, it should be clear that the capital of the society had to come partly from outside investors: Piedmontese partners accepted deposits, at least since 1247 for the Low Countries

19 On the long-standing success of the chirograph as a credit instrument for middling groups, see Howell 2018.

20 Verriest 1935, 140 and 144; Howell 2018, 19–20, no. 2. The *voir-jurés* officers were remunerated in wine for their registration of the credit transactions (Billen and Kusman 2018, 57).

21 This was a favourable legal framework for Piedmontese credit dealings. In the County of Flanders, Benedetto owned the fourth and the sixth part of the banks of Aalst and Gent respectively. The duchy of Brabant was deemed by the Piedmontese financier as riskier than the neighbouring principalities of Flanders and Hainault when it came to investing his capital. (Kusman 2012, 338). Benedetto donated all his assets to Pope John XXII in 1321–1322 and had to draw up an inventory of his partnerships.

and in 1287, the widow of the count of Flanders even went so far as to become a partner of the Lombard bank of Courtrai herself, owning a more than fair share of forty-one per cent on the total profits of the de Roero-Layolo society in Courtrai[22]. The existence of outside investors, whether burghers or members of the nobility, speaks for the banking function of Lombard lending societies at a very early stage. Piedmontese financiers could indeed mobilise very large amounts of capital, as we shall see later. The need to attract the capital of external investors explains the emphasis that Piedmontese moneylenders put on developing strong ties with honourable families of brokers-hostellers at local level, from the onset of their credit dealings, as was the case in Tournai with the Catine family[23]. In doing this, they achieved a double aim: firstly, they integrated more easily into the merchant community as quite often those brokers-hostellers were themselves former merchants and had kept their good connections with regional or international merchants. As they generally came from landlords or wealthy traders stock, these families of brokers-hostellers brought with them a good reputation, which was certainly of paramount importance to foreign ill-famed usurers such as Lombards.[24] Secondly, brokers-hostellers were themselves experts in monetary matters as well as in keeping current accounts with foreign merchants lodging with them.[25] Thirdly, Piedmontese financiers worked hand in hand with brokers-hostellers when a noble debtor proved unable to reimburse his debt. He then had to go as hostage—or substitute pledges for him—in a high-standing inn at the choice of the lenders. This practice originated in the so-called *leistinge* custom or *Einlager* custom that had feudal roots going back to the eleventh century.[26] This custom compelled the vassals of a lord that had guaranteed the payment of a debt to remain in an inn as hostages so long as their overlord was indebted to the Lombards. The vassals that were pledges for their overlord had to be accommodated in a high-standing inn, usually a hostel (*hospicium*) at their overlord's expense.

22 Bigwood 1921–1922, vol. 1, 344–348 (Douai in 1247); Kusman 2012, 82–83 and 114; Murray 2005, 166 (Bruges in 1457 but apparently rooted in a long-standing tradition).

23 Giacomo de Baieni and Giacomo de Layolo rented their house to a known hosteller and broker of Tournai, Bauduin Catine in the *Lormerie,* a district of the city where many leather crafts (sadlers and spur-makers) were living and working (Kusman 2012, 71, 75–76). He was also their neighbour. Catine had links with the most important families of landlords in Tournai (such as the *A le Take* lineage) and acted as a middleman for providing the Piedmontese financiers with a trustworthy clientele. I associate broker and hosteller because in daily practice, both occupations were often in the hands of the same person.

24 Todeschini 2007, 116–122 and 158–159.

25 Murray 2005, 132–133, 188–189, 202–205 and 213; Greve 1996, 4–9.

26 Kosto 2013, 130–162: at first, hostages are taken to guarantee a peace treaty between two feuding lords, then, the custom is extended to monetary agreements.

These hostel expenses could run very high, as the sojourn of pledges for the duke of Brabant in various hostels of Namur testified in 1311.[27]

From 1290 on, the Piedmontese families Roero and de Mirabello had developed strong ties with some major broker-hostellers in medium to big-sized cities of the Low Countries and Rhineland. In Brussels, these were the Vederman and the Tserclaes. In Mechelen, the Piedmontese moneylenders held business ties with Arnould d'Oudenghem and in Köln with Heinrich Hildegher Birklin and afterwards with the Quartermatt family. All these brokers and hostellers, with no exception, were recruited among the ranks of the urban elites, and high-profile former itinerant merchants, as it was the case with the Birklin family in Köln.[28]

The pawnbroking function was not a distinctive feature of the Tournai lending dealings.[29] Only fourteen sales of pawned objects, wares (among these, wheat) and horses were recorded, mainly between 1269 and 1279, which of course does not mean that all records pertaining to these sales were kept.[30] As said, the Piedmontese lending societies were essentially a family business: for each family partnership, two brothers and their nephews often worked together, the nephews of each family in a sort of apprenticeship-term for a couple of years before moving to another society. The daily running of the banking society lay in the hands of a so-called governor who acted as a local manager or factor. Contrary to the partners, he did not move from one society to the other, and had a small number of clerks, servants and messengers (probably one or two subordinates fulfilling all these functions) working under him.[31]

---

27 In 1310, the count of Namur and his brother Guy of Zeeland stood surety for the duke of Brabant for a debt of 12,000 Leuven pounds incurred by the duke of Brabant with the Piedmontese banker Manfredo de Viallo in 1305. The count of Namur sent four knights of his hostel to go as hostages for the debt in two inns of Namur. The total lodging expenses for two knights in one of these inns amounted to 135 pounds tournois for fifteen weeks. (State Archives in Namur, Charters of the counts of Namur, no. 321 [28/X/1305] and no. 412 [1310–1314]: account of the comital receiver).

28 Kusman 2012, 45–47, 182–184 (Köln), 308 (Mechelen) and 335–336 (Brussels).

29 The majority of these chirographs disappeared, but six of them were copied or edited. Of these six loan contracts, none of them mentioned the taking of a pawn in guarantee: State Archives in Mons, Papiers Léo Verriest, classeur no. 2, 1250–1268, chirograph of 10 December 1268, classeur no. 5, 1235–1305 chirographs dated 22 August 1254, 19 July 1267, 28 July 1273, 12 April 1273 and Bigwood 1921–1922, vol. 2, III., 266, chirograph dated from August 1261.

30 Bigwood 1921–1922, vol. 1, 358–359 but the fact that Bigwood does not mention that there were more of these sales, nor Verriest, both great practitioners of the Tournai chirographs in the 1920ies, suggests the unimportance of these sales.

31 Bigwood 1921–1922, vol.1, 348–349, Bordone et Spinelli 2005, 100–101 and Greilsammer 2009, 79.

A brief look at the career of Rainerio Roero, one of the many partners of the Tournai bank at the end of our period, highlights his multiple partnerships and his mobility (Table 3).

Table 3 Partnerships of Rainerio Roero (1276–before August 1320)*

Society	Number of main partners and family links	Date of mention
Tournai (kingdom of France)	Bonifacio and Tommaso de Baieni, brothers, Tommaso, Fiore and Berardo Roero for them and their brothers, Giorgio and Rainerio Roero, and Emmanuele Layolo, for him and his brothers, Giacomo and Huberto (10)	1276
Herentals (duchy of Brabant)	Manuele, Gavandino, Berardo (brother of Rainerio), Rainerio, Simone and Giovanni Roero (nephew of Rainerio), Vincenzo Trossello, Giorgio Garetti, Enrico and Uberto de Mercato and Godefrido de Leuven (11)	1292
Kortrijk (county of Flanders)	Rainerio and Simone Roero and associates (2)	1295
Maastricht (condominium Bishopric of Liège and duchy of Brabant)	Rainerio, Percevallo (son of Rainerio), Antonio (nephew of Rainerio), Omodeo (son of Rainerio) and their associates (4)	1293–1296
Gavere (county of Flanders)	Uberto Roero and his cousins, Rainerio Roero, Antonio Roero (nephew of Rainerio), Percevallo Roero (son of Rainerio), Ancelino Pavone, Bartolomeo and Guglielmo de Cuminiano, brothers (7)	1301–1303

* Thanks to the impressive survey of Lombard pawnshops in Germania Romania by Winfried Reichert, it is now relatively easy to reconstruct partnerships at least partially, for specific places: Reichert 2003 2/2, 296–297, 338–339, 384, 464–465 and 2/3, 741. Additional information is given in Kusman 2012, 79, n. 102 and 176–177.

This short glimpse at the career of Rainerio Roero shows that he and his partners kept an eye on commercial opportunities and political changes (Table 4).

A change of scale in the commercial strategies of the Piedmontese moneylenders is clearly discernible between the end of the thirteenth century, when the clientele of the Tournai (Fig. 3) Lombard bank was within a twenty-five-km. radius of Tournai, at the most, and the first half of the fourteenth century when its Mechelen counterpart was to build up a supra regional credit network that was to evolve into a wide-reaching bank, geared towards the financing of long-distance cloth trade from Brabant to the Avignon papal court. Indeed, when we map the borrowers of both banks, the differences in the scale of the credit undertakings are noticeable. The vast majority of the Tournai bank clients were city dwellers engaged in local trade, or, at best, in regional trade, and only a tiny number of them traded at the Champagne fairs; some well-off craft members and entrepreneurs made up the rest of the middling urban clientele while the rest of

Table 4 Adjusting quickly to the economically changing situation and looking at the political factor*

Date	Trade events	Political events	Reaction
Ca 1250–1285	Growth of Tournai exports: linen cloth, Tournai stone and pivotal function of Tournai for transit trade of woad and grains from Picardy to Flanders	–	Start of the credit activities of the Piedmontese financiers in Tournai
1274	–	Publication of decree councils of Lyon in 1274: anti-usury campaign	Sale of pawns and end of loans until 1282. Change in clientele: fewer elites and more peasants
1289	Annexion of the lordship of the Bruille by the City of Tournai: end of the special status of the Lombards. Growing political integration in the kingdom of France	Growing competition with Lille. Decline of Tournai cloth industry. City finances severely burdened by the cost of the new city walls	End of credit transactions of the lending house and redeploying in Brabant and Flanders where cloth industry is thriving
1280–1282	Aardenburg becomes trade staple for foreign merchants	Urban revolts in Bruges. Wool embargoes on exports from England to Flanders (1270–1280)	Comital privilege for Lombards in Aardenburg in 1281: Bernardo Roero and Giacomo Canelli: trade, money changing and lending
1288	–	Succession war of Limburg. Victory of duke of Brabant on count of Guelders at the battle of Wörringen. Annexion of Limburg	1293 Lombards start credit activities in the lordship of Maastricht, a condominium belonging to both the bishop of Liège and the duke of Brabant, where an important ducal mint is located
1290	Brabantine cloth merchants to England at fairs of Boston and Saint-Yves and in London in growing number	Political alliance between king of England and duke of Brabant	Enrico de Mercato, Piedmontese moneylender starts his activities in Brussels. Acts as middleman for money transfers between England and Brabant and money changing

* Information from Sivery 1980; Billen and Boone 2020; Kusman 2012, 78–82, Wyffels 1966, 37–45 and Boffa 2005, 103, no. 47.

Figure 3 The clientele of the Lombard bank of Tournai (1254–1289).

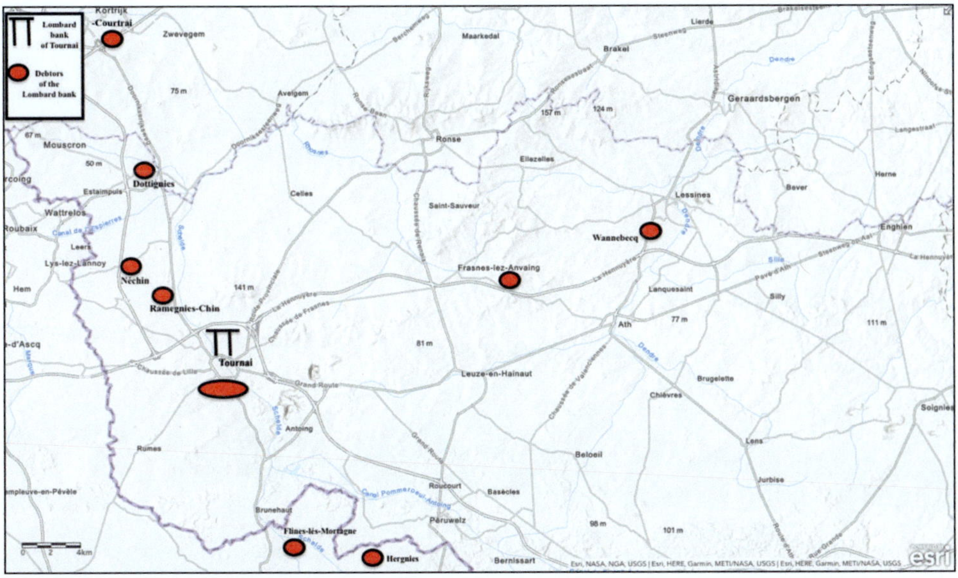

the borrowers came from the urban elites—often overlapping with the traders at the Champagne fairs—with only some peasant borrowers linked as tenants to the manorial demesnes of the Mortagne family in Mortagne, southwards of Tournai and in Kortrijk. By contrast, in Mechelen, between c. 1325 and 1345, the most important partner, Gabriele de Montemagno, could rely on partners, agents and factors working for him up to Avignon, seat of the papal court at that time and almost 900 kilometres away (Fig. 4). Other important partnerships were purchased in 's-Hertogenbosch in Brabant, Köln (in partnership with the Roero) in Rhineland and Zaltbommel in the county of Guelders, to name just a few important cities where Gabriele did invest his capital. Gabriele himself took care of financial duties for the count of Guelders thanks to his associates at the Lombard bank of Avignon.[32] In Mechelen, the bank provided capital for the needs of the high nobility or the city finances. It probably also provided capital for the cloth merchants of the city going to and returning from the papal court.[33] Still, the regional spe-

32 "Item den selven daghe sende mijn here Johannes van Ysendijc bi Gabriels brieven aen Lombarde, Gabriels vriende tot Avinon aen .ij.c. x. enghelsche (…)": State Archives in Arnhem, General Receipt of Guelders, ducal account of 1342–1343. For the partnership in Köln, see Bordone 1996, 40.

33 The commercial hostel of Gabriele de Montemagno was located next to the cloth hall and near the main market place of Mechelen. It was a strategic place for the credit dealings of his society in Mechelen (Kusman 2012, 299–316).

Figure 4 The long-distance banking network of the Mechelen Lombard bank.

cialisation pattern of the Piedmontese credit persisted throughout the fourteenth century within the duchy of Brabant in cities such as Leuven or Nivelles.[34]

Until now, we have studied the financial functions of Lombard banks from the perspective of private credit dealings. But what could be inferred from the activities of Piedmontese moneylenders in connection with the public finances? In this following part, we look at two case studies documenting this topic.

Piedmontese Financiers and Money Supply in Cities

As is well known, a distinctive feature of a modern bank lies in its ability to create money through loans and to contribute to the money supply in taking deposits.[35] Of course, in the late medieval Low Countries, various intermediaries such as hostellers, town moneychangers, Piedmontese and Jewish moneylenders, could, at times, be able to perform one of these or both functions. However, there was no sufficiently strong central power to ensure the permanent availability of this money supply, let alone the fact that no public bank existed before the *wisselbank* of Amsterdam in 1609.[36] Before the existence of such a public exchange bank, how did communities and private financiers cope with the shortage of coins in times of silver scarcity? Besides, during famine times, not only coins but simply an adequate credit supply could be of crucial importance for the town provisioning and daily commercial transactions.[37] It has been claimed that town moneychangers fulfilled, at least partly, through their town exchange offices, the role of municipal public banks: accepting deposits and being in charge of the public debt through the management of public annuities. They also extended loans to private individuals.[38] I will argue here that through their Lombard banks, Piedmontese moneylenders performed a similar function. To be able to defend this thesis, we have to

---

34 The Nivelles Lombard bank had a radius of action at most of twenty kilometres and its clientele came mostly from the middling groups and the urban and rural elites. The average loaned sum amounted to three pounds thirteen shillings of an old groat, still worth 165 daily wages of a skilled craftsman (Van Uytven 1987, 32–33). The same radius of action applies to the case of the Leuven bank with a strong presence of urban craftsmen, notably in the cloth-making sector and also many workers of the food and drink trades such as butchers and many peasants involved in the food supply of Leuven. The bulk of the loans was made up of consumption loans (Kusman 2012, 311 and 326–327 and Archivio Segreto Vaticano, Collectoria 433a, fol. 41r–v).

35 Bannock and Manser 1995, 22–23.

36 Aerts 2010, 1–3.

37 Hatcher and Bailey 2009, 138–139.

38 Aerts 2010, 10.

look first at the size of their presence in the urban network of the late medieval Low Countries. Of paramount importance indeed is the density factor of such a network of financial intermediaries. To prove my point, let us consider the example of the duchy of Brabant, occupying a central position within the late medieval southern Low Countries, and let us draw a comparison with the neighbouring county of Flanders. Around 1310, forty-five Lombard banks were operating, making the Lombard credit an ubiquitous fact. If we draw the hypothesis that the population must have numbered between 300,000 and 400,000 inhabitants, taking into account a low estimate of 300,000 inhabitants, it would have meant that for every 1,428 household units, there was at least one Lombard lending house available (Fig. 5).[39] This high density of credit institutions is strikingly similar to more late figures of fairs and markets density in sixteenth and seventeenth-century England or eighteenth-century France.[40] Even more stunning is the fact that, by contemporary standards on the number of inhabitants per bank branch, the medieval figures of households per Lombard banks are only slightly inferior to the average of bank per inhabitants in the EU twenty-eight member states in 2018.[41]

If we map the presence of Piedmontese financiers in Brabant, we observe a strong connection between the clothing industry in a given town or borough and

39 Population estimates of Brabant are based upon estimations for the beginning of the fifteenth century with an average household number of five persons: Blockmans, Pieters, Prevenier and van Schaïk 1980, 43–51 and Van Uytven 2004, 234. As there was a sharp demographic decline after the Black Death crisis of 1348–1349—given that after the plague, the population of the Low Countries lost about one third—, the low estimate of 300,000 could be an underestimation of the population number in 1300, generally assumed as the peak of the population growth in medieval Europe (Van Bavel 2010, 278–280). The map is mainly based on the general census by the king of the Romans, Henri VII, in 1309 when he summoned before him, in Köln, all factors of the Lombard pawnshops in the imperial principalities of the Low Countries for a tax collection. Edition of this important document in Van Syngel and Dillo 2000, II, no. 1514a, 1283–1291. Additional mentions are to be found in Castellani 1998, 257, for a house belonging to Guelf partners (associated with Ghibelline partners) of the Solaro family in Brussels and for the Lombard bank of Landen (Ghibelline partner) in 1308: Archivio Segreto Vaticano, Collectoria 433a, fol. 82r–82v.

40 Braudel 1979, 33–37.

41 https://www.ebf.eu/facts-and-figures/structure-and-economic-contribution-of-the-banking-sector/ consulted on 13 June 2020: in 2018 the average number of inhabitants per bank branch in the EU-28 reached almost 5,000. Of course, the average household unit in today's Europe is closest to four than to five as in the late Middle Ages: in 2019, 47 per cent of household had only one child and another forty percent just two children. Another thirteen per cent had three or more children and the rest had no children, resulting in an EU average of 2.3 children per household (https://ec.europa.eu/eurostat/statistics-explained/index.php/Household_composition_statistics consulted on 3 March 2021).

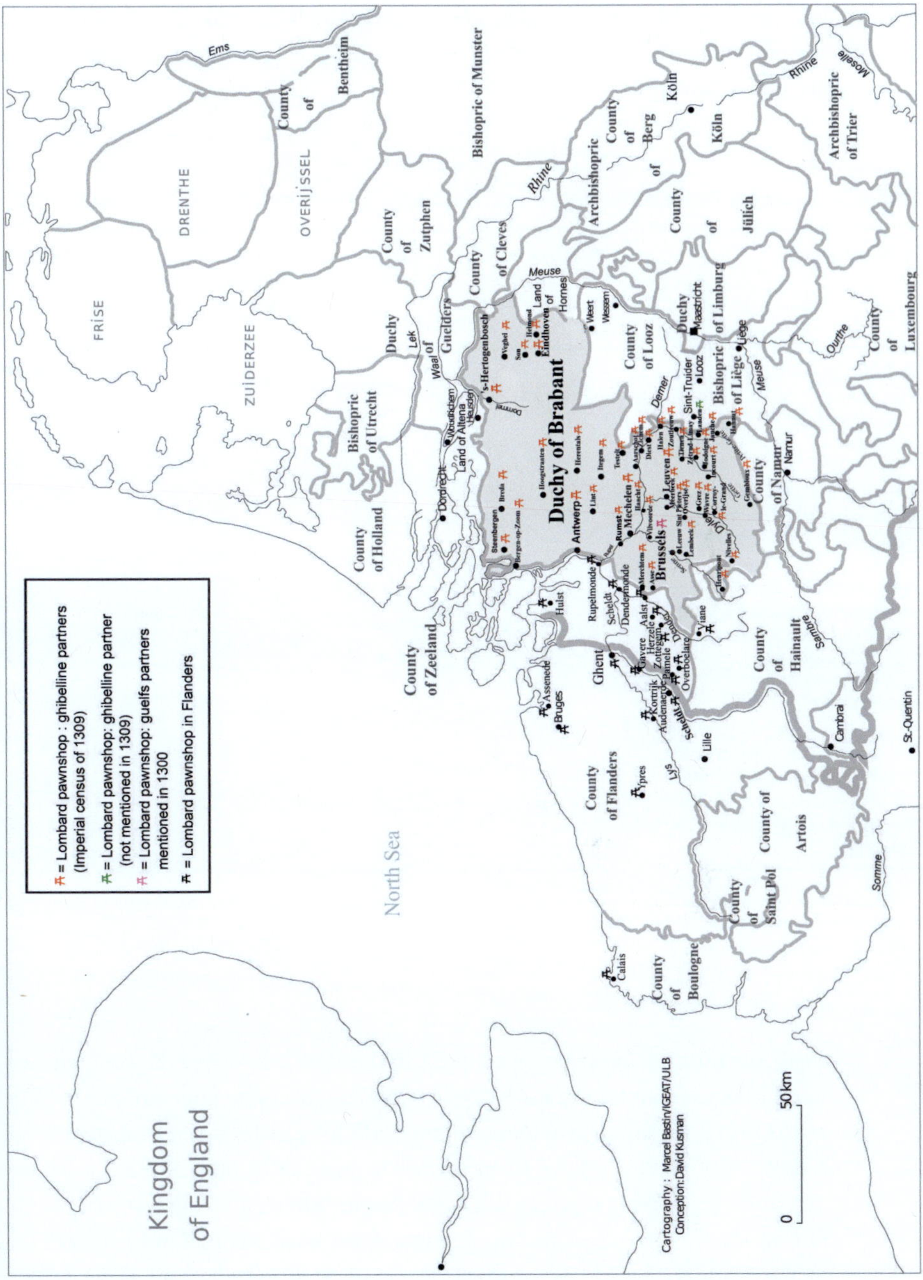

Figure 5. The network of Lombard pawnshops in 1309 in Brabant.

the presence of a local Lombard lending house. When no official market is mentioned, Piedmontese moneylenders could though still act as sellers of commodities (see Table 5).

Table 5 Ranking Brabantine towns and boroughs with Lombard banks around 1300*

City or borough	Borough without official market	Local market(s)	Cloth industry for regional market	Cloth industry for supra-regional/ international market
Antwerp, Brussels, Diest, Herentals, Leuven, Mechelen, Nivelles, s'-Hertogenbosch, Vilvoorde, Zoutleeuw **(10)**		×		×
Aarschot, Bergen-op-Zoom, Breda, Eindhoven, Helmond, Jodoigne, Tienen **(7)**		×	×	
Asse, Gembloux, Hannut, Hoogstraaten, Incourt, Jauche, Landen, Merchtem, Overijse, Steenbergen, Wavre, Zichem **(12)**		×		
Grez **(1)**		?		
Corroy-le-Grand, Haacht, Halen, Henripont, Itegem, Leeuw Sint Pieters, Lembeek, Lint, Meerbeek, Rumst, Son, Testelt, Veghel, Zétrud-Limay **(15)**	×			

* Pieces of information on the commercial functions of the mentioned towns and boroughs in Bonenfant 1962, Despy 1973, Despy 1981, Van Uytven 1992a and Van Uytven 1992b and Margue 2000.

I will advance the idea that, in contrast to the slow take-off of the Brabantine fairs cycle (Antwerp and Bergen-op-Zoom, most notably), the Lombard credit network could prove useful in providing commercial information and intermediation for traders. The Antwerp fairs seem in fact to have only been introduced between 1315 and 1325, which explains why the Tuscan merchant Francesco Pegolotti did not mention them when writing his merchant book manual but refers at length to the Flanders fairs.[42] By contrast, the county of Flanders, an even more commercialised economy around 1300, counted reportedly only seventeen Lombard

42 Limberger 2016.

banks in activity at that time.[43] Given that the population figure of the Flemish principality must have been incomparably higher than its Brabantine counterpart, this is a very low figure per household compared to Brabant.[44] In this last principality, every Lombard bank was at most—and usually at half this distance—only twenty-five kilometres away from its closest partner bank; in the South of the duchy, it was even less than that average. This meant that a road journey of going, (and sometimes returning), from one Lombard bank to another could be covered by horse in a single day, which must have certainly eased the circulation of information between agents of different banks.[45] This dense banking network undoubtedly helped pool capital from associated banks when needed for a single credit undertaking, and, by analogy with the fair network, provided scale economies.[46]

This explains undoubtedly why around 1293, all the Piedmontese banks of Brabant were in a position to loan the duke of Brabant John I the huge sum of 100,000 pounds tournois, a sum on a par with at least three years of annual receipts. This loan undoubtedly ranked these establishments among major actors such as the Florentine merchant-banking companies relying on bank deposits to venture into high finance.[47] Given the fact that the total partnerships in each society amounted probably on average to 2,000 pounds tournois, it would have meant that the vast majority of each pawnshop would have run out of cash or resorted to lending themselves. Their financing model relied, quite possibly, partly on out-

---

43 And we have to point out the fact that among these seventeen lending houses, seven were located under Imperial sovereignty: Aalst, Gavere, Herzele, Overboelare, Pamele, Viane and Zottegem with a quite high level of bank density in this region of Imperial Flanders (see Reichert 2003, 2/1, map D.I.1.A. 1301–1350 and D.I.1. 1301–1350). On the *modus operandi* of the imperial census of 1309, see Van Syngel and Dillo 2000, II, no. 1514a, 1283–1285. On the take-off of the Flemish cloth industry towards foreign markets such as the Baltic towns, Italy and England as early as the twelfth century: Van Bavel 2010, 299.

44 In 1469, the population of Flanders would have numbered 660,738 inhabitants whereas in Brabant, the population numbered 413,238 inhabitants (Blockmans, Pieters, Prevenier and van Schaïk 1980, 44–45).

45 On this common average of a day journey for trading practices since the end of the twelfth century, see for the Low Countries Jansen 1982, 162 and for England, Britnell 2006, 147.

46 Epstein 1994, 468.

47 Such as the Frescobaldi and Peruzzi: Hunt 1994 and Sapori 1947, 39–40. In 1307, the Frescobaldi issued a claim to the king of England Edouard II on their losses. Among other damages, they had to pay out all their bank deposits to their clients, amounting to a sum of 50,000 pounds sterling, a sum equivalent to at least 200,000 pounds black tournois (Spufford 1986, 209).

side deposits belonging to Robert de Nevers, son of the count of Flanders Guy de Dampierre, and, partly, on deposits belonging to rich citizens from Brabant.[48]

If we dare go one step further in our hypothesis, Piedmontese banking societies could well have fulfilled the function of public exchange banks being on the same foot than other sovereign rights such as the Mint or the Jews. It is indeed remarkable that in one of the first ducal ordinances defining the scope of his general receiver with respect to the ducal incomes, in 1284, besides the ordinary incomes of the ducal demesne, the duke John I (1268–1294) mentions the incomes of the mint as well as the incomes of the Lombards and the Jews, but no incomes whatsoever derived from money changing are mentioned.[49] Still, the control of money changing shall be deemed as an expression of the princely sovereignty in the second half of the fourteenth century.[50] At a local level, between 1303 and 1307, the loan at interest and the pawnbroking is allowed to "Lombards" in several Brabantine towns (Tienen, Antwerp, Zoutleeuw and Leuven) by a set of ducal ordinances setting the weekly interest rate at two pennies a pound, resulting in a yearly interest rate of 43.3 per cent. Interestingly enough, in the case of Tienen, no charge on money changing is allowed to Piedmontese moneylenders, which, in fact, is symptomatic of common practice.[51] The early regulation of Piedmontese credit (from 1284 on), as well as the ducal protection of Piedmontese moneylenders suggests that, in connection with the high density of this banking network, they could also have performed a public money-changing function.[52]

48 Kusman 2012, 115–117.

49 Edition in Martens 1943, no. 1, 21–23 [18 IV 1284]. A late confirmation for Brussels, of the public character of the Lombard lending house is given in an ordinance of the city of Brussels in 1383, regulating usury in the city. The ordinance states that the Lombards holding a public table of loan at interest are only a matter for the ducal officers, and that they do not fall within the town's jurisdiction: City Archives of Brussels, Ancient archives, no. 5, *Coren van Brussele,* 176–178.

50 Martens 1954, 148–150 and Uyttebrouck 1977, 234 and 250: the moneychangers had to pay an annual fee to the duke, as testified by the first ducal accounts (from 1364 onwards).

51 Kusman 2012, 237–238.

52 "Dux Brabancie est in possessione, et fuerunt sui pradecessores a tempore a quo non extat memoria, tenendi, tuendi et manutenendi Lumbardos, Tuscos, Caursinos ac alios alienigenas quoscumque mercatores habitantes in Brabantia, de suis pecuniis et mercibus mercantes et contrahentes, pro certo servicio quod sibi prestant singulis annis, et suis predessoribus prestiterunt." This affirmation of a long tradition of fiscal dues from "Lombards", to the Prince, in exchange for his protection of these foreign merchants, is stated explicitly for the first time in legal advice given by the University of Paris to a question from the duke of Brabant and the city of Brussels on the legality of lending at interest: edited in Kusman 1995, 174–175 and 220 [13 IV 1319].

The case-study of Mons, in the county of Hainault, provides us with an example of a strong position taken by the local Lombard bank in the city finances. Mons was one of the main princely residences of the count of Hainault. The city was a small city by Brabantine standards, with a population of roughly 8,000 inhabitants, which made Mons a small town in comparison with Mechelen whose population fetched about 22,000 inhabitants or Brussels whose population must have numbered around 35,000 before the Black Death of 1348–1349. Mons economy was mainly founded on its profits from the trade in wine and furs. Furs were exported to Bruges and to the fair of the Lendit in France, and the wine was imported from Gascogne and the Rhine region: all magnates in Mons belonging to the political elites derived their wealth from the import of wine or the trade in furs[53].

The Lombard credit took an important position within the city finances. The study of the current account that the Lombard bank kept with the town receiver between 1314 and 1318 shows that this current account was either in credit or in debit (Fig. 6).

Figure 6 Evolution of the current account of the Mons Lombards compared with the balance of the urban incomes between 1314 and 1318 in pounds tournois.

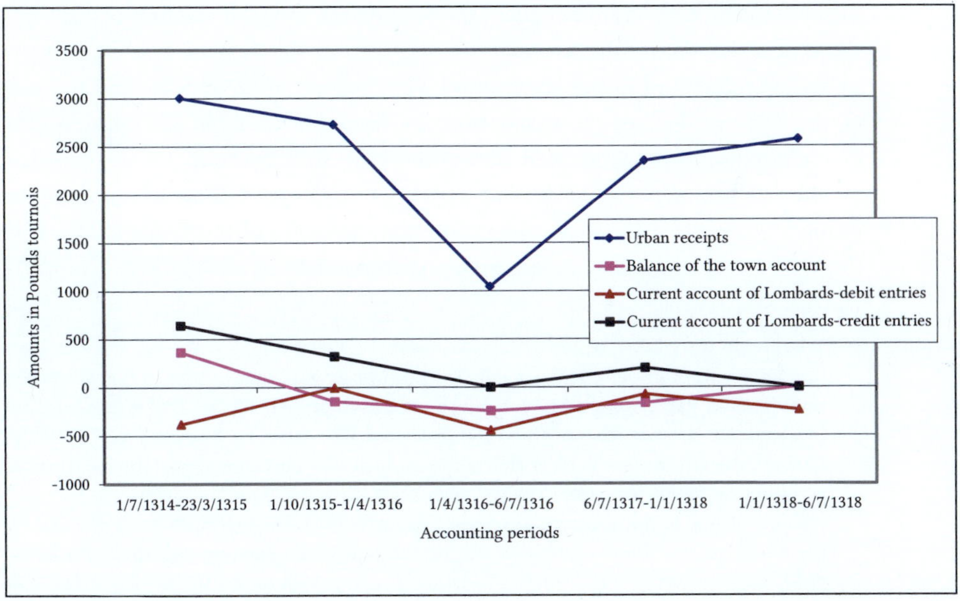

53 Deligne 2004, 256 and 272–278.

When the city incomes slump then the advances made to the city from the de Turco de Castello family rise, as in 1316, just after the great famine of 1315, when the city incomes were barely over a thousand pounds tournois: the Piedmontese financiers loaned the city 444 pounds tournois (defined here in the chart as a debit), to compensate for the loss in incomes as opposed to the previous accounting period of 1314–1315, when the urban receipts amounted to roughly 3,000 pounds tournois. A five-fold increase in grain prices in North-Western Europe was no exceptional event.[54] The motivation for the city's borrowing to the Lombard bank had diverse grounds: public works for the extension of the city walls, salaries to be paid, paying some costly life-annuities or, as in 1316, advancing grains to the city. We have to point out here that this financing scheme was cheap if we look at the interest rates: the Piedmontese financiers charged a weekly interest rate of 0.8 per cent with, on average, a median term of payment set at ten weeks: a little less than three months, again, in line with the commercial cycles of the regional fairs in Hainault and Flanders.[55] If the Piedmontese bank of Mons played a major part in the credit supply of the city in 1316, advancing roughly forty-four percent of the total incomes, the amount is certainly an underestimation of their total stake in the public debt of the city. In Mons, most of the excises levied on commercial commodities were farmed out to private financiers for a three-month term. Those farmers needed short-term credits to fill the gap between the date they paid the sum to the magistrate to collect the tax and the moment the first tax receipts came in their coffers. The tax collectors relying on the Piedmontese credit were in majority involved in the levying of taxes on sheep, grains, wine and the new cloths, some of the most profitable taxes in Mons. For example, the farmer of the new cloths excise, had received four pounds six shillings four pennies tournois for the accounting period of 6th July 1316 to 6th July 1317.[56] These advances to the farmers were often drowned within the total amounts of the farms paid out to the town receiver, so that it seems almost impossible to reconstruct a complete

---

54 We rely on the edition of Mons town accounts by Piérard 1975, I, 90–142. For the great famine, see Jordan 1996, 135 and 158. This author asserts that in 1316, the grain prices in Mons and Valenciennes had reached a very high price level and that a normal price level would be attained only in 1330 (five-fold decrease). In Brabant, in the city of Leuven, the famine is severe, with a surge in mortality and an increase in wheat prices, reaching eighteen shillings gros tournois per quarter in 1316 and returning to a normal level (nine to ten shillings gros tournois) only in 1318–1319 (Barla 2020, 164 and for the wheat prices: Royal Library of Belgium, Manuscripts section, BR. Ms. 21877 *Notae pro historia Lovaniensi ad annos 1316–1319*, fol. 247v). Miskimin 1975, 25–26, claims that there was a five-fold increase in wheat prices in Paris between May 1314 and November 1315.

55 Kusman 2014, 330.

56 Piérard 1975, I, 122 and 126.

picture of the volume of the Piedmontese credit supply to the city finances. We lack indeed any surviving private account books of these farmers that could provide us with names of their financiers.[57]

In Mechelen, the Piedmontese bank had reached a higher degree of integration in the city finances: Lombards, as they were dubbed in the city's accounts, held a specific account on the town's exchange. It allowed investors interested in credit ventures to deposit their life-annuity, or part of it, in the Lombard bank through an order given to the money changer working for them. This implied that in Mechelen, buyers of Mechelen life-annuities coming from Brussels, could use their annuity for speculative ends. However, it also allowed farmers of the excises to loan them money for farming a specific excise when they were running short of capital. We gain insight into these practices because the accounting techniques were more advanced with respect to the recording of the excises receipts as every income recorded per excise was detailed in the account (see scheme, Fig. 7).

Figure 7 The Mechelen exchange office around 1311–1314.

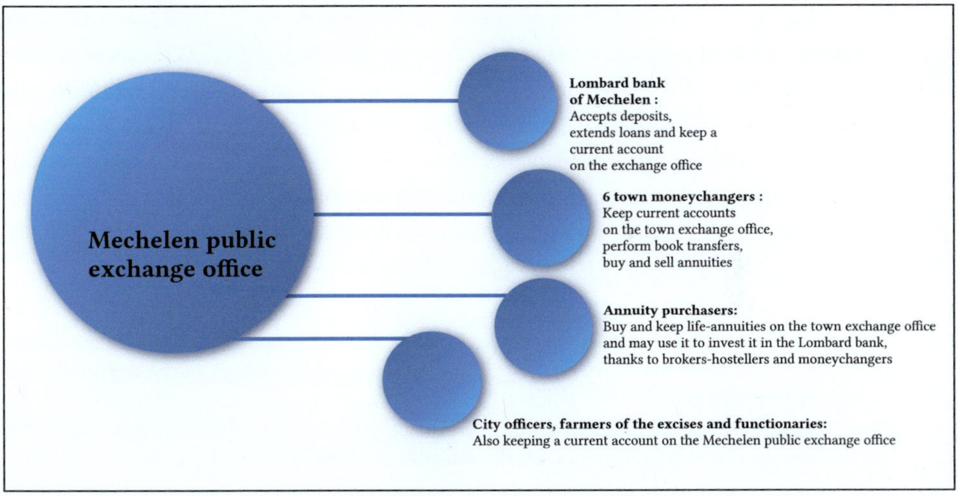

57 The town accounts do not specify the individual amounts paid out per excise: the receiver only draws a distinction between the total amount of the *menus membres des maletottes* (the minor excises) and the *maletotte dou vin* (the wine excise, deemed the major excise). Most of the time, it is the reimbursement made to the "Lombards" that is recorded by the receiver, as in the summer of 1317 when the magistrate paid back the loan that had been extended to the farmer of the mills excise, amounting to forty-five pounds tournois (Piérard 1975, I, 115 and 123).

The fact that it worked with book transfers between current accounts helped reduce the volume of transfers of metallic money and eased the money supply.

In a particularly striking example of book transfer, the Piedmontese financier Giovanni de Mirabello paid the city the sum of seventy-four pounds *payment*[58] due by the cloth-excise farmers on 22 June 1312. This sum was directly transferred to the account of the town receiver, creditor of the city for a debt to one of the moneychangers. The farmers reimbursed Mirabello from his advances on the same day.[59] Another feature of these financial practices increased the creditworthiness of the excise farmers vis-à-vis the town magistrate and the enforcement of their obligations: when the Mechelen Lombards acted as sureties for the financial obligation of the private financiers that were awarded a specific excise, the farming contract was concluded before the aldermen's house.[60] A last building block in the favourable institutional framework for the credit practices of the Piedmontese moneylenders in Mechelen was their extremely competitive weekly interest rate for the loans extended to the city: at one penny per pound, their credit was even cheaper than in Mons. It resulted in a 0.4 per cent weekly interest rate.[61]

In 1311, the Lombard bank could provide a sizeable sum to the Mechelen magistrate: 4,600 pounds *payment* or twelve per cent of the annual incomes (37,000 pounds). If we isolate this sum in the loans made by private creditors to the city (annuity-buyers excluded) then the Piedmontese came as first creditors with ninety per cent of the advance made to the city.[62] Their position is again probably underestimated because besides this direct loan to the city, Piedmontese financiers advanced sums to a number of excise farmers, as mentioned. The financial

58 The local—weak—currency of Mechelen (the "Paiement money") was used for real payments whereas the vieux gros tournois was a money of account in the town accounts (Peeters 1980).

59 Giovanni de Mirabello paid the city a sum of seventy-four pounds Paiement due by the farmers on 22 June 1312 among the various incomes of the town exchange. The sum was reimbursed by the farmers to the financier on the same day among the posts related to the incomes of the cloth excise (City Archives of Mechelen, Ancient archives, Town Accounts, SR, SI no. 1, fol. 16r and fol. 69v). This was certainly not the only credit extended by de Mirabello.

60 Examples for the mills-excise when a payment of 166 £ 15 s 6 d is recorded for Giovanni de Mirabello and his partners on 26 May 1312, matching the farming contract of 1311 guaranteed by the Lombards and similarly for the finished cloths excise, with a payment to the Lombards of 282 £ 9 s recorded on 22 May 1312, related to a farming contract concluded the previous year (City Archives of Mechelen, Ancient archives, Town Accounts, SR, SI no. 1, fol. 18r, 25r and 206r).

61 City Archives of Mechelen, Ancient archives, Town Accounts, SR, SI no. 1, fol. 155v.

62 Kusman 2012, 278–295.

backing of several excise farmers by foreign businessmen is worth noticing. It shows that the Piedmontese moneylenders were more successful in Brabant and Hainault than their counterparts were in Flanders in taking a stake—albeit indirectly—in the profitable market of the town excises farms that made up seventy-five to eighty per cent of the total urban incomes.[63]

The place taken by the Lombard banks in the city finances of Mechelen and Mons shows that these lending houses could play a pivotal role in the money supply and, certainly, in the credit supply of cities of very different size in the Late Medieval Low Countries. We have seen that in Mechelen, credit money circulated smoothly between various financial intermediaries. As is well known, the question revolving around credit money as a form of money supply remains open to debate because for the so-called monetarists, the circulating credit money had to be ultimately supported by a sufficient volume of coined money[64]. This could only be answered with certainty if we were able to rely on precise numbers with respect to the volume of mint output as in the case of the kingdom of Valencia around 1300 or in England.[65] This is alas not the case prior to the last quarter of the fourteenth century. This being said, it is difficult to obliterate from this argument the massive mint outputs of the Low Countries, and most notably from Brabant and Flanders around the 1290ties: under the duke of Brabant John I and the count of Flanders Guy de Dampierre about 90,000 pounds of sterling (imitations of sterling pennies dubbed in England crockards and pollards) were struck in their princely workshops and began circulating in England. This resulted in a massive inflow of English silver in the Low Countries in the same territorial states where these coins had been struck.[66] We also have to underline that the argument of Nightingale in favour of the importance of a sufficient coin supply is partly based upon her belief that as credit instruments could not circulate in England, they could not be counted as part of the money supply.[67] This is a disputable argument for the Low Countries. Moreover, we have seen how payments performed between current accounts could play a role of paper money.[68]

---

63 At least with regard to the city of Ghent where the little milieu of the excise farmers was totally closed to Italian merchant bankers even when these were acting as sureties (Boone 2016).

64 Nightingale 2004, 68 vs. Bolton 2012, 280–282.

65 Furio and Garcia Marsilla 2014, 520.

66 Bolton 2012, 160–161.

67 Nightingale 2004, 55.

68 Not only credit could circulate as money: see also the interesting position of Lord Smail 2018, 101, who argues that "in certain circumstances, commodities could be made to circulate efficiently as a form of commodity money".

Concluding Remarks

The Lombard credit was by no means a credit for the poor. Instead, the involvement of Piedmontese moneylenders at a very early stage with fairs and trade cycles shows that their emphasis was rather on the credit supply of a very wide cross section of the urban society, going from the middling groups to the courtiers and, at the top, the Prince. The incredibly high density of their lending houses network around 1310 in Brabant demonstrates that Piedmontese moneylenders had achieved a kind of "universal bank", very different than the one proposed by de Roover when he studied Lombards in Bruges. The variety of their financial activities, ranging from lending to money changing, banking and high finance has to be underlined as has to be reconsidered the so-called usurious rates of their credit undertakings. If we accept that their average term for loans was inferior to three months then it is clear that their interest rates have indeed to be considered anew on a weekly basis, in fact, as implied by their license to lend at interest. Just as the moneychangers, they could play a pivotal role of financial intermediaries in the capital markets by pooling important funds in the town exchanges. This means that "Lombards" ought to be looked at as public credit actors rather than simply private credit actors as it had been done in the past. The importance of their deposit banking function explains their emphasis on having good ties with brokers-hostellers since the beginning of their activities in Tournai.

Their role in credit supply and, possibly, in money supply is undisputable as shown by their role played in the city finances of Mons and Mechelen. In time of famine, they could help the city alleviate the shock of finding new networks of provisioning by providing capital on a short-term basis.[69] Their supra-regional credit networks were decisive in overcoming such situations as the famine of 1315–1316. The involvement of Piedmontese moneylenders with indirect taxation through their loans to some of the private financiers that farmed out excises demonstrates finally how instrumental they were for the growth of public finance in the Low Countries cities.

69 On the role of financial intermediaries such as the Jewish lenders to alleviate aggregate shocks, see the remarkable paper of Botticini 2000, 173.

References

Archival References

Arnhem, State Archives: General Receipt of Guelders, ducal account of 1342–1343.
Brussels, City Archives: Ancient archives, no. 5, *Coren van Brussele.*
Brussels, Royal Library of Belgium: Manuscripts section, BR. Ms. 21877.
Mechelen, City Archives: Ancient archives, Town Accounts, SR, SI no. 1.
Mons, State Archives: Papiers Léo Verriest, classeur no. 2, 1250–1268 and classeur no. 5, 1235–1305.
Namur, State Archives: Charters of the counts of Namur, no. 321 and no. 412.
Vatican City: Archivio Segreto Vaticano, Collectoria 433a.

Bibliographic References

Aerts E. 1980. "Middeleeuwse bankgeschiedenis volgens Professoor Raymond de Roover." *Bijdragen tot de Geschiedenis* 63: 49–86.

Aerts E. 2010. "The absence of public exchange banks in medieval and early modern Flanders and Brabant (1400–1800): a historical anomaly to be explained." *Financial History Review* 17: 1–27.

Aerts E. 2018, "Raymond de Roover on the Bankers of Mediaeval Bruges." *Annales Mercaturae* 4: 7–29.

Bannock G. and W. Manser. 1995 (2nd edition). *The Penguin international Dictionary of finance.* London: Penguin books.

Barla N. 2020. "Por la necessitet du povre peuple": *La gestion des crises alimentaires dans les Pays-Bas méridionaux en période d'affirmation des pouvoirs urbains et princiers (XIe–XVe siècle): chronologie des crises, analyse historiographique, étude de cas (Lille et Mons au XVe siècle),* unpublished Phd diss., Free University of Brussels-Université libre de Bruxelles-University of Antwerp.

Bautier R.-H. 1979. "Les Lombards et les problèmes du crédit en France aux XIIIe et au XIVe siècles." *Rapporti culturali ed economici fra Italia e Francia nei secoli dal XIV al XVI, Atti del colloquio italo-franceses, Roma, 1978:* 7–34.

Bernardi P. 2011. *Bâtir au Moyen Âge.* Paris: CNRS-Editions.

Bigwood G. 1921–1922. *Le régime juridique et économique du commerce de l'argent dans la Belgique du moyen âge.* 2 vol. [= Mémoires de l'Académie Royale de Belgique, Classe des Lettres et des Sciences Morales et Politiques, collection in-8°, 2e série, 2/14]. Brussels: Lamertin.

Billen C. and J. J. Heirwegh 1985. "La ville à la campagne. Le Collège des laboureurs de Tournai. " In *La Belgique rurale du moyen-âge à nos jours. Mélanges offerts à Jean-Jacques Hoebanx,* edited by Jean-Louis Delattre et alii, 253–274. Brussels: Editions de l'Université libre de Bruxelles.

Billen C. and D. Kusman 2018. "Les affaires, la clientèle et les scrupules de Jehan Biérenghier, usurier tournaisien (†1305). Crédit et usure à Tournai au XIIIe et au début du XIVe siècle." *Histoire Urbaine* 51: 41–70.

Billen C. and M. Boone. 2020. "*Pour argent et pour amour non.* Enquêtes princières et questions politico-fiscales dans les villes de Flandre et d'Artois au tournant du XIIIe et du XIVe siècle." In *Cultures fiscales en Occident du Xe au XVIIe siècle. Etudes offertes à Denis Menjot,* edited by F. Garnier et alii, 51–68. Toulouse: Presses universitaires du Midi.

Blockmans F. 1956. "Les Lombards à Anvers du XIIIe au XIVe siècle." *Tablettes du Brabant* 1: 229–285.

Blockmans W. P., G. Pieters, W. Prevenier, and R. W. M. van Schaïk. 1980. "Tussen crisis en welvaart: sociale veranderingen 1300–1500.", In *Algemene Geschiedenis der Nederlanden,* 4, edited by D. P. Blok, 42–86. Haarlem: Fibula-Van Dishoeck.

Boffa S. 2005. "L'introduction de la grosse monnaie et la transformation des administrations monétaires dans les principautés des Pays-Bas du sud à la fin du XIIIe et au début du XIVe siècle." *Revue belge de Numismatique* 151: 97–118.

Bonenfant P. 1962. "La fondation de 'villes neuves' en Brabant au moyen âge." *Vierteljahrschrift für Sozial-und Wirtschafts-Geschichte* 49: 145–170.

Boone M. and E. Lecuppre-Desjardin 2007. "Grains de blé, grains du chapelet: économie et dévotion entre Gand et Tournai à la fin du Moyen Âge." In *Campin in Context. Peinture et société dans la vallée de l'Escaut à l'époque de Robert Campin,* edited by L. Nys and D. Vanwijnsberghe, 193–204. Brussels-Valenciennes-Tournai: Presses Universitaires de Valenciennes.

Boone M. 2016. "Marché libre, rendement collectif et intérêts privés, un trio infernal? Les fermiers des assises de la ville de Gand à la fin du Moyen Âge." *Memini* 19–20: 159–175.

Bordone R. 1992. "Progetti nobiliari del ceto dirigente del commune di Asti al tramonto." *Bolletino storico-bibliografico subalpino* 90: 437–494.

Bordone R. 1996. "Una famiglia di "Lombardi" nella Germania Renana della seconda metà del Trecento: gli Asinari di Asti." In *Hochfinanz im Westen des Reiches, 1150–1500,* [= Trierer Historische Forschungen 31], edited by F. Burgard, 17–48. Trier: Verlag THF.

Bordone R. and F. Spinelli 2005. *Lombardi in Europa nel medioevo.* Milan: Franco Angeli.

Botticini M. 2000. "A tale of 'benevolent' governments: Private credit markets, public finance and the role of Jewish lenders in medieval and renaissance Italy." *Journal of Economic History*, 60: 164–189.

Braudel F. 1979. *Civilisation matérielle, économie et capitalisme* XVe–XVIIIe *siècle.* 3 vol. Paris: Armand Collin.

Britnell R. 2006. "Town life." *In A Social History of England 1200–1500*, edited by R. Horrox and W.M. Ormrod, 134–178. Cambridge: Cambridge University Press.

Buylaert F. 2011. *Repertorium van de Vlaamse adel (ca. 1350–ca. 1500).* Ghent: Academia Press.

Cannelloni F. 2015. *Credito e pegno, famiglie e "nazioni": i Lombardi tra Piemonte e Paesi Bassi (ca. 1380–1500)*, unpublished Phd diss., Università degli Studi di Padova-Katholieke Universiteit Leuven.

Castellani L. 1998. *Gli uomini d'affari astigiani. Politica e denaro fra il Piemonte e l'Europa (1270–1312).* Turin: Paravia scriptorium.

Deligne C.2007. " Petites villes et grands marchands? Pour une reconsidération de l'histoire des villes hainuyères (XIIIe–XIVe siècle)", in *Voisinages, coexistences, appropriations. Groupes sociaux et territoires urbains (Moyen Âge–16e siècle)*, edited by C. Deligne and C. Billen, 255–284. Turnhout: Brepols.

De Roover R. 1948. *Money, banking and credit in mediaeval Bruges. Italian Merchant bankers, Lombards and Money-Changers. A Study in the Origins of Banking.* Cambridge: Medieval Academy of America.

Despy G. 1973. "Les phénomènes urbains dans le Brabant wallon jusqu'au environs de 1300." In *Wavre 1222–1972 750e anniversaires des libertés communales. Colloque historique, les franchises communales dans le Brabant wallon (Wavre 23 et 24 septembre 1972), Actes*, 21–53. Wavre: Cercle Historique et Archéologique de Wavre et de la Région.

Despy G. 1981. *Les campagnes du roman pays de Brabant au Moyen Âge: la terre de Jauche aux XIVe et XVe s.* Louvain-la-Neuve: Centre belge d'histoire rurale.

Dillo M. and G.A.M. Van Synghel 2000. *Oorkondenboek van Noord-Brabant tot 1312, II. De heerlijkheden Breda en Bergen op Zoom*, 2 vol. The Hague: Instituut voor Nederlandse Geschiedenis.

Dyer C. 2005. *An age of transition? Economy and Society in England in the Later Middle Ages.* Oxford: Oxford University Press.

Epstein S.R. 1994. "Regional Fairs, Institutional Innovation and Economic Growth in Late Medieval Europe." *The Economic History Review*, New Series 47, no. 3: 459–482.

Escher M. and F. G. Hirschmann 2005. *Die urbanen Zentren des hohen und späteren Mittelalters.* Trier: Kliomedia.

Furio, A. and J. V. Garcia Marsilla 2014. "Espèces et créances en circulation. Monnaies métalliques et crédit comme monnaie dans le royaume de Valence vers 1300." In *Dynamiques du monde rural dans la conjuncture de 1300,* edited by M. Bourin and F. Menant: 493–532. Rome: Ecole Française de Rome.

Greilsammer M. 2009. *La roue de la fortune. Le destin d'une famille d'usuriers lombards dans les Pays-Bas à l'aube des Temps modernes.* Paris: Editions de l'École des hautes études en sciences sociales.

Greve A. 1996. "Hanseatic merchants: banking customs in fourteenth-century Bruges." In *Finances publiques et finances privées au bas moyen âge. Actes du colloque tenu à Gand les 5 et 6 mai 1995,* edited by M. Boone and W. Prevenier, 3–13. Leuven-Apeldoorn: Garant.

Hatcher J. and M. Bailey 2009. *Modelling the Middle Ages. The History and Theory of England's Economic Development.* Oxford: Oxford University Press.

Howell M. C. 2018. "Un réseau de credit à Ypres au XIIIe siècle. Les reconnaissances de dettes de 1249–1291." *Histoire Urbaine* 51:19–40.

Hunt E. S. 1994. *The medieval super-companies. A study of the Peruzzi Company of Florence.* Cambridge: Cambridge University Press.

Jansen H. P. H. 1982. "Handel en nijverheid 1000–1300" In *Algemene Geschiedenis der Nederlanden,* 2, edited by D. P. Blok et alii, 148–186. Haarlem: Fibula-Van Dishoeck.

Jordan W. C. 1996. *The great famine. Northern Europe in the early fourteenth* century. Princeton: Princeton University Press.

Kosto A. J. 2012. *Hostages in the Middle Ages.* Oxford: Oxford University Press.

Kusman D. 1995. "Textes concernant une consultation de l'Université de Paris par le duc de Brabant et la ville de Bruxelles en 1318–1319: Lombards et pouvoirs en Brabant au début du XIVe siècle." *Bulletin de la Commission Royale d'Histoire* 161: 171–225.

Kusman D. 2012. *Usuriers publics et banquiers du Prince. Le rôle économique des financiers piémontais dans les villes du duché de Brabant (XIIIe–XIVe siècle).* Turnhout: Brepols.

Kusman D. 2014. "Shylock reconsidéré dans le comté de Hainaut: une intéressante affaire d'usure en 1319–1321." In *Trulla et cartae. De la culture matérielle aux sources écrites. Liber discipulorum et amicorum in honorem Michel de Waha,* edited by F. Chantinne et alii. Brussels: Le livre Timperman.

Limberger M. 2016. "Regional and interregional trading networks and commercial practices at the port of Antwerp in the 14th and 15th centuries. The testimony of merchants and skippers in court records." *Nuevo Mundo Mundos Nuevos* [online]: http://journals.openedition.org/nuevomundo/69938 consulted on 3 March 2021, DOI: https://doi.org/10.4000/nuevomundo.69938.

Margue M. 2000. "Entstehung und Entwicklung der brabantischen Städte und die Straße Flandern-Köln (11.–13. Jahrhundert)." In *Städtelandschaft-Städtenetz-zentralörtliches Gefüge. Ansätze und Befunde zur Geschichte der Städte im hohen und späten Mittelalter,* edited by M. Escher et alii, 383–406. Mainz: Kliomedia.

Martens M. 1943. *Actes relatifs à l'Administration des Revenus domaniaux du Duc de Brabant (1271–1408).* Brussels: Palais des Académies.

Martens M. 1954. *L'administration du domaine ducal en Brabant au Moyen Age, 1250–1406.* Brussels: Palais des Académies.

Miskimin H.A. 1975. *The Economy of Early Renaissance Europe, 1300–1460.* Cambridge-London-New York-Melbourne: Cambridge University Press.

Murray J.M. 2005. *Bruges, cradle of capitalism, 1280–1390.* Cambridge: Cambridge University Press.

Nieuss J.-F. 2006. "Du donjon au tribunal. Les deux âges de la pairie châtelaine en France du Nord, Flandre et Lotharingie (fin XIe–XIIIe s.) (1re et 2e partie)." *Le Moyen Âge* 112, no. 1–2: 9–41 and 307–336.

Nightingale P. 2004. "Money and credit in the economy of late medieval England." In *Medieval Money Matters,* edited by D. Wood: 51–71. Oxford: Oxbow.

Peeters J.-P. 1980. "De rekenmunt in de Mechelse stadsrekeningen als getuige van de evolutie van het Brabantse muntwezen tijdens de late Middeleeuwen". *Handelingen van de Koninklijke Kring voor Oudheidkunde, Letteren en Kunst van Mechelen* 84: 103–156.

Piérard C. 1971. *Les plus anciens comptes de la ville de Mons (1279–1356),* 2 vol. Brussels: Palais des Académies.

Reichert W. 1987. "Lombarden zwischen Rhein und Maas. Versuch einer Zwischenbilanz." *Rheinische Vierteljahrsblätter* 51: 188–223.

Sapori A. 1947. *La compagnia dei Frescobaldi in Inghilterra* [= Biblioteca Storica Toscana 9]. Florence: Olschki.

Sivery G. 1980. "Le bassin scaldien et la géographie de la circulation au XIIIe siècle." *Revue Belge de Philologie et d'Histoire* 58: 797–832.

Smail D.L. 2018. "The Materiality of Credit. Debt Collection as Pawnbroking in Late Medieval Mediterranean Europe." *Histoire Urbaine* 51: 95–110.

Spufford P. 1986. *Handbook of medieval exchange.* London: Royal Historical Society.

Tihon, C. 1961. "Aperçus sur l'établissement des Lombards dans les Pays-Bas aux XIIIe et XIVe siècles." *Revue Belge de Philologie et d'Histoire* 39: 334–364.

Todeschini G. 2007. *Visibilmente crudeli malviventi, persone sospette e gente qualunque dal Medioevo all'età moderna.* Bologna: Viella.

Uyttebrouck A. 1977. "Notes et réflexions sur la structure des premiers comptes conservés de la recette de Brabant (années 1363–1364 et suivantes)." In *Centenaire du séminaire d'histoire medieval de l'Université libre de Bruxelles,* edited by G. Despy: 219–257. Brussels: La Renaissance du Livre.

Van Bavel B. 2010. *Manors and Markets. Economy and Society in the Low Countries, 500–1600.* Oxford: Oxford University Press.

Van Uytven R. 1987. "De Lombarden in Brabant in de middeleeuwen." In *Bankieren in Brabant in de loop der eeuwen,* edited by H.F.J.M. Van Den Eerenbeemt, 21–36. Tilburg: Stichting Zuidelijk Historisch Contact.

Van Uytven R. 1992a. "Brabantse en Antwerpse centrale plaatsen (14de–19de eeuw)."In *Le Réseau urbain en Belgique dans une perspective historique (1350–1850). Une approche statistique et dynamique. 15e Colloque international, Spa, 4–6 sept. 1990,* 29–79. Brussels: Crédit Communal de Belgique.

Van Uytven, R 1992b. "Les moyennes et petites villes dans le Brabant Septentrional avant 1400." In *Les petites villes en Lotharingie. Actes des 6es Journées Lotharingiennes, 25–27 octobre 1990,* edited by M. Pauly, 65–84. Luxembourg: Section Historique de l'Institut Grand-ducal de Luxembourg.

Van Uytven R. 2004. "Une population dense et une prospérité apparente". *Histoire du Brabant du duché à nos jours,* edited by R. van Uytven, 234–241. Zwolle: Waanders.

Verriest L. 1935. "Un fonds d'archives d'un intérêt exceptionnel, les chirographes de Tournai." *Annales du Cercle Archéologique de Mons* 56: 139–194.

Verriest L. 1905. *Institutions Judiciaires de Tournai au XIIIe siècle. Les registres de justice dits Registres de la Loi.* Tournai: Casterman.

Warlop E. 1975–1976. *The Flemish nobility before 1300,* vol.1–4. Kortrijk: G. Desmet-Huysman.

Weissen K. 2002. *"Dove il Papa va, sempre è caro di danari. The Commercial Site Analysis in Italian Merchant Handbooks and Notebooks from the 14th and 15th Centuries."* In *Merchant's Books and Mercantile "Practiche" from the Late Middle Ages to the Beginnings of the 20th Century,* edited by M.A. Denzel, J.-C. Hocquet and H. Witthoft, 63–73. Stuttgart: Franz Steiner Verlag.

Wyffels C. 1966. "Nieuwe gegevens bettreffende een XIIIse "democratische" stedelijke opstand: de Brugse Moerlemaye." *Handelingen van de Koninklijke Commissie voor Geschiedenis* 132: 37–142.

Picture Credits

Fig. 1: Map adapted from the map 3 in Kusman, 2012, 390.
Fig. 2: Brussels, Royal Library of Belgium, Br. Mss. 1175.
Fig. 3: Map designed by D. Kusman with the ESRI application.
Fig. 4: Map adapted from the map 8 in Kusman, 2012, 394.
Fig. 5: Map designed by D. Kusman.
Fig. 6: Figure designed by D. Kusman.
Fig. 7: Figure designed by D. Kusman.

TRADING NETWORKS, CREDIT, AND TRUST: THE HANSARDS' CAPITAL RAISING REVISITED

Ulf Christian Ewert

Abstract: Since the late twelfth century, Low-German merchants—based on privileges in London, Novgorod, Bruges, and Bergen—succeeded in largely monopolising Baltic Sea trade. The Hansards used several formal contractual schemes to raise capital, spread commercial risk, and share profits, but predominantly they traded within family networks and preferred "reciprocal trade", which was handled without formal contract and formal credit, and often even without cash transfer. By doing this, the Hansards could circumvent several shortcomings of their system of trade—a notorious scarcity of precious metals and money in Northern Europe and a lack of venture capital. "Reciprocal trade" for long was a viable institution, even promoting the Hansards' limited use of money and credit. This in turn had an adverse long-term effect on economic growth in the Baltic Sea region because the development of capital markets and sophisticated instruments of trade finance was inhibited, this restricting a further expansion of Hanseatic trade around 1500.

Keywords: network trade; reciprocal trade; Hanse; institutional analysis; path dependence; lock-in

Introduction

This article is about how late-medieval mercantile practice—in particular the merchants' use of money and credit—correlated with the institutional arrangement of the respective trading system. By taking the case of the Hansards' trade in the Baltic Sea, I attempt to explain why the Hansards used money and other financial

Published in: Stephan Nicolussi-Köhler (Ed.), Change and Transformation of Premodern Credit Markets. The Importance of Small-Scale Credits. Heidelberg: heiBOOKS 2021, 251–274. DOI: https://doi.org/10.11588/heibooks.593.c12697

instruments—to some degree at least, and differently from other merchant groups at the time—to only a limited degree, and why they, in holding on to an exchange pattern today called "reciprocal trade", not only often avoided for much of their internal commercial exchange the transfer of money in either cash or payable formal debt but also ran during the fifteenth century into an institutional "lock-in" by which the economic development in the Baltic Sea region, in particular the development of a venture capital market, was restrained. Even though the Hanse case points to the economic development of medieval towns and therefore does not mirror a rural setting, it may well serve as an example of a small loan system, for Hansards typically operated with only little capital and thus borrowed only small sums.

So, the argument I would like to bring forward in this article contributes to a long-standing debate in economic history about the impact of institutional design on economic development and economic growth in the Middle Ages[1], and I am going on from ideas about the path-dependent development of the institutional arrangement of Hanseatic trade which Stephan Selzer and I have published together.[2]

Trade in the Late-Medieval Baltic Sea Region and the Hansards

Measured in terms of monetisation and commercialisation, the Baltic Sea in the late Middle Ages presented itself as an economically rather highly developed region. During the European boom period of the high Middle Ages, immigration of western settlers into the Baltic Sea region was enormous. A dense network of towns had sprung up along the southern Baltic shore, and the colonisation of the hinterland brought about a huge expansion of arable land and sustained agricultural development.[3] Trade in medieval Northern Europe can basically be described as the commercial exchange between crafted goods such as linen and cloth from the West for raw materials like ore, wax, timber, and furs, as well as foodstuffs like grain, herrings, or dried cod, from the East and North.[4] The east-

1 Cf. North 1990; Milgrom, North, and Weingast 1990; Greif 2000; Greif 2002b; Greif 2006; Greif, Milgrom, and Weingast 1994; Ogilvie 2007; González de Lara 2008; Edwards and Ogilvie 2012; Ogilvie and Carus 2014.

2 Cf. Ewert and Selzer 2010; Ewert and Selzer 2016.

3 Cf. Jahnke 2019.

4 Cf. Hammel-Kiesow 2000; Selzer 2010; Jahnke 2014.

west transfer of goods, especially of luxuries, existed, although much less intensive, even before the turn of the millennium. Numerous trading centres of the Viking Age, which in recent decades have been excavated mainly in the western Baltic Sea region, are proof of this.[5] Then, as a result of agricultural development and population growth, Baltic Sea trade was given a significant quantitative boost throughout the thirteenth century. Even before, it had already been relocated from the early trading centres to the towns newly founded along the southern Baltic coast. Urban dwellers, some of which became quite wealthy, consumed far more than what was necessary for subsistence. Their increasing demand for necessities and luxuries could be satisfied by an intensifying commerce[6], which now was carried out via permanent and legally protected urban markets.

The new and quite closed trading system emerging in this period was based on privileges that were granted by local rulers to groups of Low-German merchants at some important markets at the periphery of the North Sea and the Baltic Sea, that is in London, Bruges, Novgorod, and later also in Bergen. After having ousted former competitors from long-distance trade in this area, the Low-German traders—better known as the merchants of the Hanse or Hansards—operated most of the Baltic Sea trade in the late Middle Ages. The Hansards predominantly traded within kinship and friendship networks, and in economic terms, their dominance of Baltic Sea trade which remained more or less unchallenged up to the late fifteenth century can be addressed as a cartel.[7]

Of course, the transfer of commodities between the Hanse's trading outposts—the *Kontore*—in Novgorod, Bruges, London, and Bergen on the one hand, and the many cities and towns in the Baltic Sea region on the other, is barely conceivable without the existence of money and credit. Hence, various gold and silver currencies existed that could be used for commercial exchange[8]. Each season, Hansards brought silver and coins to the Saint Peter's court in Novgorod as well as to the Bruges fairs.[9] Thus, the Hansards used money as a medium of exchange and as a means of storing value, and different currencies served as a computing unit—in order to address only the three essential functions of money.[10] The computing function of money is all too obvious when looking into some of the merchants' account books and ledgers that have survived from the fourteenth and fifteenth

5 Cf. Adamczyk 2013a; Adamczyk 2013b; Kleingärtner 2013; Selzer and Ewert 2021 [forthcoming].

6 Cf. Irsigler 1989; Hammel-Kiesow 2000.

7 Cf. Ewert and Selzer 2010; Ewert and Selzer 2016.

8 Cf. Adamczyk 2018; Adamczyk 2019.

9 Cf. Jenks 1982.

10 Cf. Sprandel 1975; Steinbach 2019.

centuries.[11] In wills, too, a merchant's material wealth was usually given in a certain currency or even in several different currencies—in book money as well as in real money.[12]

The Hansards' Limited Use of Money and Credit

So, why speak of a Hansards' limited use of money and credit? To answer this question, it is not sufficient to only look at the degrees of commercialisation and monetisation in the Baltic Sea region in the late Middle Ages. Undisputedly, the Baltic economy was already highly developed, as proved by a widespread and intense commercial exchange all across the region, mainly of Hansards. Moreover, as noted above, since money was available in different currencies and merchants also used book money for computing and accounting purposes, monetisation had also reached a quite advanced degree. Hence, is non-use of money therefore not a good indication of an even more commercialised economy, an economy where commercial agents can substitute cash with other financial instruments?[13] Moreover, it appears though that even high degrees of commercialisation and monetisation did not automatically produce some kind of standard or universal trading practice in the late Middle Ages, and quite obviously merchants from a different regional and cultural background developed rather different trading techniques.[14] Therefore it would be necessary to analyse how the respective merchants made use of the money available and when they substituted alternative financial instruments for money.

Limits to the Hansards' use of money and credit for trade in this broader sense are very obvious when compared to the standards that were firmly established among Italian traders at the same time. Late-medieval Italian merchants, for in-

11 See e.g. Nirrnheim H. (ed.) 1895 on the account book of Vicko von Geldersen from Hamburg; Mollwo C. (ed.) 1901 on the account book of Hermann and Johann Wittenborgfrom Lübeck); Slaski 1905, Stark 1993, and Orlowska 2012, 2020 on the account book of Johann Pyre from Gdańsk; Lesnikov M. P. and W. Stark (eds.) 2013 on the account books of Hildebrand Veckinchusen, who lived for most of his commercial life in Bruges; Koppe 2018 on the account book of Hans Wyneke from Reval.

12 A prominent example certainly is the will of Sivert Veckinchusen, written down and sealed in Lübeck on 9th May 1406, where numerous benefits in kind Sivert wanted to be given to his heirs are enlisted, each marked with its proper value in *marc lübisch* (Mark of Lübeck). See Stieda 1921.

13 Cf. Bell, Brooks, and Moore 2017.

14 Cf. Ewert 2019b.

stance, were able to use the bill of exchange a lot more virtuously than their contemporaries in Northern Europe. For Italian traders, this financial instrument was not only a common means of a sedentary merchant to change money in different currencies, or to make cashless payments abroad. They used the bill of exchange even to take out a loan, and more importantly, around 1400 they began to primarily take advantage of the arbitrage resulting from fluctuations of the exchange rate in various markets in Europe. This was a lucrative business, indeed, and some Italian merchants now traded mainly with bills of exchange, becoming merchant bankers in the process.[15] Barely anything comparable existed, however, in the Baltic Sea region.

Why was that? Reasons that are recurrently mentioned in the literature are an alleged lack of credit or even a sort of anti-credit stance of the Hansards as well as their supposed allegedly innovative backlog in all organisational, legal, and financial matters of long-distance trade.[16] These arguments can easily be disproved, and historians have done so in the past. For example, in an article published in 1982, Stuart Jenks convincingly shows that merchants of the Hanse who traded in England and Flanders quite often bought on loan and even used bills of exchange as a means of payment and also as a means of borrowing. To achieve the liquidity required for their business in Bruges, it was a standard procedure for Hansards to draw on bills of exchange of their trading partners in Cologne or Gdańsk, for example. The debt was redeemed by the proceeds of the sale of goods that were then sent to these partners.[17] Although this can primarily be shown for commercial activities of Hansards in the economically already highly developed western regions, there are no signs of either ignorance or hostility in general of Hansards vis-à-vis a use of bills of exchange or related financial instruments.[18] Quite the opposite: the Hansards were able to act extremely flexibly in financial matters, as is proved by a famous case where three Prussian merchants—Gerhard von Allen, Matthias Wyse, and Heinrich Schönhals—handled a debt of a group of English crusaders in Prussia to the Teutonic Order. To settle the debt that was acknowledged by the leader of the group, Humphrey de Bohun, in January 1363, the three merchants issued two bonds obligatory. Both letters of payment belonging to these bonds were at first brought to England by Thomas Albon, a London woolmonger, who then repaid one of them in Bruges at Easter the same year. The other letter of payment was repaid, again in Bruges, to Reynold Papen, a Hansard who was closely connected to Gerhard von Allen, the original issuer of one of the

---

15 Cf. Jenks 1982; Guidi-Bruscoli 2019.

16 Cf. Stromer 1976.

17 Cf. Jenks 1982.

18 Cf. North 1999.

bonds obligatory.[19] Resuming this latter case, it seems though that Hansards in principle were very well able to employ rather advanced techniques of finance whenever it was required. This notwithstanding, they did not systematically trade with either letters of payment or bills of exchange, so their use of financial instruments was limited, of course, in comparison to what Italian merchants commonly did.

There may have been other boundaries for Hansards to a full exploitation of available financial instruments as well—lacking capital or institutional deficiencies, for instance. Around 1400, for example, merchants from Venice, Genoa, Pisa, Siena, Florence, and other Italian cities were able to easily draw on capital from third parties for their trading activities. Italians used various forms of contract for either trade or raising capital where profits and risks were shared between partners, and guaranteed by municipal notaries. Such contractual schemes, for example, are the *rogadia, foenus nauticum, societas maris, commenda,* or *collegantia,* all of them being more or less sophisticated developments of a basic form of contract of greco-roman origin.[20] Thus, in Italian cities, something similar to a venture capital market already existed, through which traders were provided with enough capital for their sometimes risky commercial endeavours.[21] Hansards employed several formal contractual schemes, too, which had an incentive structure very similar to those used by Italian traders, the only difference being that such contracts were not certified by notaries, as was customary in Italian cities, but were legally protected by the respective town council. One of these types, much simpler of course than some of the more sophisticated Italian contracts, was the so-called *vera societas* (real partnership), by which trading capital could be raised from inactive partners. Here, the partners commonly agreed upon how they would distribute profits of trade among them, and who of them had to bear the risk of a potential loss of capital.[22] On 1 November 1358, for example, the merchants Arnold Lowe and Rudolf Wittenborch from Lübeck set up a written contract, saying that they had entered into a formal partnership where Arnold Lowe as the inactive partner paid 800 *marc lübisch* to Rudolf Wittenborch, who was to trade with this money for the benefit of both. Profits as well as losses shall be divided equally, and in case the active partner Rudolf Wittenborch died, Arnold Lowe shall be paid off with the whole sum of his deposit.[23] This *vera societas* contract was registered in the *Niederstadtbuch,* one of the town books in the

19 Cf. Paravicini 1995; Bell, Brooks, and Moore 2017.
20 Cf. Skambraks and Köhler 2019.
21 Cf. Greif 1994.
22 Cf. Cordes 1998; Cordes 1999; Cordes 2000.
23 Cf. Dollinger [4]1989.

city of Lübeck.[24] With such contracts, Hansards were able to formally raise capital for trading activities. However, even though formal contractual schemes for spreading commercial risk and sharing profits existed, a venture capital market as is observed in Italian cities, never really developed in the towns of the Hanse.[25] In addition, trade that relied on such *vera societas* contracts made up for only a smaller portion of Hanseatic trade.

Just like the Hansards' limited use of some at the time well advanced financial instruments, also their use of venture capital was thus not principally restricted by the institutional setting. These episodes might be a hint for the fact that Hansards in principle—to raise capital—could employ financial instruments and contractual schemes in a multitude of ways, but for some reason, they were not always doing it. Also, the Hansards' obvious renunciation of exploiting the full power of financial instruments and contractual schemes available to them does not mean that in return they were restricted to primarily use cash. Interestingly enough, they found something different to raise capital through informal loan and to operate commercial exchange with a minimum of cash possible, a pattern of exchange that can probably be best labelled "reciprocal trade". How this pattern worked, and why it remained in wide use even in fourteenth and fifteenth centuries will be discussed in the following sections of this article.

Reciprocal Trade: the Avoidance of Cash Transfer and Formal Credit

The focus of my considerations on why the late-medieval Hansards, all in all, have been quite reluctant in using money or credit, is therefore on this very specific Hanseatic form of bilateral exchange between merchants, the "reciprocal trade". The majority of Hanseatic businesses were self-employed merchants, and commercial exchange of Hansards in general was handled on a partnership basis.[26] Those business transactions between Hansards that were operated as "reciprocal trade" were of great importance in quantitative terms. Estimations published in literature say that such transactions may have accounted for a majority of all transactions between Hansards in fourteenth and fifteenth centuries, very likely in the order of between more than a half and two thirds. And even in the sixteenth century, this pattern of trade was still prevalent among the merchants of

24 Cf. Seggern 2019.

25 Cf. Huang and Sapoznik 2019.

26 Cf. Ewert and Selzer 2016.

the Hanse.[27] This is why it seems crucially important to analyse in particular this pattern of commercial exchange and of capital raising.

What is the Hansards' "reciprocal trade"? Business partners who operated at distant locations in the Baltic Sea region sent goods to each other, which then were sold on by the respective recipients on their own account. The commercial risks related to the transportation and sale of goods were divided between the two partners. The sender of goods had to take the risk of transportation, whereas the recipient had to care about the risk of sale. And the sender would also formally pocket the profits of sale. All this was done without a written contract between the two partners involved.[28] A very important feature of this pattern is that trading partners were often relatives or considered themselves as friends.[29] For example, the probably most prominent late-medieval merchant of the Hanse, Hildebrandt Veckinchusen, who for most of his commercial life was a trader at the Bruges market, maintained such informal trading relationships with various relatives living in Lübeck, Riga, Reval (Talinn) and Dorpat (Tartu).[30] All these relatives themselves traded as legally independent merchants. Thus, trade of single members of the broader Veckinchusen family was not the trade of a family business at all. A second important feature of "reciprocal trade" is the usually long endurance of such informal partnerships. Some of the partners involved in "reciprocal trade" exchanged goods with each other for more than twenty years. Finally, an individual merchant usually entered into several such informal partnerships at the time, as there was no formal ban of competition among Hansards.[31] In the account book of Johan Pyre from Gdańsk that covers a period of thirty-two years, for instance, more than forty trading partners are enlisted.[32]

Concerning the contractual basis as well as the spread of risk, "reciprocal trade" differed significantly from another sort of business transaction that also was regularly employed by the Hansards, and was called *sendeve* (Sent-away good). The *sendeve* was more kind of a commission business, the like it is even nowadays still in use. Here, a merchant—the commission agent—transported the goods of another merchant and sold them by order and on behalf of this merchant. The owner of goods formally instructed the sale, he had to bear all potential risk, and similar to "reciprocal trade" he also received all the profits of sale, but he had to pay for the commission agent's service.[33]

27 Cf. Stark 1984; Thierfelder 1958.
28 Cf. Mickwitz 1937; Mickwitz 1938; Stark 1984; Stark 2000; Cordes 1998; Cordes 2000.
29 Cf. Ewert and Selzer 2015.
30 Cf. Irsigler 1985; Stark 1993; Cordes 1998; Kluge 2013.
31 Cf. Sprandel 1984.
32 Cf. Sprandel 1984; Orlowska 2012; Orlowska 2020.
33 Cf. Cordes 1998; Cordes 1999; Cordes 2000.

Hence, "reciprocal trade" was a means by which the Hansards were able to avoid, by and large, the transfer of cash because usually the profits of a sale could be paid to the sender by sending back own goods to him. These return goods he then could sell at a profit at his home town market. This notwithstanding, the more clever design of the institution of "reciprocal trade" is obvious because no formal contract or formal order was required in this trading pattern, and therefore the proceeds of a sale had not to be returned to the sender immediately. Since "reciprocal trade" by definition had an enduring element in it, mutual debts could be redeemed within a longer period of time. Furthermore, as long as the recipient of the goods had not yet returned the sale's profits to the sender, it was possible for him within this period to use the sale's proceeds to buy new goods. Thus, "reciprocal trade" was also a means for Hansards to raise capital without entering into a formal contract—a financial instrument providing credit to merchants without letting them pay interest. As a consequence, as Hansards were usually involved in several such informal partnerships using "reciprocal trade" for commercial exchange, the Hansards' trading network can also be considered a credit network in which the members were connected to one another through their mutual obligations of payment.

However, it is the informal character of this trading pattern that makes the analysis of "reciprocal trade" so difficult. The lack of written contracts is why it is almost impossible for legal history to classify this specific form of partnership.[34] This notwithstanding, by taking into account that "reciprocal trade" is nonetheless an informal and implicit contract, principal-agent theory and game theory can be used to derive the incentive structure and the performance of this institutional design, at least from a theoretical perspective.[35] What makes the empirical analysis even more difficult is that "reciprocal trade" can be neither systematically nor clearly detected in the account books that have survived from merchants of the Hanse of the fourteenth and fifteenth centuries. Exactly because of lacking formal agreements between merchants, it is simply impossible for many of the entries to show that they definitely were noted in connection with an informal partnership.

34 Cf. Selzer and Ewert 2001.
35 Cf. Greif 2002a; Ewert and Selzer 2010; Ewert and Selzer 2016.

Trust and Reputation: on the Viability of "Reciprocal Trade"

Compared to the sophistication of means of financing used by other groups of merchants in the fourteenth and fifteenth centuries, the Hansards' "reciprocal trade" appears simple and outdated, of course. Since this pattern of exchanging goods between trading partners and providing each other recurrently with loans worked without a significant transfer of cash, one might also think that very likely it was inefficient. Money or equivalents of money are usually viewed as being essential to make exchange more efficient. Nevertheless, the Hansards employed this trading pattern very intensively for their business, and they held on to this practice for quite a long time. Therefore, there must have been good economic reasons why the Hansards were doing this, if one does not want to assume they were not "clever" businessmen in general. To explain this, three points are briefly outlined below which made the institution of "reciprocal trade" advantageous for both the individual merchant and for the group of all Hansards.

Firstly, the key to understanding the considerable efficiency of "reciprocal trade" as a means of exchange and of financing is that it was embedded in the broad social network of the merchants of the Hanse. This network had emerged since the late twelfth century when merchants still travelled and accompanied their goods, and it became more and more dense later on when many merchants had already settled down.[36] The key terms to focus on here are trust and reputation. Trust played a crucial role in bilateral trade relationships without a contractual basis. However, trust itself was based on reputation. Every merchant within the trade network was keen to maintain a good reputation. Once reputation was lost, due to inadequate care for goods or even fraudulent behaviour, for example, not only was a single partnership destroyed for the merchant, other merchants also no longer wanted to do business with him because of his bad reputation. Hence, betrayal within a single partnership would result in a multilateral ban.[37] In a game-theoretical approach, this central importance of reputation can be demonstrated within a game of trust, which Avner Greif has proposed for the analysis of the incentive structure of institutions used in medieval trade.[38] This simple one-shot game can be extended to an infinite game and, in accordance with the structure of "reciprocal trade", it can be modified insofar as the recipient of the goods who operates the sale on his own responsibility only achieves a positive reputation in each round if he proves able, careful, and honest—that is, selling the partner's goods at a profit and sending back own goods to him which the partner

36 Cf. Ewert and Sunder 2012; Ewert and Sunder 2018.

37 Cf. Selzer and Ewert 2001; Ewert and Selzer 2007.

38 Cf. Greif 2000.

could sell in the next round to realise his profits. With such an incentive structure, betrayal is not a real option for rationally behaving merchants because fraudulent behaviour would very soon result in a loss of all trading partnerships and thus in the economic "death" of the betrayer.[39] News of a merchant's bad reputation spread through the network—not necessarily very quickly, but nevertheless reliably—and thus ensured a properly working multilateral reputation mechanism.[40] Being embedded in the social network of Hansards, "reciprocal trade" proved then to be a self-enforcing and therefore viable institution.[41]

Secondly, because of this self-enforcing character, "reciprocal trade" produced manifest economic benefits for the individual merchant. In this trading practice essential components of the transaction costs remained relatively low, in particular information costs, cost of contract enforcement, and financing costs.[42] In their trusted relationships it was not necessary for Hansards to procure their own information if they wanted to send goods to a partner for sale. Commonly, the trading partner had enough information about what was going on in his home town market. Merchants could also trust that a trading partner would sell the goods at a profit in his own interest because he wanted to send his own goods back. There were no costs for the enforcement of contracts because with "reciprocal trade" there was no contract in a legal sense. Mutual fairness, however, resulted from embedding "reciprocal trade" into a network structure through which reputation was communicated. Financing costs were also low because little capital was needed to be able to trade at all and because the proceeds from the sale of the goods received from the trading partner were used as a loan to buy new goods. In terms of transportation costs only, there was likely no particular saving in "reciprocal trade" compared to other conceivable forms of trade because the goods had to be transported in any case. All in all, "reciprocal trade" made the merchants extremely flexible because easy-to-establish contacts with many other merchants in the network enabled everyone to offer a wide range of products without having to spend a lot of capital or transfer cash, and also to easily obtain small loans for own trading activities. In addition, little start-up capital was required to start trading, and young merchants typically started trading small quantities only within the network until they had gained enough reputation to do bigger business.[43]

---

39 Cf. Ewert and Selzer 2010; Ewert and Selzer 2016.

40 Cf. Selzer and Ewert 2001; Ewert and Selzer 2010.

41 Cf. Ewert and Selzer 2016.

42 Cf. Selzer and Ewert 2001; Selzer and Ewert 2005; Jenks 2005; Ewert and Selzer 2010; Ewert and Selzer 2016.

43 Cf. Ewert and Selzer 2010; Ewert and Selzer 2016.

Thirdly, "reciprocal trade" had noticeable positive effects at the group level, as well, and was thus of economic benefit for the whole Baltic Sea region. The Hanse's system of trade was extremely effective in distributing the goods across space. The network, consisting of many bilateral relationships, made it possible to distribute goods all across the Baltic Sea region. Like in a relay, goods could be sent on from town to town.[44] In addition, by using this trading pattern, the Hansards as a group were able to compensate in part for the lack of venture capital and the lack of a single currency in the Baltic Sea region, and the difficulties that resulted from the fact that the existing currencies were valid only locally or regionally. From an economic point of view, money or currency has to be understood as a public good. Because of potential 'free-riding' the incentive structure is quite unfavourable for any individual engagement. So, typically communities or states become responsible for both the provision and maintenance of public goods.[45] However, the central administrative structure of the Hanse was not yet so developed in the fifteenth century. Therefore the Hanseatic League, which was a loose and by no means permanent association of towns, had not only repeatedly great problems in reacting unanimously to all sorts of external threats[46] but also to credibly guarantee a universal and Northern-Europe-wide currency. However, shortcomings of the monetary system in the Baltic Sea region were only of secondary importance for the viability of "reciprocal trade". In their bookkeeping, the Hansards used the existing currencies to determine the value of the goods they sent away, but these were mostly paid for in kind—with the goods received from the trading partner in return.

Yet, around 1400 there were no economic reasons for giving up "reciprocal trade" and replacing it with newer trading and financing techniques, even more so because the estimated average margin of around fifteen per cent that could be earned in Hanseatic trade was not small, compared with the profit rates of Italian traders at the time.[47] As the institution of "reciprocal trade" proved to be efficient and viable, also the Hansards' limited use of money and credit seems to have been simply a rational choice.

---

44 Cf. Selzer and Ewert 2001; Ewert and Selzer 2010; Ewert and Selzer 2016.

45 Cf. Ewert 2019a.

46 Cf. Ewert and Selzer 2016.

47 Cf. Stark 1985.

Adverse Effects of the Hansards' Limited Use of Money and Credit

It is quite obvious that the pattern of "reciprocal trade" which the Hansards predominantly employed for commercial exchange within long-lasting informal partnerships had several desirable properties, indeed. As argued above, this institution was efficacious, efficient. and, because of its self-enforcing character, also viable. To keep business alive, neither the transfer of money between distant markets was necessary, nor that of financial instruments by which merchants could draw on credit. So, why should the Hansards have given up such an advantageous institution?

Maybe this is simply the wrong question to ask. In the fifteenth century, we see increasing signs that the merchants of the Hanse were beginning to lose some of their economic potential compared to other merchants in Europe. Only three points are mentioned here as examples: firstly, around 1400 the Hansards' did not enter the Italians' newly evolving trade with letters of exchange. Whether the Hansards in principal were unable to exploit this new business is not quite clear. Stuart Jenks is able to convincingly show that special circumstances in the Bruges market in late 1399 and early 1400—a regulation of the city's magistrate with the clear aim at coping with the shortage of coins, saying that bills of exchange shall be redeemed by paying in cash only—helped the Italian merchants a lot in promoting this new business while at the same time, the diet of the Hanseatic League had forbidden Hansards in Bruges to buy on loan.[48] However, in the further course of the fifteenth century, there were no attempts by the Hansards to organise anything comparable within the internal trade of the Hanse. Secondly, the famous *Venedyssche selscop* (Venetian society) which some members of the Veckinchusen family had founded to trade furs from Russia and Finland in Venice soon developed into a financial disaster and went bankrupt within a short period of time.[49] There were of course many reasons for this, but it was certainly also decisive that the Hansards in Venice operated outside their usual trading network, and so they lacked reputation to borrow money from other merchants than the Hansards. Finally, when the centre of Western European trade moved from Bruges to Antwerp around 1500, the merchants of the Hanse were unable to assert themselves against the emerging strong competitors from Upper Germany, who had much more capital at hand. As a result, the Hansards could neither maintain

48 Cf. Jenks 1982.

49 Cf. Stieda 1894; Kluge 2013.

their cartel regarding long-distance trade in the Baltic Sea region furthermore, nor gain a foothold in the new and capital-intensive transatlantic trade.[50]

Yet, it appears likely more adequate to ask: Why did the merchants of the Hanse not basically adopt the more modern techniques of raising capital which their Italian contemporaries already employed? Both groups of merchants came into contact regularly with each other in Bruges and in London, and due to these contacts, the Hansards knew about the Italian techniques of trade and finance. Nevertheless, apart from a few single cases that were discussed above, such an adoption cannot be observed in general, but especially not for the Hanse's internal trade.

At this point, path dependence comes into play. In economics, this concept was formulated in connection with the aim at explaining why technical standards prevail and still dominate even when they are no longer efficient. The starting conditions play a decisive role here, as they structure the further development.[51] Thus, developments of institutions and institutional arrangements are path-dependent as well.[52] Applied to medieval trading systems, this means that initial conditions of these systems are reflected in the design of institutions, and their further development often remains tied to the path that was taken at the time they were created. Therefore, path dependence is a theoretical concept that argues also with the past, which is why it seems suitable to explain institutional developments in medieval long-distance trade. The dominance of a particular institutional solution is typically promoted early in the development process by a large number of users. This creates a network effect and makes switching to other institutions costly and thus unattractive, because users typically value the expected returns from competing institutional solutions lower than the costs of switching. As a consequence, and contrary to any simple economic logic, inefficient institutions cannot simply be modified or replaced. Often, either modification or replacement of individual institutions within an institutional arrangement are difficult or even impossible because of their interdependence which had evolved in the process. A typical consequence of such a quasi-irreversibility is the so-called "lock-in" of the institutional arrangement.[53]

Exactly this happened in the Hanse's system of trade and of raising capital. As a result of a path-dependent institutional development, in the fifteenth century this system seems to have been trapped in such a "lock-in". The Hansards'

---

50 Cf. Ewert and Selzer 2010; Ewert and Selzer 2016; Kypta 2015; Hammel-Kiesow and Selzer (eds.) 2016.

51 Cf. David 1985; Arthur 1989.

52 Cf. David 1994; Sydow, Schreyögg, and Koch 2009.

53 Cf. Ewert 2019b.

preference to trade mainly within kinship and friendship networks still in the fourteenth and fifteenth centuries was path-dependent, of course. And so was the lasting dominance of "reciprocal trade". This specific pattern of trade thus reflected in many ways the initial conditions that once in the thirteenth century had promoted the emergence of the Hanse's reputation-based network organisation of trade, namely the huge regional differences in economic development that existed across the Baltic Sea region, a traditional shortage of precious metals and coins, the common practice of privileging entire merchant groups according to their region of origin, and an only weak legal system.[54] Furthermore, since the information and coordination problems typical of cartels could be solved rather easily via contacts based on relatives and friends, the trade network remained stable even after many of the merchants of the Hanse had settled in the late Middle Ages. For the Hansards, the network was a powerful vehicle to organise and maintain their trading cartel in the Baltic Sea region.[55] However, both network organisation and "reciprocal trade" not only developed path-dependently, they were also mutually dependent, in particular so because "reciprocal trade" was embedded in the social network of Hansards. Operating commerce through kinship and friendship networks promoted the pattern of "reciprocal trade" insofar as the network enabled merchants to easily get in contact with a lot of other merchants from the same Low-German speaking background—to trade with them and to obtain informal loans from them. In this respect, the Hanse can very well be understood as a "small world", a large but fragmented network, where nonetheless distant subgroups are loosely connected through "bridging persons".[56] The network also enhanced fairness among its members, thus members were protected by the multilateral reputation mechanism, which was pivotal for "reciprocal trade" to work properly.[57] In turn, through "reciprocal trade", trusted relationships were created which increased the number of possible connections and further intensified the cohesion of the whole network.[58] As a consequence of the mutual interdependence of Hanseatic institutions of trade, a single Hansard could not simply quit the Hanse's system of trade and adopt instead trading habits and financing techniques of other European merchant groups at the time, namely those of Italian merchant bankers. This would have meant losing all connections within the Hansards' network, renouncing from all benefits coming from it, and giving up business after all. It should be clear though, why the Han-

54 Cf. Ewert and Selzer 2010; Ewert and Selzer 2016.
55 Cf. Ewert and Sunder 2012; Ewert and Sunder 2018.
56 Cf. Watts 1999; Selzer and Ewert 2001; Ewert and Selzer 2016.
57 Cf. Selzer and Ewert 2001; Ewert and Selzer 2010; Ewert and Selzer 2016.
58 Cf. Ewert and Selzer 2010; Ewert and Selzer 2016.

sards did not switch to alternative means of raising capital and alternative techniques of financing trade.

That the merchants of the Hanse were not able to substantially change the institutional arrangement of their internal trade in the fifteenth century is also a result of the fact that the practice of "reciprocal trade" affected economic development adversely, especially the development of capital markets and a sophisticated finance of trade. As argued above, for "reciprocal trade" usually not much capital was required, which is why in the short term, newcomers could start a trading business quite easily. In the long run, however, such common low-capital trading among Hansards inhibited both the development and growth of a venture capital market in the towns of the Hanse.[59] It is no surprise, of course, that even in the fifteenth century, larger companies did not emerge and most of the Hanse's trading businesses were self-employed merchants or small firms, which in turn meant that the merchants were very well used to operating with only little capital.[60] The same was true for the development of more complex financial instruments because such instruments simply were not necessary, neither for the exchange of goods nor for borrowing within trusted relationships.[61] Hence, the majority of Hansards—those who did not trade at either the market of Bruges or London—had simply no opportunity within their own business to exploit the manifold financial possibilities that bills of exchange can provide. These serious deficits in the commercial development of the Baltic Sea region in the late Middle Ages therefore neither reduced the significance of "reciprocal trade", nor did this specific pattern become redundant. Quite the reverse: the practice of "reciprocal trade" was even more enhanced by this. Thus, commercial exchange with merchants from outside the Hanse—the so-called *butenhansen*—in general remained difficult, as in such cases the multilateral reputation mechanism was ineffective, and financing techniques were often not compatible with each other. This "lock-in" was stabilised furthermore because to keep the network of the Hansards closed, many towns of the Hanse prohibited formal trading companies with partners from outside the Hanse, who of course could have provided Hansards with more capital.[62] In addition, to protect the Hanse's privilege, the Bruges *Kontor* repeatedly banned purchases on loan, which to some extent exacerbated the notorious lack of credit and financing there.[63] It seems reasonable therefore why many Hansards held on to "reciprocal trade" in the late fifteenth century and even be-

59 Cf. Schonewille 1998.
60 Cf. Jenks 2013.
61 Cf. Ewert and Selzer 2010; Ewert and Selzer 2016.
62 Cf. Jenks 1996.
63 Cf. Jenks 1982.

yond, and did not make any attempt to employ more sophisticated techniques of capital raising and of finance. In the early sixteenth century, the Hansards finally had too little venture capital available and their financing techniques were too simple to really be able to enter into the then emerging capital-intensive transatlantic trade.[64]

Conclusions

With the rapidly progressing commercialisation and monetisation of the economy in various regions of Europe during the high and late Middle Ages, the use of money and credit within trade also changed accordingly. All across Europe merchants developed techniques to circumvent the notorious shortage of precious metals and an ever rising diversity of local currencies. Within long-distance trade, merchants began to use book money, they minimised the number of risky coin transfers, and finally tried to avoid payments in cash. And they also deployed more sophisticated means to finance trade. Like in other European regions, too, trade in Northern Europe had also reached this "new" level of economic development—that is merchants substituted financial instruments for cash wherever and whenever possible, which also meant that they had to rely more and more on loans to handle commercial exchange.

As with other merchant groups, the Hansards used book money and reduced the number of cash transfers to a minimum. However, the Hansards did not employ sophisticated financial instruments like e.g. Italian merchants did. And even though they knew about the more modern financing techniques that came in use in Mediterranean trade, there was barely an attempt to copy these techniques. Within much of their internal trade, the Hansards held on to a practice called "reciprocal trade" which allowed them to avoid the transfer of real money. Interestingly enough, this informal pattern of trade was so simple and lean that sophisticated financial instruments, by which merchants can draw on credit or transfer payable debts, were not necessary either. Thus, the Hansards' use of money within long-distance trade was extremely limited, indeed, but as "reciprocal trade" was embedded in a kinship and friendship network based on trust and reputation, this practice proved for long to be efficient and viable.

It was only around 1500, when European trade changed radically, that Hanseatic "reciprocal trade" had actually become inefficient and seriously inhibited

64 Cf. Ewert and Selzer 2010; Ewert and Selzer 2016.

both the development of credit markets and economic growth in the Baltic Sea region. This is why this pattern of commercial exchange and capital raising should have been replaced by a more efficient institutional arrangement, of course. However, due to the mutual interdependence of their trading network and their practice of "reciprocal trade", the Hansards found themselves trapped in a so-called "lock-in" of their system of trade, where it was barely possible to adopt more modern techniques of finance and to significantly increase venture capital by loans. Trust and reputation were perfect means to back-up financial obligations within a relatively small group of merchants where each merchant handled relatively small exchanges only, but they were poor when commercial exchange became more complex and capital-intensive. So, taking a step further to reach an even "higher" level of economic development, where finance turned out to be the key element of business expansion, was for Hansards simply impossible.

References

Bibliographic References

Adamczyk D. 2013a. "Fernhandelsemporien, Herrschaftszentren, Regional- und Lokalmärkte: Die ökonomischen Funktionen von Silber, oder wie lässt sich der Grad der Monetarisierung in den frühmittelalterlichen Gesellschaften des Ostseeraumes 'messen'?". In *Economies, Monetisation and Society in the West Slavic Lands AD 800–1200,* edited by T. Bogucki and M. Rębkowski, 115–136. Szczecin: Wydawnictwo IAE PAN.

Adamczyk D. 2013b. "Wollin und sein Hinterland im kontinentalen und transkontinentalen Beziehungsgeflecht um das Jahr 1000". In *Geschichte, um zu verstehen. Traditionen, Wahrnehmungsmuster, Gestaltungsperspektiven. Carl-Hans Hauptmeyer zum 65. Geburtstag,* edited by H. Düselder, D. Schmiechen-Ackermann, T. Schwark, M. Stöber and C. Schröder, 299–317. Bielefeld: Verlag für Regionalgeschichte.

Adamczyk D. 2018. "How and why did Dirhams flow to Scandinavia during the Ninth Century?" *Quaestiones Medii Aevi Novae* 23: 139–151.

Adamczyk D. 2019. "The Use of Silver by the Norsemen of Truso and Wolin: The Logic of the Market or Social Prestige?" In *Social Norms in Medieval Scandinavia,* edited by J. Morawiec, A. Jochymek and G. Bartusik, 19–34. Leeds: Arc Humanities Press.

Arthur W.B. 1989. "Competing Technologies, Increasing Returns, and Lock-in by Historical Events". *The Economic Journal* 99, no. 394: 116–131.

Bell A. R., C. Brooks, and T. K. Moore 2017. "The Non-Use of Money in the Middle Ages". In *Money and its Use in Medieval Europe. Three Decades on Essays in Honour of Professor Peter Spufford* [= Royal Numismatic Society Special Publication 52], edited by M. Allen and N. J. Mayhew, 137–151. London: Royal Numismatic Society.

Cordes A. 1998. *Spätmittelalterlicher Gesellschaftshandel im Hanseraum*, Quellen und Darstellungen zur hansischen Geschichte, Neue Folge 45. Cologne: Böhlau, 1998.

Cordes A. 1999. "Einheimische und gemeinrechtliche Elemente im hansischen Gesellschaftsrecht des 15.–17. Jahrhunderts. Eine Projektskizze". In *"kopet uns werk by tyden." Beiträge zur hansischen und preußischen Geschichte. Festschrift für Walter Stark zum 75. Geburtstag*, edited by N. Jörn, D. Kattinger, and H. Wernicke, 67–71. Schwerin: Thomas Helms Verlag.

Cordes A. 2000. *Wie verdiente der Kaufmann sein Geld? Hansische Handelsgesellschaften im Spätmittelalter* [= Handel, Geld und Politik 2]. Lübeck: Schmidt-Römhild.

David P. A. 1985. "Clio and the Economics of QWERTY". *American Economic Review* 75, no. 2: 332–337.

David P. A. 1994. "Why are Institutions the 'Carriers of History'? Path Dependence and the Evolution of Conventions, Organizations and Institutions". *Structural Change and Economic Dynamics* 5, no. 2: 205–220.

Dollinger P. [4]1989. *Die Hanse*. Stuttgart: Kröner.

Edwards J. and S. C. Ogilvie 2012. "What Lessons for Economic Development Can We Draw from the Champagne Fairs?," *Explorations in Economic History* 49, no. 2: 131–148.

Ewert U. C. 2019a. "Collective Goods in the Middle Ages". In *Methods in Premodern Economic History: Case Studies from the Holy Roman Empire, c. 1300–c. 1600*, edited by U. Kypta, J. Bruch, and T. Skambraks, 64–67. London: Palgrave Macmillan.

Ewert U. C. 2019b. "Pfadabhängigkeit und 'Lock-in'—Fernhandelspraxis im Hanseraum jenseits italienischer Vertragsstandards". In *Italien als Vorbild? Ökonomische und kulturelle Verflechtungen europäischer Metropolen am Vorabend der "ersten Globalisierung" (1300–1600)* [= Forum Mittelalter—Studien 16], edited by J. Oberste and S. Ehrich, 151–166. Regensburg: Schnell & Steiner GmbH.

Ewert U. C. and S. Selzer 2007. "Netzwerkorganisation im Fernhandel des Mittelalters: Wettbewerbsvorteil oder Wachstumshemmnis?". In *Unternehmerische Netzwerke. Eine historische Organisationsform mit Zukunft?*, edited by H. Berghoff and J. Sydow, 45–70. Stuttgart: Kohlhammer.

Ewert U. C. and S. Selzer 2010. "Wirtschaftliche Stärke durch Vernetzung. Zu den Erfolgsfaktoren des hansischen Handels". In *Praktiken des Handels. Geschäfte und soziale Beziehungen europäischer Kaufleute in Mittelalter und früher Neuzeit,* edited by M. Häberlein and C. Jeggle, 39–69. Constance: UVK Verlagsgesellschaft.

Ewert U. C. and S. Selzer 2015. "Chapter 5: Social Networks," In *A Companion to the Hanseatic League* [= Brill's Companions to European History 8], edited by D. J. Harreld, 162–193. Leiden/Boston: Brill.

Ewert U. C. and S. Selzer 2016. *Institutions of Hanseatic Trade: Studies on the Political Economy of a Medieval Network Organisation.* Frankfurt/Main: Peter Lang Edition.

Ewert U. C. and M. Sunder 2012. "Trading Networks, Monopoly, and Economic Development in Medieval Northern Europe: An Agent-based Simulation of Early Hanseatic Trade". In *Raumbildung durch Netzwerke? Der Ostseeraum zwischen Wikingerzeit und Spätmittelalter aus archäologischer und geschichtswissenschaftlicher Perspektive* [= Zeitschrift für Archäologie des Mittelalters, Beiheft 23], edited by S. Kleingärtner and G. Zeilinger, 131–153. Bonn: Rudolf Habelt Verlag.

Ewert U. C. and M. Sunder 2018. "Modelling Maritime Trade Systems: Agent-based Simulation and Medieval History". *Historical Social Research* 43, no. 1: 110–143.

González de Lara Y. 2008. "The Secret of Venetian Success: A Public-order, Reputation-based Institution". *European Review of Economic History* 12, no. 3: 247–285.

Greif A. 1994. "On the Political Foundations of the Late Medieval Commercial Revolution: Genoa during the Twelfth and Thirteenth Centuries". *Journal of Economic History* 54, no. 2: 271–287.

Greif A. 2000. "The Fundamental Problem of Exchange. A Research Agenda in Historical Institutional Analysis". *European Review of Economic History* 4, no. 3: 251–284.

Greif A. 2002a. "Chapter 52: Economic History and Game Theory". In *Handbook of Game Theory with Economic Explanations, vol. 3,* edited by R. Aumann and S. Hart, 1989–2004. Amsterdam: North Holland.

Greif A. 2002b. "Institutions and Impersonal Exchange. From Communal to Individual Responsibility". *Journal of Institutional and Theoretical Economics* 158, no. 1, 168–204.

Greif A. 2006. *Institutions and the Path to the Modern Economy: Lessons from Medieval Trade.* Cambridge: Cambridge University Press.

Greif A., P. Milgrom and B.R. Weingast 1994. "Coordination, Commitment, and Enforcement: The Case of the Merchant Guild". *Journal of Political Economy* 102, no. 4: 745–776.

Guidi-Bruscoli F. 2019. "The Florentines and European 'Capitals' at the Dawn of the 'First Globalisation'". In *Italien als Vorbild? Ökonomische und kulturelle Verflechtungen europäischer Metropolen am Vorabend der "ersten Globalisierung" (1300–1600)* [= Forum Mittelalter—Studien 16], edited by J. Oberste and S. Ehrich, 137–150. Regensburg: Schnell & Steiner GmbH.

Hammel-Kiesow R. 2000. *Die Hanse.* Munich: C.H. Beck.

Hammel-Kiesow R. and S. Selzer (eds.) 2016, *Hansischer Handel im Strukturwandel vom 15. zum 16. Jahrhundert* [= Hansische Studien 25]. Trier: Porta Alba Verlag.

Huang A. and A. Sapoznik 2019. "Fremdes Geld. Auswärtige Kapitalbeziehungen des Braunschweiger Rentenmarktes im 15. und 16. Jahrhundert". *Vierteljahrschrift für Sozial- und Wirtschaftsgeschichte* 106, no. 1: 29–66.

Irsigler F. 1985. "Der Alltag einer hansischen Kaufmannsfamilie im Spiegel der Veckinchusen-Briefe". *Hansische Geschichtsblätter* 103: 75–99.

Irsigler F. 1989. "Der hansische Handel im Spätmittelalter". In *Die Hanse. Lebenswirklichkeit und Mythos. Eine Ausstellung im Museum für Hamburgische Geschichte in Verbindung mit der Vereins- und Westbank,* edited by J. Bracker, 518–532. Lübeck: Museum für Hamburgische Geschichte; Vereins- und Westbank.

Jahnke C. 2014. *Die Hanse.* Stuttgart: Reclam.

Jahnke C. 2019. "Lübeck: Early Economic Development and the Urban Hinterland". In *A Companion to Medieval Lübeck* [= Brill's Companions to European History 18], edited by C. Jahnke, 226–252. Leiden/Boston: Brill.

Jenks S. 1982. "War die Hanse kreditfeindlich?". *Vierteljahrschrift für Sozial- und Wirtschaftsgeschichte* 69, no. 3: 305–337.

Jenks S. 1996. "Hansisches Gästerecht". *Hansische Geschichtsblätter* 114 (1996), 2–60.

Jenks S. 2005. "Transaktionskostentheorie und die mittelalterliche Hanse". *Hansische Geschichtsblätter* 123: 31–42.

Jenks S. 2013. "Small is Beautiful: Why Small Hanseatic Firms Survived in the Late Middle Ages". In *The Hanse in Medieval and Early Modern Europe* [= The Northern World 60], edited by J. Wubs-Mrozewicz and S. Jenks, 191–214. Leiden/Boston: Brill.

Kleingärtner S. 2013. *Die frühe Phase der Urbanisierung an der südlichen Ostseeküste im Frühmittelalter* [= Studien zur Archäologie des Ostseeraums 13]. Neumünster: Wachholtz.

Kluge M.F. 2013. “Zwischen Metropole, Fürst und König: Die Venedische Handelsgesellschaft der Kaufleute Veckinchusen und ihr Niedergang”. *Hansische Geschichtsblätter* 131: 33–76.

Koppe G. 2018. “Hans Wynekes Revaler Handlungsbuch (1490–1497). Ein Beitrag zur Ausbildung hansischer Kaufleute”. In *Menschen—Märkte—Meere. Bausteine zur spätmittelalterlichen Wirtschafts- und Sozialgeschichte zwischen Hamburg, Lübeck und Reval* [= Contributiones 6], edited by S. Selzer, 123–179. Münster: Verlag für Wissenschaft.

Kypta U. 2015 “Die Hanse und die Krise des Spätmittelalters. Überlegungen zum Zusammenspiel von wirtschaftlichem und institutionellem Wandel”. In *Wirtschaftskrisen als Wendepunkte,* edited by D. Adamczyk and S. Lehnstaedt, 159–184. Osnabrück: fibre Verlag.

Lesnikov M.P. and W. Stark (eds.) 2013. *Die Handelsbücher des Hildebrand Veckinchusen: Kontobücher und übrige Manuale* [= Quellen und Darstellungen zur hansischen Geschichte, Neue Folge 67]. Cologne: Böhlau.

Mickwitz G. 1937. “Neues zur Funktion hansischer Handelsgesellschaften”. *Hansische Geschichtsblätter* 62: 191–201.

Mickwitz G. 1938. *Aus Revaler Handelsbüchern. Zur Technik des Ostseehandels in der ersten Hälfte des 16. Jahrhunderts,* [= Societas Scientiarum Fennica. Commentationes Humanarum Litterarum IX/5]. Helsinki: Akademische Buchhandlung.

Milgrom P.R., D.C. North, and B.R. Weingast 1990. “The Role of Institutions in the Revival of Trade: The Law Merchant, Private Judges, and the Champagne Fairs”. *Economics and Politics* 2, no. 1: 1–23.

Mollwo C. (ed.) 1901. *Das Handlungsbuch von Hermann und Johann Wittenborg.* Leipzig: Dyk.

Nirrnheim H. (ed.) 1895. *Das Handlungsbuch des Vicko von Geldersen.* Hamburg: Voss.

North D.C. 1990. *Institutions, Institutional Change and Economic Performance.* Cambridge/New York: Cambridge University Press.

North M. 1999. “Kreditinstrumente in Westeuropa und im Hanseraum” In *“kopet uns werk by tyden”. Beiträge zur hansischen und preußischen Geschichte. Festschrift für Walter Stark zum 75. Geburtstag,* edited by N. Jörn, D. Kattinger and H. Wernicke, 43–46. Schwerin: Thomas Helms Verlag.

Ogilvie S.C. 2007. “‘Whatever Is, Is right’? Economic Institutions in Pre-industrial Europe”. *Economic History Review* 60, no. 4: 649–684.

Ogilvie S.C. and A.W. Carus 2014. “Chapter 8: Institutions and Economic Growth in Historical Perspective”. In *Handbook of Economic Growth,* vol. 2A, edited by P. Aghion and S. Durlauf, 403–513. Amsterdam: North Holland.

Orlowska A. P. 2012. "Handel in einem Kaufmannsnetz: Der Danziger Johann Pyre". In *Vertraute Ferne. Kommunikation und Mobilität im Hanseraum,* edited by J. Mähnert and S. Selzer, 32–39. Husum: Husum Druck- und Verlagsgesellschaft.

Orlowska A. P. 2020. *Johan Pyre. Ein Kaufmann und sein Handelsbuch im spätmittelalterlichen Danzig. Darstellung und Edition* [= Quellen und Darstellungen zur Hansischen Geschichte, Neue Folge 77]. Cologne: Böhlau.

Paravicini W. 1995. *Die Preussenreisen des europäischen Adels. Part 2.* [= Beihefte der Francia 17/2]. Sigmaringen: Thorbecke.

Schonewille M. 1998. *Risk, Institutions and Trade. New Approaches to Hanse History.* Nijmegen: Univ. Nijmegen.

Seggern H. von 2019. "The 'Niederstadtbuch'. A Source of History of Private Life of Lübeckers around 1500". In *A Companion to Medieval Lübeck* [= Brill's Companions to European History 18], edited by C. Jahnke, 352–371. Leiden/Boston: Brill.

Selzer S. 2010, *Die mittelalterliche Hanse.* Darmstadt: Wissenschaftliche Buchgesellschaft.

Selzer S. and Ewert U. C. 2001. "Verhandeln und Verkaufen, Vernetzen und Vertrauen. Über die Netzwerkstruktur des hansischen Handels". *Hansische Geschichtsblätter* 119: 135–161.

Selzer S. and U. C. Ewert 2005. "Die Neue Institutionenökonomik als Herausforderung an die Hanseforschung". *Hansische Geschichtsblätter* 123: 7–29.

Selzer S. and U. C. Ewert 2021. "Nord- und Ostsee, 500–1600". In *Globale Handelsräume und Handelsrouten von der Antike bis zur Gegenwart,* edited by M. A. Denzel and M. Häberlein. Berlin: De Gruyter. [forthcoming]

Skambraks T. and S. Köhler 2019. "Medieval Trade and Credit Contracts: *foenus nauticum, commenda* and *compagnia/societas*". In *Methods in Premodern Economic History: Case Studies from the Holy Roman Empire, c. 1300–c. 1600,* edited by U. Kypta, J. Bruch, and T. Skambraks, 157–159. London: Palgrave Macmillan, 2019.

Slaski W. von 1905. *Danziger Handel im 15. Jahrhundert auf Grund eines im Danziger Stadtarchiv befindlichen Handlungsbuches geschildert.* Heidelberg: Beisel.

Sprandel R. 1975. *Das mittelalterliche Zahlungssystem nach hansisch-nordischen Quellen des 13.–15. Jahrhunderts* [= Monographien zur Geschichte des Mittelalters 10]. Stuttgart: Anton Hiersemann Verlag.

Sprandel R. 1984. "Die Konkurrenzfähigkeit der Hanse im Spätmittelalter," *Hansische Geschichtsblätter* 102: 21–38.

Stark W. 1984. "Über Platz- und Kommissionshändlergewinne im Handel des 15. Jahrhunderts". In *Autonomie, Wirtschaft und Kultur der Hansestädte. Jhannes Schildhauer zum 65. Geburtstag* [= Hansische Studien 6—Abhandlungen zur Handels- und Sozialgeschichte 23], edited by K. Fritze, E. Müller-Mertens and W. Stark, 130–146. Weimar: Böhlau.

Stark W. 1985. *Untersuchungen zum Profit beim hansischen Handelskapital in der ersten Hälfte des 15. Jahrhunderts.* Weimar: H. Böhlaus Nachfolger.

Stark W. 1993. "Über Techniken und Organisationsformen des hansischen Handels im Spätmittelalter". In *Der hansische Sonderweg? Beiträge zur Sozial- und Wirtschaftsgeschichte der Hanse* [= Quellen und Darstellungen zur hansischen Geschichte, Neue Folge 39], edited by S. Jenks and M. North, 191–201. Cologne–Weimar–Vienna: Böhlau.

Stark W. 2000. "Über Handelstechniken auf dem Brügger Markt um die Wende vom 14. zum 15. Jahrhundert". In *Hansekaufleute in Brügge, Part 4. Beiträge der Internationalen Tagung in Brügge April 1996,* edited by N. Jörn, W. Paravicini and H. Wernicke, 97–107. Frankfurt/Main: Peter Lang.

Steinbach S. 2019. "What is Money?" In *Methods in Premodern Economic History: Case Studies from the Holy Roman Empire, c. 1300–c. 1600,* edited by U. Kypta, J. Bruch and T. Skambraks, 132–145. London: Palgrave Macmillan, 2019.

Stieda W. (ed.) 1921. *Hildebrand Veckinchusen. Briefwechsel eines deutschen Kaufmanns im 15. Jahrhundert.* Leipzig: S. Hirzel Verlag.

Stieda W. 1894. *Hansisch-Venetianische Handelsbeziehungen im 15. Jahrhundert. Festschrift der Landes-Universität Rostock zur zweiten Säcularfeier der Universität Halle a.S.* Rostock: Dr. v. Adlers Erben.

Stromer W. von 1976. "Der innovatorische Rückstand der hansischen Wirtschaft". In *Beiträge zur Wirtschafts- und Sozialgeschichte des Mittelalters. Festschrift für Herbert Helbig zum 65. Geburtstag,* edited by K. Schulz, 204–217. Cologne–Vienna: Böhlau.

Sydow J., G. Schreyögg, and J. Koch 2009. "Organizational Path Dependence: Opening the Black Box". *Academy of Management Review* 34, no. 4: 689–709.

Thierfelder H. 1958. *Rostock-Osloer Handelsbeziehungen im 16. Jahrhundert. Die Geschäftspapiere der Kaufleute Kron in Rostock und Bene in Oslo* [= Abhandlungen zur Handels- und Sozialgeschichte 1]. Weimar: H. Böhlaus Nachfolger.

Watts D. 1999. "Networks, Dynamics, and the Small-World Phenomenon". *American Journal of Sociology* 105, no. 2: 493–527.

CONTRACT AND TRUST IN FIFTEENTH-CENTURY CHURCH COURTS

Hannah Robb

Abstract: This chapter looks at the relationship between the ecclesiastical courts and the customs of credit in fifteenth-century England. It suggests that the church courts in particular shaped the language and performative ritual used at the point of contracting credit. Though court records and household inventories suggest that written instruments were used when contracting credit, ecclesiastical jurisdiction over credits sworn on oath in the later medieval period placed greater emphasis on the declarations and performance of trust than the written record as a form of proof. The commutation of the oath from the sacred to the profane, marked by the rise of oral credit contracts in the secular courts of the sixteenth and seventeenth centuries, highlights the significance of ecclesiastical jurisdiction in shaping credit contracts and the emergence of a language of faith that continued to underpin contracts.

Keywords: credit, law, custom, oaths, courts.

Introduction

The record of credit in late medieval England is multifaceted. We have in the fifteenth century evidence of sealed instruments, written contracts, and private household account books coexisting with, and often enforced by, oral agreements, sworn oaths, and physical and customary displays of concord and friendliness to confirm an exchange. The primary source from which the interplay between the written and oral contract can be discerned is itself a product of the shifting rela-

Published in: Stephan Nicolussi-Köhler (Ed.), Change and Transformation of Premodern Credit Markets. The Importance of Small-Scale Credits. Heidelberg: heiBOOKS 2021, 275–292. DOI: https://doi.org/10.11588/heibooks.593.c12698

tionship between the written and spoken contract. Courts in late medieval England increasingly favoured written and material forms of proof.[1] Cases of disputed land ownership recorded in manorial court rolls increasingly favoured charters and deeds as primary forms of proof, taking precedence over the collective memory of the community.[2] By the close of the fourteenth century, evidence from manorial courts suggests that the court roll itself was consulted as a form of proof, a witness to the original contract of sale. The same cannot be said, however, in pleas of debt. Manor courts were rarely used as a means to record credit. Instead, the testimony of witnesses appears to have been the most popular recourse for the expediency of justice.[3] The courts of the later medieval period were driving the ways in which credit and sales were conducted and the evidence collected by the parties at the point of exchange. Ecclesiastical courts of the fifteenth century, under the plea of breach of faith, placed emphasis on the words spoken on oath in a promise to adhere to a contract. Unlike manorial court rolls, we have detailed depositions from the church courts that recall oral agreements and the use of written contracts. They reconstruct credit agreements couched in a language of trust, honesty, and truth inherent to the Christian practice of oath-taking. The church courts of the fifteenth century supported the oral credit economy and in placing emphasis on witness testimony and the words spoken that bound creditor and debtor, shaped the culture of credit.

The depositions of the consistory court of York reveal the details of credit agreements. The consistory court was held at York Minster and heard cases originating from within York and on appeal from the wider prebendal courts of which there were over one hundred operating in fifteenth-century Yorkshire. The depositions are found in the cause papers held at the Borthwick Institute of York, with each "cause" holding all documents pertaining to the case including interrogatories, depositions, appeals, and outcomes. Instances relating to credit and debt appear under pleas of breach of faith, defamation, and testamentary. Though few in number, they describe the writing and signing of contracts, the speaking of oaths, and terms of repayment. The testimonies not only reflect the integration of legalistic concepts in the language used by witnesses to frame their account at court but also the infiltration of the language of the court in credit agreements and the ways in which trust and obligation were conceptualised and used in practice. The narratives of debt litigation provide more than a reconstruction of a single credit agreement and instead present a discourse of debt that considered trust,

1 Schofield 2012, 79–81.
2 Beckerman 1992, 221–222.
3 Schofield 2012, 80.

reputation, and ideals of Christian neighbourliness.[4] Recent historiography on the concept of trust has highlighted the significance of the language of truth and honesty in defining social organisations and hierarchies in late medieval society. Ian Forrest's study on the role of "trustworthy men" in local church administration has traced the role of trust in medieval society and the development of a discourse of trust, troth, faith, and trustworthiness in the church records that identified men of good reputation, defining communities in late medieval England. The term "faith" embodied all of its secular and religious meanings. It was applied to contracts, promises, securities, and oaths as well as belief in God.[5] Most significantly, in pleas of debt brought before the church courts it indicated an "ethic of constancy in behaviour and belief that derived from the legal sense of equity".[6] There is then a particularly Christian notion of faith invoked in the promises made on oath when buying and selling on credit that was repeated in the language used in litigation. The "good", "honest", and "trustworthy men" who promised on their "good faith" to repay a debt identified themselves as part of that trusted network of Christians bound by their collective relationship to God. Tyler Lange's study on the role of excommunication in pleas of debt in later medieval France explores the extent of ecclesiastical jurisdiction and argues excommunication was a successful deterrent to the breaking of contracts in part because it threatened exclusion from wider society; "the sacramental community was also an economic entity".[7] At the fore of these debates lies the relationship between the courts and social and economic institutions. There appears a long-standing trope that the close of the fifteenth century witnessed a significant transition from faith in individuals to faith in institutions to enforce the terms of contract. This was echoed in a move from oral to written contracts and the greater circulation of credit with the exchange of credit instruments. The works of Muldrew and Wrightson identify the secular courts of early modern England as an institution that increasingly came to impose social ideals of neighbourliness in response to an ever increasingly complex and commercialised web of interdependency. Faith was no longer held in the contracting individuals, bound by a belief in God and a desire to maintain Christian harmony and sociability, but in the power of institutions to legally enforce promises.[8] The fifteenth century thus stands at an apex as legal institutions shifted and the power of the church to act as an adjudicating authority in economic matters was increasingly challenged.

---

4 For a discussion of the preconstruction of witness testimony, see Johnson 2014.

5 Forrest 2018, 28–29.

6 Forrest 2018, 31.

7 Lange 2016, 278.

8 Craig Muldrew 1996; Wrightson 2002.

This chapter first explores the evidence for written accounts of credit using court records, probate inventories, and household accounts. It looks at the materiality of credit contracts and the ways in which written proof of credit was used in the legal process. The second part of this chapter looks to the oral customs surrounding the contract. It suggests that legal custom informed the language used in oath-making in credit contracts and deferred sales. The evidence is drawn from the depositions of the ecclesiastical courts in the archbishopric of York and the act books of the lower ecclesiastical courts in the Yorkshire region. Within these papers, deponents describe a culture of oral credit that was shaped by the legal customs of the church court. The language used to describe the binding nature of the oral promise and the symbolism of ritual associated with oath-taking highlights the significance of the church as both a formal institution enforcing the terms of agreement and as a social institution regulating the morality of the marketplace. In doing so, this chapter explores the relationship between the law, legal formulae, and practice in the credit economy of the fifteenth century.

Evidence for a Record of Written Credit

Written contracts, bonds, and sealed instruments were routine in mercantile trade. The extent to which there was a written record of credit that facilitated day-to-day trade is, however, less clear. Though there were notaries operating within York, the role was limited.[9] Court records suggest they presided over contracts, recorded the instalments of repayments, and drafted summons to court yet no separate archive for the recording of credit was maintained as was common across mainland Europe where notarial guilds grew in number in the late medieval period.[10] Two cases cite payments having been made with the public notary resident at York Minster and summons to court appear to have been displayed within this public office.[11] There clearly existed a desire to record credit and it would appear that competing authorities held jurisdiction over such matters. Of-

---

9 Though no separate notarial archive was maintained in York, studies cataloguing the various notarial signatures across a range of documents show notaries were present and played a significant role in the verification of private documents and court proceedings. See Purvis 1957.

10 Hardman 2014; Ogilvie, Küpker, and Maegraith 2012.

11 CP. F. 251, John Wyntryngham v. John Huett, 03/02/1469–28/04/1470, Borthwick Institute of York (from here on in "Borthwick"), CP. F. 274, testamentary and debt, Gilbert Lacey and Percival Amyas v. John Lacey, 1489, Borthwick.

ficers for the Wapentake appear to have acted in a notarial capacity and are recorded as having witnessed agreements and repayments in a rural village in the Harthill Wapentake, East of York.[12] The courts of York Minster also appear to have performed the role of a register when credit was agreed. The Chapter Act Book and Deed Register of York Minster functioned as a register of bonds for the city of York from the mid fourteenth century, functioning alongside the secular courts of the merchant statute staple and the mayor's court, suggesting not only that the court was acting as a written record of credit but was part of a wider system of written obligations in later medieval York.[13]

The surviving probate inventories of York suggest that written accounts were being kept by some households. The extent of the debts listed in the inventories suggests a written record was available to the elected appraisers and executors. Debts owed to the deceased were often described in detail. Thomas Gryssop, a chapman in York, was owed 13 *s.* 4 *d.* by a pledge of three spoons, three basins, and three jars.[14] Thomas Brystall and John Stolys owed £36 for herring to Robert Schylbotyll.[15] Objects that facilitated accounting in the home appear fairly frequently throughout the inventories. Both Robert Talkan, a girdler in York, and William Ledale, a chaplain also residing in York, were recorded as owning counters, and the inventory of Geoffrey Couper listed a reckoning board in the aula.[16] In the inventory of Thomas Crake, a gentleman in Beverley, the debts owed were not listed in the inventory but rather it was recorded that the names and debts were to be found in "a bill in the custody of the executors".[17] Two probate inventories make specific reference to formal accounts. The appraisers of the skinner Roger Burton valued his shop and store room in York and listed "receipts" as a separate category in the inventory which detailed a mixture of agreements. John Kirkeby had numerous pledges amounting to £3 13 *s.* 4 *d.*, the Duke of Northumberland had paid in part for ten books, and Walter Luket, also a skinner, appears to have borrowed a number of tools for his trade including iron andirons, lime, and a

12 CP. F 210, Thomas Harrison v. John Papedy, 03/07/1465–14/10/1465, Borthwick.

13 Chapter Act Book and Deed Register 1343–1368, from f. 71 Jan 1349/50, York Minster Library, H1/2.

14 "Gryssop, Thomas, York, Chapman, 1446 [BIHR, Dean and Chapter of York, Original Wills, 1383–1499]", Stell 1999, 569.

15 "Schylbotyll, Robert, Scarborough, 1409 [BIHR, Cause Papers, folio 69]", Stell 1999, 526.

16 "Talkan, Robert, York, Girdler, 1415 [BIHR, Dean and Chapter of York, Original Wills, 1383–1499]", Stell 1999, 524; "Ledale, William, York, Chaplain, 1438 [BIHR, Exchequer Wills, 15th century", Stell 1999, 556; "Couper, Geoffrey and idonea, York, 1402 [YML, Probate Jurisdiction, Inventories, L1 (17)24]", Stell 1999, 507.

17 "Crake, Thomas, Beverley, Gentleman, 1488 [YML, Probate Jurisdiction, Inventories, L1(17)28]", Stell 1999, 660.

pair of bellows.[18] In the inventory of John Carter, a tailor operating in York, the debts collected were taken from "the book of debts".[19] John Carter was operating a large business. He had two workshops listed in his inventory, one for western cloth and one for southern cloth, with a shop attached in which he kept the tools of his trade; shaping boards, trestles, shears, and pressing irons and shelves on which he displayed his cloth. A note from the appraisers states that the executors refused to allow the book of debts to be appraised within the inventory. The total debts outstanding listed from the book of debts totalled £17 3 *s.* 0.5 *d.*, more than the stock in each of his individual workshops.[20] The accounts appear to have been a valuable commodity for the business and were held onto by the family after the death of Roger Burton.

Written records of credit and debt seemed to have been prevalent and written instruments are listed in those debts outstanding. Pledges and bonds appear across the inventories of York Minster. But this evidence is static. We have no real sense of how those bonds or pledges listed in the inventories were contracted, where they were subsequently stored or how often they were consulted. Written contracts are also found in the details of the depositions in the cause papers of the Consistory Court. What we learn from the depositions is the ways in which contracts were agreed and the circumstances in which they were signed. We can also glimpse the material significance of the written contract as depositions describe how they were handled and utilised as a form of proof where debts were contested.

A dispute over an unpaid debt of £5 6 *s.* 11 *d.* listed in the will and inventory of James Fawcett and contested by Richard Newman, executor of the will of John Simpson, and Richard Fawcett, James Fawcett's son and executor, holds two additional documents that detail the debts and accounts of the deceased James Fawcett. Richard Fawcett appears to have produced two additional documents proving that the debt owed by his father was, in fact, held in outstanding credit agreements. It would appear that James Fawcett had purchased grain in large sums from John Simpson to sell on in smaller portions. The inventory of business debts points to a series of smaller sales to individuals who appear to have formed part of the kinship group of James Fawcett. Thomas Ellyson appears three times in the accounts purchasing grain from James Fawcett. His brother, John Ellyson, who was a priest, witnessed the will of James Fawcett and was left 6 marks 6 *s.*

18 "Burton, Roger De, York, Skinner, 1428 [BIHR, Dean and Chapter of York, Original Wills, 1383–1499]", Stell 1999, 550.

19 "Carter, John, York, Tailor, 1485 [YML, Probate Jurisdiction, Inventories, L1(17)6]", Stell 1999, 650–651.

20 "Carter, John", Stell 1999, 650–651.

8 *d.* to "pray and syng for hym".[21] He was also entrusted, along with John and Roger Knoll, whose brother Thomas Knoll owed money on outstanding accounts, to value the goods of James Fawcett in the inventory. The debts listed as "incomplete" in the account amount to the £5 6 *s.* 11 *d.* listed as an outstanding debt in the will of John Simpson. In providing the accounts at court, Richard Fawcett was attesting to the fact that the debts were owed by other members of the business network and not directly by his father. The debts were chased for a long period of time. The executor of the will of John Simpson appears before the bishop's court in 1517 pursuing unpaid debts from the will and inventory of James Fawcett. The will of James Fawcett is included with the cause papers and is dated 24 April 1511 and was publicly proved just two weeks later in May. Richard Fawcett was found not guilty and was absolved of the accusation and Richard Newman was left to pay the legal fees and expenses. The accounts appear to have been successful in absolving Richard Fawcett of the obligation. Though we cannot know whether the obligation to pay the outstanding debts passed to those individuals who owed the money to James Fawcett, the accounts presented at court offered tantamount proof that the debt owed was part of a longer chain of credit agreements and Richard Fawcett was not liable to pay.[22]

In a plea of debt and defamation brought by William Barton against John Partryngton in 1434, Barton sought to defend his reputation after Partryngton accused him of reneging on the terms of a credit agreement. William Barton and John Partryngton had entered a written bond, witnessed before a group of jurors. The exchange was sealed with a surety valued at £3 13 *s.* 4 *d.* which was safely stored in a box along with the bond and held in the custody of John Partryngton and his wife.[23] The deal was undone when Partryngton publicly accused Barton of breaking the terms of their contract; seizing the box containing the surety and bond from Partryngton's wife. The objects exchanged represented the promise of both parties to be bound by the terms of their agreement, and signalled the concord between creditor and debtor as Partryngton's wife was entrusted with the surety. When this bond was undone, it was the objects that were forcibly seized. Yet it was not the written obligation that was presented as proof at court. Instead, the plea of defamation and debt challenged the denigration of the good character of Barton who was accused of stealing the surety. Witnesses gave depositions attesting to the binding oaths sworn by Barton and Partyngton and the damage inflicted on Barton's good character when the accusation of theft was made. Despite

---

21 CP. G. 85, Richard Newman v Richard Fawcett, 1508–1517, Borthwick.

22 CP. G. 85, Newman v Fawcett, 1508–1517, Borthwick.

23 CP. F. 332, William Barton v. John Partryngton, 06/10/1434–02/12/1434, Borthwick.

the signing of the bond, the credit contract was bound by oath and regulated by a desire to maintain a good reputation.[24]

In a plea of breach of faith between Thomas Harrison and John Papedy in 1465, the depositions reveal the significance of written documents in the credit agreement. The two men signed a written obligation agreeing to a loan to be repaid in three instalments. When the payments were not forthcoming, a written reminder, described in the deposition as a "demand for monetary fines", was issued to Papedy, recalling the original agreement. The reminder was countersigned by those who had been witness to the original credit agreement. When this was ignored, two of Papedy's horses were seized to the value of the loan. The written word held an important role in the credit contract. Yet the depositions suggest that it was not the contract itself, the "abstraction" of the agreement from the physical exchange to a written document, but the ritual surrounding the agreement that marked its binding nature.[25] Papedy swore on oath "to firmly oblige himself to the said Thomas Harrison" and agreed "to fulfil the promise based on trust to repay" the 12 *s.*[26] The deal was struck as John Papedy offered his "faithful right hand to the said Thomas Harrison" and swore on his "good faith and character" before this group of "faithful and worthy people" to repay the 12 *s.*[27] The spoken word was legally binding and the memories of the witnesses recalling the oath legitimated the contract. At no point does the contract appear to have been produced as evidence in the case. The dates for payment were seemingly structured around the local calendar with 3 *s.* 4 *d.* due at the feast of Raspaldingmore, named after the local village. The credit agreement was firmly embedded in the rhythms of the local communal calendar and engraved in the memories of fairs and feasts. Though the dispute between Newman and Fawcett suggests that written proof could be presented at court, it appears to have been rare in the fifteenth century. In the case of Newman and Fawcett, the documents attached to the cause were held alongside the testimonies of witnesses who considered not just the obligation to repay but the onus upon the executors to perform their role truthfully and honestly as sworn on oath. The church courts were a popular forum for petty credit disputes in the fifteenth century in part because witness testimony was tantamount. The legal custom of the church courts took what was

---

24 Robb 2018.

25 MacNeil 2006, 323.

26 "Et ad promissas solutoes fid[el]it[er] admiplenda idem Johannes Papedy de visu et audita istius jurati ut dicit fide sua media et praestita in manus dicti Thome Herryson firmite se astrinxit et jurato suo vallauit", CP. F. 210, Harrison v. Papedy, Borthwick.

27 "praefatus Johannes Papedy fidem suam in manum dexteram dicti Thome Herryson", CP. F. 210 Harrison v. Papedy, Borthwick.

commonly held and believed to be the truth as proof.[28] The emphasis on witness testimony shaped the custom of the oath in credit transactions and the materiality of the contract.

Truth, Trust, and Honesty; Oral Contracts in the Church Courts

Church courts held jurisdiction over those contracts predicated on trust and made binding by a promise or oath. Calling on God in the bargaining process to attest to the truth of the contracting parties and the trustworthiness of their promises invoked the "theory of the sanctity and irrevocability of promises".[29] Legal tracts of the twelfth century described the promise as sacred. The *Decretum* stated that to break a promise was to be more feared than to break a vow.[30] The extent of the influence of ecclesiastical law over those promises accompanied by an oath is to be found in the emergence of cases of *assumpsit* in English secular law. The same defining features of the oath that appeared in pleas of breach of faith in the church courts went on to define the basis of the contract in the plea of *assumpsit* in the courts of the King's Bench in the sixteenth and seventeenth centuries. The action of *assumpsit* was predicated on a notion of trespass on the case, the defendant having *"assumspit fideliter promisit"* "assumed and faithfully promised" to perform an act or exchange in sale.[31] The language of faith central to the Christian oath was transposed from the plea of breach of faith to *assumpsit.* Oath-taking in credit agreements did not decline but instead was adopted by the secular courts. The process of the transition of the oath from the sacred to the profane can be traced in the decline of pleas of breach of faith in the church courts and the rise of *assumpsit* in the secular courts.[32] Richard M. Wunderli has suggested that changes in civic litigation allowing for plaintiffs to pursue oral contracts in the secular courts in the early modern period diverted cases of breach of faith from the church courts in London and into the city courts. By the close of the fifteenth century, cases of breach of faith had virtually disappeared from the commissary court records in London, a trend paralleled in Lichfield, Hereford, Chichester, and Exeter.[33]

---

28 Helmholz 2004.
29 Hogg 2011, 78.
30 Cited by Hogg 2011, 80.
31 Ibbetson 1999, 131.
32 Spurr 2001.
33 Wunderli 1981, 104.

The language of trust, truth, and faith defined the oral contract in both ecclesiastical and secular courts. The "good", "honest", and "trustworthy men" who promised on their "good faith" to repay a debt identified themselves as part of the Christian community.[34] In the case of Harrison and Papedy, the "faithful promise" based on trust had been made "in the presence of friends".[35] In a plea of breach of faith, the defendant Richard Reade had made a "faithful and public pledge" to promise the delivery of grain to the attorney Thomas Williamson, "to honestly fulfil the deed".[36] In 1449, Robert Laton had been brought to the consistory court for failure to repay a debt owed in an instance of deferred sale. The agreement had been made as Laton had bought goods on deferred payment from John Skathelok to the value of £13 4 *d.* which he was unable to satisfy when the goods were delivered. The agreement was made in the hall of Robert Laton's home. Robert had made himself "faithfully committed to that sum [...] by his hand to lay a pledge for the money of John".[37] At the church in Ripon, William Myreschewe apprehended Jacob Ketton in the knave of the church, near the font, where he queried an outstanding payment. Jacob Ketton "gave his faith" to William in the church to pay 3 s by the feast of Saint Michael Archangel, witnessed by William Forsett. Sealed by a spoken oath, the promise was made in the knave without formal written documentation.[38] The credit described in the cause papers was based on oral agreements. It was couched in a language of trust, and contracts were confirmed by ritual and custom in a culture of oath-taking. In 1440, Elizabeth Radwell, widow of William Radwell, pursued Robert Tippling for failure to make payments for a horse purchased from her husband prior to his death for £17.[39] The payment was said to have been divided into three sums and paid in instalments. Those witness to the original agreement described how they watched through the shop window

34 Fontaine 2014, 60.

35 "ac neguit retinet in praesenti in anime suo grave periculum [damage] que Thome dampnum non [damage] et gravaemen", CP. F. 210, Harrison v. Papedy, Borthwick.

36 "predictus dictus Ricardu Reade se fide sua media pleges et fideuissorem fuisse quod prefatus quarter grana omnia et singula fuisset dicte Thome Wright ad temporis et locus predictus saluo et secure per dictus Thoma Williamson", CP. F. 266 Thomas Wright v. Richard Reade, 27/07/1484, Borthwick.

37 "quo termino tunc ibidem per dicte Johanem concesso ibidem Robertus manu sua le.ata pro misit per fides sua solide dicte Johani predicte summam xiij solidinis iiij denaris", CP. F. 216 John Skathelok v. Robert Laton, 05/02/1449–17/11/1450, Borthwick.

38 "dicit quod interfuit quando Jacobus Ketton de Ripon de prebuit fidem Willelmo Myreschewe, in navi ecclesiae, prope fontem, quod solverert et iijs. in festo Sancti Michaelis Archangeli ex tunc prox sequent"', William Myreschew v. Jacob Ketton, 8 July, 1460, Acts of the Chapter, Ripon, 91–92.

39 "p[re]dicte Robertis tu[n]c ib[ide]m ut di[ci]t manu le nata p[er] fide[s] suam se astrinxit obligauit", CP. F. 217, Elizabeth Radwell v. Robert Tippling, 1440, Borthwick.

of John Walker. Though they did not hear at the time the words spoken, they were later informed by witnesses who had heard Robert Tippling promise "by his good faith" to make the payments and that he had "faithfully observed" the first instalments.[40] The witnesses were able to attest to having seen the rituals of exchange, but their testimony to the words spoken was derived from what was common knowledge from trusted sources within the community. Repeated and conferred to memory, the words spoken conformed to the language and ritual of the Christian oath.

The intent behind the oath and the words spoken were as important as the ritual. In 1496, Richard Rawson accused Thomas Vicars of failing to make a payment, having allegedly promised to pay for grain that his wife had purchased on credit. The case was presented at court under perjury legislation as Thomas Vicars stood accused of having deliberately misled Richard Rawson and made a false promise.[41] The initial agreement of sale was conducted in the home of Thomas Vicars in the village of Strensall, north of the city of York. Richard Rawson agreed to sell to the wife of Thomas Vicars fifteen quarters of malt for the price of 26 *s.* 8 *d.* before a group of free jurymen, which included the vicar of Strensall and William Brannisby. Amongst the witnesses recalled at court was William Brannisby's wife. Thomas Vicars was to pay 12 *d.* in advance of the delivery of the malt, and his wife the 26 s and 8 d upon receipt of the goods. However, William Jackson, witness to the exchange, claims Thomas Vicars and his wife made false and counterfeit promises. According to Jackson, when Richard Rawson queried Thomas Vicars' commitment as he "have yet none obligation", Vicars responded "By my feith ye shall be content and paid the said money at the fest of pentecost next to come or I shall lay my land in pledge for the money".[42] Vicars' wife also offered similarly vague promises, "this malt must thorow my hande and I shal besis me to see ye be content".[43] Unlike those cases above brought before the judge under a "breach of faith", there is no mention of accompanying gestures declaring a binding oath. Focus is instead placed on the intent behind the promise to pay and whether the agreement was conducted honestly and in good faith. As such, the dispute focuses on the language of the promise. Contrary to the deposition provided by William Jackson in which Vicars was accused of offering false and counterfeit promises, the prosecution proctor asserts that Vicars had in those words firmly promised to pay for the malt on behalf of his wife. The promises made by Vicars and his wife were guaranteed only by their good character and it is the intent behind their

---

40 CP. F. 217, Radwell v. Tippling, 1440, Borthwick.
41 DC. CP. 1496/2 Richard Rawson v. Thomas Vicars, Borthwick.
42 DC. CP. 1496/2 Rawson v. Vicars, Borthwick.
43 DC. CP. 1496/2 Rawson v. Vicars, Borthwick.

promises which they appear to be defending when they were accused of deceiving Richard Rawson in the sale.

Summons to court echoed the orality of the contract and enforced the reputation mechanism that regulated the credit economy. Read aloud in the marketplace or before the congregation, displayed in civic and ecclesiastical buildings alike, they punctuated the visual and auditory landscape of the market. John Huett of Marr appeared before the consistory court of York having been impeached in his home for the alleged failure to pay a deferred rent. Witnesses recalled that prior to the arrest, the summons to court had been displayed in "a certain hall of the court chaplain to the ecclesiastical court of Presholme, circulated around Presholme and produced in the house and dwelling of Richard of York Castle".[44] The legal documents of the court infiltrated daily life. Summons were delivered to the defendant before two witnesses or publicly declared in the parish church. These documents of the early stages of the plea, their written word as well as their physical impression on the scape of the church and civic buildings could lead to an out-of-court settlement between two parties from the threat of legal action alone. At the lower ecclesiastical court of Ripon in Yorkshire, 23 per cent of those cases recorded never proceeded beyond citation, and a further 27 per cent were settled by a licence of concord.[45] The figures seem to reflect a wider trend for out-of-court settlement in cases of debt litigation. A significant proportion of debt litigation heard before the court at Newmarket Suffolk was settled out of court. Over 35 per cent was settled through request for licence of concord whereby both parties sought private reconciliation. A further 23 per cent of debt litigation disappeared from the records after a defendant had appeared with no outcome listed and over 13 per cent disappeared following the initial plea at court.[46]

Trust, as noted by Forrest, did not exist outside institutions.[47] The church courts held limited authority to exact a repayment. Unable to seize assets and land, the authority of the church lay in its ability to lean on social institutions. Arbitration was a popular form of mediation in the church court. The process, both when ordered within the court and when settled outside the court, solidified the notion of "trustworthy men" as those elected arbitrators who embodied the authority of the judge. Mediation invoked a language of neighbourliness that instilled trust in a collective of faithful individuals and enforced more widely the notion of a body of Christian believers as part of one social and economic entity. The cases in the deposition books speak only of instances where arbitration had collapsed, but it

44 CP. F. 251, Wyntryngham v. Huett, Borthwick.
45 Fowler 1875, Acts of the Chapter, Ripon, 1452–1506.
46 Davis 2012, 356.
47 Forrest 2018, 53–62.

is clear that being a good neighbour and of good faith was of paramount importance. Arbitration in pleas of debt contributed to a language of harmony. In a plea of breach of faith in the church court of Ripon in 1453, Thomas Hebwyn brought a plea of breach of faith against Thomas Hardwyck for 2 *s*. When Hardwyck failed to attend a hearing in the church court, the plaintiff Hebwyn submitted a petition to court. After Hardwyck and Hebwyn consulted friends, a day for arbitration, described in the record as an agreement of hope, was reached.[48] Providing fair and friendly mediation was central to the success of arbitration. In a plea of breach of faith appealed at York Minster, doubt was cast over the intentions of one neighbour elected as mediator. The original credit agreement had been overseen by the local vicar William Brannisby who had acted as a "friendly mediator" to an exchange of malt between Thomas Vicars and Richard Rawson.[49] When Vicars failed to make the payment, William Brannisby was called upon to act as a mediator in a case of arbitration to end hostilities between the two until a future date when it was agreed payment would be made, obliging them both under pain of punishment. The arbitration presided over by the vicar Brannisby was also witnessed by William Jackson. During the process of appeal, the proctor acting on behalf of Vicars submitted an exception to the witnesses and their statements, stating that of the two men summoned before the court having been witness to the agreement and acting in the process of arbitration, one provided "friendly mediation" between the two parties whilst one was "not of good faith" to have been called as witness. In the deposition, Jackson was referred to as an enemy, *hostis,* of Thomas Vicar's and his wife.[50] The proctor went on to state that "he holds no moderate faith in that party to act as witness" and called for Vicars to be absolved. The church court drew on the social institutions in late medieval society when it ordered parties to arbitration, but the practice of out-of-court settlement was an integral branch of the formal institution of the legal process. In a plea of breach of faith brought before the prebendal court at Ripon, the litigants were ordered to subject themselves to "obey and yield to arbitration" concerning "all manner of actions, quarrels, debts, and demands [...] and disturbances".[51] Though the Church courts leaned on social institutions to deliver outcomes in debt litigation, the process of mediation was no less formal or coercive than the judgements delivered in court.

The sharing of wine and the breaking of bread, as described in the case between Harrison and Papedy, or the holding out of the "right and faithful hand"

48 "Thomas Hebwyn v Thomas Hardwyck, November 1453", Acts of the Chapter, Ripon, 25.
49 DC. CP. 1496/2 Rawson v. Vicars, Borthwick.
50 DC. CP. 1496/2 Rawson v. Vicars, Borthwick.
51 'Thomas Swwtyng v Katherine Smyth, 1468', Acts of the Chapter, Ripon, 132.

of John Huett to swear a "promise on his name", all acted as a performative contract.[52] Expressing concretely the abstractions which lay beneath the exchange, "they both evidenced and brought about the creation of the new relationship, and frequently imparted a sacral character to it, and they served to reveal conceptual connections between apparently dissimilar institutions."[53] The physical rituals associated with gift exchange served to solidify credit agreements. The remnants of the rituals of feasting and pledging bear credence to the transition of the physical exchange of property, in the likes of the earlier medieval symbolic exchanges of turf in the livery of seisin or the Germanic tradition of the exchanging of twigs, to the public display of ritual which drew those bearing witness into the transaction themselves.[54] These gestures no longer conveyed the exchange itself, but publicly attested to the imposition of future obligations on one or both parties.

Conclusion: Performing Trust

The increasing use of written contracts in credit represented the abstraction of the exchange, from a performative ritual to an impersonal exchange.[55] It distanced the creditor and debtor and simultaneously introduced a material object of the written obligation that could be exchanged in itself. According to Jack Goody, it reflected the shifting nature of the relationship between creditor and debtor from kin-based relationships in a society with a shared communal knowledge of credits and reputations to an economic exchange between anonymous actors.[56] It also, however, coincided with a shift in legal preferences. The ecclesiastical courts, once a popular forum for petty debt litigation under the guise of breach of faith, witnessed a dramatic decline in business in the sixteenth century. In the secular prerogative courts of equity and requests in the sixteenth and seventeenth centuries, disputes over unpaid debts rose and were increasingly centred around the use of a written bond or sealed instrument. Once the debt was repaid, the written bond was required to be physically cancelled by the creditor, either marked and crossed out, to indicate the debt had been repaid, marked, and returned to the debtor to make a complete contract or destroyed. As such, the written obligation

52 CP. F. 210, Harrison v. Papedy, Borthwick, CP. F. 251, Wyntryngham v. Huett, Borthwick.

53 Ibbetson 1992, 4–5.

54 Ibbetson 1999, 4–5; Ibbetson 1992, 7.

55 MacNeil 2006, 323.

56 Goody 1986, 144–148.

held greater sway and was more closely guarded by creditor and debtor alike as vital proof if needed in court.[57]

Oral contracts were the norm in fifteenth-century England, in part, because it was the testimony of witnesses that were the most widely accepted and authoritative form of proof at court. Performing the ritual of the oath was commonplace because it permitted the hearing of the case under the guise of breach of faith in a church court thereby increasing the legal routes open to the creditor in a legally pluralistic society. Though a promise was made on faith and declared to be truthful and honest, both creditor and debtor looked ahead to the possibility of legal action, inciting the language that might grant greater recourse to legal restitution. The legal code of church courts in medieval England had developed to support the oral contract. The courts prioritised the testimony of witnesses over written evidence and in doing so cultivated a language of trust and fealty that characterised the solemnity of the oath and underpinned the oral contract. There was no clear shift from an oral credit economy to a written one, indeed historiography on early modern credit networks has done much to assert the continued importance of oral agreements for the maintenance of market exchange in the sixteenth and seventeenth centuries. The co-existence of both oral and written agreements in the fifteenth century was the most effective means of creating a communal knowledge of the economic activities of the community.[58] The written contract gained its importance by its materiality; where it was signed, who viewed it, and how it was handled in a process of ritual and custom around the speaking of oaths. Parallels are to be drawn in the ways in which written court documents gained authority. Summons to court were circulated, delivered to defendants, read aloud to their neighbours, displayed in civic halls, or read from the pulpit; their legitimacy derived from the mark they made in the auditory landscape of medieval society. There was no clear ascendancy of written evidence either at court or in the credit economy, rather custom ascribed an almost sacral meaning to a written document whose validity as a form of proof was derived from its performance and basis in a collective memory.

---

57 Stretton 2013, 194.

58 Forrest 2018, 345.

References

Archival References

H1/2, Chapter Act Book and Deed Register 1343–1368, York Minster Library.

CP. F. 210 Thomas Harrison v. John Papedy, 03/07/1465–14/10/1465, Borthwick (= Borthwick Institue of York).

CP. F. 216 John Skathelok v. Robert Laton, 05/02/1449–17/11/1450, Borthwick.

CP. F. 217 Elizabeth Radwell v. Robert Tippling, 1440, Borthwick.

CP. F. 332 William Barton v. John Partryngton, 06/10/1434–02/12/1434, Borthwick.

CP. F. 251 John Wyntryngham v. John Huett, 03/02/1469–28/04/1470, Borthwick.

CP. F. 266 Thomas Wright v. Richard Reade, 27/07/1484, Borthwick.

CP. F. 274 Gilbert Lacey and Percival Amyas v. John Lacey, 1489, Borthwick.

CP. G. 85 Richard Newman v Richard Fawcett, 1508–1517, Borthwick.

DC. CP. 1496/2 Richard Rawson v. Thomas Vicars, Borthwick.

Bibliographic References

Beckerman J. S. 1992. "Procedural Innovation and Institutional Change in Medieval English Manorial Courts". *Law and History Reviews* 10, no. 2: 197–252.

Davis J. 2012. *Medieval Market Morality: life, law and ethics in the English marketplace, 1200–1500.* Cambridge: Cambridge University Press.

Fontaine L. 2014. *The Moral Economy: Poverty Credit, and Trust in Early Modern Europe.* Cambridge: Cambridge University Press.

Forrest I. 2018. *Trustworthy Men, How Inequality and Faith Made the Medieval Church.* Princeton: Princeton University Press.

Fowler J. T. 1875. *Acts of the Chapter of the collegiate church of SS. Peter and Wilfrid, Ripon, 1452–1506* [= The publications of the Surtees Society 64]. Durham: Andrews and Co.

Goody J. 1986. *The Logic of Writing and the Organization of Society.* Cambridge: Cambridge University Press.

Hardman E. L. 2014. "Regulating interpersonal debt in the bishop's court of Carpentras: litigation, litigators and the court, 1486 and 1487". *Journal of Medieval History* 40, no. 4: 478–498.

Helmholz R. 2004. *The Oxford History of the Laws of England. Volume I. The Canon Law and Ecclesiastical Jurisdiction from 597 to the 1640s.* Oxford: Oxford University Press.

Hogg M. 2011. *Promises and Contract Law Comparative Perspectives.* Cambridge: Cambridge University Press.

Ibbetson D.J. 1999. *A Historical Introduction to the Law of Obligations.* Oxford: Oxford University Press.

Ibbetson D.F. 1992. "From Property to Contract: The Transformation of Sale in the Middle Ages". *Journal of Legal History* 13, no. 1:1–22.

Johnson T. 2014. "The Preconstruction of Witness Testimony: Law and Social Discourse in England before the Reformation", *Law and History Review* 127: 127–147.

Lange T. 2016. *Excommunication for Debt in Late Medieval France The Business of Salvation.* Cambridge: Cambridge University Press.

MacNeil H. 2006. "From the memory of the act to the act itself. The evolution of written records as proof of jural acts in England 11th to 17th century", *Archival Science,* 6, no. 3–4:313–328.

Muldrew C. 1996. "The Culture of Reconciliation: Community and the Settlement of Economic Disputes in Early Modern England". *The Historical Journal* 39, no. 4: 915–942.

Ogilvie S., M. Küpker, and J. Maegraith 2012. "Household Debt in Early Modern Germany: Evidence from Personal Inventories". *The Journal of Economic History* 72, no. 1: 134–167.

Purvis J.S. 1957, *Notarial Signs from York Archiepiscopal Records,* London: St. Anthony's Press.

Robb H. 2018. "Reputation in the fifteenth century credit market; some tales from the ecclesiastical courts of York". *Cultural and Social History* 15, no. 3: 297–313.

Schofield P.R. 2012. "Credit and its Record in the Later Medieval English Countryside. In *Cities-Coins-Commerce* [= Studien zur Gewerbe- und Handelsgeschichte der vorindustriellen Zeit 31], edited by P.R. Rössner, 77–88. Stuttgart: Frank Steiner Verlag.

Stell P.M. 2006, *Probate Inventories of the York Diocese 1350–1500.* York: York Archaeological Trust.

Spurr J. 2001. "A Profane History of Early Modern Oaths". *Transactions of the Royal Historical Society* 11: 37–63.

Stretton T. 2013. "Written Obligations, Litigation and Neighbourliness, 1580–1680". In *Remaking English Society. Social Relations and Social Change in Early Modern England* [= Studies in Early Modern Cultural, Political and Social History 14], edited by S. Hindle et alii, 189–209. Woodbridge: Boydell Press.

Wrightson K. 2002. “Earthly Necessities Economic Lives in Early Modern Britain 1470–1750”. New Haven and London: Yale University Press.
Wunderli R. M. 1981. *London Church Courts and Society on the Eve of the Reformation.* Cambridge: Medieval Society of America.

STRATEGIES OF SURVIVAL: PAWN-BROKING AND CREDIT RELATIONS IN ROME AND PERUGIA (15TH AND 16TH CENTURIES)

Tanja Skambraks

Abstract: This article deals with the instruments and forms of small-scale credit and pawn-broking organised by the Monti di Pietà of Rome and Perugia in the fifteenth and sixteenth centuries. These pawnshops offered small-scale credit for little interest and formed a crucial part of the strategies of survival of the working poor in late medieval and early modern Italian towns. This article analyses examples from the account books of the Roman Monte from the years 1585 to 1595 to show the manifold forms of credit and interpersonal credit networks created between the inhabitants of Rome at the end of the sixteenth century. The social structure of the Monte's clientele will be studied as well as the essential role of pawn objects, mostly household items and clothes as stores of value, enabling the working poor to transform them into cash when needed. Using an approach that is inspired by anthropological works on the role of objects, this article aims at contributing to new perspectives of studying pre-modern small-scale credit.

Keywords: pawn-broking, credit instruments, pawn-objects, working poor

Published in: Stephan Nicolussi-Köhler (Ed.), Change and Transformation of Premodern Credit Markets. The Importance of Small-Scale Credits. Heidelberg: heiBOOKS 2021, 293–331. DOI: https://doi.org/10.11588/heibooks.593.c12699

Lamento dei poveretti by Giulio Cesare Croce (1590)

Mala cosa è la pigion,
Per colui che l'ha a pagare,
Ma per quel che l'ha a tirare
Gli è una gran consolation,
Mala cosa è la pigion.

A bad thing is the rent
For the one who has to pay;
But for the one who collects it,
She is a great comfort.
A bad thing is the rent.

E si scopre questo male
Per Agosto e per Natale,
Che si vedon camminare
I patroni a visitare
Quei che stan ne' lor camini,
In botteghe e magazzini,
Acciò faccian provvision,
Mala cosa è la pigio

And this bad thing happens
In August and at Christmas,
When you see walking around
The landlords who visit them,
In their fireplaces,
Shops and warehouses
And who then have to pay.
A bad thing is the rent.

E si sentono i lamenti
Che fan tutti i pigionanti,
Che già son sotto alle feste,
E non hanno panni né veste,
Che le legne, il pane, e 'l vino
Non li lassano un quattrino,
E non vi è compassion,
Mala cosa è la pigion.

And you hear the wailing
Of all tenants,
Who are already celebrating,
But have neither cloth nor dress,
Wood, bread and wine,
Not one penny left,
And for whom there is no pity.
A bad thing is the rent.

Quanti poveri meschini
Con la moglie e figliuolini
Non han fuoco da scaldarsi,
E né pan da sostentarsi,
E la sera e la mattina
Stanno a far la tremarina
A caval de dui carbon?
Mala cosa è la pigion

How many poor men
With wives and children
Have no warming fire
And no nourishing bread either,
And in the evening as well as in the morning
They tremble
By the fire of two coals?
A bad thing is the rent.

Chi ha impegnato il ferraiolo,
Chi la cappa, chi un lenzuolo,
Chi l'anel de la mogliera,
Chi ha venduto la lettiera,
Chi il giuppon' e le calzette,
Le banzolle e le cassette,
Le carieghe e i credenzon,
Mala cosa è la pigion.

Who pawned the priest's robe,
Who the cape, who a tablecloth,
Who the ring of the wife,
Who sold the bed drawer,
Who the doublet and the socks,
The big and small boxes,
The chairs and the chests of drawers.
A bad thing is the rent.

[...]
Nota ben quel ch'io t'insegno,
Primamente, piglia un pegno,
Che sia tanto d'importanza
Quanto monta la sostanza,
E poi va' con lieta fronte
A portarlo tosto al Monte,
Che t'havran compassion.
Mala cosa è la pigion

[...]
Remember well what I teach you,
First, take a deposit,
Which is of such value,
As the number of belongings is increasing,
And then go with a happy head
Go and bring everything to the Monte,
Where they feel pity.
A bad thing is the rent.

Introduction

In his poem *Lamento dei poveretti*[1], first printed in 1590 by Benedetto Ossanna in Mantova, the Bolognese blacksmith and poet Giulio Cesare Croce describes the experience of poverty and consequently the use of pawn-broking as an instrument of poor relief. The poem deals with the difficulties people have paying their rent (*pigione*) every August and Christmas. The text not only points to the weak standard of living in a dilapidated house and the difficult communication with an unwilling landlord, it also mentions the process of pawn-broking at the Monte, bringing some temporary relief from the pressure of paying the protagonist's bills. Those lacking money were forced to pawn different objects with the local Monte di Pietà, like hats, bedding, shoes, frocks, furniture, or their wedding rings.

The witty description of the tense economic situation of a member of the local crafts in this text depicts the ubiquitous problem in an early modern town: the shortage of money on the one hand and the lack of social security on the other hand.

This article starts with this problem and furthermore deals with the broad question of how the working poor in the late medieval and early modern society survived in times of crisis. As Laurence Fontaine has shown for seventeenth- and eighteenth-century France[2], the working poor relied on a variety of means to secure their income in an economy of precariousness, lacking the nets of social security we know in today's western European societies. According to Fontaine, people had various jobs and professions, they borrowed from their closer social circles, subleased flats or chambers, invested money in charitable institutions to secure their livelihood in their old age, and so on. In short, people in the pre-modern epoch were quite versatile: they used multiple and creative ways of gaining and saving money to cope with crisis. From this perspective of the poor as active economic actors emerges a more complex and manifold picture of the working poor, a group that made up 50 per cent to two thirds of a town's population in the later Middle Ages.[3] The term 'working poor' is mostly associated with the epoch of industrialisation of the eighteenth and nineteenth centuries. In contrast to this viewpoint, I would like to suggest, as Sven Rabeler has done already[4], taking into account that in the late medieval and early modern towns there was already a substantial group of working men and women, who—although employed—were

---

1 Croce 1982, 151–158.

2 Fontaine 2013, 43–50.

3 Pullan 1978, 988–997; Boglioni, Delort and Gauvard (eds.) 2002; Gutton 1971, 53; Gazzini 2017, 67–75; more generally: Soisson 1999, 9–29; Braunstein 1999, 91–103.

4 Rabeler 2015, 75–111; Schubert 2001, 659–697 as well as Groebner 1993, passim.

under a constant threat of slipping from precariousness into poverty by different phenomena related to economic crisis and life cycle (rising prices, temporary unemployment, age, plagues, etc.).

Starting from the hypothesis of the manifold survival strategies of the working poor, I will take a closer look at how those strategies are related to small credit, deposits, and the practice of pawn-broking at the Monti di Pietà.

These 'mountains of piety' were communal pawn-broking institutions providing small loans (usually up to 5 or 6 florins) for a short period of time (6 months up to one year) to town inhabitants in need, like craftsmen, lay labourers, and petty traders.[5] The first Monte was established in Perugia in 1462, the first of over 200 foundations in the whole of Italy until the middle of the sixteenth century.[6] The Observant Franciscans were promoters and often also co-founders of the Monti, supported by the local town governments. As urban preachers and confessors of the city elite, they took a decisive role in the spreading of innovative ideas on the use of money and the taking of interest, whereby they became forerunners of an economic ethic fostering a more flexible understanding of the term usury.[7] The installation of the Monti di Pietà can thus be interpreted as a means of the late medieval urban 'moral economy' induced by some Franciscan friars closely cooperating with the urban political elite involved in business and trade to provide easily accessible credit for those whose income would not be sufficient to cover costs in times of need and hardship.

This paper will study source material from the Roman Monte (founded in 1539) and the Monte of Perugia from the fifteenth century and will focus on two topics: the emergence and function of a new institution providing relatively cheap small credits on the one hand and the saving possibilities provided by deposit banking on the other.

The variety of small-scale credit can be traced very well in the account books of the Monte di Pietà, the Libri Mastri (below LM)[8], providing detailed information on the deposits people made in the Monte's bank in the second half of the sixteenth century. These ledgers inform us not only about the use of the Monte

---

5 Muzzarelli 2001a, Idem. (ed.) 1994; Avallone (ed.) 2001; Montanari (ed.) 1999; Holzapfel 1903; Todeschini 2009; Carboni and Muzzarelli (eds.) 2008; Menning 1993; Pullan 1971; Banchi pubblici, banchi private e Monti di Pietà nell' Europa preindustriale. Atti del Convegno, Genova 1–6 ottobre 1990, Genua 1991.

6 A catalogue of all foundations until the middle of the sixteenth century is given Terpstra (eds.) 2012.

7 See, for instance Skambraks 2017, 169–190; Muzzarelli 2013, 135–148; Id. 2001, 17–29; Id. 2000, 77–94; older fundamental works are Noonan 1957 and Langholm 1992. Terpstra (eds.) 2012.

8 ASR, Archivio Sagro Monte di Pietà, Libri Mastri 1585–1595.

as an institution of money transfer and investment but also—and this is where its actual source value proves itself—about the manifold credit and debt relations of the inhabitants of Rome at the end of the sixteenth century. The entries show in detail *what* the Romans spent money on, beyond purely quantitatively calculable sums of money.[9]

This information includes forms of small loans with varying degrees of formalisation, contracts on debts, the method of debt repayment as well as purchase transactions, and some price data for grain, livestock, labour services, wages, and rents. The ledgers also provide some valuable information on the structure of the Monte's clientele since they sometimes contain the clients' professions and places of living and/or origin.

The second part of this article will deal with the fundamental role of pawns as circulating objects in late medieval society, as for instance Valentin Groebner, Maria Guiseppina Muzzarelli, and Daniel Smail have already emphasised.[10] Pawn objects, mostly household items or clothes, were stores of value ("Wertspeicher") in the economy of lower social strata, strongly depending on the repeated exchange of those goods for money. To show which objects were used and how they worked as stores of value, this paper will analyse a list of auctioned pawn objects of the Perusian Monte di Pietà from the year 1469/70 kept in the state ar-

---

9 The following types of currency and money are mentioned in the sources:
As general currency of account: 1 fiorino = 100 baiocchi = 20 solidi = 240 denari
Coins used in Rome in the 16th century:
1 giulio (= 3.2 grams of silver) = 10 baiocchi
1 giulio = 50 quattrini (copper coin)
1 scudo d'argento (= 30 g of silver) = 10 giuli
1 scudo d'argento = 100 baiocchi
1 baiocco = 5 quattrini
conversions:
1 lira = 20 soldi
1 ducato = 60 soldi = 3 Lire
1 baiocco = 0,2 solidi = 2,4 denari
1 quattrino = 4 denari
Measures and weights used:
1 *staio* equals 25.92 litres
1 *quaderno* equals 14.83 litres
1 *quarto* equals ca. 6 litres
1 *rubbia* (grain) contained ca. 45 litres
1 *barile* = ca. 63.39 litres

10 Groebner 1993, 235–243 and Id. 2004, 175, 179; Muzzarelli 2012a, 9–19; Carboni and Muzzarelli (eds.) 2012; Smail 2017. A pioneering study on the subject of pawn objects was written by Zdekauer 1896, 63–105; For the early modern period and referring to Groebner and Fontaine, see Siebenhüner 2015, 167–187.

chive of Perugia[11] and until now only partly printed. By analysing this list (naming the borrowers and the buyers, the value of objects in money, and attributing their condition) quantitatively as well as qualitatively, we can trace an economy of small but essential objects circulating from household to household.

1 Types of Loans and Credit Relations in Early Modern Rome

The first part of this article will show the different strategies by means of which the customers of Monte di Pietà secured their survival through various small loans. It will not only show what types of loans they took, under what conditions, and with whom they did so but also that they were involved in an 'economy of obligation', so well described by Craig Muldrew[12], who pointed out the social ties by means of variable credit and debt relationships.

The Roman Libri Mastri record all money deposits and transfers of customers through the Monte, sorted by year and in chronological order. The books in the Roman State Archives are complete from 1584 to the nineteenth century. My analysis is based on a sample of the ten years from the first volume of 1584/85 to 1595.[13] Regarding the development of deposit and ergo credit business transacted by the Roman Monte in this decade, we can see a steady rise in the absolute number of transactions:

Deposits were the second line of business of many Monti, trying to foster their stock of capital and consequently enabling the provision of small loans to the working poor. In Rome, the Monte began this activity in the year 1552, thirteen years after its foundation. The investments yielded between 2 per cent to 8 per cent interest.

All payments were acknowledged with a *cedola,* i.e. a promissory note or voucher. These receipts are lost for Monte di Roma, while they are still present in other places, such as Naples, and can be seen in their original form of storage—

---

11 ASCP, Archivio della Commune di Perugia, Miscellanea di Computisteria n. 3 (1469–1470), Libro de vendete de pegni del Monte.

12 Muldrew 1998.

13 The books of 1585 and 1586 are the only ones available together with registers of names. While the register for 1585 contains 1166 names, the register for 1586 contains 1083 names. The register of 1585 mentions 114 women's names—about 10 per cent of female clients. Only 17 Jews explicitly named as *hebreo* appear, which corresponds to a rounded figure of 1.5 per cent.

Figure 1 Number of transactions in the Libri Mastri

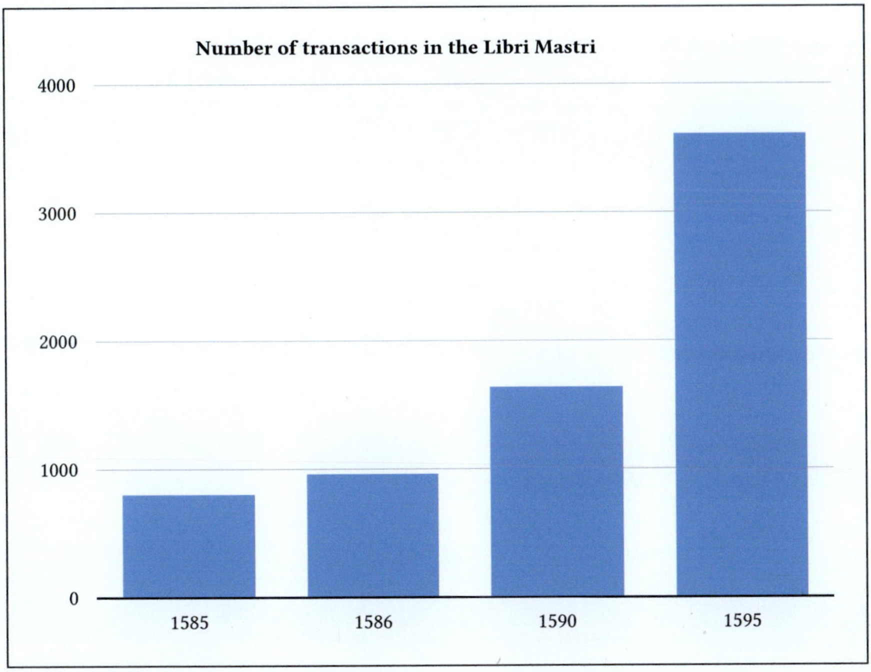

piled up on a rope (see Fig. 1).[14] One *cedola* was given to the payer and had to be provided by the person who withdrew the sum of money later.

The amounts of money are indicated in scudi, bolognini, and denari, whereby the type of coins deposited such as *quattrini, cartocci,* etc. is also given. The entry *reco contanti* is almost always shown—a clear sign for the money transfer of cash.

Many entries provide all details of the credit agreements, such as the duration, total amount, modalities of repayment, etc., which indicates the legal obligation of these entries and the cash books as well as the practice of the complete copying of the *cedole* text. Hence, the entries in accounting books could probably also be used in court. Auditors from the Monti's management committee of the *sindici* and *deputati* monitored the quality and accuracy of the income and expenditure, as is shown, for example, by a more detailed account at the end of the LM of 1590.

14 In addition—and this is decisive for the bookkeeping—the payments into the account are listed on all recto pages (right), which are marked with Roman numerals, while the opposite verso pages (left) contain the withdrawals. The cashier also inserted monthly overviews. They are designed as lists and record the individual names and their payments in short form.

Figure 2 Cedole and account books of the Banco di Napoli, Cartastorie, Museo dell'Archivio Storico del Banco di Napoli (own photo).

From the entries, various outstanding debts or credits emerge, which require a closer contextualisation and analysis, since their terminology is often blurred. They appear under various names such as *risposta, census, compagnia d'offitio, canone, sublastatione, piggione* and are used in a manner that does not clearly differentiate between all of them. Real estate credit transactions and purchase transactions on credit appear very frequently, and certain forms of annuities are also commonplace. To explore the contemporary meaning of these different forms, additional sources, like legal tracts are also used for a better understanding.[15]

Besides, we can draw conclusions about the actors and their credit relations on an urban micro-level, as well as about their practices of payment (deferral, payment by instalments) and sanctioning of unpaid debts. Another significant aspect of qualitative analysis is that the sums recorded can be used to draw very concrete conclusions about the current prices of houses, vineyards, land, rents and consumer goods, raw materials, tools and animals, as well as work performance. By means of these price data, questions about the standard of living of the lower and middle classes in Rome during the period under study can be answered at least from a microscopic perspective.

I turn to the example of the account book of 1585. Looking at the amounts of money mentioned in the Libro Mastro of 1585 and their quantitative distribution, the following picture emerges:

Clearly, the most frequently mentioned investments range between 5 to 10 or 10 to 20 scudi[16], hence small amounts. With 475 entries, these figures together comprise approx. 60 per cent. On the other hand, the entries of higher sums (like over 300 or 1000 scudi) are rather rare. There are only 25 entries in this book. Ten

---

15 For example, a *tractatus* for confessors by the Dominican Agostino Montalcino from 1590. *Agostino Montalcino, Lucerna dell'anima. Somma de case di conscientia necessaria a i confessori, & molto utile a i penitenti,* Venice 1590.

16 Looking at contemporary wages and prices allows for some preliminary conclusions on the purchasing power. Reliable wage data from Rome for the sixteenth century have been handed down mostly from the building sector and offer a further starting point for research into the living standards of the working population. Some examples: a master builder received a daily wage of 8 giulii, his assistant received half the sum. A master mason earned 4–6 giulii (= 40 to 60 baiocchi) per day, his assistants received 25 to 30 baiocchi. The pope's barber earned about 20 baiocchi per day. See the data in Delumeau 1957/1959. Comparing some price data for bread, wine, oil, wheat, and cheese, one could calculate the following costs for food per day per person:
1 loaf of bread (8 ounces) for 1 baiocco
1 pound of cheese for 6 baiocchi
0.5 pound of lamb for 1.5 baiocchi
0.5 litre of white wine for 1.18 baiocchi
0.38 litres of oil for 2.6 baiocchi
Total: about 12.28 baiocchi.

Figure 3 Frequency of sums (in scudi) mentioned in the LM 1585

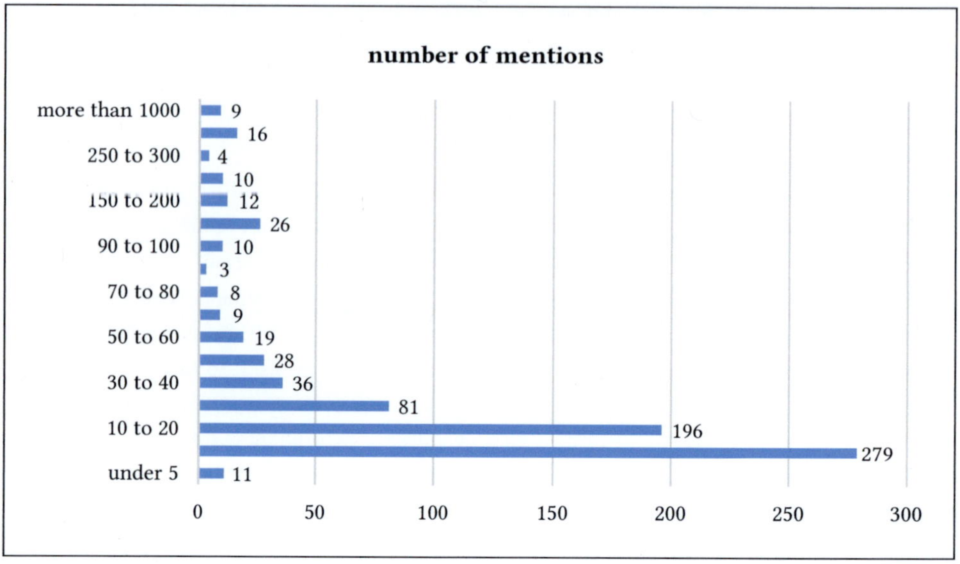

years later, the picture had changed, as obvious from the account book of 1595. There, the sums of money paid into the Monte are often much higher, pointing to the Monte's shift in function and clientele, which became more and more a bank of the Vatican, with Cardinals and well-off Roman nobles emerging among this clientele.

1.1 Types of Credit Transactions

The variety of money transactions mentioned, which the Monte made possible, is shown in table 1, which compares the purposes for the years 1585, 1586, and 1590. This overview shows that the vast majority of the payments involved rent payments for houses or workshops. They make up 25 per cent of all 2,873 transactions, similar to the unspecified debts with 23 per cent. Annuities, property taxes for vineyards, plots of land, farm huts or barns in the vicinity of Rome as well as house purchases sum up to 10 per cent. Thus, real estate as a circulating store of value was a widespread means of securing loans and pensions in Rome. Land ownership and agricultural yields secured the lives of most city dwellers. In addition, houses were leased, very often by widows or heirs.

In addition to this numerical information, a closer look at the source entries illustrates the different types of transactions. Three examples will be presented

Table 1 Overview of the purposes of money transactions of the years 1585, 1586, and 1590

Purpose of use	1585	1586	1590
Undefined debts (*promessa fatta, per tanti pretende, a suo creditore*)	136	236	293
Rents for a house or flat (*pigione per una casa, per una bottegha*)	245	238	248
Unclear	105	113	181
Annuity, lease, taxes (*census, risposta, canone, affitto*)	51	93	148
At his/her free disposal (*a suo piacere*)	17	42	73
House purchase, vineyard, land	57	62	64
Purchase of raw materials, tools	16	23	20
Inheritance	6	19	20
Loan secured by office (*compagnia d'offitio*)	–	19	19
Legal disputes (*lite*)	35	18	18
Unspecified purchase (*causa mercede, mercatore*)	20	24	18
Purchase of clothing	15	14	18
Pension	8	5	9
Purchase of wine	15	7	8
Purchase of animals (horses, cows, mules, lambs, goats)	12	11	8
Dowry (*dote*)	–	2	8
Building work, wages	20	11	7
Purchase of grain	5	2	5
Sequestration (*sequestra*)	–	2	0
Purchase of jewellery	1	1	–
Purchase of a carriage	1	–	–
Total	766	942	1165

and analysed in more detail. The first type of transaction is the so called *compagnia d'offitio*[17], a form of obligation secured by the office of a person, which seems to have been quite common in Rome at that time. An example from 24 January 1585[18] illustrates the details of such an agreement. In this example, Martino Riccio paid a rather large sum of 132 scudi, which the deceased Giovanni Maria Riccio, possibly a relative, owed to a lady named Virginia Bonsignori from a loan (*compagnia d'uffio*):

> *Martio Riccio deve havere a di 24 di gennaio scudi centotrentadoi di moneta reco contanti disse per tanti che deve a Virginia Bonsignori per sorte et per il resto de frutti d'una compa' d'uffi fatta seco sopra d'uffo de m. Giovanni Maria Riccio, con l'obligo et recognitione della bona fede per una rata de Gioronimo Visconte per l'atti del bruto predetto sotto, di 22 di dicembre 1582 [...].*

The payment *per sorte e per il resto de' frutti* was thus the proceeds and the interest of a probably much higher original loan (the book mentions 209 scudi, 69 baiocchi at the end of the page), which had been taken out on December 1582. In contrast to the life and perpetual annuity (*census*), which is dealt with below, no real estate or

17 Agostino Montalcino described it in his treatise for confessors, Lucerna dell' anima, from the year 1590 originally as a form of loan given out by officers of the curia. Their reputation or status—and thus also their income—was used as a security for a debt. See Montalcino 1590, 672 f.:
Si ritrovanno nella Corte di Roma, & in alcuni altri luoghi d'italia certi offitii molto utili, & fruttuoli, iquali quantunque talvolta habbino per loro fondamento opere, o attioni di cose, & negotii spirituali, o a quelle sieno annessi, & congionti, come e v.g. il maneggiare l'annate, o le date de beneficii ecclesiastici, o altre simili entrate di santa Chiesa, o l'adoperarsi nello scrivere, i segnare, riverdere, o registrare, riconoscere, i sigillare Bolle, o brevi Apostolici in materia di dispense, gratie, i giustitie, ci rivediamo pero tanto di corporale, & temporale, che e stato con gran ragione anticamente giudicato che detto offitii sieno vendibili, come sono hoggi, & troviamo essere stati gia lunghissimo tempo. Quindi nasce che l'camerlenghato della molto Rever. Camera Apostolica si vendeva gio 50 & 60 milla, el'Notario 10 mila, & altri officii minori molto meno, come i segretariati Apostolici 8 mila, & gli abbreviatori maggiori, & minori, & scrittori di piu forte giu mano in mano, o in palazzo di N.S. o in Cancelleraia, i a Ripa, o altrove, Cavalierati di San Pietro, & di San Paolo, & infinito altri si vendono hor piu hor meno, secondo che fa la piazza di banchi co'l ministerio di sensali, & venditori, & comperatori, come avviene in tutte l'altre mercantie; & pero che accadera talvolta che uno il quale ha voglia d'uno di questo officii, & e atto ad essercitarlo, non ha tanti denari che lo possa pagare interamente solo, si gli concede che possa pigliare qualche altro compagno, che concorrendo alla spesa tiri anch'egli i frutti dell'offitio per rata del danaio che ci impiega, sottentrando alle medesime condituoni di danno; & pericolo, o riscio non altrimenti che si facesse il primo offitiale a cui dice l'officio, havendolo egli in petto.

18 ASR, Archivio Sagro Monte di Pietà, Libro Mastro 1585, fol. 18v.

piece of land appears as security in the source text, which seems characteristic for this special form. The *compagnia d'offitio* was thus a form of loan granted without material security or pledge. The entry further indicates the transfer or repayment of the sum by the survivors of the deceased Giovanni, recording the renewal of the loan on 15 May 1584.[19] Finally, the cash book contains the entry on the seizure (*sequestra*[20]) of the goods of Profisia de Bastis, Virginia and Laudonia de Riccio—possibly the widow and her daughters—for the sake of the creditor Virginia de Bonsigniori. The repayment of the debts took place on the second of March of the same year by Martio, who paid the money to the procurator of Virginia, Giovanni Francesco Alfonso.

Figure 4 Credit transactions

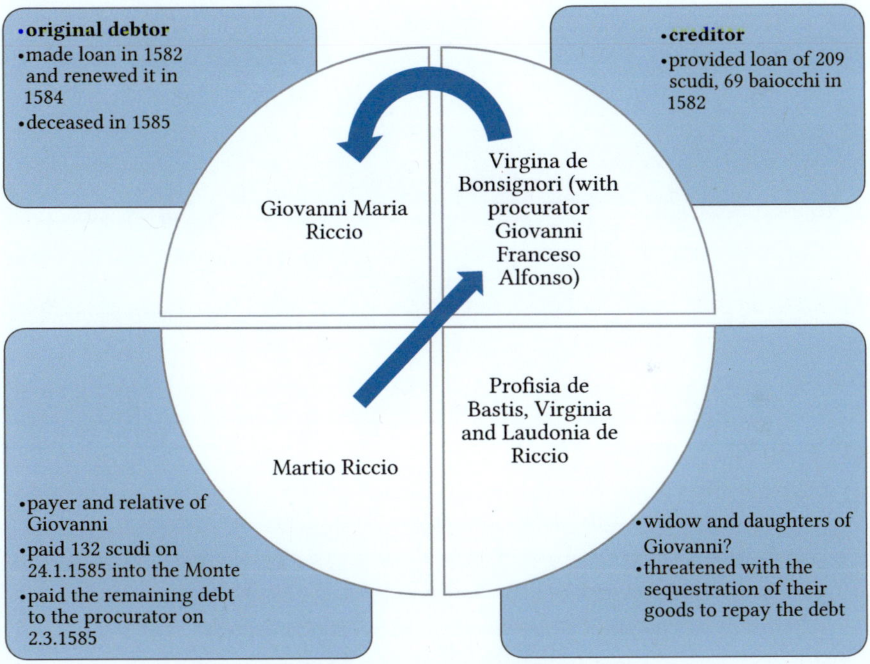

19 *"[...] et poi rifatta per li medi. atti sopra il suo offitio sotto di 15 di maggio 1584 stante la morte di detto Giovanni Riccio suo procuratore, et haremo a pagarli a detta Virginia ogni-volta che sara cassati detti fructi et haverea annuistiti detti denari et ad impito tutto quel-lo si contiene nella detta compagnia fatta come sopra de che ce ne haremo a stare alle fede di detto notare, sara pagaremo come sopra ad a chi ne sara ordinato in pie della nostra ce-dola da mons. A.C. O suo luogha. . . . . 132."* Ibid.

20 Ibid.: *Sequestro fatto a stanzi de Porfisia de Bastis et de Virginia e Laudonia de Ricci con m.ª Virginia di bonsigniori per li atti del Valerio.*

The second example describes the *census consignativus*[21] as a late established form of annuity in Rome.

Figure 5 Extract from the Libro Mastro of the Roman Monte di Pietà 1586.

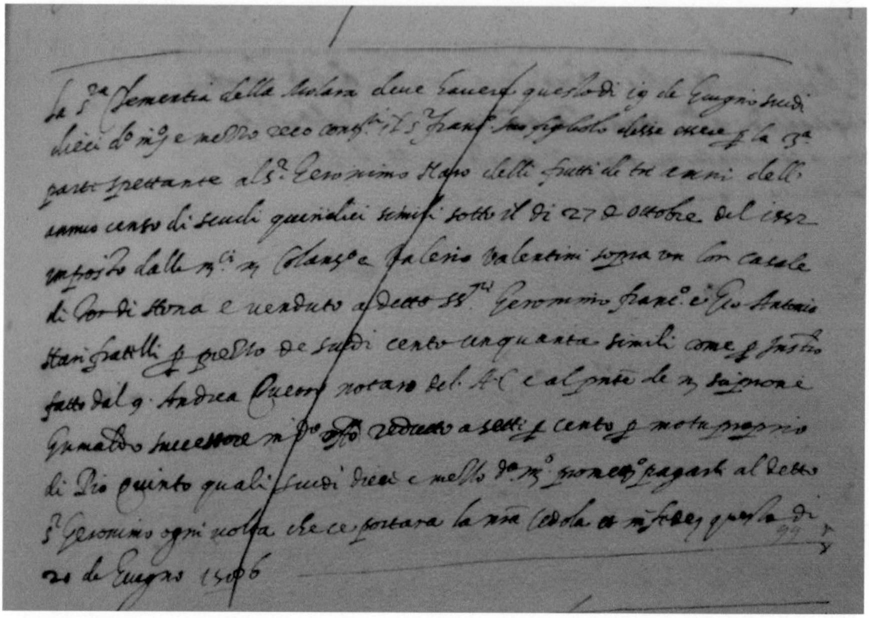

The transcription reads:

> *La signora Clementia della Molara deve havere questo di 19 di giugnio scudi*
> *dieci di moneta e mezzo reco conti il Signore Francesco suo figliolo disse essere per la terza*
> *parte spettante al Signore Geronimo Naro delli frutti de tre anni dell'*
> *annuo censo di scudi quindici simili sotto il di 27 di ottobre del 1552*
> *imposto dalla M. Colanso e Valerio Valentini sopra un lor casale*
> *di Torre di Nona e venduto a detto signori Geronimo, Francesco e Giovanni Antonio*
> *Nari fratelli per prezzo de scudi cento cinquanta simili come per instanza*
> *fatto dal G. Andrea Querro notaro del A.C. e al presente de M. Scipione*
> *Gumaldo successore in detto offitio redutto a setti per cento per motu proprio*
> *di Pio Quinto quali scudi dieci e mezzo detta moneta prometto pagarli al detto*

21 See Vaquero Pineiro 2006, esp. 257–259.

S. Geronimo ogni volta che ce portara la nostra cedola et infra questa di 20 de Giugno 1586 · *12*[22]

The transaction documented on fol. 95r of the cash book of 1586 was concluded between Clementia della Molara and Geronimo Naro as the lender. The entry shows a transaction in which annual payments of 15 scudi plus interest (*frutti*) were made resulting from a rent. This rent worth 150 scudi had long ago, namely in 1552, been sold by Colanso and Valerio Valentini to Geronimo Naro (and his two brothers) and had been secured by real estate, namely a house in Torre di Nona. So we learn that Geronimo Naro lent the sum of 150 scudi in form of a rent of 15 scudi per year to the Valentinis, who obviously resold the rent to Clementia. The son of Clementia, Francesco, now paid an amount of 10.5 scudi into the Monte on 19 June 1586. Furthermore, we learn that the business was certified by the notary Andrea Querro. And that a new interest rate of 7 per cent had been fixed by Pius V. This corresponds exactly to the 10.5 scudi that the son of Clementia paid in. The running time of the credit amounted to three years and the new contract had been fixed on 27 October 1582.

It is important to notice that this case of the *census consignativus* was a property-based annuity without transfer of rights of usage of a good. Consequently,—one could interpret here—the source does not mention any information on the possible usage of the house by the Naros. It also remains silent on the relationship between the Valentini brothers and Clementia della Molara. It seems that only the monetary annuity (secured by a property) was subject of the contract. It was therefore a mortgage loan. A lender A 'buys' an annuity from borrower B, who pays him an annual money supply/annuity for the (borrowed) sum.

In contrast, the *census reservativus*[23] transfers the right to use an object, e.g. a house, to the lender in addition to the annuity, thus providing the chance to extract some extra profit (interest). According to the legal historian Manuel Vaquero Pineiro, the *census consignativus* as a loan instrument and investment opportunity—in contrast to Northern Europe—did not become established in Italy until the first half of the sixteenth century.[24] As one reason, the author suggests the stronger and longer lasting focus of economic actors in Italy on the management of agricultural goods and the different organisation of trade. He concludes that the *census consignativus* spread mainly after the Sacco di Roma 1527 and in places where 'the interests of the urban circles disturbed the traditional socio-economic structures in a less lasting way'. Thus, it became a complementary instrument

22 ASR, Sagro Monti di Pietà, Libro Mastro 1586, fol. 95r.
23 See Alonzi 2008, 343–388.
24 Vaquero Piniero 2006, 265f., 277.

of income for those who were able to invest some money. Interestingly, also the Roman middle class and not only the urban elite used this possibility, as the analysed example has shown.

The third example[25] from the year 1585 provides an insight into the sequestration of goods of a debtor in default and the solving of a dispute about outstanding debts by the local court. In this case, the seizure obtained by the fiscal court is documented in the course of debt repayment. The entry of 7 May 1585 in the LM informs us as follows[26]:

> *Messer Giovanni Antonio Custo deve havere a di 7 di maggio scudi cinquantanove et bolognini 78 di moneta de gli diecie per scudi reco contanti disse per resto de scudi 67 altrevolte depositati nel suo offico del notariato del detto C. a 13 de marzo 1572 da messer Fabrizio Valeraris con messer Battestino piniatore et Giovanna moglie di Nicolo [...] il honora che i detti furono consigliati a messer Ambrosio Barbadella sotto di 20 marzo 1572 et Giovanni per detto se ritiene per mercede di detto deposito, e disse depositarli in vistu de un mutuo relassato dal Illustrissimo G. senatore di Roma a stanza del fiscale del Populo Romano per l'atti del Barattano, et per evitar' l'esecutione et spese d'essa et in ogni altro meglior [...] per pagarli a chi in pie della nostra cedola ne sara ordinato da detto G. senatore et insieme dal Romana Apostolica Curia o suo luogho dal un tribunale detto deposito per offende li tanti pero predetto messer Nicolo brunone sequestratio per scudi di 16 dicembra 85 et messer Bastiano de Moreo sequestratio per scudi 60 et altri interessati, tanto nelli atti di detto illustissimo senatore come di detto Custo et suo altrimente et revocati detti sequestatii per anzi sartorio 59.78*

On 7 May, 59 scudi and 78 bolognini were deposited by Giovanni Antonio Custo. He was in debt with Fabrizio Valeraris and Giovanna. Both of them had obviously obtained the repayment of the debts in court. This was the partial payment of a larger sum which he owed them and which had already been partially paid with 67 scudi on 13 March 1572 in the office of a notary. On March 20 1572, the creditors Fabrizio Valeraris as well as Mr. Battestino and Giovanna, wife of Nicolo, were advised by Ambrosio Barbadella. Giovanni had made the debts in order to buy goods (*per mercede*). Unfortunately, we do not know exactly which goods were bought. Interestingly, some of the debtor's goods were also confiscated, as can be seen from the terminus *sequestro.* The seizure had been ordered by the Roman fiscal court. Exceptionally, this case describes in great detail some characteristics of debt practice, including repayment terms and sanctions. The loan of approximately 127 scudi (including interest) was not fully recovered until 13 years after

25 ASR, Sagro Monte di Pietà, Libro Mastro 1585.
26 Ibid., fol. 51r.

the payment of a first instalment in 1572. Therefore, it seems that long-time credits were quite common, but creditors nevertheless held on to their claims for years and then resorted to judicial assistance, so that the debtor was ultimately forced to repay.

These three examples—representing only a tiny fraction of the mass of entries in the Roman Libri Mastri—show the use of different credit instruments by the inhabitants of Rome in the late sixteenth century. These instruments had specific forms suitable for various financial needs and maybe also for different social groups. More generally speaking, the sources also show that during their lifetime as well as afterwards, people were closely entangled in networks of small credits resulting from buying and selling land, houses, and goods. They mutually sought to secure loans by *immobilia* or reputable offices and were often forced to pay back their debts by courts appointed by creditors. In short: it seems everybody in Rome was indebted to everybody. Thus, by looking at the sources from the Roman Monte as a deposit bank, we indirectly gain insights into the manifold system of urban credit networks pointing to the aforementioned versatility as one strategy of survival.

2 Some Information about the Monte's Clientele Drawn from the Libri Mastri

In addition to the information concerning the purposes and types of loans, the cash books also provide insights into the investment bank's clientele structure. Who used the Monte as a deposit bank and for transfers of money? Is there a certain distribution among social groups and to what extend does the group of bank users coincide with the users of the pawnshop? The accounts also contain information on the sex, the geographical origin within Rome and Italy or Europe, and religious affiliation and thus enable further conclusions on the spatial and social distribution of the clients. Furthermore, they could also contribute to answering the question as to whether the Monte was still a bank of the poor in the late sixteenth century or whether the functional expansion of its services through the investment business also brought about a change in its client structure.

2.1 Distribution of inventors among professional groups (from the Libro Mastro 1585)

Of the total of 787 entries in the main cash book of 1585, by no means all of them mention the profession of a money investor. Nevertheless, in many cases the professions of the Monte's customers are mentioned. Striking at first glance is the diversity of 57 different professions in this one book alone.

A closer look at the distribution according to specific professions reveals the following picture: in cases where the professions of investors are mentioned, bakers are most frequently represented with 19 mentions, followed by landlords with 17 mentions and fruit dealers. Butchers are mentioned 9 times. Investors generally referred to as merchants (*mercante*) appear 9 times, as do tailors and blacksmiths. Cow breeders follow with 8 mentions. The vast majority of the investors mentioned with a professional title thus belonged to the urban crafts, with the food trades (including millers, winegrowers, grain, and wine carriers) and gastronomy accounting for the largest share of customers. The building trade is also represented by bricklayers, carpenters, stonemasons, and architects, and the textile sector by cloth cutters, a weaver, and a button carver. Members of the literate class such as notaries, churchwardens, or treasurers as well as booksellers and printers appear rather seldom (altogether: 11 mentions). Further occupational groups are: doctors, barbers and (6) painters (*pitore*) as well as old clothes dealers, glassblowers, saddlers, and stove builders.

The naming of certain professions such as cleaver, crossbow maker, perfumer, spice dealer, lint maker, or also prickler/picker and mending artist refer to a highly specialised craft especially in the field of textile production and processing as well as in the manufacture and production of weapons and the distribution of luxury goods in early modern Rome. If one relates the professions to the intended use of their payments, there is often a direct link between the money spent and the work of the customers. In addition to the purchase of raw materials, in very many cases the remittances are rent payments for the houses in which both their homes and their workshops or shops were located.[27]

---

27 An interesting example of the payment of a shop rent by a non-tradesman can be found in the LM of 1586. On 21 August, the banker Antonio Donati (*banchero in banchi*) paid 10 scudi for the rent of his exchange bank to the pharmacist Daniele Angelieri. This brief entry not only shows once again the extent to which different professional and social groups were linked by debts but above all, it proves the coexistence of different forms of credit services which private bankers offered as a matter of course. Although this insight may seem banal, it should be emphasised that it clearly shows an expansion of the credit landscape rather than a replacement or suppression of certain institutions by others. LM 1586, fol. 141r: *"peggione del semestre del loco che tiene per cambiare moneta da Daniele Angelieri grogheri in banchi."*

Figure 6 Numerical distribution of professions in the LM 1585.

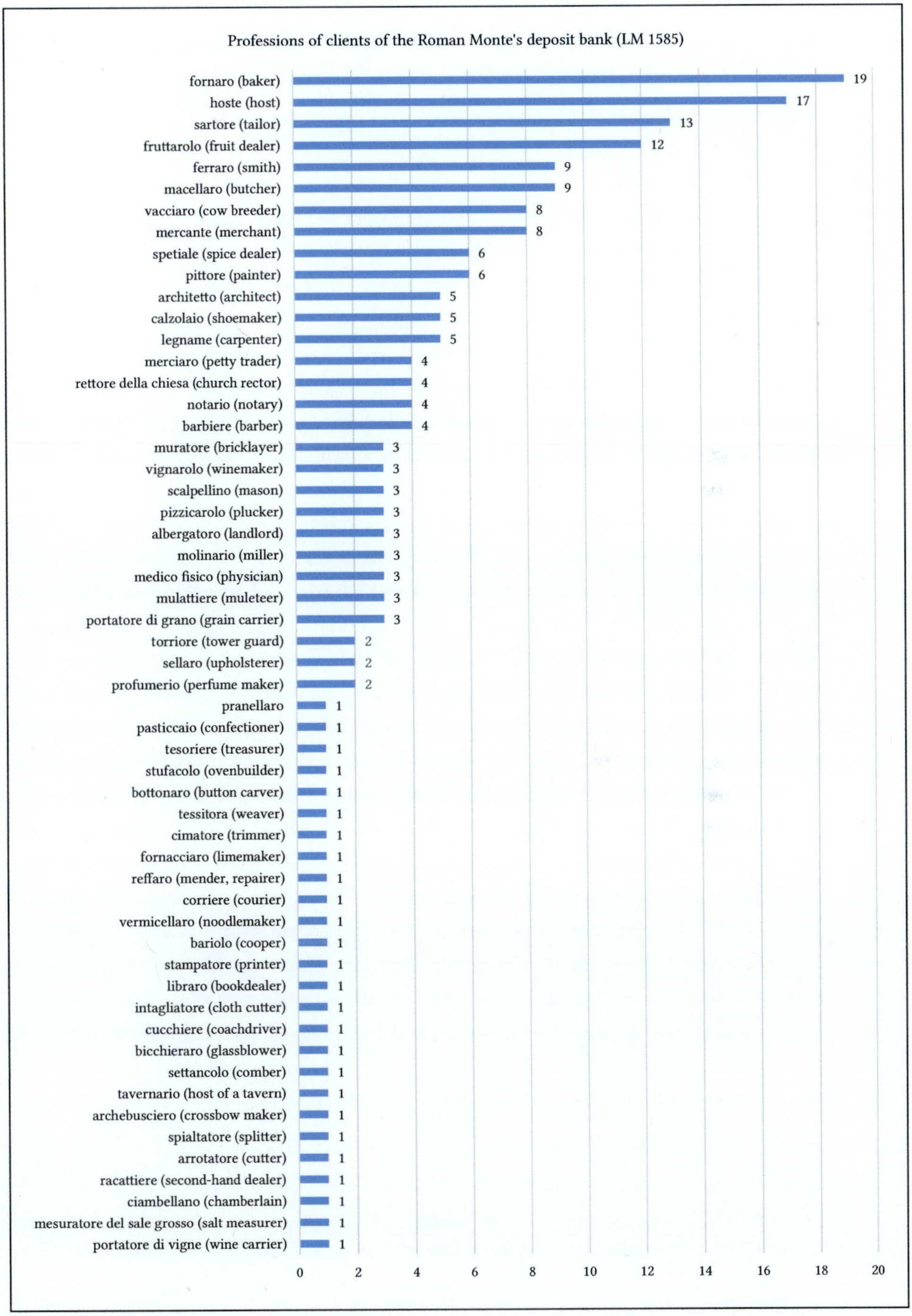

2.2 Investors by Sex, Religion, and Institution

In a second step, in addition to the distribution of clients according to professional groups, the composition of clients according to gender, religious affiliation, and institutional membership can be revealed.

Women

In the 787 entries (interrupted by 16 interim accounts) of the 1585 book, only 81 investors are female, including a Hersilia de Monti, who appears in this book as an investor four times[28]. She paid 6 scudi on 22 December 1584 for a payment concerning a vineyard. Almost a year later, on 23 November, she paid 11 scudi *in virtu di un mandato relassato,* three days later, on 26 November, she paid 22 scudi and 23 denarii for the *risposta del anno della sua vigna.* The 12 scudi which were deposited on 11 December were also dedicated to the same purpose. For the term *risposta,* it is difficult to find an adequate meaning in modern Italian. It could mean a kind of tax or compensation payment that was always due on the lease of the vineyard at the end of the year. It is also interesting that these were different amounts. In 1584, there were 6 scudi, while one year later a total of 34 scudi was due. Most of the female customers paid rents and leases using the Monte just like the men. Only rarely do we learn about their professions, as in the case of the landlady (*hostessa*) Madalena Tolona, who on 18 January paid 18 scudi to pay for clothes she had bought from Allessandro Colutio.[29] It is possible that she also worked as an old clothes dealer. Occasionally daughters and widows appear as heiresses. In another case, the Roman woman Liana de Altis paid 25 scudi on 2 July to settle a dispute about a border wall between two houses with her neighbour Antonio Francesco dalla Città di Castello.[30] Another Roman woman, Vasolina de Gradi, paid a dowry of 100 scudi to the daughter of her niece Costanza on 9 July, with note that the money would be paid out as soon as she married, but not without the bride's husband's prior guarantee of her dowry.[31] Margarita Lamberti, the wife of the confectioner Giovanni di Boccardo, deposited 22 scudi and 65 denarii on 17 July, which she should have at her free disposal.[32] The same purpose was also applied to the considerable 289 scudi paid by Orsolina, wife of

---

28 Ibid., fol. 6r; 173r; 175r; 184r.

29 Ibid., fol. 17r.

30 Ibid., fol. 80r.

31 Fol. 92r: *"Per la dote de M. Vasola filgliola di Costanza sua nepote per pagarli a detta M. Visola ogni volta che se mariata, overo e suo marito che la sposara assecurando suo prima."*

32 Fol. 95r.

Mutio del Ago, on 24 July[33] and the 330 scudi paid by Cecilia Tremezzina on 20 September[34] In the case of the Spanish Isabella Perez, she transferred 150 scudi to a certain Nicolo Sebiavone[35] on 10 September. The same, now called the wife of Reale Fasoritto, paid her dowry of 200 scudi to the Monte on 24 December. These few selective glimpses also show the variety of financial transactions that women and men carried out via the Monte. Not only lease payments, rents, and loan rates as well as dowries were of course financed by women but also whole house purchases. For example, the Roman Camilla Grannotti paid 200 scudi on 4 October for a house in the Piazza de Branchi[36] and 200 barrels of wine were paid by the Roman Orsolina with 135 scudi on 6 October.[37] These few sums once again make it possible to estimate contemporary prices for food, property, or even services, as already discussed in the first part of this article.[38] Summarising these results, it is clear that although women as clients are less frequently mentioned in the sources, they carried out exactly the same types of transactions at the Monte. Little can be said about the associated legal autonomy. If a woman was married, this also appears as a note of her identity in the main cash register, as does her profession or place of origin.

Jews

As the analysis of the pawnshop registers shows[39], the Monte was of course also used by Jewish customers. This also applies to the investment business, as can be seen from the Libri Mastri. Among the investors in 1585 there were 18 Jewish customers. The Jew Melunio Aronetto appeared several times during the year, paying twice his rent of 15 scudi for 6 months, as did most other Jewish investors, who mainly paid rent for houses or shops. In one case, on 19 July, three brothers

33 Fol. 97r. also in the words: *"per rihaberli a suo piacere."*

34 134r.

35 Fol. 126r.

36 Fol. 143r.

37 Fol. 145r.

38 If, for example, the 200 barrels of wine at a price of 135 scudi are taken as the basis for a simple calculation, the result is a barrel price of 1 scudo and 48 denari. It is well known that house prices in the Middle Ages often fluctuated strongly, so the price of 200 scudi for a house—which is quite average for the house prices in the Libro—does not even seem to be that high if compared with the 200 barrels of wine. Another shaky comparison: Gemma Monutini paid 190 scudi on 16 October for several purposes at once, namely for the protection/decoration of her houses (*para de case*), for clothes and the services of an accountant (*raggioniere*). Ibid., fol. 151r. Craftsmen services for 15 scudi were paid to the bricklayers and carpenters Pietro and Giuseppe de Sandi by Hersilia Cicolini on 25 October: ibid. fol. 157r.

39 See Skambraks 2018; Terpstra (eds.) 2012.

named Benjamin, Vitale and Manuele de Campagniano together paid 70 scudi to pay off their debts to various creditors.[40] The same was done by Salomon de Isaac Coreona and Dattilo Beanfri on 22 August with the 15 scudi, and Mainie di Laszaro da fiorentino and Leone Selviglia on 4 September with the 18 scudi they deposited with Monte.[41] A quite high amount of 115 scudi was paid by Ismael Pirnensale on 23 October—also to settle debts.[42] The Jewish customers—although in smaller numbers—naturally appear in the sources as actors who used the Monte as an investment and remittance institution. Once again, one can see from the Libri Mastri that the Monti were by no means only an institution for Christians. Contrary to the polemic of legal opinions or Franciscan preaching during the dispute among experts, they were pragmatically constituted institutes of money transfer.

Fraternities and Monasteries

Some entries in the books also mention groups of customers, such as heirs or several family members acting together, as in the case of the three brothers mentioned above. When heirs are named, it is often a routine matter of managing the inheritance of money or outstanding debts of a deceased person. It is also worth noting the use of the Monte as a remittance or investment institution by 10 different guilds, companies, and monasteries of Rome: in addition to the Compagnia of the Banner Bearers (gonfalone) of Rome, which paid the rent and the census of 12 scudi on 10 January, the Compagnia di S. Alò[43] del Arte de fabbri and the Guild of Chefs are mentioned as professional representatives. In the case of the former, the payment of 6 scudi was an annual interest payment (lucrum) to the heirs of Giovanni Filippo. During his lifetime, he had lent a sum of money to the Compagnia whose amount, unfortunately, was not mentioned.[44] The Compagnia del Sacro Sacramento di San Giovanni paid 11 scudi for work done on a house in the Borgo[45] on 13 July and, together with the heirs, paid 30.31 scudi, i.e. the costs for mobile goods, medicine, and finally the funeral of Matteo Labioloa, rector of the Church of Santi Vincenzo e Anastasio near the Fontana di Trevi, on 14 September.[46]

The brotherhoods and congregations of Santa Maria (330 scudi), San Gregorio di Ripetta (9 scudi *per un censo overo canone*), Del Salvatore (8.1 scudi for debts

---

40 Fol. 96r.

41 Fol. 113r., 124r.

42 Fol. 156r.

43 S. Alò stands for the saint Eligius, the Patron of the blacksmiths/smiths and the jewellers. His Italian name is Eligio. See Christian Hülsen, Le chiese di Roma nel medio evo. Cataloghi ed appunti, Hildesheim/New York 1975 (= NP Florenz 1927), 120, 264.

44 Fol. 35r.

45 Fol. 94r.

46 Fol. 130r.

made by virtue of declaration), and Casa Pia (1811.25 scudi for a house) and the monasteries of the nuns of S. Lucia nelli Monti (10 scudi) and the Chapter of the Church of Santa Maria Maggiore (9 scudi) each paid different amounts for rent, house purchase, and to settle debts.[47]

Among all the customers of 1585, the mentioned brotherhoods and monasteries make up a very small percentage with only 9 entries. The Compagnia e Congregatione de Mon. Casa Pia, which paid the amount of 1811 scudi and 25 denarii on 24 November, stands out *per il resto del prezzo di una casa dove al ponte il mont. promessali.*[48]

2.3 Places of Origin

The LM show a variety of geographical origins of the monte's customers. The entries point to the manifold group of inhabitants and/or visitors (here the sources do not give any clear indications) from different places of origin, from all over Italy and also from other European countries such as Germany, Spain, Portugal, Bulgaria, France, and Ireland. Among the Italian cities, there is a predominance of central and northern Italian cities, including some metropolises such as Genoa, Venice, Milan, and Bologna. The heartland of the Monti—Umbria—is represented by places like Perugia, Foligno, Norcia, and Todi. Nevertheless, these few mentions are not representative enough to allow us to conclude that the Monti were very popular as a credit institution already known to customers from their home towns. Among the cities of southern Italy appear Naples, Taranto and Cesaria, of which only Naples had had a Monte since 1539.

From the entire Roman urban area, various districts are mentioned as places to live and/or work: the Borgo, Ponte Sisto, Campo Marzio, Trastevere, Monti, Piazza Fontanara, Fontana di Trevi, Porta del Popolo, Regola, S. Pietro, Piazza di Sciarra, Piazza di Siena, Paradiso, S. Croce, S. Maria in Val Negra, Monte Giorgio, Corso, Via di Ripetta, La Rotunda, Piazza Montanara, San Lorenzo, Piazza del Duca, Campo di Ferro, La Spada, Torre di Nona, Ripa (banks), and Vallicella.

Popular and central market places such as the Rotunda (the Pantheon), the square around the Trevi Fountain, the Ponte Sisto, Campo Marzio, as well as var-

47 The following companies and monasteries are mentioned: the Compagnia del Gonfalone di Roma; La Santa Compania di S. Alò del Arte de Fabri; La Venerabile Compagnia del Salvatore di Roma; La venerabile Compagnia del Sacro Sacramento di S. Giovanni; La Venerabile Compagnia di San Gregorio de Ripetta; Le monache de S. Lucia nelli Monti; Capitulo et Canonici Di Santa Maria Maggiore; La Compania dei Cuochi di Roma; La venerabile Compagnia di Santa Maria.

48 Fol. 174r.

ious places close to the Tiber and famous artisan districts such as Trastevere, Monti, or San Lorenzo can be directly related to the professional structure of the Monte's clientele in or very close to the Via dei banchi vecchi (the seat of the Monte), which also largely handled their investment transactions and transfers through it.

Having provided a snapshot of the forms of small-scale credit used by the citizens of Rome towards the end of the sixteenth century as well as some exemplary information on the social status of the Montes deposit bank's clientele, the third part of this article will deal with the Monte as a pawn-broking institution, and the role of pawns as circulating objects enabling the practices of loan-taking and consumption in particular. I will analyse this by studying one specific source from the second half of the fifteenth century from Perugia, namely a list of sold objects at an auction in 1469/70.

3 Objects as Stores of Value

A history of small-scale credit can be told as a story of institutions and their genesis, the people working in them, and the organisation of their work, but it can also be told by looking at the material side of credit, namely the objects that made these credits possible.[49] Using them, debtors could take out small loans and thus inject new capital into the money cycle by investing in new tools, clothing or food, or simply—as in Giulio Cesare Croces poem—for the payment of rent.

As Valentin Groebner has pointed out, the objects themselves became capital bearers. They replaced money in a debt economy in which credit was omnipresent. The medieval 'economy without the house' of which Groebner speaks, demanded tactics and strategies for the survival of a part of the population without many resources. I would like to take these assumptions as a starting point for the analysis of a part of the Monte's administrative sources, namely the pawn-broking registers and sales lists. I will tackle the following questions: What kind of objects emerge in the sources and what conclusions can be drawn from their quality about the actors involved, i.e. the debtors and the buyers and for the more pre-

49 Carboni and Muzzarelli (eds.) 2012, 11. The authors write about the significance of objects in relation to their owners: "Le cose, oltre a testimonare la lora stessa storia, rivelano tratti della storia degli uomini e delle donne che le hanno prodotte, volute, utilizzate. Le cose contano per quello che valgono oltre che per quello che significano."; Caboni and Terpstra (eds.) 2012; Zdekauer 1896, 2036–4660. For the early modern period and referring to Groebner and Fontaine, cf. Siebenhüner 2015, 167–187.

cise characterisation of what we call small-scale credit? The list of sold pawns from the year 1469/70, used here, contains 553 entries naming 703 unredeemed objects.[50]

The Monte's efforts to bring the unpaid pawns back into circulation became visible. Auctions took place twice a month on three consecutive days. In addition to the dates given in the list, we also find the exact description of the objects according to their condition, style, colour, etc. as well as the names of the former owners and the buyers.

In addition, the entries in the left column show the number of the pledge in the Monte as well as a first instalment made by the buyer marked with the entry *per arra* (= *caparra* = advance payment). The sale of the object was confirmed by the abbreviation *stab* for *stabilitum* (completed, established). The form of the entries is very clear: the sums of money are set off on the right side, which increases the clarity regarding the profit earned from the sales.[51]

Figure 7 Extract from the list of auctioned pawn objects, Perugia 1469/70.

147	*Bernadino d'Antonio di Tomasso*	*ff. 2 s. 12*
	Uno vestito novo da donna	
	Uno gonellino rosso panno manecho	
Per arra	*Tre mantelle, e una tovaglietta cremonesa*	*ff.1–f. 35s.*
	Die 24 aprilis nemo. Die 26 nemo. Die 27	
	Ugo Crostimbanis di perusio promisit flor. Duos et solidum	
Stab.	*55 cui fuit stabilitum*	*ff. 2–f. 55 s.*

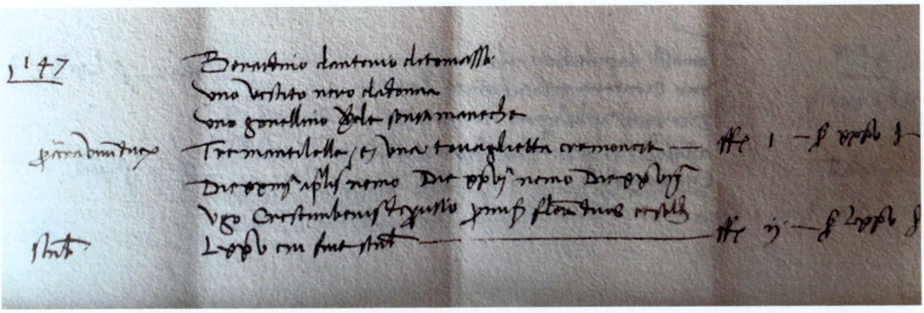

50 The list was partly edited by Majarelli and Nicolini in 1962. The edition contained 135 entries. I have now transcribed the complete list of all 553 entries and made a quantitative evaluation of the 703 items mentioned.

51 ASCP, Archivio della Commune di Perugia, Miscellanea di Computisteria n. 3 (1469–70), Libro de vendete de pegni del Monte, fol. 19r.

Of the 703 items mentioned, only 68 were not auctioned. This corresponds to a percentage of about 9.7 per cent. In addition to the compensation for non-refunded loans, the Monte naturally made great efforts to remove the objects from its depot in order to make room for new pawns.

3.1 The Distribution of Types of Pawns In the Auction List

Regarding the types of sources emerging in the list, we see the following distribution (see table 2):

Most of the items sold were garments. Coats (*vestite*) for men and women are the most frequently mentioned with 123 entries. These are followed by small and large tablecloths (with 69 and 47 entries respectively) and towels (*stuckatoii*) with over 60 mentions. Belts and undergarments (*camorre*), overgarments, jackets, coats, and books are also frequently mentioned. Rarely mentioned, i.e. less than ten times, are pieces of jewellery such as gold rings, coral, or amber necklaces or precious stones, like sapphires. Pieces or bales of cloth (*tessuto, un stampolo di panno*) are to be found quite often, pointing to the practices of pawning by members of certain crafts such as tailors or cloth makers, and thus placing the small-scale credit of the Monti in the context of urban textile production and the precarious living conditions there, which often forced the producers to pledge unfinished goods or products in order to obtain cash. The armaments and weapons look exotic, as does the oven door (*porteletto de forno*), which was pledged by Elpapa Bailo for 20 shillings and bought at auction on 28 June 1469 by Antonio Angeli, the baker, for 21 shillings.[52]

3.2 Monetary and Intangible Values of Pawn Objects

The majority of objects had a rather small value with less than or up to 1 florin. At the lower edge of the price range, there are objects like a carving knife (*coltello*), which was pawned for 16 shillings, a piece of cloth or garment (*stregnietoio*) of cotton and green ribbon for 18 shillings, or a small tablecloth and a towel (*tovaglia pichola e uno sciuchatoio*) for 15 shillings. While tablecloths, bed linen and headscarves were usually only sold for 1 florin, more precious items of clothing, especially women's dresses, could achieve prices of between 2 and up to 14 florins. Looking at the objects listed in the Perusian index and the amounts of money allo-

52 ASCP, Commune di Perugia, miscellanea di computerista n. 3, 1469, fol. 35r.

cated to them, the overall picture is divided into two parts: items of clothing seem to achieve the highest monetary value, whereby certain objects also achieved a rather high monetary value here. Elaborately crafted women's and men's dresses and textiles made of precious fabrics produced around 6 florins, whereas armour pieces or weapons, such as crossbows with at most 1 florin, had a lower value.

Generally, the sales value of all objects auctioned was above their estimated value at the pawnshop. Thus, the auctions guaranteed the Monti the recovery of the amount lent and the interest (between 4 and 10 per cent), as provided for in the statutes. The object with the highest monetary value appearing in the list was a group of objects consisting of a men's coat and a black velvet jacket. Both—originally pledged by a wool merchant/weaver (*lanaio*) named Nucenzio de Giapocho for 6 florins, 52 shillings, and 6 denari—were auctioned for an impressive 12 florins to a certain Permatheus de Cavaceppis:[53]

Nucenzio de Giapocho lanaio:	
uno mantello pagonazo da homo e uno	
giupetto de velluto nero	*ff. 6 s. 52 d. 6*
Die 20 aprilis nemo; die 21 aprilis nemo;	
die 8 maii Permatheus de Cavaceppis	
promisit fl. 12, cui fuit stabilitum	*ff. 12 s. — d. —*
Die 13 maii de voluntate predicti Per-	
mathei fuit predictum pignus restitutum	
per dictos offitiales Ludovicho Iasonis	
lanario p.S. recipienti pro dicto Nucien-	
tio de licentia ipsius Nocentii.	

Good prices were also achieved by a velvet ribbon 'Cremosine-style' with 6 florins and 50 shillings, decorated with silver and engraved in the *niello* fashion[54] (the loan sum was: 2 florins, 17 shillings, and 6 denari[55]), a book by Lactance for 6 florins and 50 shillings, as well as another bound book with the title 'Bartholo'[56], which was auctioned by Ansininus de Visso for 5 florins, 12 shillings, and 6 de-

53 Nr. 57, Majarelli and Nicolini 1962, 356 f.

54 This is a colouring goldsmith's technique still known today, in which a blue-black (lat. *nigellus* = blackish) material is melted onto metal, usually silver, to emphasise the contrast between the two colours.

55 *"Una fietta cremosi (cremisi = scarlet red) vellutata cum ariento orato et niellato"*: Majarelli and Nicolini 1962, 356.

56 Possibly this book was an encyclopaedic work written by Batholomäus Anglicus around 1240 with the title *De proprietatibus rerum,* which found widespread reception after it was first printed 1470 in Cologne.

Table 2 Types of pawns in the Perusian list, 1469/70.

Terms in the source	Translation	Number of mentions
vestito	dress, robe	123
tovaglietta	small tablecloth	69
asciuchatoio	towel or scarf	63
camorra, gamorra	undergarment	49
tovaglia	tablecloth	47
cintura	belt	44
un stampolo di panno	a roll of fabric	40
giornea	overgarment	36
tessuto	cloth	32
libro	book	23
mantella	coat	18
capuccio	coat with hood	14
paio di lenzoli, lenzuolo	bedlinen	11
gonellino, gonella	overcoat	10
guranello	coat	7
berrettino	cap	7
giupparello, giubbotto, farsetto	lined waistcoat	7
tazza	cup	6
guardanappo	napkin	6
anello d'oro	golden ring	6
cupizo di panno	piece of cloth	5
tramaglio	net to catch birds	5
un paio di calze	a pair of shoes	4
mantilotto	small veil	4
balestra	crossbow	4
saccetto	small sachet	4
pantiera	belt (military)	4
veste	jacket	3

Terms in the source	Translation	Number of mentions
una gumisia, camicia	shirt	3
vergetta d'oro	stick of gold	3
braccia di panno	one cubit of cloth (60 cm)	3
paia de fianchali	arm protection	3
coltello	small knife	2
coralliera	coral necklace	2
capellino	small cap, hat	2
un palo de pettene da lanare	a pair of combs	2
filaia d'ambra	amber necklace	1
bacino	basin	1
coperchio	cover	1
guanchale, guanciale	cuschion, pillow	1
una berrecta di grana	carmine hat	1
pezzo di seta	a piece of silk	1
panno bigio	a piece of rough fabric	1
diamante	diamond	1
tenevello grosso e una zappa pichola	drill and hoe	1
taffeta da grano/grana	silky textile made of carmine fabric	1
nove quinterne de carta bambagina	nine pieces of Amalfi paper	1
piedano	carpenters tool	1
una ongarescha cum guaina	pottery: cup or bowl mounted on a low foot	1
una coltre azura	blue duvet	1

nari after 4 days. His pawnbroker's value, which messer Antonio da Pucci had received, was originally 2 florins and 12 shillings. After initial restraint on the first day, this book had been the subject of several days of competition among the bidders, as the entry shows:[57]

6569	*Messer Antonio da Pucci: un libro chiamato Bartholo* *sopra la prima parte de Reforcato. Die 14 martii,* *nemo; die 15 martii dominus Iacobus de Montefiascone* *promisit fl. 3;* *die 16 dominus Iohannes Basilii de Spoleto promisit* *fl. 4;* *Perioannes Francisci promisit fl. 4, 2 s., contra prefatus* *dominus promisit fl. 5; die 20 martii dominus Ansini-* *nus de Visso* *promisit fl. 5, s. 12, d. 6,*	*ff. 2 s. 12*
stabilitum	*die 23 martii fuit stabilitum predicto domino Ansini-* *no pro*	*ff. 5, s. 12, d. 6.*

Three supposedly learned bidders before Ansininus as the final buyer on 20 March appear successively in the list on 15 and 16 March 1469. This example shows the high value that could be attributed to a coveted object—here possibly an encyclopaedic work of high renown—in the course of an exchange act. As a result, its monetary value was more than doubled. But books were by no means always sought-after objects for sale. For example, three books (including Ciceros *De Senectute,* his *Retorica,* and a book called *Statuta*) by the debtor messer Felitiano de Gostantino with a total value of 1 florin, 27 shillings, and 6 denari were not auctioned.

From these data we can conclude on the appreciation of the objects by the debtors and buyers, sometimes as prospective pledgers, in an economy of circulating valuables. My hypothesis is that as soon as for instance clothes were disposable, i.e. not needed due to weather and season, they could be converted into cash. The same was true for (still) unsold handicraft products.

The objects themselves also raise the question of the social status of the borrowers. If we take a closer look at the individual entries on the deposit list, we also see the professions of debtors and buyers which enable us to locate the majority of the Monte's clientele in the stratum of the working poor. Let us take a closer look at these professions:

57 Majarelli and Nicolini 1962, 339.

Table 3 Professions of debtors and buyers mentioned in the source

Terms in the source	Translation
bambachaio	cotton weaver
sartore	tailor
merciaio	haberdasher
fabro	blacksmith
lanaiolo	wool trader
tentore/tintore	dyer
barbiere	barber
cimatore	bricklayer
spetiali	spice dealer
macellatore	butcher
polaiolo	poulterer
funaio, fornaio	baker
calzolaio	shoemaker
piliraio, pelliciaio?	furrier

In addition, the list's content refers to the lively trade in second-hand clothing, into which other items were fed from the auction of surplus clothing. Musettus Mussetti, a second-hand clothes dealer (*riggatiere*), bought several quite precious ladies' dresses. With prices of up to 10 guilders, these were quite high and consisted of precious fabrics such as silk and were especially decorated. But not only old clothes dealers bought the objects, also craftsmen, like the baker (*furnarius*) Antonio Angelus (who appears several times as a buyer), seem to have bought objects again and again, which they could then resell or pledge themselves.

Additionally, the above-mentioned examples of messer Antonio da Pucci and messer Felitiano de Gostantino show that not only craftsmen, day labourers, and farmers were among the Monte's customers. The clients designated as of higher social rank ("messer") can probably be assigned to the learned or wealthier class. At first glance, those frequently pledged garments also refer to an upscale middle-class clientele that was capable of acquiring such status objects and, in case of doubt, was able to do without them. Beside the use of the Monte as a 'temporary external closet', other entries show the pledging of worn and used garments, pointing to clients from lower social strata and the monte's core business of small-scale credit. As Martha Howell proved for Flanders and England in the fourteenth century on the basis of wills and inventories[58], wealthy heads of households gladly bequeathed their partly worn clothes to relatives, but also to servants and employees. Or they passed them on during their lifetime when they were worn out and no longer in the best condition, as Muzzarelli describes.[59] She, on the other hand, also confirms the hypothesis that not only the poor constituted the clientele of the Monti but also wealthier customers used the Monte as a safe depository for their valuables or also the winter wardrobe.

Hence, in the sphere of pawn-broking, household objects of everyday use and seemingly little monetary value gained an essential role as means to secure survival in times of need. If sold, they could re-emerge in the circle of commodities on a second-hand market and might later be again transformed into pawn objects. This leads to the aspect of the construction of an object's value beyond its mere monetary value. Anthropological studies such as Appadurai's assumption of the 'social life of things'[60] provide promising approaches concerning the role of objects in human societies. Based on the assumption that objects are used for exchange against other objects, their value results from the attribution of the actors whose desire for certain objects was awakened. According to this theory, the object's raw material value, on the other hand, would play a subordinate role, so that value asymmetries arise that can multiply the original value of an object, e.g. a piece of clothing, achieved through material and invested work. Moreover, the value of the objects is not fixed from the outset but is constituted in the act of exchange.

Taking into account the hypothesis of value generation through attribution, a detailed reading of the vocabulary by means of which the pledged objects are described in the sources is carried out below—following Smail's categories[61]. The following categories are recorded: age, condition, colour, material, style, in the case of clothing, cut, and fabric. Here you can find detailed and differentiated descriptions that also allow interesting insights into Renaissance fashion. Apart from the usual colours black, grey, green, brown, and white, the following are frequently mentioned: turquoise, red, azure blue, pale blue, yellow, lilac, semi-coloured, striped, purple, marmorated fabrics, and clothing. The fabrics of the garments are also always mentioned: silk and velvet are less common, with

---

58 Howell 2010, 177–181.

59 Muzzarelli 2012b, 25: "Many ornate and expensive garments, when used and consumed or not well conserved, were passed on by their wealthy owners to servants, clients, or second-hand dealers who then sold them to the poorer people".

60 Appadurai 1988 (ND 2006).

61 Cf., Smail 2017, passim.

the majority of the garments consisting of simpler fabrics such as linen or wool, *bigio* (grey, rough fabric) or *bruschino* (a kind of fleece). The frequently used formula *ariento ornato* also refers to the ornamentation of objects, especially belts with silver borders.[62]

As shown, the value of an object was not only constituted by its immediate monetary value. The attributes ascribed to it also convey the appreciation of the objects for the borrowers, since the precise identification at the moment of redemption enabled customers to recapture their belongings. Not to forget the reliability of the Monte's services in keeping the objects in good condition (and not selling them, etc.) that surely played an important role as well. The importance of these household objects for survival becomes clear in the extremely precise description in the sources, naming the age, the condition, colours, materials, and styles of the objects in pawn registers and lists, pointing out the value the objects possessed for their owners beyond their mere monetary value.[63]

4 Conclusion

Summing up, economic historians can narrate the history of small-scale credit as a story of a political economy, of the permeation of the urban elites' business practices, who supported by the Franciscans established institutions providing financial means for poorer members of society. Approaching the topic of small-scale credit from the perspective of cultural history and anthropology, I would like to suggest here that it is possible to add new dimensions to the study and understanding of the great narratives of the emergence of credit and banking structures in the late Middle Ages. Then, as now, it seems, it was small-scale credit that made the transformation of universal patterns of consumption of the working poor possible.[64] Economically flourishing towns and cities of the later Middle Ages provided a variety of desirable consumer goods in different qualities, which were appreciated by consumers of all social backgrounds, including humbler ones.

---

62 Cf. for a detailed explanation of colours and cuts as well as a useful glossary see: Muzzarelli 2008; Muzzarelli and Carboni 2012, 9–19 and with case studies Rinaldi, 2012, 71–114, 111 f.

63 The condition of these objects is often described with attributes such as new (*nuovo*), old (*antico*), white (*biancho*), stained (*macchiato*), good (*buono*), dirty (*sporraccio*), torn (*stracciato*), and worn (*usato*). The clothes mostly seemed to have been in a more acceptable condition than the household textiles, which were often already somewhat shabby.

64 Kowaleski 2006, 238–259.

These loans were based on the accumulation of certain mobile goods that could purposefully be turned into money when needed. The objects as stores of value were thus part of a household economy of lower classes supported by the Monti to survive and bridge crises.

The pawned clothes were not just status symbols that had fallen into the hands of poorer people (or been pledged by richer ones). They were circulating stores of value that ensured the survival of the less fortunate needy, as Giulio Cesare Croce described.

More generally—returning to Laurence Fontaine's studies on the moral economy and the market—the borrowers of the Monti's small-scale credits thus actively participated in the pre-modern market. Additionally, I have shown that the working poor as active economic actors were involved in manifold forms of informal loans and credits as an essential human practice of survival as well as ubiquitous social bonds in pre-modern times.

It became clear that the until then neglected Libri Mastri of Roman Monte are a highly valuable and informative source for the city's credit and micro-credit history, for the history of everyday life, prices, and wages and for the entire social topography of the city. The number of transactions carried out via the Monti increased continuously, pointing to the increasing success of the Monti not only as a pawnshop but also as a deposit bank. In addition to the payments related to everyday business, however, the main cash registers also contain most valuable information on certain forms of credit by means of which the inhabitants of Rome were connected to each other by overlapping and intertwined credit relationships, as shown above. Although it is possible to identify and describe some of these in more detail using contemporary legal sources, it must be noted that the terminological fuzziness in the entries undermines a clear distinction and delimitation of the various forms of pensions and interest in particular.

The analysis furthermore showed the Monti's predominantly urban, male clientele, who can be assigned mainly to the milieu of craftsmen, small traders, and day labourers.[65] Conclusively, the constant circulation of household objects as well as the manifold loan transactions increasingly formalised through small-scale credit institutions like the Monti di Pietà also point to the successful survival strategies used by the working poor in late medieval society.

---

65 But also curial officials used the services of the Monte as a financial institution. Last but not least, the slow transformation of Monte di Roma into a kind of state bank of the Vatican begins here.

References

Archival References

ASR (Archivio di Stato di Roma), Archivio Sagro Monte di Pietà, Libri Mastri 1585–1595.

ASCP (Archivio della Commune di Perugia), Miscellanea di Computisteria n. 3 (1469–1470), Libro de vendete de pegni del Monte.

Bibliographic References

Alonzi L. 2008. "La lunga durata del census reservativus. Forme di credito e contratti agrari tra medioevo ed eta' moderna." *Nuova Rivista Storica* 92, no. 2: 343–388.

Appadurai A. (ed.) 1988 (RP 2006). *The social Life of things. Commodities in cultural perspective.* Cambridge: University Press.

Avallone P.(ed.). 2001. *Il "povero" va in Banca. I Monti di Pietà negli antichi stati Italiani (secc. XV–XVIII).* Napoli: Edizioni Scientifiche Italiane.

Banchi pubblici, banchi private e Monti di Pietà nell' Europa preindustriale. Atti del Convegno, Genova 1–6 ottobre 1990 [= Atti della Società Ligure di Storia Patria 31 (105), no. 1], Genua 1991.

Boglioni P., R. Delort and Claude Gauvard (eds.) 2002. *Le petit peuple dans l'occident médiéval: terminologies, perceptions, réalités.* Paris: Editions de la Sorbonne. DOI: 10.4000/books.psorbonne.13848

Braunstein P. 1999. "La pauvreté au quotidien: apports et limites des sources medievales." In *Les Niveaux de vie au Moyen Age. Mesures, perceptions et representations: actes du colloque international de Spa,* edited by J.-P. Sosson, C. Thiry, S. Thonon and T. van Hemelryck, 91–103. Louvain-La-Neuve: Academia-Bruylant.

Carboni M. and M. G. Muzzarelli (eds.) 2008. *I Conti dei Monti: Teoria e Pratica amministrativa nei Monti di Pietà fra medioevo ed Età Moderna.* Venezia: Marsilio.

Carboni M. and M. G. Muzzarelli (eds.) 2012. *In pegno. Oggetti in transito tra valore d'uso e valore di scambio (secoli XIII–XX).* Bologna: Il Mulino.

Carboni M.and N. Terpstra (eds.) 2012. *The Material Culture of Debt. Renaissance and Reformation. Special Issue* 35, no. 3.

Croce G. C. 1982. "Lamento de' poveretti i quali stanno a casa a pigione, e la convengono pagare 1590." In *Storie di vita popolare nelle canzoni di piazza di G. C. Croce, Fame fatica e mascherate nel '500*, edited by Monique Rouch, 151–158. Bologna: Editrice Clueb.

Delumeau J. 1957/1959. *Vie economique et sociale de Rome dans la seconde moitié du XVIe siecle. Vols. 1 and 2* [= Bibliotheque des écoles francaises d'athenes et de Rome 184]. Paris: Ecole francaise de Rome.

Felloni G. 1991. "Kredit und Banken in Italien. 15.–17. Jahrhundert." In *Kredit im spätmittelalterlichen und frühneuzeitlichen Europa*, edited by M. North, 9–24. Köln/Wien: Böhlau.

Fontaine L. 2013. "Survivre en temps de crise. Une perspective historique". *C.E.R.A.S. Revue Projet* 5: 43–50.

Gazzini M. 2017. *Storie di vita e di malavita. Crimonali poveri e altri miserabili nelle carceri di Milano.* Firenze: University Press. DOI: 10.36253/978-88-6453-615-6.

Groebner V. *1993. Ökonomie ohne Haus. Zum Wirtschaften armer Leute in Nürnberg am Ende des 15. Jahrhunderts.* Göttingen: Vandenhoeck und Ruprecht.

Groebner V. 2004. "Mobile Werte, informelle Ökonomie. Zur Kultur der Armut in der spätmittelalterlichen Stadt." *Vorträge und Forschungen im Mittelalter* 85: 165–187. DOI: https://doi.org/10.11588/vuf.2004.0.17393

Gutton J.-P. 1971. *La societé et les pauvres: l'exemple de la généralité de Lyon, 1534–1789,* Paris: Societé d'edition "Les belles Lettres".

Holzapfel H. 1903. *Die Anfänge der Montes Pietatis (1462–1515).* München: J. J. Lentner.

Kowaleski M. 2006. "A consumer economy." In *A social history of England, 1200–1500,* edited by R. Horrox, 238–259. Cambridge: University Press.

Langholm O. I. 1992. *Economics in Medieval Schools: Wealth, Exchange, Value according to the Paris Theological Tradition.* Leiden: Brill.

Majarelli S. and U. Nicolini 1962. *Il Monte die Poveri di Perugia. Periodo delle origini (1461–1474).* Perugia: Banca del Monte di credito.

Martini A. 1883. *Manuale di Metrologia ossia misure, pesi e monete in uso attualmente a anticamente presso tutti i popoli.* Torino: Ermanno Loescher.

Meneghin V. 1986. *I Monti di Pietà in Italia dal 1462 al 1562.* Vicenza: L.I.E.F. Edizioni.

Menning C. B. 1971. *Charity and State in Late Renaissance Italy: The Monte di Pietà of Florence.* Ithaca: NCROL.

Montalcino A. 1590. *Lucerna dell'anima. Somma de case di conscientia necessaria a i confessori, & molto utile a i Penitenti.* Venice.

Montanari D. (ed.) 1999. *Monti di Pietà e presenca ebraica in Italia (secoli XV–XVIII).* Roma: Bulzoni.

Muldrew C. 1998. *The Economy of Obligation. The Culture of Credit and Social Relations in Early Modern England.* Basingstoke: Palgrave Macmillan.

Muzzarelli M. G. (ed.) 1994. *Banchi ebraici a Bologna nel XV secolo.* Bologna: Il Mulino.

Muzzarelli M. G. 2000. "Un 'deposito apostolico' per i meno poveri, ovvero l'invenzione del Monte di pietà." In *Povertà e innvazioni istituzionali in Italia,* edited by V. Zamagni, 77–94. Bologna: Il Mulino.

Muzzarelli M. G. 2001a. *Il denaro e la salvezza: l'invenzione del Monte di Pietà.* Bologna: Il Mulino.

Muzzarelli M. G. 2001b. "Il credito che 'cura': il Monte di pietà." In *Il povero va in banca: i monti di pietà negli antichi stati italiani,* edited by P. Avallone, 17–29. Napoli: Edizioni Scientifiche Italiane.

Muzzarelli M. G. 2008. *La guardaroba medievale. Vesti e società dal XIII al XVI secolo,* Bologna: Il Mulino.

Muzzarelli M. G. 2012a. "Considerazioni preliminari. Un cumulo, anzi un Monte di pegni." In *In pegno. Ogetti in transito tra valore d'uso e valore di scambio (secoli XIII–XX),* edited by M. G. Muzzarelli and M. Carboni, 9–19. Bologna: Il Mulino.

Muzzarelli M. G. 2012b. "From the closet to the wallet: pawning clothes in Renaissance Italy." *Renaissance and Reformation: The Material Culture of Debt. Special Issue* 35, no. 3: 23–38.

Muzzarelli M. G. 2013. "I Monti di Pietà fra etica economica e economica politica." In *Orientamenti e tematiche della storiografia di Ovisio Capitani,* editey by M. C. de Matteis and B. Pio, 135–148. Spoleto: Fondazione CISAM.

Noonan J. T. 1957. *The scholastic analysis of usury.* Cambridge/Mass.: Harvard University Press.

Pullan B.. 1971. *Rich and Poor in Renaissance Venice: The Social Institutions of a Catholic State, to 1620.* Oxford: Blackwell.

Pullan B. 1978. "Poveri, mendicanti e vagabondi (secoli XIV–XVII)." In *Storia d'Italia, Vol. 1: Dal feudalesimo al capitalismo,* edited by R. Romano, 988–997. Turin: Einaudi.

Rabeler S. 2015. "Pauperismus in der Vormoderne. Beobachtungen zur Existenz und Wahrnehmung der 'labouring poor' in Städten des 14. bis 16. Jahrhunderts." In *Arm und Reich: zur gesellschaftlichen und wirtschaftlichen Ungleichheit in der Geschichte,* edited by G. Schulz, 75–111. Stuttgart: Steiner.

Rinaldi R. 2012. "Amministrazione e traffico deo beni pignoranti a Bologna e nel contado tra duecento e trecento." In *In pegno. Ogetti in transito tra valore d'uso e valore di scambio (secoli XIII–XX),* edited M. Carboni and M. G. Muzzarelli, 71–114. Bologna: Il Mulino.

Schubert E. 2001. "Erscheinungsformen der Armut in der spätmittelalterlichen deutschen Stadt" In *Die Stadt als Kommunikationsraum. Beiträge zur Stadtgeschichte vom Mittelalter bis ins 20. Jahrhundert. Festschrift für Karl Czok zum 75. Geburtstag*, edited by H. Bräuer and E. Schlenkrich, 659–697. Leipzig: Universitätsverlag.

Siebenhüner K. 2015. "Juwelen. Kostbare Objekte zwischen Alltagökonomie und Sinnstiftung." *Historische Anthropologie 23, no. 2:* 167–187.

Skambraks T. 2017. "Expertise im Dienste der Caritas. Die Monti di Pietà zwischen gelehrtem Wissen und Erfahrungswissen." In *Wissen und Wirtschaft: Expertenkulturen und Märkte vom 13. bis 18. Jahrhundert,* edited by M. Füssel, P. Knäble and N. Elsemann, 169–190. Göttingen: Vandenhoeck & Ruprecht.

Skambraks T. 2018. "Zwischen Kooperation und Konkurrenz. Jüdische Pfandleihe und Monti di Pietà in Italien." In *Ökonomische Glaubensfragen. Struktur und Praktiken jüdischen und christlichen Kleinkredits im Spätmittelalter,* edited by G. Fouquet and S. Rabeler, 99–120. Stuttgart: Steiner.

Smail D. L. 2017. *Legal Plunder. Households and Debt Collection in Late Medieval Europe.* Cambridge/Mass.: Harvard University Press.

Sosson J.-P. 1999. "Les niveaux de vie au bas Moyen Age: en guise d'introduction" In *Les Niveaux de vie au Moyen Age. Mesures, perceptions et representations: actes du colloque international de Spa,* edited by J.-P. Sosson, C. Thiry, S. Thonon and T. van Hemelryck, 9–29. Louvain-La-Neuve: Academia-Bruylant.

Todeschini G. 2009. *Franciscan Wealth: From Voluntary Poverty to Market Society,* translated by D. Melucci. Saint Bonaventure, NY: Franciscan Institute, Saint Bonaventure University.

Vaquero Pineiro M. 2006. "Die Rentenkaufverträge im spätmittelalterlichen und frühneuzeitlichen Italien." *Quellen und Forschungen aus italienischen Archiven und Bibliotheken* 86: 252–293.

Zdekauer L. 1896. "L'interno d'un Banco di Pegno del 1417 (con documenti inediti)." *Archivio storico italiano* 17, no. 1: 63–105.

Picture Credits

Fig. 1: Figure designed by Tanja Skambraks.

Fig. 2: Cedole and account books of the Banco di Napoli, Cartastorie, Museo dell'Archivio Storico del Banco di Napoli (by Tanja Skambraks).

Fig. 3: Figure designed by Tanja Skambraks.

Fig. 4: Figure designed by Tanja Skambraks.
Fig. 5: Extract from the Libro Mastro of the Roman Monte di Pietà 1586 (by Tanja Skambraks).
Fig. 6: Figure designed by Tanja Skambraks.
Fig. 7: Extract from the list of auctioned pawn objects, Perugia 1469/70 (by Tanja Skambraks).

Printing and Binding
Books on Demand GmbH, Norderstedt, Germany